YouTube® and Video Marketing

An Hour a Day

Greg Jarboe

WILEY

Wiley Publishing, Inc.

Senior Acquisitions Editor: WILLEM KNIBBE
Development Editor: PETE GAUGHAN
Technical Editor: BRAD O'FARRELL
Production Editor: LIZ BRITTEN
Copy Editor: JUDY FLYNN
Editorial Manager: PETE GAUGHAN
Production Manager: TIM TATE
Vice President and Executive Group Publisher: RICHARD SWADLEY
Vice President and Publisher: NEIL EDDE
Book Designer: FRANZ BAUMHACKL
Compositor: CHRIS GILLESPIE, HAPPENSTANCE TYPE-O-RAMA
Proofreader: WORDONE, NEW YORK
Indexer: TED LAUX
Project Coordinator, Cover: LYNSEY STANFORD
Cover Designer: RYAN SNEED
Cover Image: PATAGONIK WORKS / DIGITAL VISION / GETTY IMAGES, INC.

Advance Praise

Jam-packed with wisdom, this book will reward anyone willing to put in the time to become a viral video master.
   —SETH GODIN, author, *Tribes*

YouTube and Video Marketing: An Hour A Day is the definitive guidebook for anyone serious about online video marketing. A masterpiece! Greg Jarboe sets the gold standard for books on YouTube. His YouTube book should be a part of everyone's Internet marketing library.
   —SHARI THUROW, author of *Search Engine Visibility* and *When Search Meets Web Usability*

Whether your budget is zero or tens of thousands of dollars, Greg Jarboe shows you how to get the best bang for your online marketing buck. In his book, YouTube and Video Marketing: An Hour A Day, *Greg takes you beyond basic techniques to professional promotion and advertising strategies—everything you need to market your business on YouTube.*
   —MICHAEL MILLER, author, *YouTube for Business*

This is a must-read book for any marketer considering adding video to their company's online marketing initiatives. Jarboe has written an easy-to-read book that fuses valuable tactical best-practice information for YouTube marketing with how to strategically and successfully integrate YouTube into the corporate marketing plan.
   —AMANDA WATLINGTON, Ph.D., APR, Owner, Searching for Profit

Greg Jarboe has reported on online video for Search Engine Watch, spoken about how to optimize for search and engage the community at Search Engine Strategies conferences, taught our YouTube and video marketing workshop, and produced more than 300 videos for SESConferenceExpo's Channel on YouTube. He's compressed four years of experience into his book, debunked a lot of conventional wisdom, lead marketers on a path to gaining actionable insights, and added new case studies I hadn't read before.
   —MATT McGOWAN, VP, Publisher, Incisive Media

Sure you've heard about SEO, but what do you know about YTO? YouTube optimization is a brand new science, and almost no one knows more about it as Greg Jarboe. The quirky, revolutionary YouTube is nothing like Google—even if they are part of the same company. But with this book, you can now learn how to optimize—and get the most out of—YouTube. The Internet is going video, YouTube is synonymous with video on the Internet, and now with this book you've got everything you need to profit from these megatrends. Congratulations to Greg Jarboe for making such a complex topic easy to understand, and actionable as well!
   —JIM LOUDERBACK, CEO Revision3

With Marketers struggling to keep up with the rapidly emerging tools of the trade, this book is a must read. YouTube and Video Marketing: An Hour A Day breaks down critical marketing components into logical steps and backs it up with great examples of companies that have demonstrated the power of social media. What some continue to call a 'new form of marketing' is quickly becoming the standard. This is not a fad; it is the new reality.

 —George Wright, VP Marketing and Sales, Blendtec

Influencing people ain't what it used to be. Mediums are different, opportunities are new and numerous, the faith-based initiatives of yore are increasingly less effective. One vibrant and empowering medium for Marketers to keep it real and create Brand Evangelists is YouTube. Greg has a ton of practical experience, with dirty hands to prove it, and in this book he shares his wisdom and guidance. I have no doubt you'll rethink Video Marketing 20 pages into this wonderful book!

 —Avinash Kaushik, author, *Web Analytics: An Hour A Day*

From the early days of personal computer software to today's white-hot web and social media environment, Greg Jarboe has not only stayed up with modern marketing techniques—in many cases, he has invented them. These pages don't just talk theory; they offer a practical, step-by-step guide on how to get the most out of online video marketing. Don't be surprised if you start wanting to spend more than an hour a day; this is a page-turner that will bring you real results.

 —Michael Kolowich, President and Executive Producer, DigiNovations / North
  Bridge Productions

What makes YouTube and Video Marketing: An Hour A Day *a must-read is Greg's storytelling abilities. After all, it is the millions of stories that are told on YouTube every day by people like you that make it such a powerful marketing medium. If you won't find an hour a day to invest in learning to make it work for you, don't worry your competitors will tell the story of their success.*

 —Bryan Eisenberg, *New York Times* best-selling author of *Call to Action* and
  Always Be Testing

'Master Story Teller', that's how I would describe Greg Jarboe, someone I've known in the internet marketing and PR world for several years. Now he's pioneered yet another essential digital marketing channel: online video. In YouTube and Video Marketing: An Hour A Day, Greg has assembled a priceless collection of insights, examples and practical tips for companies that want, that need, to understand how to use video marketing to grow their business. You cannot afford to miss this story.

 —Lee Odden, CEO TopRank Online Marketing

To my family, friends, and community

 # Acknowledgments

I could not have written this book without the help and support of many people.

First, I need to thank my wife, Nancy, for putting up with me during the past eight months—especially when I was in the "Batcave," our nickname for the family room in the basement where I worked on this book evenings and weekends. To make it up, I will watch *Seinfeld* and *Countdown with Keith Olbermann* with you for the next eight months. And thanks to my kids, Andrew, Brendan, and Kelsey; you listened to me talk about YouTube and video marketing for 3 percent of your lives. I will listen to you talk about the Boston Red Sox, Massachusetts politics, and overthrowing the patriarchy, as specified by the Equal Time rule. And thanks to Andrew's wife, Melanie, for joining our speech and debate team just as I disappeared into the Batcave or headed over to the Sweet Bites Bakery & Café for "the usual."

Next, I need to thank my business partner, Jamie O'Donnell, and my colleagues at SEO-PR: Nell Connors, John Mulligan, Byron Gordon, Sergei Fyodorov, Nathan Groom, Jean Sexton, John Zukowski, Chris Halcon, Danya Abt, Adam Macbeth, and Monarch. You helped me keep my day job and watched my back during the swing shift. I'm taking all of you to Joe's Cable Car Restaurant in San Francisco.

I need to thank SEO-PR's clients for sharing their case studies. This includes Matt McGowan, vice president and publisher for Incisive Media's Interactive Marketing Group, which includes Search Engine Strategies (SES), Search Engine Watch, and ClickZ; Carl Mehlhope, SVP, integrated sales and marketing at STACK Media; Tamir Lipton, senior marketing manager, Meredith; Deni Kasrel, director, Web & publications, Office of University Communications at the University of Pennsylvania; and Al Eccles, SEO manager of Yell. You've helped me to make "Stone Soup."

I want to thank the three people who shared their success stories for this book: Arun Chaudhary, new media road director of Obama for America; John Goldstone, producer of *Monty Python and the Holy Grail* (1975), *Monty Python's Life of Brian* (1979), and *Monty Python's The Meaning of Life* (1983); and George Wright, vice president of marketing and sales for Blendtec. And I apologize for putting your success stories in Chapter 11. I'm calling it the eleventh chapter so no one gets the wrong idea.

I also want to thank four people at YouTube and Google who helped me with this book: Suzie Reider, Ricardo Reyes, Aaron Zamost, and Karen Wickre. It takes a village to teach these lessons.

And I want to thank several people who shared their input and feedback. This includes Seth Godin, Amanda Watlington, Michael Kolowich, Kayden Kelly, Charles Davis, Joe Christopher, Alexandra Tran, Ken Colborn, Lee Odden, Sally Falkow, Mike McDonald, Abby Johnson, Bill Hunt, Sage Lewis, Bill Tancer, Matt Tatham, Grant Crowell, Amber Naslund, and Michael Miller. I get by with a little help from my friends.

I want to thank Stewart Quealy, Marilyn Crafts, Jackie Ortez, Kevin Ryan, Mike Grehan, Andrew Goodman, the SES Advisory Board, and Search Engine Watch for putting me on panels about online video at SES conferences. And I should thank my fellow panelists for sharing their expertise: Chase Norlin, Steve Espinosa, Matthew Scheybeler, Gregory Markel, Ed Kim, Barbara C. Coll, Shari Thurow, Liana Evans, Henry Hall, and Matthew Liu. If I'm known as an expert on this topic, it's because I've spent less than 20 percent of my time speaking at SES and more than 80 percent listening to you.

I should thank my colleagues at Market Motive: Avinash Kaushik, Michael Stebbins, John Marshall, Scott Milrad, Tyler Link, Byran Eisenberg, Matt Bailey, Todd Malicoat, Dr. Alan Rimm-Kaufman, Jessica Bowman, Mary Huffman, and Mark Evans. There's a reason why we've been called the "Internet marketing dream team." But I can't remember it.

Finally, I should thank the folks at Sybex, an imprint of John Wiley & Sons. This includes Willem Knibbe, Pete Gaughan, Brad O'Farrell, Liz Britten, and Judy Flynn. I have come to the conclusion that the making of books is like the making of sausages: the less you know about the process, the more you respect the result.

If I've forgotten anyone, then I hope you will forgive me. As Mel Brooks says, "God willing, we'll all meet again in *Spaceballs 2: The Search for More Money*."

About the Author

Greg Jarboe is president and cofounder of SEO-PR (www.seo-pr.com), a search engine optimization firm, public relations agency, and video production company. He is a frequent speaker at Search Engine Strategies and other conferences. He is also the news search, blog search, and PR correspondent for the Search Engine Marketing News Blog at Search Engine Watch.

Jarboe is a member of the Market Motive faculty, which has been called the "Internet marketing dream team." He is a principal in the ChannelOne Marketing Group, a virtual team of nationally recognized experts with deep experience in video production and Web marketing. He is also one of the experts who sat down to talk shop with Michael Miller for the book *Online Marketing Heroes: Interviews with 25 Successful Online Marketing Gurus* (Wiley, 2008).

According to Virginia Nussey, associate writer of the SEO Blog on Bruceclay.com, "Greg is considered an expert on everything from news search to video search to linkbait and beyond. If you don't know him, your introduction is long overdue because Greg has his fingers on the pulse of the Internet marketing industry."

Cofounded in 2003 by Jarboe and Jamie O'Donnell, SEO-PR has offices in San Francisco, California, and Greater Boston, Massachusetts. Larry Chase's *Search Engine for Marketers* named Jarboe and O'Donnell to its "Who's Who in SEO Experts." Market Motive adds, "Regarded as the pioneers and leading authorities on online publicity, Greg and Jamie of SEO-PR continue to blaze new trails on one of the best kept secrets in Internet marketing: Online publicity." SEO-PR has worked with a variety of clients and helped generate the following results:

- $2.5 million in ticket sales for Southwest Airlines in 2004
- 1.3 million searches on SuperPages.com for "florists" in 2005
- 450,000 unique visitors to *The Christian Science Monitor* in 2006
- 1,100 attendees to the Wharton Economic Summit in 2007
- 36% increase in searches for *Better Homes and Gardens* in 2008
- 859 inlinks to Parents.com Toy and Product Recall Finder in 2009

SEO-PR has also produced, optimized, and promoted hundreds of online videos for *Better Homes and Gardens*, Marvell Technology Group, Search Engine Marketing Professional Organization (SEMPO), Search Engine Strategies, STACK Media, the University of Pennsylvania, and Yell.com.

Jarboe has also taught online training courses for Market Motive, including "Video Strategy: Basic Planning" and a full-day workshop for CBS Sports. At SES San Jose 2009, he taught the "YouTube and Video Marketing Workshop."

In 2005, SEO-PR won the Golden Ruler Award with Southwest Airlines from the Institute for Public Relations and *PR News*. In 2008, SEO-PR was a finalist for SES awards in three different categories: Best Social Media Marketing Campaign, Best Business-to-Business Search Marketing Campaign, and Best Integration of Search with Other Media.

Before cofounding SEO-PR, Jarboe was vice president and chief marketing officer for Backbone Media, vice president of marketing for WebCT, and director of corporate communications for Ziff-Davis. At Ziff-Davis, he helped launch dozens of new media, including ZDTV and The Site, hosted by Soledad O'Brien, on MSNBC.

Before that, Jarboe was president of Jarboe Communications and director of marketing for *PC Computing* and director of corporate communications at Lotus Development Corp. Prior to that, he held PR, marcom, and public affairs positions at Data General, Sequoia Systems, Stratus Computer, and Wang Laboratories.

In the 1970s, he was a radio newscaster, newspaper editor, and cohost of the *Marcie and Me* show on the public access channel of Continental Cablevision in Lawrence, Massachusetts. He won two New England Press Association awards while editor of *The Acton Minute-Man*.

Jarboe graduated from the University of Michigan in 1971, attended the University of Edinburgh, and completed all the course work for his master's at Lesley College. He lives in Acton, Massachusetts, where he has been elected to the board of selectmen.

Jarboe is frequently interviewed about online video by journalists and bloggers. You can watch "Greg Jarboe of SEO-PR discusses YouTube and Video Marketing at SES London 2009" at www.youtube.com/watch?v=iiBkobaP2w8. Or, go to:

http://videos.webpronews.com/2009/03/24/mysteries-of-online-video-revealed

to discover "Mysteries of Online Video Revealed."

Contents

Chapter 7   Month 5: Engage the YouTube Community   209

Foreword

The setting was the Roosevelt Hotel in Manhattan. It was a TV/digital video upfront event attended by 500 media and advertising agency executives. For 10 minutes the conversation was YouTube and a video that had been created by two Domino's employees. The video referenced was a short clip of two employees using very poor judgment, playing around with food in a Domino's kitchen. These two turkeys, as my 11-year-old daughter called them, shot the video and then posted the video on YouTube. What ensued was an uncontrollable storm that flashed across the Internet, local television networks, *Good Morning America*, *AdAge*, and dozens of blogs and video sharing sites.

The conversation about the posting of the video was telling. As I listened to the people in the room state their opinions, reflect on the occurrence, and debate how they would have managed this had it been their own franchise or corporation, I listened for signs of any real understanding of how YouTube works. I didn't hear any. There was confusion about the videos themselves and who can post and who controls the content. There was no sense of the tools and functionality that YouTube has developed for marketers to leverage, there really wasn't any base understanding of where a marketer would begin, when in crisis mode or otherwise.

Had Greg Jarboe been standing in the doorway, *YouTube and Video Marketing* in hand, he'd have moved his first 500 copies.

When Jarboe called me in the fall of 2008 and let me know that he intended to write a book on YouTube, it was hard for me to imagine a printed book that could capture the power of YouTube as a marketing vehicle. Why? Because to look through the videos (meaning beyond the video itself) and understand the rhythm of what goes on in this vast ocean of content one is constantly clicking on links and ending up with something like this in the browser: www.youtube.com/watch?v=JZNGpB9A2js.

I was having a hard time visualizing reading a book that had one turning to the keyboard every few moments and typing 35 characters, mixed caps and lower case...

In reading the early chapters, as Jarboe sent them feverishly through over email, I am struck by how graciously he has woven the fundamental principles of marketing into this unpredictable platform called YouTube. He has done a brilliant job of understanding *the way it all works in 2009* while remaining grounded in the core of what any marketer strives to achieve as they parse their marketing budget.

Marketing has changed, forever—and will change more in the next few years than it has changed in the last 50 years. Marketing is changing, media is changing, and all we have to do is watch the media consumption habits of our kids (I have a tween focus group of two in my home...) to know just how real and startling this is and how rapidly it is occurring.

Yet, while YouTube may be current and innovative, what a marketer requires of their activations and marketing programs is plain old *traditional* and can be found in the pages of the books that college graduates heading into advertising, marketing, and communications careers read today and have read for 30 years. It always has been and always will be about connecting with one's consumer/customer and ultimately selling whatever it is that needs to be sold. Texts like *Ogilvy on Advertising* (Crown, 1983), but culled from advertising/marketing practices applied in the 1950s and 1960s (think AMC's *Mad Men*), resonate today.

Advertising and marketing are still about coaxing a consumer to buy Nike's $160 Air Jordon Fusion 9, "connect to everything you love in life" (Blackberry's tag line) through a Storm 9530, or recognize the virtue of Unilever's *big mouth* jar for the mayonnaise that "that brings out the best" (Hellmann's tag line is "bring out the Hellmann's and bring out the best").

In 2009, what is required of marketing and advertising is the same as what it was in 1957 when Dove ran its first spots for the cleansing bar made of ¼ cleansing cream. What are altered forever are the tools, platforms, medium, vehicles, and technology by which a marketer can actually market. And today, a marketer is challenged to create a dialog with the consumer, to engage the consumer versus washing over them with their branding and advertising.

Jarboe focuses on the fundamental requirement of a marketer to connect with their consumer. He also talks about the changes a marketer must make. Think for a moment about Nike. As a consumer you see Nike+ (enables runners to track their pace, distance, etc. on their iPod or a Nike sport band and then upload it to a Nike running site), NikeiD (design your own shoes), Nike Women to engage with them. Every year *Advertising Age* tracks the spending of the top 100 marketers in the country. A few years ago, Nike spent only 33 percent of its $678 million U.S. advertising budget on actual ads with television networks and other traditional media companies. That is down from 55 percent 10 years ago. Nike has figured it out.

The Internet gave marketers the opportunity to innovate. YouTube has given marketers a platform for celebrating and amplifying nearly every marketing activation. Yet often marketers are missing the opportunity to give their programs transformative new wings.

When Red Bull launched its Soap Box Derby in San Francisco's Dolores Park this past October (2008), about 100,000 people converged to see 30 teams fly down Dolores Street at 38 miles an hour. As I watched the day unfold, I reflected on how Red Bull missed the opportunity to have 100 million people feel the rush of the derby and the irreverent, fast, outrageous sense of Red Bull. The tools exist on YouTube, and YouTube is where the people are.

Blue Shield had a similar miss when it launched its Uncovered campaign in September 2008. For several days, six or seven beautiful, stoic, startling bronze statues spaced about four feet apart stared out from the sidewalk. I'd estimate 20 people walked by and noted the figures. Call it 120 people an hour during peak hours, perhaps 1,200 people each day. Even with a dozen or so activations across the state, quick math doesn't have the numbers adding up fast enough. While Blue Shield did launch a website (www.letsshieldcalifornia.com) with the objective of raising awareness and starting a conversation, it was seemingly unaware of the tools that exist on YouTube, many of them free of charge, that could ignite this movement across the Web. *YouTube and Video Marketing* details the precise functionality that could have carried this very powerful activation miles farther and engaged millions of Californians unaware of the fact that one in five of us are not insured.

While there are dozens of examples where a marketer could have taken a campaign farther, Jarboe highlights many real wins.

When I think about the most important learnings over the past few years, it is as simple as our locking into the importance of engagement and dialog over "advertising." The program that Shaun Farrar, VP media at Digitas, drove on Cingular's behalf wasn't simply an ad campaign. The program was called the Cingular Underground, and it was a call to unsigned bands to upload their music videos. The community voted, the finalists appeared on *Good Morning America* and toured on the Gibson Guitar Tour Bus, and there was a record contract signed. Cingular took advantage of the new without losing the best of the old.

There is a wonderful video on YouTube, which you can find by searching for "The Christmas Broadcast, 1957." TheRoyalChannel is the official presence on YouTube for the queen of England. Her Christmas message truly sums up where we are today.

Happy Christmas.

Twenty-five years ago my grandfather broadcast the first of these Christmas messages. Today is another landmark because television has made it possible for many of you to see me in your homes on Christmas Day... I very much hope that this new medium will make my Christmas message more personal and direct... That it is possible for some of you to see me today is just another example of the speed at which things are changing all around us. Because of these changes I am not surprised that many people feel lost and unable to decide what to hold on to and what to discard. How to take advantage of the new life without losing the best of the old. But it is not the new inventions which are the difficulty. The trouble is caused by unthinking people who carelessly throw away ageless ideals as if they were old and outworn machinery.

I've thought a lot about the people in the room at the Roosevelt Hotel, (many of them TV executives and buyers) and wondered what voice or approach would be most effective in bringing them along and helping them understand what YouTube is really all about (as a marketing vehicle). Jarboe has done an outstanding job detailing how to make the most of what YouTube has to offer to brand managers, account directors, media planners, marketers, and yes, senior executives in traditional media companies. Over 400 million people around the world spend time on YouTube every month—seems like a good time to learn what Jarboe has to teach.

SUZIE REIDER,
YouTube Head of Advertising

Introduction

The first video on YouTube was shot by Yakov Lapitsky and features Jawed Kim, one of the company's founders, at the San Diego Zoo. Entitled "Me at the zoo," it is 19 seconds long.

That video (`www.youtube.com/watch?v=jNQXAC9IVRw`) was uploaded on Saturday, April 23, 2005, at 8:27 p.m. At that time, YouTube's headquarters was above a pizzeria and Japanese restaurant in San Mateo, California.

In front of the elephants, Kim says, "The cool thing about these guys today is that they have really, really, really long, um, trunks." An annotation added more than three years later asks, "Can you hear the goat? MEEEEEEEEEEEH!" As of May 2009, "Me at the zoo" had more than 684,000 views. The video had also received over 4,400 ratings, been favorited more than 3,100 times, created one video response, and generated close to 5,200 text comments.

Why is this ordinary moment so extraordinary? In spite of what Kim says, it's not the elephants or their trunks. And despite the annotation, it's not the goat. In fact, you can't see the reason this ordinary moment became so extraordinary by watching "Me at the zoo." The founders of YouTube weren't trying to "capture special moments on video" themselves. They were trying to empower YouTube users "to become the broadcasters of tomorrow."

That's why the real story is what happened next. And it's only in hindsight that we can see why YouTube went on to become the world's most popular online video community.

YouTube users like Cobaltgruv (`www.youtube.com/cobaltgruv`) started putting up videos. On his Channel, Cobalt, 31, says, "Well, I'm an average dude who found YouTube the very first month it was out—user 42 or something. Think I even left the first comment on this site!"

And among the early YouTube celebrities were Anthony Padilla and Ian Hecox, the stars of Smosh. Both members of the comedy duo are from Carmichael, California, and were born in the fall of 1987. Yes, they're that young.

On November 19, 2005, they uploaded three videos to the Smosh Channel (`www.youtube.com/smosh`): "Mortal Kombat Theme" (which had more than 15 million views as of May 2009), "Power Rangers Theme" (over 4.4 million views), and "The Epic Battle: Jesus vs. Cyborg Satan" (more than 1.3 million views).

Smosh also uploaded a video in which they lip-synched and danced to the Pokemon theme song. It was one of the most viewed videos on YouTube for almost a year, but it had to be removed due to copyright infringement. According to Brad O'Farrell, the technical editor of this book, "It's *the* reason they're popular." I'll take his word for it because I'm not their target demographic.

Their video "Smosh Short 2: Stranded" won the 2006 YouTube Award for Best Comedy. The 72 videos on Smosh's channel had almost 236 million views as of May 2009, making it the #3 most viewed comedy channel of all time. With almost 807,000 subscribers, it was also the #3 most subscribed channel of all time.

All this gave YouTube the early reputation as a small video sharing site where any wanna-be director with a video camera and an internet connection could upload their quirky and unusual amateur content for an audience of 18- to 24-year-olds to discover, watch, and share. Well, that's what it was back in 2005.

So, let's move beyond YouTube's early reputation to today's online video market.

Today's Online Video Market

Over 300 million people worldwide discover, watch, and share videos on an estimated 6 million to 9 million YouTube channels each month. YouTube acts as a distribution platform for original content creators and advertisers large and small and provides a forum for people to connect, inform, and inspire others across the globe.

In the United States, 98.8 million viewers watched 5.3 billion videos on YouTube.com in February 2009, according to data from the comScore Video Metrix service. That's 53.8 videos per viewer.

In Canada, more than 1.6 billion videos were viewed by 18 million viewers on YouTube.com that month, representing nearly 90 videos per viewer.

The average online video viewer in the United States watched 312 minutes of video in February 2009, while the average online video viewer in Canada watched 605 minutes of video that month.

As Bob and Doug McKenzie would say, "Hosers, eh?"

According to U.S. site stats from Nielsen/NetRatings for December 2008, the YouTube audience is more diverse than you may think:

- Eighteen percent of YouTube users are under the age of 18
- Twenty percent are 18 to 34
- Nineteen percent are 35 to 44
- Twenty-three percent are 45 to 54
- Twenty percent are over the age of 55

Nearly half of YouTube users have annual incomes of $75,000 or more:

- Six percent make less than $25,000
- Twenty percent make $25,000 to $49,999
- Twenty-five percent make $50,000 to $74,999
- Nineteen percent make $75,000 to $99,999
- Eighteen percent make $100,000 to $149,999
- Ten percent make $150,000 or more

Fifty-two percent are male and 48 percent are female. Forty-two percent have some form of higher education degree, and 13 percent hold postgraduate degrees. As my wife, Nancy, would say, "That's 'wicked smart,'" although this would sound like "wicked smaht," since she has never lost her Boston accent.

As YouTube's audience has become larger and more diverse, the range of content on the video sharing site has become larger and more diverse too.

For example, YouTube now includes television shows and movies from partners like CBS, Crackle, Lionsgate, MGM, Starz, and others. To help users navigate through the thousands of television episodes available for users to watch, comment on, favorite, and share, YouTube introduced a new tab to its masthead on April 16, 2009. The Shows tab allows users to browse shows by genre, network, title, and popularity. At the same time, YouTube also announced an improved destination for movies to help users navigate through the hundreds of movies.

YouTube also includes premium content from more than 3,000 YouTube partners, including the Smithsonian, Encyclopedia Britannica, Library of Congress, Blah Girls, Total Beauty TV, Fix My Recipe, and Painting and Drawing.

And YouTube includes video content from small businesses like Harmony Ridge Lodge, which is located in Nevada City, California, adjacent to Tahoe National Forest. Check out "Dog Does Yoga, Drives a Car," which introduces Monarch, and "Silly Pet Smackdown: Monarch vs. Kelly" on HarmonyRidgeLodge's channel (www.youtube.com/ HarmonyRidgeLodge).

Jamie O'Donnell, who is the owner of the lodge and Monarch as well as my business partner at SEO-PR, produced the videos to promote his pet and dog-friendly lodging. And the videos of Monarch have generated referrals and brought in guests. As YouTube says on its own advertising brand channel, it has truly grown quickly into "the world's largest magazine rack."

According to YouTube internal data for January 2009, channel subscriptions and user uploads had doubled over the previous year. And that was before YouTube introduced a new Subscriptions tab in April 2009 that grants logged-in users one-click access to fresh content from their favorite creators. Later that month, YouTube also launched a Subscription Center for users without any subscriptions (www.youtube.com/my_subscriptions). Users who visit the Subscription Center see some suggestions of a random set of popular channels to help them get started using this YouTube feature.

According to YouTube internal data for February 2009, more than 15 hours of video were being uploaded to YouTube every minute. With hundreds of thousands of new videos uploaded daily, it's not surprising that 51 percent of YouTube users go to the video sharing site weekly or more often to discover "what's new."

And with YouTube making it so simple to share videos and offering so many Share options, it's not surprising that 52 percent of 18- to 34-year-olds share videos often with friends and colleagues. And that was before YouTube added a Share To Twitter button under the Share options in March 2009 and, in April, launched RealTime, a toolbar that lets you discover what your friends are doing on YouTube.

What Are Ad Buyers Waiting For?

But what are the buyers of video advertising waiting for? And, are the producers of online video making money?

In the summer of 2008, a reporter asked TubeMogul what percentage of its users was actively monetizing their videos. Since TubeMogul sells viewership analytics rather than an advertising platform, it had no data to turn to. So, TubeMogul sent a poll to its users to get a fuller picture of what is going on.

An anonymous survey was sent to 11,919 TubeMogul users, and 1,114 completed it. On August 7, 2008, TubeMogul reported that 51.1 percent of those who responded said yes, they were currently monetizing their videos.

Out of these users who were monetizing their content, 47.4 percent of the producers were joining revenue-sharing programs on video sharing sites like YouTube and taking a rare sponsorship deal when and if they could get it. At the other end of the spectrum were 23.4 percent of the producers who were popular professionals selling their own, exclusive ads. About 29.2 percent fell in the middle somewhere.

The reported cost per thousand (CPM) impressions varied widely, from pennies to over $100, averaging $12.39 across all surveyed. With 20.4 percent of all surveyed actively selling ads into their content, the picture looked hopeful.

In terms of ad formats, overlays were the most popular. The industry seemed split between product placement used by 29.4 percent of those surveyed and pre-roll used by 31.2 percent.

Who were the 48.9 percent surveyed that did not monetize their videos at all? Many of these people said their videos were ads (i.e., movie previews or corporate-seeded viral videos) or they were putting out their content for fun (i.e., family videos).

Nine of TubeMogul's users are among the 100 most viewed channels on YouTube: Machinima, Mondo Media, Fred, Hot for Words, Athene Wins, Barely Political, sxephil, Nuclear Blast Europe, and Venetian Princess. But, we don't know if prominent TubeMogul users shared their ad revenue numbers, so the results may not be representative of the broader marketplace.

Plus, a lot has changed since August 2008—in addition to the global economy, housing market, financial institutions, and auto industry.

In October 2008, YouTube announced a collaboration with iTunes and Amazon.com that offered the YouTube community direct access to buy and download music, games, and other products with a few clicks of a mouse. That month, YouTube also started to test full-length programming, enabling CBS and other partners to embed in-stream video ads, including pre-, mid- and post-rolls, in some of these episodes.

In November 2008, YouTube announced promoted videos, a self-serve advertising platform that displays the most relevant, compelling videos alongside YouTube search results. These videos are priced on a cost-per-click basis.

In December 2008, Brian Stelter of *The New York Times* wrote an article entitled "YouTube Videos Pull in Real Money." He wrote, "One year after YouTube, the online video powerhouse, invited members to become 'partners' and added advertising to their videos, the most successful users are earning six-figure incomes from the Web site."

Stelter interviewed Cory Williams, 27, a YouTube producer known as smpfilms on YouTube. Williams said his big break came in September 2007 with a music video parody called "The Mean Kitty Song." The video, which introduces his evil feline companion, had been viewed more than 20 million times as of May 2009.

With more than 250,000 subscribers to smpfilms's channel, Williams said he was earning $17,000 to $20,000 a month via YouTube. Half of the profits come from YouTube's advertisements, and the other half come from sponsorships and product placements within his videos, a model that he has borrowed from traditional media.

On February 23, 2009, Asjylyn Loder of the *St. Petersburg Times* wrote an article entitled "St. Petersburg man makes living sharing tinkering talents on Web." She wrote, "Kip Kedersha's fuzzy Havanese puppy paid for himself in 43 seconds, by shoving himself headfirst into a square hole while his owner chronicled his efforts in a video titled 'Round Dog vs. Square Hole.'"

The video has been viewed more than 357,000 times as of April 2009 on kipkay's channel. More than 97,500 people subscribe to Kedersha's channel. Loden added, "The channel is also how Kedersha makes a living. He earns thousands of dollars a month as part of YouTube's Partner Program, which places advertisements along the bottom of Kedersha's videos."

In March 2009, YouTube started posting partner success stories to its website. The first featured Demand Media, which had launched the ExpertVillage's channel in April 2006. Demand Media's channel was accepted into YouTube's Partner Program in 2007. And as of May 2009, the 139,000 videos on ExpertVillage's channel had more than 540 million views, making it the #3 most viewed channel of all time.

Demand Media has launched over 20 YouTube branded channels housing more than 150,000 videos, including eHow's channel, livestrong's channel, Golflink's channel, and Greencar's channel. In 2008, subscriptions to Demand Media's YouTube channels increased by more than 1,000 percent to over 250,000 subscribers.

As of January 2009, Demand Media's channels generated over 2 million video streams per day. "What originally began as a marketing-driven syndication effort has now turned into a seven figure revenue stream," Steven Kydd, EVP of Demand Studios, Demand Media's content creation division, said in the YouTube partner success story.

On April 9, 2009, *Ad Age* reported that YouTube was selling ads against 9 percent of its video views. Although that figure sounds unimpressive, it was triple the "3 percent" figure reported by Zachary Robers of ClickZ on July 23, 2008.

So, the buyers of video advertising aren't waiting anymore and the producers of online video are making money.

New Source of Competition

YouTube also has to contend with competition from a new source: Hulu.

As this was being written, comScore had just released April 2009 data from the comScore Video Metrix service reporting that YouTube ranked #1. More than 107 million Americans had watched 6.8 billion videos on YouTube.com in April 2009, representing a 40.4 percent share of all videos viewed that month. Hulu ranked #2 with 40.1 million viewers watching almost 397 million videos, a 2.4 percent share. MySpace ranked #3 with 49 million viewers watching 387 million views, a 2.3 percent share.

A year earlier, comScore reported that YouTube ranked #1. More than 82 million Americans had watched 4.1 billion videos on YouTube.com in April 2008, representing a 37.3 percent share of all videos viewed. MySpace ranked #2 with 46 million viewers watching 481 million videos, a 4.4 percent share. Yahoo! Video ranked #3 with 37.3 million viewers watching 328 million videos, a 3.2 percent share. Hulu didn't rank in the top 10 United States online video properties.

And as this was being written, ABC, a unit of Disney, had just announced that it would join NBC Universal and Fox as a part owner in Hulu. Brad Stone and Brian Stelter of the *New York Times* wrote an article on April 30, 2009, entitled "ABC to Add Its Shows to Videos on Hulu."

Stone and Stelter wrote, "The deal is a blow to YouTube, owned by Google and by far the largest video site on the Web. It also courted Disney but struck a deal to display only short clips from shows on ABC and ESPN. People familiar with the negotiations said talks between Disney and YouTube broke down over how a deal would be structured, with Disney insisting on owning a stake in any joint venture."

Let Me Sum Up

So, as Inigo Montoya says in *The Princess Bride* (1987), "Let me 'splain. No, there's too much. Let me sum up." The market for online video has grown very large. The buyers of video advertising aren't waiting anymore, and the producers of online video are making money. And the competitive landscape has changed. So, as Westley says in the movie, "That doesn't leave much time for dillydallying."

Who Should Read This Book

This book is for veteran marketers. Internet marketers, search engine marketers, business marketers, sports marketers, event marketers, product marketers, and corporate marketers should read this book because they didn't learn about video marketing in college—because there were no courses on this topic a couple of years ago—and their marketing jobs and marketing careers are rapidly being reshaped by YouTube.

This book is also for new YouTubers. Comedians, directors, gurus, musicians, partners, and politicians should read this book to learn how to market and promote their YouTube videos more effectively.

Finally, this book is for entrepreneurs. Do-it-yourselfers and small business owners should read this book to debunk popular myths and gain actionable insights from their YouTube and video marketing efforts.

What You Will Learn

This book will show you how to implement a successful video marketing strategy in a relatively new and rapidly changing field. It focuses on YouTube, which is the top online video website, but it also covers Google Video and other video search engines as well as MySpace Video and other video sharing sites. It focuses on the United States, but it also covers Canada, where YouTube is also the top video destination.

What Is Covered in This Book

YouTube and Video Marketing: An Hour a Day is organized to provide you with proven, practical guidelines for developing and implementing video marketing for your organization. My extensive experience in this field also enables me to provide clear, detailed, step-by-step instruction on crucial topics.

Here's a relevant guide to understanding video marketing tactics, developing a strategy, implementing the campaign, and then measuring results. You'll find extensive coverage of keyword strategies and video optimization, strategies for distributing and promoting to other sites and blogs, YouTube advertising opportunities, and crucial metrics and analysis.

- Written in the popular "Hour a Day" format, breaking intimidating topics down into easily approachable tasks
- Covers previously undocumented optimization strategies, distribution techniques, community promotion tactics, and more
- Shows you what is and isn't successful and helps you develop a winning strategy
- Explores the crucial keyword development phase and best practices for creating and maintaining a presence on YouTube via brand channel development and customization
- Examines effective promotional tactics, how to optimize video for YouTube and search engine visibility, and metrics and analytics
- Includes case studies, additional resources, a glossary, information about creating and editing video, step-by-step guides, and valuable hands-on tutorials

YouTube and Video Marketing: An Hour A Day gives you the tools to give your clients or your organization a visible, vital marketing presence online.

What's Inside?

This book is an eight-month-plus program for developing, implementing, and tracking a video marketing strategy. The months are divided into weeks, and these are divvied into days that focus on tasks that are estimated to take about an hour each. Depending on your circumstances, your familiarity with the subject matter, and the sophistication of your clients and organization, it may take you more or less time to complete certain tasks. The book is divided into 12 chapters:

Chapter 1, "A Short History of YouTube," introduces you to the world's most popular online video community. Founded in February 2005, YouTube allows millions of people to discover, watch, and share originally created videos. In this chapter, you will learn why YouTube took off the way it did, how video sharing sites differ from video search engines, and who might blurt out, "God, this is going to be all over YouTube."

Chapter 2, "The Online Video Market," points out that the online video market is very large, but it doesn't work like a "mass market." In this chapter, you will learn who discovers, watches, and shares new videos; what categories or types of new video they watch; when they discover new videos; where they share new videos; why few new videos go viral; and how video marketing works. Finally, you will learn that it's okay to admit, "I still don't have all the answers, but I'm beginning to ask the right questions."

Chapter 3, "Month 1: Map Out Your Video Marketing Strategy," starts by showing you how to identify your target audience first. In this chapter, you will learn how to identify opinion leaders on YouTube and other online video sites. You will also learn why the old communication model should be reversed to map out your video marketing strategy. This quest will require all of the imagination, passion, and discipline of Don Quixote plus the practicality, realism, and cleverness of Sancho Panza.

Chapter 4, "Month 2: Optimize Your Video," shows you how to ensure that your video will be found when Americans conduct more than 2.9 billion "expanded search queries" on YouTube each month. In this chapter, you will learn how to research keywords, how to optimize video for YouTube and the Web, and what to do when someone asks, "Have you tried searching under 'fruitless'?"

Chapter 5, "Month 3: Create Viral Video Content," is about creating content that hopefully informs, inspires, and entertains. In this chapter, you'll watch the best viral videos of 2007 and 2008 to learn how to make original content worth watching and compelling content worth sharing. After you've learned how to create a viral video, you can tell your close friends, "I can't wait to see what you're like online."

Chapter 6, "Month 4: Create a Channel," encourages you to create a channel on YouTube, but don't stop there. YouTube should be the center, but not the circumference, of your video marketing strategy. In this chapter, you will learn how to set up a basic YouTube channel, how to create and customize a brand channel, and how to distribute videos to other sites—although this may not stop people from making comments like, "When I was a boy, I had to walk five miles through the snow to change the channel."

Chapter 7, "Month 5: Engage the YouTube Community," shows you how to help friends and colleagues discover videos you think they'll want to watch. In this chapter, you'll be taught how to become a fully vested member of the YouTube community, study the most discussed YouTube Live highlights, find out why you should add YouTube to your site and share videos, and learn the latest lessons of viral marketing. You'll also discover the comic irony of one sheep saying to another, "Sure, I follow the herd—not out of brainless obedience, mind you, but out of a deep and abiding respect for the concept of community."

Chapter 8, "Month 6: Learn Video Production," tells you why you should learn video production even if YouTube is designed to make producing videos as easy as possible. This encourages some people to shoot first and ask questions later. They tell others, "I figure we can blue-screen the kids in later." For those who would rather ask questions first and shoot later, this chapter will help you learn the basics of video production, get video production tips, master video production techniques, and answer frequently asked questions.

Chapter 9, "Month 7: Become a YouTube Partner and Video Advertiser." In this chapter, you will learn how to become a YouTube partner, which gives you the ability to share in ad revenue from your YouTube videos. You will also take a look at some of the YouTube ad opportunities to discover how your brand can converse with this vibrant community. Finally, you will learn why this model is a natural fit, which is why you will never hear a YouTube Partner say, "Unfortunately, a few years back we had to start accepting advertising."

Chapter 10, "Month 8: Trust But Verify YouTube Insight." Galileo once wrote, "*Count what is countable*, measure what is measurable. What is not measurable, make measurable." In this chapter, we will look at what is countable by YouTube Insight and what is measurable by TubeMogul and Visible Measures. We'll also look at other tools that make measurable what is not measurable by TubeMogul and Visible Measures. But we will need to continue explaining, "The chart, of course, is non-representational," until currently available metrics get more robust.

Chapter 11, "Measure Outcomes vs. Outputs." Although it is useful to measure views and ratings, how many of these "outputs" do you need to make the cash register ring? In this chapter, we'll look at six individuals or organizations that have used YouTube and video marketing to generate measurable "outcomes." But before we do that, we'll question the dude at the watercooler with sunglasses who says, "When you're nailing the numbers, they don't ask questions."

Chapter 12, "Mysteries of Online Video Revealed." This book took me eight months to write and it's supposed to take you an hour a day for eight months to read. So I'm not surprised if you are saying, "Enough storyboarding. Let's shoot something." But, whether you learn by reading or learn by doing, you will quickly discover there's always more to learn. New developments at YouTube and continual changes in video marketing mean the mysteries of online video can never be revealed once and for all. So in this chapter, we will look at the right questions that you need to continue asking in the days, weeks, and months ahead.

Glossary of Terms, Tips, and Tubers. Not only does the YouTube community have its own language, YouTubers have their own culture, customs, and folk heroes. You need to learn how to "walk the walk" of video marketing as well as how to "talk the talk" of YouTube. That's why I've assembled a glossary of terms, tips, and Tubers instead of just appending a typical glossary of terms. But let me warn you here and now that exploring YouTube and video marketing isn't like learning Latin and Roman history. Just when you think you've defined a term, described a tip, or depicted a Tuber, "shift happens."

How to Contact the Author

I welcome feedback from you about this book or about books you'd like to see from me in the future. You can reach me by calling SEO-PR's San Francisco office at 415-643-8947, sending an email to greg.jarboe@seo-pr.com, or following me on Twitter at http://twitter.com/gregjarboe. For more information about SEO-PR, please visit our website at www.seo-pr.com.

Sybex strives to keep you supplied with the latest tools and information you need for your work. Please check their website at www.sybex.com, where we'll post additional content and updates that supplement this book if the need arises. Enter *YouTube and Video Marketing* in the Search box (or type the book's ISBN—9780470459690), and click Go to get to the book's update page.

A Short History of YouTube

1

Founded in February 2005, YouTube is the world's most popular online video community, allowing millions of people to discover, watch, and share originally created videos. In this chapter, you will learn why YouTube took off the way it did, how video sharing sites differ from video search engines, and who might blurt out, "God, this is going to be all over YouTube."

Chapter Contents:

First Mover and Fast Followers
YouTube Nation
Video Search Engines, Then and Now
Video Sharing vs. Video Search
Google and YouTube

First Mover and Fast Followers

The improbable history of YouTube begins way back in the wrong place at the wrong time. And if things had turned out differently, this book would be titled *Singingfish and Video Optimization: An Hour a Day.*

A decade ago, the first-mover advantage belonged to Singingfish. Founded in mid-1999, it was one of the earliest search engines to focus on audio and video content. A public alpha version of Singingfish was unveiled in June 2000, and the company was acquired by Thomson Multimedia in November 2000.

Singingfish employed its own web crawler, Asterias, which was designed to ferret out audio and video links across the Web. It also used a proprietary system to process each of the links it discovered, extracting what little metadata it could find and then enhancing it prior to indexing.

Singingfish first appeared on Infospace's Dogpile and Metacrawler sites as well as Internet AG's Swiss Search in the summer of 2001. At that time, it was the dominant multimedia search engine. No competitor indexed as much of the audio and video content available on the Web or provided more relevant query results.

However, Singingfish had the misfortune of going to market just as the dot-com bubble was bursting. So, even as it was being launched, Singingfish was being downsized dramatically by Thomson Multimedia.

Although AOL acquired Singingfish in October 2003, the first mover continued to shrink. The last members of its staff were laid off in December 2006 and its traffic was redirected to AOL Video in February 2007.

Now, a first mover isn't always able to capitalize on its advantages. Plus, a first mover often faces higher R&D and marketing costs because it is creating products and markets from scratch.

That's why many companies pursue a fast-follower strategy. Fast followers try to learn from the first mover what works and what doesn't. Then they try to use their resources to make superior products or outmarket the first mover.

Singingfish saw a lot of that kind of competitive behavior as it was slowly being folded into AOL Video.

For example, blinkx was founded in 2004 and launched its video search engine in 2005. Protected by 111 patents, blinkx has an index of over 35 million hours of searchable video and more than 450 media partnerships.

Google Video was launched in January 2005. Although this video search engine receives a small percentage of videos from user uploads, it gets the vast majority of them by crawling the web.

And Yahoo! Video was launched in May 2005 as a video search engine, but it was relaunched in June 2006 with the ability to upload and share video clips. In February 2008, Yahoo! Video moved away from crawled video content.

We'll take closer looks at these video search engines later in this chapter and again in Chapter 4. But all three are now *also-rans* with market shares in the low single digits.

Being the first mover didn't work for Singingfish, and being fast followers didn't work for Google Video, Yahoo! Video, or blinkx. So why did YouTube become the world's most popular online video community?

That's the question I'll try to answer in this chapter.

YouTube Nation

According to comScore Video Metrix, over 107 million Americans watched 6.8 billion videos on YouTube in April 2009. YouTube had another 315 million viewers in other countries that month, making it the world's most popular online video community. If YouTube were a nation with a population of over 422 million, it would rank #3—behind China and India, but ahead of the United States and Indonesia.

YouTube has its own language, which is why you'll find a glossary of terms in the back of this book. For example, a YouTuber, or Tuber, is a member of the YouTube community. And it has its own quaint expressions, such as "Leave Britney Alone!" and, as Figure 1.1 illustrates, "God, this is going to be all over YouTube."

YouTubers have their own culture and customs. For example, Tubers enjoy mixing Mentos and Coke and share funny views of the "Evolution of Dance." They were also the first to embrace the "Free Hugs Campaign" and the first to confess "I got a crush…on Obama!"

"God, this is going to be all over YouTube."

Figure 1.1 "God, this is going to be all over YouTube." (Cartoon by Marshall Hopkins in *The New Yorker*, December 25, 2006.)

And YouTube Nation has its own folk heroes. For example, Weezer's "Pork and Beans" video features a "multitude of YouTube celebrities," including Tay Zonday (Chocolate Rain) and Lauren Caitlin Upton (Junior Miss South Carolina). And "Welcome to the YouTube Nation" from SuicideFriendly mentions Brookers, Renetto, and more than a dozen other "new stars of the day."

If all this seems a little foreign to you now, it will soon appear as American as baseball and apple pie, or as Canadian as possible under the circumstances. In fact, go to www.youtube.com/watch?v=FM_R27QfqKs and watch the music video captured in Figure 1.2. "Welcome To The YouTube Nation" from SuicideFriendly could become the unofficial anthem of this era the way "This Land Is Your Land" by Woody Guthrie became the unofficial anthem of a previous era.

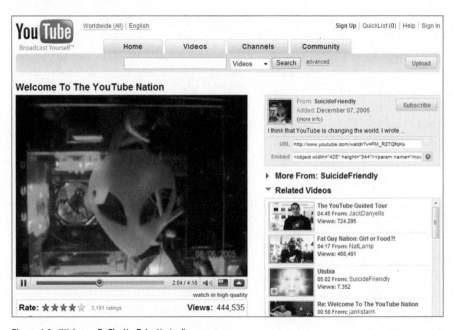

Figure 1.2 "Welcome To The YouTube Nation"

The lyrics can be downloaded at www.7thfilms.com/YouTube.doc; here is the opening stanza and chorus:

> *A Shifting Paradigm, you'd better heed the call or you'll be left behind.*
> *A Worldwide community, there's no borders in this reality.*
> *Say goodbye to the world you (knew). It gives a voice to all, not just the*
>   *chosen few.*
> *If you think I'm wrong, think hard. The other side of the world is in*
>   *your backyard.*
> *Forget what you've known before. Leave it behind and close the door.*
> *It's a new day. Celebrate your liberation.*
> *Welcome to the YouTube Nation. Welcome to the YouTube Nation.*

A Tale of Two Paradigms

For many veteran marketers and lots of new YouTubers, YouTube Nation seems to contain almost as many contradictions as the opening paragraph of Dickens's *A Tale of Two Cities*.

The four-and-a-half-year history of YouTube is short; a 22-minute video is long. The reach of YouTube is wide; the reach of the typical video is narrow. New YouTube features are being developed at lightening speed; new video marketing concepts are getting adopted at a glacial pace. More search activity is observed on YouTube than on any other expanded search entity except Google; the video sharing site is not a video search engine.

Let me define a few terms. I call the overall category *online video sites*. It includes two subcategories with radically difference paradigms:

- *Video sharing sites* like YouTube and MySpaceTV
- *Video search engines* like Google Video and blinkx.

Now that I've defined the terms, let's consider the question, Is it the best of times or is it the worst of times to launch a YouTube and video marketing campaign?

According to Hitwise, YouTube accounted for 79 percent of all U.S. visits to 60 online video sites in February 2009. Google Video ranked second with 4.6 percent followed by MySpaceTV with 4 percent, Hulu with 2.5 percent, Yahoo! Video with 1.6 percent, MetaCafe with 1.4 percent, Daily Motion with 1 percent, MegaVideo with 0.8%, MSN Video with 0.7%, and Veoh with 0.7 percent.

With YouTube the clear leader in online video, this is the best of times to get started. So lots of new YouTubers are tempted to shoot first and ask questions later.

They aren't alone. As of April 2008, YouTube was hosting about 83.4 million videos. And in January 2009, YouTube CEO Chad Hurley said that YouTube was receiving 15 hours of new video from users every minute. This makes it the worst of times to get started. With so many competing videos vying for attention, the odds that the typical video will "go viral" aren't good. Consider these statistics for videos in their first month on YouTube:

- Seventy percent get at least 20 views.
- Fifty percent get at least 100 views.
- Fewer than 20 percent get more than 500 views.
- Fewer than 10 percent get more than 1,500 views.
- Three percent get more than 25,000 views.
- Around 1 percent gets more than 500,000 views.

The stats in Figure 1.3 are based on an analysis of a large dataset from the third and fourth quarters (Q3 and Q4) of 2007 by Rubber Republic.

How many views should you expect for a YouTube video?

We indexed a large number of YouTube videos and counted how many views they had in the first month:

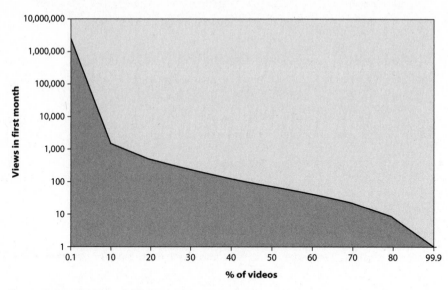

Figure 1.3 How many views should you expect for a YouTube video?

So getting excited that you've just uploaded a new video to YouTube is just as funny today as Navin R. Johnson (played by Steve Martin) getting excited that "The new phone book is here, the new phone book is here!" in the 1979 movie *The Jerk*:

Harry Hartounian: "Boy, I wish I could get that excited about nothing."

Navin R. Johnson: "Nothing? Are you kidding? Page 73 - Johnson, Navin R.! I'm somebody now! Millions of people look at this book (every day)! This is the kind of spontaneous publicity—your name in print—that makes people. I'm in print! Things are going to start happening to me now."

This brings me back to my earlier question: Is it the best of times or the worst of times to launch a YouTube and video marketing campaign?

Would you consider your YouTube and video marketing campaign a success if *most* of your YouTube videos achieve a relatively low number of views but *some* achieve very high viewing figures?

For some search engine optimizers and public relations managers, this might be considered perfectly normal results. And for a few early adopters and entrepreneurs, this might be considered a reasonably acceptable risk.

However, for most marketing managers, these ordinary outcomes don't cost-justify creating a YouTube account. And for lots of new YouTubers, these modest benefits don't seem to be worth the effort.

If you want to improve your chances of success, if you need to increase your return on marketing investment, it will take time—an hour a day—to learn how YouTube works and unlearn irrelevant video marketing concepts. That's what this step-by-step guide is all about.

YouTube Founded in 2005

The YouTube backstory is short. In fact, the company history on its website is less than 200 words long, and the video on the page entitled "Company History" is only 3 minutes and 36 seconds long.

YouTube was founded by three former PayPal employees: Chad Hurley, Steve Chen, and Jawed Karim. According to Jim Hopkins in *USA Today* (Oct. 11, 2006), the idea for what became YouTube sprang from two very different events in 2004: Janet Jackson's "wardrobe malfunction" during the Super Bowl XXXVIII halftime show and the great Sumatra-Andaman earthquake, also known as the Asian Tsunami or Boxing Day Tsunami.

In February 2005, it was difficult to find and share online videos of either event. At a San Francisco dinner party, Karim proposed to Hurley and Chen that they create a video-sharing site. "I thought it was a good idea," Karim told Hopkins.

Within a few days, the three agreed to develop the idea and then divided work based on their skills: Hurley designed the site's interface, while Chen and Karim split the technical duties for making the site work. None of the three had strengths or interests in marketing. In May 2005, a public beta test version of YouTube went live.

Note: Later, when the cofounders divided up management responsibilities, Hurley became CEO, Chen became CTO, and Karim assumed an advisory role after leaving YouTube to get a master's degree in computer science at Stanford.

Although YouTube didn't spend much time or effort communicating with the wide, wide world of marketers in 2005, the company did a great job of communicating with users. In fact, the YouTube Blog was created in July 2005 "in an effort to communicate improvements and changes," and they communicated just that throughout that summer by introducing the following features:

- Searching by username
- Linking videos from other web pages
- Showing related videos within comments
- Introducing channels, categorizing and grouping similar content
- Embedding the YouTube video player into other web pages
- Rating videos between one and five stars

Is Time Long or Is It Wide?

So, why did YouTube become the world's most popular online video community? It's difficult to explain, but it's important to understand.

In her recorded piece "Same Time Tomorrow," Laurie Anderson asks the question: Is time long, or is it wide? In other words, are new developments most influenced by history (long) or by everything that is happening at that moment (wide)?

Or is this the wrong question? Maybe YouTube has evolved because of both, or neither. In other words, did YouTube engineers and developers act as if time was short and narrow?

As the YouTube Editors commented in a July 2005 post, "You know, I really can't believe the pace that we're releasing new features. I mean, it really does seem like just yesterday we launched something and, yet, here we are again…back with more." In other words, time is short.

Or, as the Editors commented a month later, "Once again, many of these changes are in direct response to your feedback, so please keep them coming." In other words, time is narrow.

It is also important to understand that the users providing feedback to YouTube were not a random sample of average consumers, nor were they a select group of leading content providers. The early adopters of YouTube were what Everett Rogers, the author of *Diffusion of Innovations*, calls opinion leaders.

Opinion leaders have the technical competence and social accessibility to informally influence other members of a community. They play an important role in what Rogers calls "diffusion networks"—particularly in reaching critical mass in the diffusion of interactive innovations like the fax in the 1980s, the Internet in the 1990s, and YouTube in this decade.

As Figure 1.4 illustrates, *critical mass* is the tipping point at which enough individuals in a system have adopted an interactive innovation so that the innovation's further rate of adoption becomes self-sustaining.

Rogers says, "The benefits from each additional adoption of an interactive innovation increase not only for all future adopters, but also for each previous adopter." For example, with each additional adopter of the Internet, email became slightly more valuable to everyone as a larger number of other people could be reached by email.

"So, the benefits of an interactive innovation flow backward in time to previous adopters, as well as forward in time to future adopters," Rogers concludes.

In a vacuum, the rapid development of innovative features will produce hits and misses. But when rapid development of an interactive innovation is combined with a laser focus on opinion leaders, critical mass is reached more rapidly.

This is what enabled YouTube to get a winning horse to the starting gate in record time. In November 2005, YouTube received funding from Sequoia Capital. One month later, YouTube was officially launched.

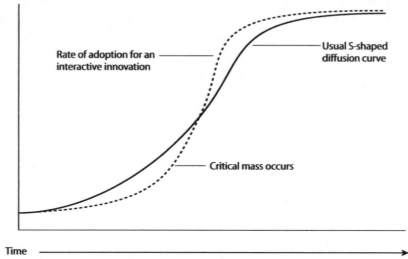

Adoption from 0 to 100%

Rate of adoption for an interactive innovation

Usual S-shaped diffusion curve

Critical mass occurs

Time

Figure 1.4 The rate of adoption for an interactive innovation, showing the critical mass

Video Search Engines, Then and Now

As I said, YouTube didn't communicate extensively to marketers back in 2005, but several of its competitors did—especially to search engine marketers. For example, three executives from video search engines spoke during the "Video Search" session (moderated by Chris Sherman) at the Search Engine Strategies (SES) conference in Chicago on December 5, 2005:

- Suranga Chandratillake, the cofounder and CTO of blinkx

- John Thrall, head of Multi-Media Search Engineering at Yahoo! Search

- Karen Howe, vide president of AOL Search and general manager of Singingfish.

In Chapter 4, I'll discuss how you should optimize video today. But I want to repeat what was said in that session (which I covered for *Search Engine Watch*), even though Singingfish is no longer publicly available and many of these tips and tricks are now out-of-date. Why would I repeat useless information and revisit irrelevant advice? Because I can't tell you how often I've heard these urban legends retold as if nothing had changed in the past four years. So it's important to understand that what worked then doesn't always work now.

Chandratillake kicked things off by asking, "What is blinkx.TV?" He then answered his rhetorical question by saying that blinkx.TV was a video search engine.

This is still true. But, if you go to www.blinkx.tv today, you will be redirected to www.blinkx.com. This is as clear a signal as you can get that other things have changed.

For example, back then blinkx.TV used metadata, speech recognition, visual analysis, text on the page, and other factors to determine what content to display when a search is conducted.

Today, blinkx takes a holistic approach to video search: It uses every characteristic of the video itself to understand the content. For example, blinkx now listens to the sound track using speech-to-text technology, looks at the images on screen using advanced video analytics, and reads other information embedded into the file by using media-analysis plug-ins to extract closed captioning. And blinkx's index of over 32 million hours of video is searchable to a much deeper degree than the weak, manually created, metadata-based approaches to video search of the past.

Next, Thrall spoke about Yahoo! Video. Back in December 2005, Yahoo! Video used a combination of factors to enable consumers to find and view different types of online video. These factors included Yahoo's media crawling and ranking technology and its content and media relationships as well as its support for Media Really Simple Syndication (Media RSS), a self-publishing specification for audio and video content.

Today, Yahoo! Video has moved away from crawled video content. The site now consolidates all premium video from across Yahoo! properties with user-generated uploads and premium partner content. Yahoo! Video's home page contains editorially selected videos that change daily and skew toward comedy, viral videos, talented users, odd stuff, animation, and premium entertainment content.

Finally, Howe spoke about Singingfish. As Figure 1.5 illustrates, Howe told the SES attendees back in 2005, "Metadata makes you visible and thumbnails don't hurt." And she listed the most important fields for accurate recall:

- Title
- Author, performer, creator of the content
- Description
- Copyright information
- Creation date
- Duration
- Keywords

Howe also said secondary metadata fields—like publisher, notes, and publication location—could add value. She said the Sfmedia RSS 2.0 module, a specification for multimedia content description, added over 30 fields of information. Designed for sites with hundreds of streams, it worked for audio, video, podcasts, video blogs, and flash.

That was then. Today, Singingfish has ceased to exist as a separate service. So what works now?

As Figure 1.6 illustrates, only the title, description, video category, and tags are required fields on YouTube. The next time you hear that other metadata makes you visible, remember, that and 50 cents won't buy you a cup of coffee anymore.

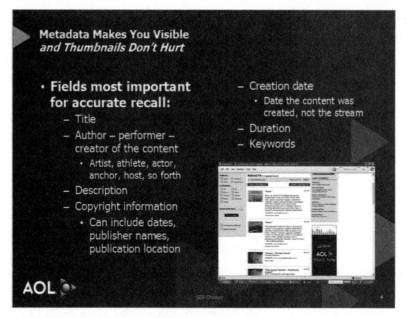

Figure 1.5 Metadata makes you visible *and thumbnails don't hurt.*

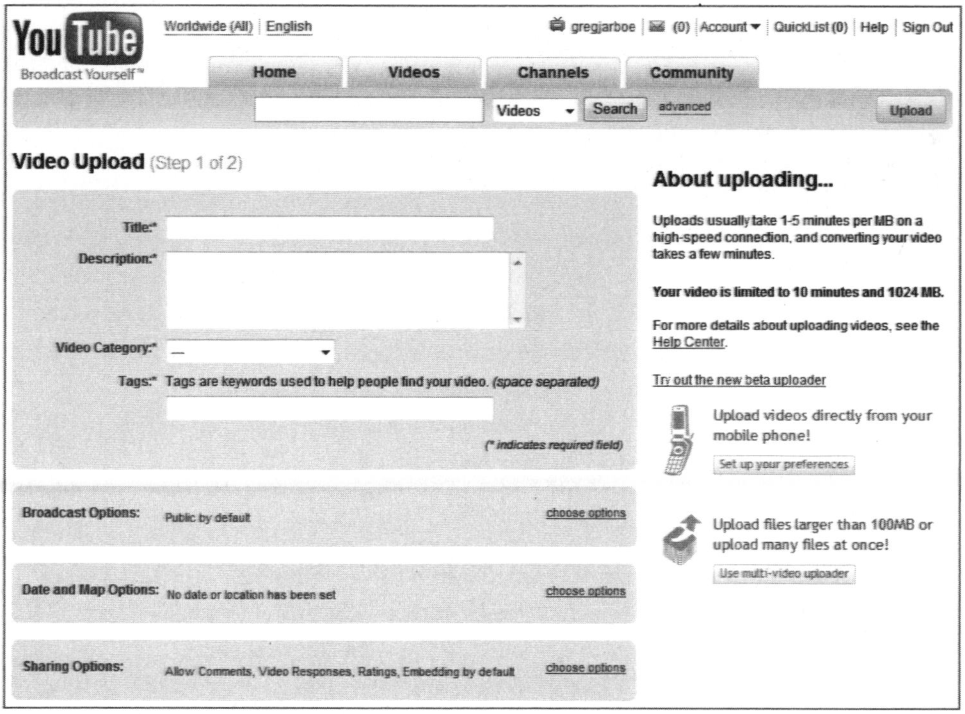

Figure 1.6 Video Upload

Diet Coke and Mentos

During the session, I learned what happened when you dropped mint-flavored Mentos candies into a two liter bottle of Diet Coke. When I returned home from SES Chicago, I was able to impress Andrew and Kelsey, two of my three kids, by showing them a geyser of soda spew into the air. My third kid, Brendan, home from college for the holidays, was not amused. He had seen the Diet Coke and Mentos Eruption videos the month before on YouTube.

Despite this "heads-up" from Brendan, when I sat down to write my special report on the session for *Search Engine Watch*, I advised marketers, "While it is still 'early days' for video search, this is the perfect time to start creating and optimizing content for this emerging category." But I was so focused on reporting what three executives from video search engines had said at the conference that I totally missed the emerging power of a new video sharing site that wasn't represented on the panel.

Video Sharing vs. Video Search

In December 2005, the online video market was still a wide-open field. It included YouTube, MySpace Video, and other video sharing sites as well as video search engines, like Yahoo! Video and Google Video. This made it very difficult to handicap what was expected to be a very long horse race.

But 10 months later, the horse race was over: YouTube had won going away. On October 9, 2006, Google Inc. announced that it had agreed to acquire YouTube for $1.65 billion in a stock-for-stock transaction.

On a conference call and webcast to discuss the acquisition, Eric Schmidt, Google's chairman and chief executive officer, was asked why Google had acquired YouTube when it already had Google Video. Schmidt answered that Google Video was doing well, but YouTube was a clear winner in the social networking side of video.

Yahoo! had also been in the bidding war for YouTube, until very close to the end. The other leading video search engine in the horse race recognized the benefit—or necessity—of having the leading video sharing site in its stable too.

It's worth spending a little time understanding what happened during the 10 short months that followed SES Chicago 2005.

Lazy Sunday

YouTube emerged from relative obscurity shortly after December 17, 2005, when a video entitled "Lazy Sunday"—which was a copy of a Saturday Night Live skit "The Chronicles of Narnia Rap"—was uploaded to the video sharing site.

On December 27, Dave Itzkoff of the *New York Times* reported that "Lazy Sunday" had already been downloaded more than 1.2 million times.

The next day, LeeAnn Prescott, who was the research director at Hitwise at the time, posted her analysis of the hot video of the past week on her Hitwise Intelligence

Analyst Weblog. Visits to YouTube, where people could discover, watch, and share "The Chronicles of Narnia Rap," shot up 83 percent in one week—and surpassed visits to Google Video.

As Figure 1.7 illustrates, Prescott's examination of clickstream data for YouTube revealed the viral nature of videos: Many of the top upstream sites that sent visitors to YouTube the previous week were either community sites like MySpace or web email services.

Weekly Upstream 'Computers and Internet' sites to 'YouTube' – 12/24/05

The following list of web sites appeared in 'Computers and Internet' industry rankings by 'sessions' and delivered traffic to 'You Tube'

Rank	Domain	More	Share	
1.	MySpace	▶	11.31%	
2.	Yahoo! Mail	▶	8.73%	
3.	Google	▶	6.32%	
4.	Xanga	▶	4.70%	
5.	My Space - Mail	▶	4.25%	
6.	MSN Hotmail	▶	3.39%	
7.	LiveJournal.com	▶	2.19%	
8.	Yahoo!	▶	1.98%	
9.	Gaiaonline.com	▶	1.22%	
10.	MSN	▶	1.10%	

Figure 1.7 Weekly upstream "computers and Internet" sites to "YouTube" 12/24/05

She added, "Not surprisingly, given the nature of the video and the upstream traffic, visitors to YouTube are overwhelmingly young." For the four weeks ending December 24, 2005, 45 percent of the visitors to YouTube were in the 18–24 age group. By comparison, 24 percent of the visitors to Google Video and 35 percent of the visitors to Yahoo! Video Search were in the 18 to 24 bracket.

By the end of January, Prescott reported, "Since my post last month on YouTube and the SNL Chronicles of Narnia rap, YouTube has continued to gain market share against other video search sites, and since surpassing Google Video, it has also surpassed Yahoo! Video Search."

On February 16, 2006, almost two months after "Lazy Sunday" had been uploaded to YouTube, the video was removed from the video sharing site. The YouTube Editors posted this explanation on the YouTube Blog: "Hi Tubers! NBC recently contacted YouTube and asked us to remove Saturday Night Live's 'Lazy Sunday: Chronicles of Narnia' video. We know how popular that video is but YouTube respects the rights of copyright holders. You can still watch SNL's 'Lazy Sunday' video for free on NBC's website."

The YouTube Editors added, "We are happy to report that YouTube is now serving up more than 15 million videos streamed per day—that's nearly 465 million videos streamed per month with 20,000 videos being uploaded daily."

"Lazy Sunday" may have helped YouTube to take the early lead right out of the gate, but it wasn't the only video fueling the growth of the video sharing site. In fact, after "Lazy Sunday" was removed, YouTube continued to gain market share.

In other words, YouTube wasn't dependent on a single hit.

Ten Minutes of Fame

YouTube's growth also continued the following month, even after the video sharing site implemented a 10-minute limit for video uploads.

On March 26, 2006, Maryrose, one of the YouTube Editors, posted this on YouTube Blog: "This change won't impact the vast majority of our users. We know that over 99% of videos uploaded are already under 10 mins, and we also know that most of our users only watch videos that are under about 3 minutes in length."

If most users were uploading and watching short-form video clips, then why did YouTube even bother to make the change?

Maryrose explained, "If you've followed our blog postings or any of the press articles, you know we're constantly trying to balance the rights of copyright owners with the rights of our users. We poked around the system a bit and found that these longer videos were more likely to be copyrighted videos from (TV) shows and movies than the shorter videos posted."

MySpace Videos

Ironically, the only threat to YouTube's lead came five days later, on March 31, 2006, when the market share of visits to MySpace Videos increased by 1,242 percent, according to Hitwise, sending it far ahead of YouTube, Yahoo! Video, and Google Video. What had happened?

The night before, the *Financial Times* reported that MySpace had removed 200,000 "objectionable" profiles from its site as it stepped up efforts to calm fears about the safety of the social networking service for young users.

Ross Levinsohn, head of News Corp's Internet division, told Joshua Chaffin and Aline van Duyn of FT.com that some of the material taken down contained "hate speech." Some of it, he said, was "too risqué." The FT.com story got 1,319 Diggs.

On April 6, Prescott posted this in her Hitwise Intelligence Analyst Weblog: "I'd like to know if anyone has insight into what MySpace did on March 31 to send MySpace Video's traffic though the roof—our clickstream data shows that before March 31, about 82% of traffic to MySpace Video was coming from MySpace, and on March 31 and thereafter it's been at about 95%. So obviously MySpace is promoting their video capabilities within the site."

As Figure 1.8 illustrates, YouTube traffic didn't suffered that week, and it was still receiving the same amount of upstream traffic from MySpace. This prompted Prescott to ask, "What has MySpace got up its sleeve?"

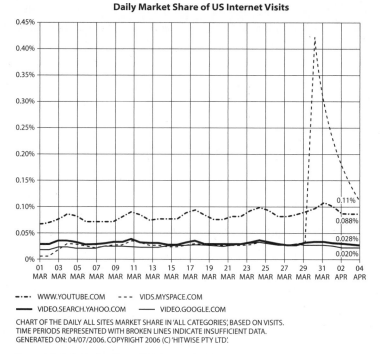

Daily Market Share of US Internet Visits

---·--- WWW.YOUTUBE.COM ---- VIDS.MYSPACE.COM

—— VIDEO.SEARCH.YAHOO.COM ——— VIDEO.GOOGLE.COM

CHART OF THE DAILY ALL SITES MARKET SHARE IN 'ALL CATEGORIES', BASED ON VISITS.
TIME PERIODS REPRESENTED WITH BROKEN LINES INDICATE INSUFFICIENT DATA.
GENERATED ON: 04/07/2006. COPYRIGHT 2006 (C) 'HITWISE PTY LTD'.

Figure 1.8 Daily Market Share of U.S. Internet Visits

Maybe lots of occasional MySpace users had suddenly rushed to see which of their favorite videos, trailers, movies, TV shows, music videos, and clips had survived the purge. Or, maybe MySpace's promotion of MySpace Videos suddenly became more effective. Or, maybe it's a little from column A and a little from column B.

Whatever it was, YouTube recaptured the lead by mid-April, although MySpace Videos remained in second place well ahead of Yahoo! Video and Google Video.

Stephen Colbert

On April 29, 2006, Comedy Central's Stephen Colbert appeared as the featured entertainer at the White House Correspondents' Association dinner. Colbert's 16-minute podium speech and a 7-minute video presentation were broadcast live on C-SPAN.

Standing a few feet from where President George W. Bush was seated, Colbert roasted the president and the White House press corps. His performance—a parody of conservative pundit Bill O'Reilly—immediately went "viral."

James Poniewozik of *Time* magazine wrote that "days after Stephen Colbert performed at the White House Correspondents' dinner, this has become the political-cultural touchstone issue of 2006—like whether you drive a hybrid or use the term 'freedom fries.'" One of my kids, who came home that weekend from college, told me about the videos of the event on YouTube and we watched them together on the PC in our family room.

On May 4, the YouTube Blog announced that the videos of Stephen Colbert roasting President Bush had been taken down at the request of C-SPAN. Yet after the C-SPAN videos were removed, YouTube continued to gain market share. Its rate of adoption had become self-sustaining.

Blind Men and the Elephant

In May 2006, Hitwise issued a press release on the growing popularity of the category and the dominance of YouTube in it. However, in the headline of the press release, the term *video search sites* was used to describe the category, but in the lead paragraph, the term *online video sites* was used.

Now, I'd don't blame Matt Tatham, the Hitwise PR guy, for this confusion. It was created by a broader clash of competing paradigms that continues to confuse many marketers and even some YouTubers today. That's why I defined a few terms earlier in this chapter. But when that press release appeared, most people were still groping for clear definitions.

It reminds me of the poem by John Godfrey Sax, "The Blind Men and the Elephant." One feels the tusk and says, "An elephant is very like a spear." Another seizes the tail and says, "The elephant is very like a rope." And four other guys touch the elephant's side, trunk, knee, and ear and conclude that it is a wall, snake, tree, and fan, respectively.

But the whole elephant is much more than just one of these things. And I believe that YouTube became the world's most popular online video site by being radically different and not just a faster follower of the early pioneers that came before it.

While video search engines were working to help people discover videos, YouTube enabled millions of people to discover, watch, *and* share originally created videos. While video search engine crawlers were trying to extract what little metadata they could find, YouTube was empowering millions of people to enrich the data by watching, sharing, and commenting on videos. While the video search engines seemed focused on competitive strategies, YouTube was focused on building a new community.

Now, that's a lot to get your arms around. So, are there any questions?

> **Search Engine Marketer:** "Let me get this straight. If I've optimized the pages on my website that contain videos, then I've optimized them for video search engines, but this won't help my videos get discovered, watched, or shared on YouTube."

That is correct. YouTube does not crawl the Web trying to index videos posted on millions of websites. So if you haven't uploaded your videos to YouTube, they won't be found when 91 million Americans watch 5 billion videos on YouTube each month.

> **YouTube Director:** "Wait a minute. YouTube isn't a video search engine, but doesn't it still make sense to optimize my videos for searches conducted on YouTube itself? Isn't that the way that a lot of videos get discovered in the first place?"

You are absolutely right. In fact, comScore qSearch calls search activity on YouTube and other video sharing sites expanded search queries. And, there are almost 3.2 billion expanded search queries conducted on YouTube each month.

> Entrepreneur: "Hold on, hold on! If there are almost 2.6 billion expanded search queries conducted on YouTube each month, how can viewers watch 5 billion videos on YouTube each month? Is this some kind of fuzzy math?"

No, this isn't fuzzy math. YouTube videos are discovered more than one way. They can be found through a YouTube search, a Google search, an embedded player, an external link, related videos, or some other way.

Now that we've addressed the elephant in the room, let's return to the Hitwise press release of May 2006.

Hitwise Tracking

Although the terminology may have been confusing, the Hitwise data in the press release was crystal clear. Overall visits to the 10 leading online video sites had increased by 164 percent over the previous three months. And as Table 1.1 illustrates, YouTube had the most traffic among online video sites, accounting for 43 percent of category visits.

▶ **Table 1.1** Top 10 Video Search Sites by Market Share of Visits

Rank	Name	Share of Visits
1	YouTube	43%
2	MySpace Videos	24%
3	Yahoo! Video Search	10%
4	MSN Video Search	9%
5	Google Video Search	6%
6	AOL Video	4%
7	iFilm	2%
8	Grouper	0.7%
9	Dailymotion.com	0.2%
10	vSocial.com	0.1%

Week ending May 20, 2006. Source: Hitwise.

The Hitwise release also noted, "Social networking giant MySpace provided more than 20% of YouTube's traffic in February and March, before MySpace widely launched its own video sharing service by placing a 'videos' link on every profile page beginning March 31."

Why didn't the MySpace move slow down YouTube's growth? YouTube's average session time for the week ending May 20, 2006, was 13 minutes 20 seconds, nearly three times greater than MySpace Video's average session time of 4 minutes 41 seconds, "demonstrating a high level of engagement between YouTube's content and its visitors."

In May 2006, Hitwise's Prescott posted some additional data to her weblog. She said that another way to gauge visitor engagement was the site's market share of page views. As Table 1.2 shows, share of page views tells a very different story than share of visits. YouTube was serving more than three times as many pages as MySpace Video, and the latter's wide launch a few weeks earlier didn't bring its share of page views very close to YouTube's at all. Also, Yahoo! Video was consistently serving more pages than MySpace Video.

▶ **Table 1.2** Top 10 Video Search Sites by Market Share of Page Views

Rank	Name	Share of Page Views
1	YouTube	54%
2	Yahoo! Video Search	19%
3	MySpace Videos	15%
4	Google Video Search	5%
5	MSN Video Search	2%
6	iFilm	2%
7	AOL Video	2%
8	Grouper	0.4%
9	Dailymotion.com	0.3%
10	vSocial.com	0.1%

Week ending May 20, 2006. Source: Hitwise.

Prescott concluded, "Sometimes looking at market share of visits to competitive websites does not tell the whole story—it can be revealing to look at share of page views as well as session times to get a clearer picture of what is happening on a site." I agree.

The 100 Million Mark

On July 16, 2006, YouTube told Reuters that viewers were watching more than 100 million videos per day on its site, marking a surge in demand for its "snack-sized" video fare.

Since springing from out of nowhere in late 2005, YouTube had come to hold the leading position in online video with 29 percent of the U.S. multimedia entertainment market, according to the most recent weekly data from Hitwise.

MySpace, another video sharing site, had a nearly 19 percent share of the market according to Hitwise. Yahoo!, Microsoft's MSN, Google, and AOL each have 3 percent to 5 percent of the online video market. In other words, the four major video search engines had a smaller collective share than either YouTube or MySpace did alone.

In June, 2.5 billion videos were watched on YouTube. In July, more than 65,000 videos were uploaded daily to YouTube, up from around 50,000 in May.

Viral Videos

Even if only 1 percent of these new videos went on to get more than 500,000 views in their first month on YouTube, this means that 650 videos a day—or close to 20,000 videos a month—were going "viral" in July.

To give you an idea of the range of videos that were going viral, let's look at half a dozen that were uploaded to YouTube from the beginning of January to the end of July 2006. Five went on to win 2006 YouTube Video Awards. The sixth was revealed to be a hoax in September 2006.

Virginia Heffernan of the *New York Times* didn't like the 2006 Awards. And I'm not crazy about the idea of putting stars on the doors of a few YouTube videographers either. But it's difficult to discuss the range of content that was engaging the YouTube community without providing some examples. So let me splice my black-and-white descriptions of these videos with some of Heffernan's color commentary from her March 27, 2007, article about the awards.

Best Series: "Ask A Ninja Question 1 'Ninja Mart Store'" was uploaded to the Digitalfilmakers's channel on January 7, 2006. It had over 600,000 views as of April 2009, and the 63 videos in the series had more than 35 million. So, what's your impression, Virginia? *"The Ninja plays older brother, offering advice and pushing Net neutrality, the so-called First Amendment of the Web."*

Best Commentary: "Hotness Prevails/Worst Video Ever" was uploaded to TheWineKone's channel on May 31, 2006. It had more than 3.2 million views as of April 2009. Tell our readers what you really think about this guy and his commentary, Virginia. ***"The Wine Kone, a handsome guy with a steady gaze and a wheezy chortle, holds forth there on belly-button issues."***

Musician of the Year: "Say It's Possible" was uploaded to TerraNaomi's channel on June 16, 2006. It had over 3.6 million views as of April 2009. And how do you feel about that choice, Virginia? *"That's a wonderful choice. The song has got a sustained ache to it, and the visual setup for the video—the singer at the guitar crowding the camera, before an unused keyboard—is painterly, in the tradition of the best YouTube bedroom guitar videos."*

Also nominated: "First Blog / Dorkiness Prevail" was uploaded to lonelygirl15's channel on June 16, 2006. This video had more than 1.9 million views as of April 2009, and the 395 videos in the LG15 series had more than 118 million views as of April 2009. The YouTube community really hated lonlygirl15, Virginia, but they told all of their friends about her. *"The widespread animus toward 'lonelygirl15,' the hit online series that got its start on YouTube but then seemed to grow too big for its britches, also seems to be alive and well at the YouTube Awards, where it was nominated for several awards but won nothing."*

Most Adorable: "Kiwi!" was uploaded to Madyeti47's channel on June 27, 2006. It had more than 22 million views as of April 2009. The awards tell us a lot about the YouTube community, Virginia. *"YouTube's winners also reveal the site's mystified attitude toward animation, in the form of the sweet but dull 'Kiwi!' cartoon, which takes the most adorable video prize."*

Most Creative: "OK Go—Here it goes again" was uploaded to OkGo's Channel on July 31, 2006. It had more than 46 million views as of April 2009. So, Virginia, do you have any final comments about the OK Go guys and their funny music video on treadmills. *"I like their pluck, but it's too MTV for YouTube."*

Allen's Listening Tour

The following month, a new video was uploaded to YouTube that got far fewer views than any of the examples that we've just looked at. But it became "a signature cultural event of the political year," according to op-ed columnist Frank Rich of the *New York Times*.

On August 11, 2006, U.S. Senator George Allen (R-Virginia) appeared before a crowd of white supporters. His re-election campaign seemed to be a mere formality. Allen had a double-digit lead over Jim Webb, his Democratic challenger, and some Beltway insiders were calling Allen the most likely Republican presidential nominee in 2008. S. R. Sidarth, a 20-year-old Webb campaign worker of Indian descent, was tracking Allen with a video camera.

Rich described what happened next in his column that November. He wrote, "After belittling the dark-skinned man as 'macaca, or whatever his name is,' Mr. Allen added, 'Welcome to America and the real world of Virginia.'"

On August 15, "Allen's Listening Tour" was uploaded to the WebbCampaign's channel on YouTube. According to Rich, "The one-minute macaca clip spread through the national body politic like a rabid virus. Nonetheless it took more than a week for Mr. Allen to recognize the magnitude of the problem and apologize to the object of his ridicule."

Allen claimed later that he had no idea that the word, the term for a genus of monkey, had any racial connotation. Nevertheless, it soon became clear that Senator Allen was in serious trouble. Even conservative pundits faulted him for running an "awful campaign." And in November, Allen was defeated by Webb.

Rich concluded, "The macaca incident had resonance beyond Virginia not just because it was a hit on YouTube. It came to stand for 2006 as a whole."

But, it wasn't as big a hit as the 2006 YouTube Award Winners. As of April 2009, "Allen's Listening Tour" had over 380,000 views.

Nevertheless, it provides the real punch line to the *New Yorker* cartoon back in Figure 1.1. It encapsulates the new paradigm that most politicians, to their peril, had not yet heard about from their children: "God, this is going to be all over YouTube."

Critical Mass

On August 16, 2006, Bill Tancer, the general manager of global research at Hitwise, posted the chart in Figure 1.9 to his analyst weblog comparing YouTube to MySpace Video, Google Video and Yahoo! Video.

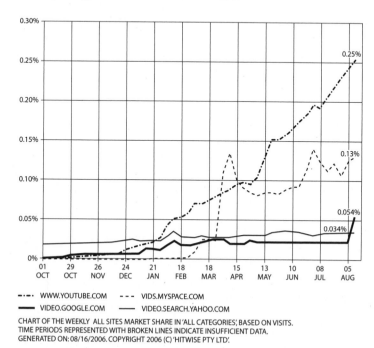

CHART OF THE WEEKLY ALL SITES MARKET SHARE IN 'ALL CATEGORIES', BASED ON VISITS.
TIME PERIODS REPRESENTED WITH BROKEN LINES INDICATE INSUFFICIENT DATA.
GENERATED ON: 08/16/2006. COPYRIGHT 2006 (C) 'HITWISE PTY LTD'.

Figure 1.9 Market share of visits to YouTube, MySpace, Google Video and Yahoo! Video

On August 30, 2006, an article by Lee Gomes in the *Wall Street Journal* took a closer look at YouTube. The following passage is from that article:

I did a scrape of YouTube a month ago and found there were 5.1 million videos. By Sunday, the end of another scrape, that number had grown by about 20% to 6.1 million. Because we know how many videos have been uploaded to the site, the length of each, and how many times it has been watched (total views were 1.73 billion as of Sunday), we can do a little multiplication to find out how much time has collectively been spent watching them.

Later in his article, Gomes added:

While YouTube's messaging software is rudimentary, and often doesn't work, many users nonetheless rely on it to stay in touch with each other. That gives YouTube—and other Web locales—some of the "social network" characteristics usually associated with the likes of MySpace. And it's another reason that established players like Yahoo and Google are ramping up their video-sharing competitors.

So, what did Gomes find? He found, "The total time the people of the world spent watching YouTube since it started last year. The figure is—drum roll, please—9,305 years!"

That is *critical mass*! This is why "Lazy Sunday" and the Stephen Colbert videos could be removed from YouTube and it would move right along as though nothing had happened.

Google and YouTube

The YouTube juggernaut was attracting the interest of many others, including Warner Music Group, which announced a partnership with the video sharing site on September 18, 2006.

On that day, Powers posted this to the YouTube Blog: "The cool thing is that Warner will be posting top music videos, interviews with your favorite artists and behind-the-scenes footage, and more. You'll be able to enjoy and share these videos without concern that they could be removed."

He added, "What's even better is that Warner is the first record label to embrace and support your creativity by authorizing use of their music content for free, in partnership with your favorite artists!"

Google Rumors

On October 6, 2006, Prescott reported, "Today's rumor that Google might be buying YouTube strikes me as highly unlikely, but deserves some analysis."

Although YouTube had surpassed Google Video in early 2006 and YouTube had a market share of visits four times greater than Google Video, Prescott also observed, "Google is YouTube's second most important source of traffic other than MySpace. In September 2006, 10.7% of YouTube's upstream visits came from Google, while MySpace accounted for 16.2% of YouTube's upstream traffic."

Prescott also looked at the data from Google's perspective. She noted that Google had begun sending more traffic to YouTube than Google Video in late June.

Next, Prescott contrasted the audiences for Google Video and YouTube. Google Video's audience skewed more male and older than YouTube. YouTube's average session time was double that of Google Video's, at 18 minutes 33 seconds in the month of September versus 9 minutes 9 seconds for Google Video. She observed, "YouTube is just plain sticky compared to Google Video."

Prescott concluded, "If there is any truth to this rumor, my feeling is that Google, with its great engineering team, could eventually build all the features of YouTube and make it even better for far less money than it would take to buy it, if indeed the going price is over $1 billion. However, YouTube has an amazingly large video library and seemingly loyal user base that is only six months old, which would be nearly impossible to replicate. That alone could be worth $1.6 billion, especially since Google is getting into the video ad space. Let's see what happens next week."

In other words, YouTube's critical mass of videos and the loyalty of the opinion leaders in its online video community had become more valuable than all of the video sharing site's innovative features put together.

Google Acquires YouTube

On October 9, 2006, Google announced it planned to acquire YouTube for $1.65 billion in stock. Two days later, Bill Tancer, the general manager of global research at Hitwise, posted a chart to his analyst weblog that demonstrated YouTube's "quick growth from obscurity in October 2005 to market dominance in mid-2006."

The chart in Figure 1.10 depicts the market share of visits to YouTube based on all Internet visits in the United States. It looks remarkably similar to the one in *Diffusion of Innovations* that Rogers used to illustrate the rate of adoption for an interactive innovation, showing the critical mass.

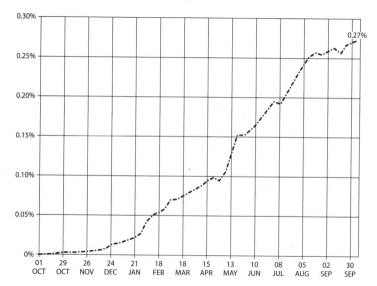

-·-· WWW.YOUTUBE.COM

CHART OF THE WEEKLY ALL SITES MARKET SHARE IN 'ALL CATEGORIES', BASED ON VISITS.
TIME PERIODS REPRESENTED WITH BROKEN LINES INDICATE INSUFFICIENT DATA.
GENERATED ON: 10/11/2006. COPYRIGHT 2006 (C) 'HITWISE PTY LTD'.

Figure 1.10 Market share of visits to YouTube

Tancer added, "One phenomenon that we've found in the adoption of 2.0 sites is that the difference in site demographics from the early days to market dominance demonstrates who the early adopters of 2.0 apps are. YouTube is a perfect example of that."

He then compared a snapshot of YouTube's demographics in January 2006 with YouTube's demographics for the four weeks ending October 7, 2006. It highlighted the fact that YouTube has gone mainstream, with an audience that now closely mirrors the demographic of the U.S. online population. For example, 52 percent of YouTube users are male and 48 percent are female. And 22 percent are 55 or older, 22 percent are 45 to 54, 19 percent are 35 to 44, 18 percent are 18 to 34, and 18 percent are under 18.

This was a perfect illustration of opinion leaders and their followers. In fact, the headline of his post was "Of YouTube, Web 2.0, and Early Adopters."

On November 13, 2006, Google closed its acquisition of YouTube. In a press release, Eric Schmidt said, "We look forward to working with content creators and owners large and small to harness the power of the Internet to promote, distribute, and monetize their content." Chad Hurley added, "The community will remain the most important part of YouTube and we are staying on the same course we set out on nearly one year ago."

Google Video and YouTube

After Google officially bought YouTube, it was asked about what would happen next. Google said that Google Video and YouTube would "continue to play to their respective strengths."

But YouTube's respective strength had been kicking sand in the face of Google Video's respective strength for more than 10 months.

So, on January 25, 2007, Google provided a bit more detail. Its online press release said, "Google's strength—and its history—is grounded in search and in innovating technologies to make more information more available and accessible. YouTube, meanwhile, excels at being a leading content destination with a dynamic community of users who create, watch and share videos worldwide."

But that wasn't news; we knew that already. Three paragraphs into the announcement, Google finally told us something we didn't know: "Starting today, YouTube video results will appear in the Google Video search index: when users click on YouTube thumbnails, they will be taken to YouTube.com to experience the videos."

As Google had stated previously, YouTube would remain an independent subsidiary and would continue to operate separately. Google would support YouTube by providing access to its search and monetization platforms as well as its international resources when YouTube launched internationally. Finally, the YouTube team would continue to create innovative new ways for people to "broadcast themselves."

Google added, "Ultimately, we envision most user-generated and premium video content being hosted on YouTube so that it can further enhance the YouTube experience. We also envision YouTube benefiting from future Google Video innovations—especially those involving video search, monetization and distribution."

The rest isn't history. The appropriate term is *current events*. In April 2009, YouTube accounted for more than 99 percent of all videos viewed at Google Sites, according to comScore. Although Google Video hadn't been sent to the guillotine, the video search engine was as good as dead in the online video market. Its place had been taken by a video sharing site.

Now that you've learned why YouTube took off the way it did, how video sharing sites differ from video search engines, and who might blurt out, "God, this is going to be all over YouTube," let's take a quick look at online video marketing.

The Online
Video Market

The online video market is very large, but it doesn't work like a "mass market." In this chapter, you will learn what journalists can teach marketers about marketing. You will also learn who discovers, watches, and shares new videos; what categories or types of new video they watch; when they discover new videos; where they share new videos, why few new videos go viral; and how video marketing works. Finally, you will learn that it's okay to admit, "I still don't have all the answers, but I'm beginning to ask the right questions."

Broadcast Yourself?

So, how does YouTube work (Figure 2.1)? Why does it work? What can veteran marketers and new YouTubers accomplish by using it?

©Cartoonbank.com

"*I still don't have all the answers, but I'm beginning to ask the right questions.*"

Figure 2.1 "I still don't have all the answers, but I'm beginning to ask the right questions."

If YouTube were simply a new television network, then video marketing would be simple. You could simply apply all the old mass marketing techniques that you learned in college to a new medium. However, YouTube doesn't work like a television network, despite its slogan, "Broadcast Yourself." It works like a video sharing site.

Mass marketing assumes a large number of individuals watch the same video at the same time. Everett Rogers, in Chapter 8 of his book *Diffusion of Innovations*, calls this model of communication "the hypodermic needle model." It presumes that the mass media has "direct, immediate, and powerful effects on a mass audience."

However, video marketing uses what Rogers calls "the two-step flow model." In the first step, opinion leaders use a video sharing site to discover videos uploaded there. In step two, opinion leaders share videos they like with their followers. While the first step involves a transfer of *information*, the second also involves the spread of interpersonal *influence*.

Most of us didn't learn how video sharing sites work in college. We didn't learn why they work. And we're still trying to figure out what can be accomplished by using them.

That's why this book is about video marketing as well as YouTube. However, before we can tackle video marketing, you must (as Yoda would say) "unlearn what you have learned" about mass marketing.

My Father's Oldsmobile

In Chapter 1, I mentioned the role my kids played in helping me learn how YouTube works. In this chapter, let me share the role that my dad played in helping me learn how marketing works.

My dad was the director of marketing for Oldsmobile. Coincidentally, he was the director of marketing in the 1980s when Oldsmobile launched the ad campaign that claimed, "It's not your father's Oldsmobile."

When my dad graduated from college in the 1950s, television was changing the media landscape of his generation. As a marketer in the mass media era, he learned the importance of focusing on product, price, place, and promotion. When I graduated from college in the 1970s, newspapers were setting the political agenda of my generation. As a journalist in the Watergate era, I learned the importance of asking who, what, where, when, why, and how.

In the 1980s, I moved from journalism into public relations, and my dad saw this as an opportunity to start a conversation between peers, since public relations was part of marketing. One of the things we discussed was the difference in perspectives between marketers and journalists. Marketers focus on the four Ps of the marketing mix: product, price, place and promotion. Journalists ask the five Ws and an H for getting the full story about something: who, what, when, where, why, and how.

Table 2.1 compares these two paradigms.

▶ **Table 2.1** Marketing and Journalism

Classic Marketing	Classic Journalism
Product	Who
	What
	When
Place	Where
Price	Why
Promotion	How

Classic journalism has the added advantage of this poem, found within Rudyard Kipling's story *The Elephant's Child*, to validate its point of view:

I keep six honest serving-men

(They taught me all I knew);

Their names are What and Why and When

And How and Where and Who.

My father and I quickly recognized that marketers weren't focusing on two fundamental questions that journalists were asking: who and when. As we kicked this around, we both had some pretty powerful insights.

The reason classic marketing didn't focus on "Who" was it was actually "mass marketing." It assumed that everyone was a prospect for products that were mass produced. That may have worked in 1909 when Henry Ford said, "Any customer can have a car painted any color that he wants so long as it is black." But it stopped working in 1924, when Alfred Sloan unveiled GM's famous market segment strategy of "a car for every purse and purpose."

My dad understood the power of market segmentation and recognized the importance of adding a fifth P to the marketing mix: the prospect.

"When" was another blind spot for mass marketing. My dad had started his career in the auto industry during the era of planned obsolescence. Each and every fall, a new line of cars was introduced—whether they featured cosmetic changes or fundamental improvements.

In contrast, I was starting a new career in the computer industry during an era when the price/performance of microprocessors was doubling every 18 months. I understood the power of Moore's Law and recognized the importance of adding a sixth P to the marketing mix: the pace of change.

Diffusion of Innovations

Our conversations helped prepare me for what came next: In 1989, I became the director of marketing for *PC Computing*. Coincidentally, the magazine's publisher back then was Michael Kolowich, and one of our inside sales representatives was Suzie Reider. Kolowich, who is now president of DigiNovations, shares some of his observations later in this chapter and in one of the case studies in Chapter 11. And Reider, who is now the director of ad sales at YouTube, shares one of her presentations later in this chapter and wrote the forward for this book.

When I joined the magazine, we conducted some market research on how the readers of *PC Computing* informally influenced the purchase of innovative PC products and applications by their colleagues at work and friends in their neighborhood. We called our magazine's readers PC Champions.

When I presented our findings to an advertiser in Silicon Valley, she surprised me by asking, "Have you read *Diffusion of Innovations* by Everett Rogers?" I hadn't, so she lent me her copy of her marketing textbook for a graduate-level course at Stanford University. I was blown away.

Rogers segmented markets by combing who and when into *earlier adopters* and *later adopters* of innovations. As Figure 2.2 illustrates, diffusion forms an S-shaped curve when you looked a cumulative adoption or a bell-shaped curve if you looked at adoption per time period.

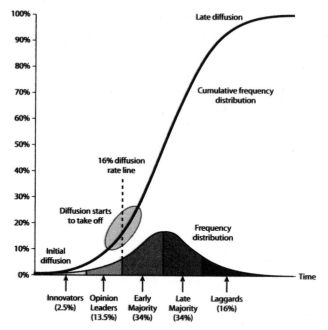

Figure 2.2 The S-curve and bell curve. (Although this image is adapted from ones in *Diffusion of Innovations*, it captures many of the key findings in the book.)

I had seen markets segmented into the classic pyramid—with a few big customers at the top and lots of little customers at the bottom. But Rogers turned this point of view on its side. The most important customers weren't the biggest ones on the top of the pyramid; the most important customers were the early adopters on the left side of the S-curve.

Even more important, his two-step flow model introduced a new dynamic into the process of deciding whether or not to adopt an innovation. Rogers showed that, in addition to the big brands communicating to the mass market through the mass media, the individual members of diffusion networks are also communicating with each other.

The most important people in these peer-to-peer conversations are opinion leaders. According to Rogers, "The diffusion curve is S-shaped because once opinion leaders adopt and begin telling others about an innovation, the number of adopters per unit of time takes off in an exponential curve."

And his two-step flow model implied that the mass media were neither as powerful nor as directly influential as had previously been thought. He said, "Mass communication channels are primarily knowledge creators, whereas interpersonal networks are more important in persuading individuals to adopt or reject."

Five Ws and an H

Now, video marketing is far more complicated than just two steps. But the two-step flow model illuminates the two blind spots that cannot be seen while looking forward or through either the rear-view or side mirrors of mass marketing: who and when.

So, let's apply the five *W*s and an *H* to the online video market to ensure that we getting the full story about video marketing. Let's ask the following questions:

- **Who** discovers, watches, and shares new videos?
- **What** categories or types of video do they watch?
- **When** do they discover new videos?
- **Where** do they share new videos?
- **Why** don't more new videos go viral?
- **How** does marketing with video work?

And, as Bette Davis warned in *All About Eve*, "Fasten your seatbelts; it's going to be a bumpy night!"

Who Watches Online Video?

There's lots of data on who watches online video.

For example, comScore Video Metrix reported that 145 million viewers in the United States watched online videos in February 2009, which was 76 percent of the total online population in America. In Canada, 21 million viewers watched online videos that month, which was 88 percent of the total online population.

In the United States, the online video audience watched 13.1 billion online videos in February 2009, an average of 90 videos per viewer. In Canada, the online video audience watched more than 3.1 billion online videos that month, an average of 147 videos per viewer.

On October 3, 2008, the eMarketer Daily newsletter featured an article titled, "Where Is Online Video Headed?" As Figure 2.3 illustrates, eMarketer foresees the number of U.S. online video viewers—defined as individuals who download or stream video (content or advertising) at least once a month—growing to 190.0 million in 2012.

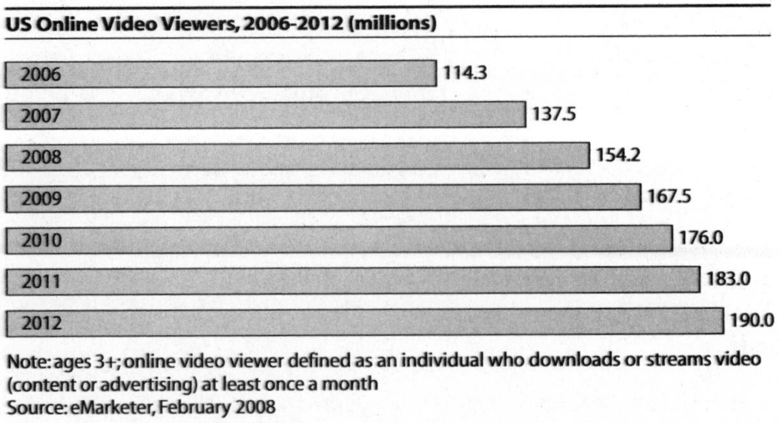

US Online Video Viewers, 2006-2012 (millions)

Year	Viewers
2006	114.3
2007	137.5
2008	154.2
2009	167.5
2010	176.0
2011	183.0
2012	190.0

Note: ages 3+; online video viewer defined as an individual who downloads or streams video (content or advertising) at least once a month
Source: eMarketer, February 2008

Figure 2.3 U.S. online video viewers, 2006–2012. (Source: eMarketer Daily newsletter.)

Now, this would be a mass marketing opportunity of Olympic proportions *if* audiences in the social media era sat down in front of their computers to watch online videos the same way that audiences in the mass media era sat down in front of their televisions to watch TV shows. But times have changed. Back in 1978, the vast majority of television viewers in the United States were watching one of just three TV channels during primetime: ABC, CBS, or NBC. As of April 2008, the vast majority of online video viewers were watching one of the 3.75 million user channels on YouTube alone.

Who Discovers and Shares New Videos?

More important, the process of discovering new content and sharing it with others has also shifted dramatically.

Forty years ago, there were only a handful of new TV shows each week worth talking about around the water cooler at work or over the phone at home. So the odds were good that anywhere from a third to a half of your colleagues and friends had also seen the new TV show last night. Although the rest of those who listened to the conversation couldn't rush home and watch a rerun back then, some might tune in the following week. There was a social component to mass media, but it was often indirect, delayed, and limited.

Today, there are around 15 hours of video uploaded to YouTube every minute. If the average video is 3.5 minutes long, then more than 250 videos a minute, 15,000 an hour, 360,000 a day, or 2,520,000 a week are being uploaded to the leader in online video. Nobody can watch even one in a thousand. That's why discovering and sharing a video has such an impact.

When you send a new video by email to your colleagues in the office or post it to MySpace for your friends to see, the odds are very good that nobody else in your social network has seen it yet. And they can watch it without delay and then relay it quickly to their other social networks. And so on, and so on. So, social media has a direct, immediate, and powerful impact on a mass audience.

As Rogers wrote, "The hypodermic needle model postulated that the mass media had direct, immediate, and powerful effects on a mass audience." However, he observed, "the mass media were neither as powerful nor as directly influential as had previously been thought." This led him to conclude that the hypodermic needle model was "too simple, too mechanistic, and too gross to give an accurate account of media effects. It ignored the role of opinion leaders."

Who Are the Opinion Leaders?

One of the right questions to ask is not necessarily, Who watches online videos? One of the right questions to ask is, Who are the opinion leaders in the online video market?

The only market research I've seen that even begins to ask the right questions was conducted by the Pew Internet & American Life Project. The findings were made public on July 25, 2007, in an online video report written by Senior Research Specialist Mary Madden (Table 2.2).

► **Table 2.2** Online Video Gets Social: How Users Engage (Percentage of Video Viewers Who Do Each Activity)

Activity	Total	Men	Women	18–29	30–49	50–64
Receive video links	75%	75%	75%	76%	77%	71%
Send video links to others	57	59	54	67	55	45
Watch video with others	57	58	57	73	58	34
Rate video	13	15	10	23	11	4
Post comments about video	13	15	10	25	9	5
Upload video	13	16	9	20	12	5
Post video links online	10	12	9	22	7	2
Pay for video	7	8	6	10	7	3

Source: Pew Internet & American Life Project Tracking Survey, February 15–March 7, 2007

One of the key findings was this: "The desire to share a viewing experience with others has already been a powerful force in seeding the online video market. Fully 57% of online video viewers share links to the videos they find online with others. Young adults are the most 'contagious carriers' in the viral spread of online video. Two in three (67%) video viewers ages 18–29 send others links to videos they find online, compared with just half of video viewers ages 30 and older."

Now, 57 percent of online video viewers can't all be opinion leaders. If they were, then every Don Quixote would have only one Sancho Panza as a follower. So, sharing links to the videos they find online with others is a necessary but not sufficient condition of opinion leadership.

According to the Pareto principle, which is also known as the 80-20 rule or the 90-10 rule, no more than 10 to 20 percent of online video viewers should be opinion leaders. Rogers also observed that "the S-shaped diffusion curve 'takes off' at about 10 to 20% adoption, when interpersonal networks become activated so that a critical mass of adopters begins using an innovation."

We need to dig deeper into the Pew report to discover other social behavior that would be "just right" to identify opinion leaders: "Video viewers who actively exploit the participatory features of online video—such as rating content, posting feedback or uploading video—make up the motivated minority of the online video audience. Again, young adults are the most active participants in this realm." The findings from the Pew report are as follows:

Nineteen percent of video viewers have either rated an online video or posted comments after seeing a video online. Madden wrote, "One of the features popular on many video sites is the ability to rate or post feedback about the content on the site. For instance, during the now legendary run of Lonelygirl15 videos on YouTube, viewers used the comments field to debate the authenticity of the diary-style videos in which the young girl shared her thoughts and daily drama with the world." If you look at the Pew rating and commenting data separately, 13 percent of video viewers have rated video, and the same percentage posted comments after viewing video online. Unsurprisingly, those who engage with online video by rating and commenting tend to be young; video viewers ages 18 to 29 are twice as likely as those ages 30 to 49 to do so.

Thirteen percent of video viewers have uploaded a video file online for others to watch. Young adults also trump older users in their experience with posting video content; 20 percent of viewers ages 18 to 29 have uploaded videos, compared with 12 percent of those 30 to 49 and roughly 5 percent of viewers age 50 and older who have posted video for others to watch.

Ten percent of video viewers share links with others by posting them to a website or blog. Madden wrote, "Some who feel compelled to share the video content they find online prefer to do so in a more public way." Again, younger users have a greater tendency to share what they find; although 22 percent of video viewers ages 18 to 29 post links to video online, just 7 percent of those ages 30 to 49 do so. Madden added, "The flurry of link sharing by younger users has helped to shape the most-viewed, and top-rated lists on popular video sharing sites. Many young adults and teenagers, who are avid users of social networking sites and blogs, post videos to their personal pages and profiles, which then get linked to or reposted by many other users."

What Categories of Video Do They Watch?

In addition to asking who discovers, watches, and shares new videos, you should also ask, What categories or types of video do they watch?

Several organizations have conducted surveys to identify the most popular types of online video content, including Advertising.com, Burst Media, Frank N. Magid Associates, Ipsos Insight, the Online Publishers Association, the Pew Internet & American Life Project, Piper Jaffray, and TNS. As Figure 2.4 illustrates, eMarketer looked at all this data and estimated in February 2008 that *news/current events* was the most popular genre of video, followed closely by *jokes/bloopers/funny clips (comedy)*.

According to the July 2007 Pew report that I cited earlier, 37 percent of Internet users have watched news videos, with 10 percent watching this genre of video on a typical day. In addition to the plethora of news content posted on video sharing sites like YouTube, Pew reported, "news-related video can now be found on virtually any website associated with major network TV news channels, cable TV news, and on most mainstream newspaper websites. Additionally, blogs, video podcasts, personal websites and social networking websites also feature news-related video."

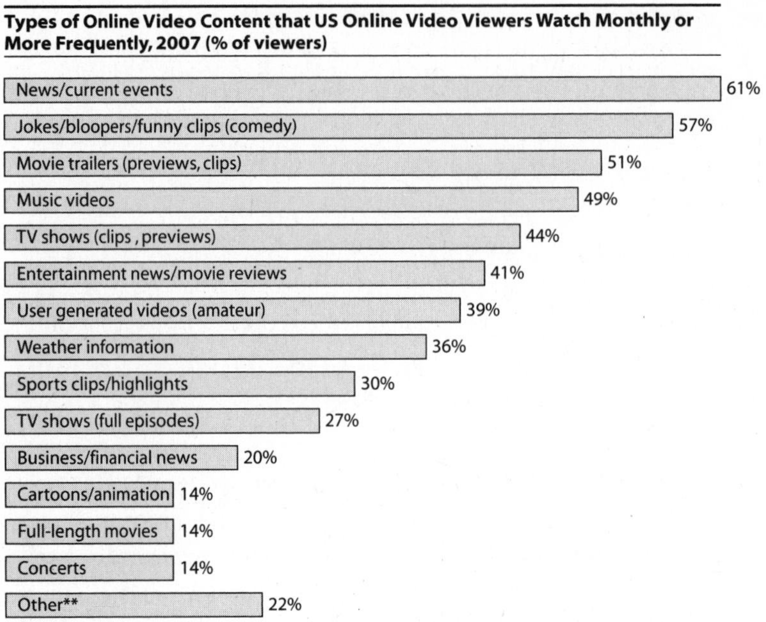

Types of Online Video Content that US Online Video Viewers Watch Monthly or More Frequently, 2007 (% of viewers)

News/current events	61%
Jokes/bloopers/funny clips (comedy)	57%
Movie trailers (previews, clips)	51%
Music videos	49%
TV shows (clips , previews)	44%
Entertainment news/movie reviews	41%
User generated videos (amateur)	39%
Weather information	36%
Sports clips/highlights	30%
TV shows (full episodes)	27%
Business/financial news	20%
Cartoons/animation	14%
Full-length movies	14%
Concerts	14%
Other**	22%

Note: excludes advertising or marketing video content; *based on a weighted average of 2007 survey data from Advertising.com, Burst Media, Frank N. Magid Associates, Ipsos Insight, Online Publishers Association (OPA), Pew Internet & American Life Project, Piper Jaffray and TNS; **includes game content, instructional, travel, live sporting events, educational, political, cooking and adult
Source: eMarketer estimates*, February 2008

Figure 2.4 Types of online video content that U.S. online video viewers watch monthly or more frequently (2007, % of viewers). (Source: eMarketer.)

Comedy and humorous videos are the second-most-viewed genre of online video among the total population of online adults; 31 percent of Internet users have watched or downloaded comedic or humorous videos and 7 percent do so on a typical day. For young adults, *comedy* is the most popular category. However, on a typical day, young adult Internet users are equally as likely to view news and comedy; 15 percent of those 18 to 29 report viewing in both categories on the average day. "Indeed, much of the content viewed by young adults, such as clips from *The Daily Show* or *The Colbert Report* blurs the line between news and comedy," reported Pew.

Music videos are another popular category. Like news, music videos can also readily cross over into the comedy category. Weird Al Yankovic's "White and Nerdy" music video is one of the most-viewed videos of all time on YouTube and is listed in both the music and comedy category. Overall, 22 percent of adult Internet users watch or download some type of music videos online and 4 percent do so on a typical day.

Videos with educational content are also popular. Overall, 22 percent of Internet users watch educational videos, and 3 percent do so on a typical day. Sometimes referred to as "how-to" or "DIY" videos, these clips range from those that provide practical everyday tips, such as "How to fold a tee-shirt perfectly," to those that visually illustrate theories or concepts, as is done in "Web 2.0...The Machine is Us/ing Us."

When Do They Discover New Videos?

This brings us to the next question: When do opinion leaders discover new videos worth sharing with their followers?

According to the Pew report, 19 percent of viewers watch online video on a typical day. However, "Few are consistently finding content that's compelling enough to share on a daily basis—just 3% send video links to others every day—but roughly one in three online video viewers will share links at least as often as a few times per month."

Now, if the 3 percent of online video viewers who share links on a daily basis is "too small"—and the 33 percent who share links a few times per month is "too large"—then what percentage would be "just right" to answer the question, When do opinion leaders discover new videos worth sharing with their followers?

I'm just spitballing here, but I think opinion leaders are watching online video on a daily basis and discovering new videos worth sharing with others a few times per week.

As Rogers noted, "One role of the opinion leader in a social system is to help reduce uncertainty about an innovation for his or her followers. To fulfill this role, an opinion leader must demonstrate prudent judgment in decisions about adopting new ideas."

Pew also found that those watched video "yesterday" reported more social viewing when compared with those who did not watch online video on the day prior to the survey. In other words, watching new videos on a daily basis enables opinion leaders to prudently share a few of them with others on a weekly basis.

This behavior is consistent with the following observation by Rogers: "The interpersonal relationships between opinion leaders and their followers hang in a delicate balance. If an opinion leader becomes too innovative, or adopts a new idea too quickly, followers may begin to doubt his or her judgment."

This behavior is also consistent with the way people spread rumors. In the *Boston Sunday Globe* on October 12, 2008, Jesse Singal observed, "Aside from their use as a news grapevine, rumors serve a second purpose as well, researchers have found: People spread them to shore up their social networks, and boost their own importance within them."

Researchers have also found that "negative rumors dominate the grapevine" and that "people are rather specific about which rumors they share, and with whom."

So, does discovering and sharing a new video demonstrate more prudent judgment than discovering and sharing rumors? You be the judge.

For example, the #1 most viewed video of all time is "Avril Lavigne - Girlfriend" from RCA Records. It was added to YouTube on February 27, 2007, and had more than 118 million views as of April 2009.

Tune out the Avril Lavigne song and pay attention to the data below it:

- The song had over 383,000 text comments, making it the #3 most discussed YouTube video of all time.

- It had been favorited over 258,000 times, making it the #14 top favorited of all time.

- It had over 315,000 ratings.

In addition, I used Yahoo! Site Explorer to discover that about 13,700 pages link to the pop music video's URL.

In other words, a lot of people on other YouTube channels, MyBlogLog communities, and Avril Lavigne fan sites shared a link to "Girlfriend" with their other friends. Does this demonstrate prudent judgment? If I were the target demographic, then I could render an impartial opinion.

Where Do They Watch New Videos?

This brings us to the next set of questions. One of them is, Where do opinion leaders watch new videos? Another is, Where do they go to watch them? And the third is, Where do opinion leaders share some of the new videos they've watched?

Why ask multiple questions? Because in addition to the two actions (finding and sharing videos), "where" can mean either a physical place or a virtual one.

Where Do They *Go* to Watch Videos?

We've already established that people don't watch new videos today the same way that people watched the final episode of *M*A*S*H*. That episode ("Goodbye, Farewell and Amen," February 28, 1983) was viewed by 106 million Americans—77 percent of the television viewers that evening—making it the most watched episode in U.S. television history, a record that still stands.

According to legend, "Goodbye, Farewell and Amen" was watched by so many people that the sewage systems of several major cities were broken by the tremendous number of toilets being flushed simultaneously right after the end of the two-and-a-half-hour long episode. Now, even the YouTube video "Avril Lavigne - Girlfriend" hasn't had that kind of sudden impact.

Once again, the only market research I've seen that even begins to ask some of the right questions is the Pew report on Online Video by Mary Madden:

www.pewinternet.org/pdfs/PIP_Online_Video_2007.pdf

According to the Pew report, 59 percent of online video consumers watch at home, and 24 percent report at-work viewing. In addition, 22 percent watch online video from a "third" place other than home or work.

Where is this "third" place? Well, for a road warrior, it could be a hotel room. For a homebody, it could be a library. For a college student, it could be a dorm room. And for any of these, it could be a coffee shop or mobile phone.

Nevertheless, these percentages are all too large to identify opinion leaders. However, when asked where they watched online video yesterday, 19 percent reported at home, only 6 percent reported at work, and just 3 percent reported a third place. Opinion leaders may be watching videos at home the day before and then watching at work a few times per week.

Where Do They *Browse* to Watch Videos?

No matter where opinion leaders are when they watch new videos, you will also want to know where they go to watch them. Although this sounds like a line from the cult film *The Adventures of Buckaroo Banzai Across the Eighth Dimension*, it isn't. Buckaroo said, "No matter where you go, there you are." I'm asking, "Whether you are at work, at home, or someplace else, which online video site do you go to in order to watch new videos?"

For the answer, let's look as some recent market research by comScore Video Metrix. As Table 2.3 shows, more than 147 million U.S. Internet users watched an average of 101 videos per viewer in January 2009. This means Americans viewed more than 14.8 billion videos that month. As my mom, who was a math teacher, used to say, "That's more than you can shake a stick at."

▶ Table 2.3 Top U.S. Online Properties Ranked by Videos Viewed, January 2009

Property	Videos (000)	Share (%) of Videos
Total Internet : Total Audience	14,831,607	100.0
Google Sites	6,367,638	42.9
Fox Interactive Media	551,991	3.7
Yahoo! Sites	374,161	2.5
Viacom Digital	287,615	1.9
Microsoft Sites	267,475	1.8
Hulu.com	250,473	1.7
Turner Network	195,983	1.3
AOL LLC	184,808	1.2
Disney Online	141,152	1.0
Megavideo.com	102,857	0.7

Total U.S. - Home/Work/University locations. Rankings based on video content sites; excludes video server networks.

Source: comScore Video Metrix

Now, comScore reported that Google Sites ranked as the top U.S. video property with 6.4 billion videos viewed—representing a 42.9 percent share of the online video market. But, as I mentioned at the beginning of this chapter, YouTube accounted for more than 99 percent of all the videos viewed at Google Sites.

And at the bottom of the press release announcing this data, comScore reported that100.9 million viewers watched an average of 62.6 videos per viewer on YouTube— for a total of 6.3 billion videos that month. This gave YouTube a 42.6 percent share of the online video market.

The comScore press release also reported that 54.1 million viewers watched an average of 8.7 videos per viewer on MySpace—for a total of 473 million videos. This gave MySpace a 3.2 percent share of the online video market.

Here's the *net* net: If YouTube is #1 with more than a 42 percent share and MySpace is #2 with only 3 percent, then YouTube will make you or break you and the other online video sites can only have impact collectively, not individually.

Where Do They Share New Videos?

Now let's ask, Where do opinion leaders share new videos? This brings us a surprising finding in the Pew report, "Online video consumers are just as likely to have shared a video viewing experience in person as they are to have shared video online. The picture of the lone Internet user, buried in his or her computer, does not ring true with most who view online video."

The Pew report found that 57 percent of online video viewers have watched with other people, such as friends or family. Young adults were the most social online video viewers; 73 percent of video consumers ages 18 to 29 have watched with others.

Once again, this is too large a percentage to identify opinion leaders. But there are ways to spot them through *observation*.

For example, Brian Stelter of the *New York Times* wrote an article on January 5, 2008, that observed, "In cubicles across the country, lunchtime has become the new prime time, as workers click aside their spreadsheets to watch videos on YouTube, news highlights on CNN.com or other Web offerings."

He added, "In some offices, workers coordinate their midday Web-watching schedules, the better to shout out punch lines to one another across rows of desks. Some people gravitate to sites where they can reliably find Webcasts of a certain length—say, a three-minute political wrap-up—to minimize both their mouse clicks and the sandwich crumbs that wind up in the keyboard."

So, go take a walk around your office at lunchtime. When you stumble across five people who are on some sort of site that is not work related, don't interrupt them. It's okay. It's lunchtime.

But observe the social motivation—the desire to share a viewing experience with someone else—which influences the way users experience online video. Then, watch closely to see if one member of the small group does the driving while others sit in the passenger seats. Could this opinion leader have discovered some of these new videos at home yesterday?

Why Don't More New Videos Go Viral?

Now, if this were a map of the online video market, then this would be the spot where you'd read the warning, "Here be dragons!" In other words, we're about to enter dangerous or unexplored waters. Why? Because there is at least some market research that asks the question, Why do some new videos go viral? But, there is no market research I know about that even begins to ask the right question: Why don't more new videos go viral?

It seems that market researchers know that most of their paying clients want to hear about successes stories. But this can give you a skewed view of the online video market. This tendency to overestimate the success rate of online videos is called the Lake Wobegon Effect because it assumes that "all the women are strong, all the men are good looking, and all the children are above average."

But, "In some cases, nothing succeeds like failure." That headline in the December 10, 2006, *Boston Globe* caught my eye. The headline appeared over an article by Robert Weisman about Gustave Manso, a Brazilian-born finance professor at MIT's Sloan School of Management.

Weisman wrote, "Manso thinks it's nearly impossible for companies to develop breakthrough products, processes, or approaches without encouraging the kind of trial and error that inevitably generates failures as well as successes. For him, the challenge is to craft incentives that will make creative people comfortable with thinking big and taking risks."

And he quoted Manso as saying, "To induce employees to explore new ideas, you have to tolerate early failure and reward long-term success."

Get it? Got it? Good.

So, let me share a story with you of an early failure in YouTube and video marketing that my long-time friend Michael Kolowich had the courage of integrity to share with readers of his Web Video Expert blog. It's the story of the Internet TV channel that Michael's firm, DigiNovations, created in January 2007 for the Mitt Romney for President campaign. Mitt TV is widely acknowledged to be the first comprehensive video channel for a presidential campaign.

However, on February 7, 2008, Romney suspended his campaign for the presidential nomination following the results of the 2008 Super Tuesday primaries—despite raising $110 million for his campaign ($45 million in personal loans and $65 million from individual donors). In other words, winning your party's nomination and getting elected president involves much more than just raising campaign contributions.

Lessons from Mitt TV

On February 10, 2008, Kolowich posted "Ten Lessons from Mitt TV." I encourage you to read the entire post on his Web Video Expert blog. But here's a sampling of lessons that you will want to know about and discuss with others:

YouTube is a two-edged sword. A lot of the 2008 presidential campaigns relied on YouTube channels generously "given" to them by the video site. And there's no question that a lot of independent traffic saw their clips based on YouTube searches. But if part of the idea was not just to inform but also to inspire people to act (give money, sign up, give us their email, etc.), then Kolowich thinks YouTube was weak at the "call to action" part. That was certainly true in 2007 and early 2008, although YouTube's "call to action" offerings got stronger in October 2008, when "click to buy" links were added to the watch pages of thousands of YouTube partner videos.

A YouTube channel is necessary but not sufficient. Because of #1, the Romney campaign decided to invest in its own very rich channel that eventually had more than 400 video clips on it, which were closely associated with their "calls to action" in the campaign. And, according to Kolowich, the most remarkable statistic of all is that more people watched the Romney campaign's clips on Mitt TV than on its YouTube channel. Other marketers have reported similar results.

A content-managed video platform is vital to success. Kolowich believed that a content-managed web video publishing system was vital to building something as sophisticated as Mitt TV. But he didn't realize at the time that the share of market of the video search engines that crawled this platform was getting smaller each and every month.

Seeds and feeds build viewership. Although the Romney campaign had its share of "I want my Mitt TV" people tuning in every day to see what was new, the key to building Mitt TV's audience (which got as high as 70,000+ viewings a day in the late stages of the campaign) was outreach—to bloggers, through press releases, through RSS feeds. The result was that there were more than 23,000 references to Mitt TV on Google and more than 2,800 sites linking to Mitt TV. However, the vast majority of videos that appeared in Google universal search results from May 2007 through November 2008 came from YouTube, not video search engines or individual websites.

Don't believe everything you read about clip length. The conventional wisdom is that video clips need to be under 2 minutes to have a prayer of getting watched. But looking over the viewing statistics, Kolowich saw that many of the most popular clips were complete speeches or events that were as long as 20 minutes or even more. It's also worth noting that the duration of the average online video viewed at Megavideo was 24.9 minutes in January 2009, according to comScore Media Metrix.

Listen to the data. According to Kolowich, one of the advantages of having their own Internet TV channel was that they could get a tremendous amount of data about what worked and what didn't. Since YouTube Insight wasn't available until March 2008, Kolowich could watch patterns of viewership and correlate it to different outreach efforts in 2007. He could see which clips were being viewed and for how long. And he could see where traffic was coming from. All this was useful in making Mitt TV a more effective channel.

So, why didn't more of Romney's new videos go viral?

For starters, Kolowich says the goal of Mitt TV wasn't to go viral. As he said, the objective was "to inspire people to act (give money, sign up, give us their email, etc.)." And Mitt TV reached this goal.

As Kolowich revealed in a post on April 23, 2008: "Without disclosing specific numbers, we found that when we could use web video to bring a viewer to the campaign website and call them to action, the payoff—in terms of contributions, volunteer sign-ups, referrals, event attendance, etc.—was orders of magnitude more than the cost of serving up the video. That's why we favored video on our own website over the many clips we posted on YouTube."

But the other reasons why so few of Romney's new videos went viral can be found in the previous paragraph: the campaign treated online video like it was just a new type of infomercial and it favored video on its own website over the clips it posted on YouTube.

Was this the right video marketing strategy? Would the Romney campaign have done any better if its goal had been to change people's presidential preference instead of prompting them to give money, sign up, and provide their email? Would the Romney campaign have done any better if it had favored YouTube over Mitt TV?

I still don't have all the answers, but I'm beginning to ask the right questions: If online video is better at informing, inspiring, and connecting than it is at direct response, then in addition to preaching to the choir on Mitt TV, shouldn't the Romney campaign have also spent more time reaching out bring more people into the church? Should the Romney campaign have spent more effort reaching out to opinion leaders and trying to win the "invisible caucus" that was held on YouTube in 2007?

What's an invisible caucus? As Linda Feldmann of the *Christian Science Monitor* reported on February 26, 2007, there was a lot of media buzz about "what's come to be known as the 'invisible primary'—the early jockeying for money, top campaign staff, and high-profile endorsements that winnow the presidential field long before any caucuses or primaries are held."

On June 15, 2008, the Pew Internet Project reported 35 percent of Americans have watched online political videos—a figure that nearly triples the reading Pew got in the 2004 presidential race. And Pew also found that supporters of Barack Obama outpaced supporters of both Hillary Clinton and John McCain in their usage of online video.

So, I'm calling the early jockeying for opinion leaders in YouTube's news and politics category an "invisible caucus." And it is worth asking, Did winning it help a former community organizer's presidential campaign "take off" while skipping it hurt a former CEO's chances of getting a critical mass of opinion leaders to share his videos with others?

Who knows? Nevertheless, on April 23, 2008, Kolowich posted this to his blog:

> *Both the Romney and Obama campaigns understood the power of video not only to get the message out but also to attract, engage, and actuate supporters on the main campaign website.... It may be pure coincidence that the candidates' fundraising performance correlates with their sophistication on Internet video, but our experience suggests that sophisticated use of web video certainly has an impact on keeping an active, vibrant base of supporters who visit often and want to stay involved.*

How Does Marketing with Video Work?

That leaves just one more question to ask: How does marketing with video work? This is the question that 9 of the 10 remaining chapters in this book will tackle. (In the final chapter, we'll revisit the five *W*s and an *H*.)

To help set the agenda for the next 90 percent of this step-by-step guide, let me share the highlights of Suzie Reider's presentation at The Edge, a creative event thrown on September 19, 2008, by the Boston AdClub. Her presentation was entitled "Marketing with Video."

Reider told the luncheon crowd about the lessons she had learned from her time with one of the world's largest social media communities. And from her point of view, YouTube is the combination of "both media and community."

As Figure 2.5 illustrates, Reider said there are six concepts to keep in mind when marketing with video:

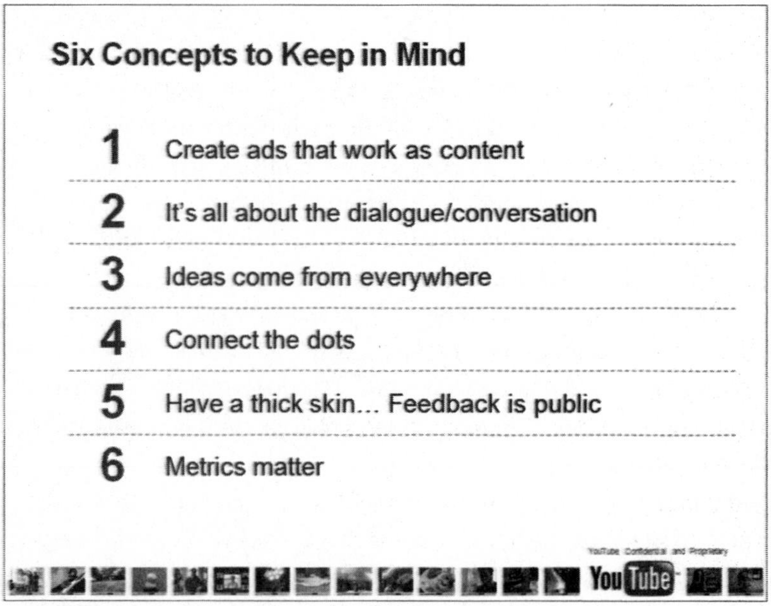

Six Concepts to Keep in Mind

1 Create ads that work as content

2 It's all about the dialogue/conversation

3 Ideas come from everywhere

4 Connect the dots

5 Have a thick skin... Feedback is public

6 Metrics matter

Figure 2.5 Suzie Reider's six concepts for marketing with video

Create ads that work as content She showed "Amazing Ball girl catch," a Gatorade commercial directed by Baker Smith of Harvest Films, that was posted in June 2008 and had almost 2 million views in April 2009.

It's all about the dialogue/conversation She showed "Tiger Woods 09 - Walk on Water." After Levinator25 posted a video of "the Jesus shot," a glitch in Tiger Woods PGA TOUR 08, the folks at EA SPORTS uploaded a funny response on August 19, 2008, that had over 3 million views as of April 2009.

Ideas come from everywhere She showed "Battle at Kruger," the most viewed "pets and animals" video of all time, with 42.8 million views in April 2009. The viral hit has become the subject of a National Geographic Channel documentary.

Connect the dots She showed the Heinz "Top This TV" Challenge, a YouTube contest that generated nearly 4,000 qualified contest entries, 105,000 hours of interaction with the brand, and an increase in ketchup sales.

Have thick skin... Feedback is public She showed "Dove Evolution," the Ogilvy spot created by Tim Piper, which had over 8.7 million views as of April 2009 and inspired the "Slob Evolution" spoof, which had almost 1.3 million views as of that date.

Metrics matter She showed YouTube Insight, a free tool that enables anyone with a YouTube account to view detailed statistics about the videos that they upload to the site.

Reider closed her presentation with a surprising example of who is marketing with video: The Royal Channel, the official channel of the British monarchy.

The royal household launched its channel on YouTube in December 2007 and had 80 videos in April 2009. The channel showcases both archive and modern video of the queen and other members of the royal family and royal events. The most viewed video was "The Christmas Broadcast, 1957," or "Queen's Speech." The access to this restricted footage was granted to mark the 50th anniversary of the first televised Christmas Broadcast. As of April 2009, it had more than 1 million views, over 3,500 ratings and had been favorited more than 1,500 times.

Now, if the British monarchy has been marketing with video for more than a year and a half, then it's time for even the most traditional organization to get started.

And like the kids in the *New Yorker* cartoon by Lee Lorenz back in Figure 2.1, we still don't have all the answers, but we are beginning to ask the right questions:

- **Who** discovers, watches, and shares new videos?
- **What** categories or types of video do they watch?
- **When** do they discover new videos?
- **Where** do they share new videos?
- **Why** don't more new videos go viral?
- **How** does marketing with video work?

And that's a great way to get started.

Month 1: Map Out Your Video Marketing Strategy

3

In the previous chapter, you learned about opinion leaders. In this chapter, you will learn how to identify opinion leaders on YouTube and other online video sites. You will also learn why the old communication model should be reversed to map out your video marketing strategy. This quest will require all of the imagination, passion, and discipline of Don Quixote plus the practicality, realism, and cleverness of Sancho Panza.

Chapter Contents

Tilting at Windmills

Week 1: Identify Opinion Leaders on YouTube

Week 2: Find Opinion Leaders on Other Video Sites

Week 3: Reverse the Old Map of Mass Media

Week 4: Follow the New Map of Social Media

Tilting at Windmills

When mapping out their video marketing strategy, many veteran marketers start by setting their marketing goals and advertising objectives. But riddle me this: How can you set practical goals and realistic objectives if you haven't identified your target audience first?

And many new YouTubers will start by shooting first and asking questions later. But riddle me that: If you haven't identified your target audience first, how can you hope to get at least 100 views?

This is why I'll talk about creating compelling video content in Chapter 5 and setting your goals and objectives in Chapter 9 after identifying your target audience in this chapter. As Figure 3.1 illustrates, it may appear that I'm tilting at windmills.

Figure 3.1 Don Quixote is followed by Sancho holding a camcorder and microphone boom.

But I'm just borrowing a page from classic marketing, which starts by determining the needs and wants of target markets. Actually, I'm just borrowing a paragraph from "Marketing Myopia," the classic article by Theodore Levitt published in the *Harvard Business Review* in 1960. According to Levitt:

> *Hollywood barely escaped being totally ravished by television. Actually, all the established film companies went through drastic reorganizations. Some simply disappeared. All of them got into trouble not because of TV's inroads but because of their own myopia....Hollywood defined its business incorrectly. It thought it was in the movie business when it was actually in the entertainment business. 'Movies' implied a specific, limited product. This produced a fatuous contentment that from the beginning led producers to view TV as a threat. Hollywood scorned and rejected TV when it should have welcomed it as an opportunity—an opportunity to expand the entertainment business.*

Although this was written almost 50 years ago, it should still be required reading today. Only now, television seems to be playing the old role Hollywood once played and online video is playing the role of TV.

Levitt added, "Had Hollywood been customer oriented (providing entertainment) rather than product oriented (making movies), would it have gone through the fiscal purgatory that it did? I doubt it."

So, let's not make the same mistake that "decimated the old movie companies and toppled the big movie moguls." Instead, let's start by identifying who our target viewers are—and what they are seeking, when they seek it, where they seek it, and why they seek it—before we decide how to inform, persuade, or entertain them.

Week 1: Identify Opinion Leaders on YouTube

In the mass marketing era, less effort needed to be spent identifying who your target viewers were. They seemed to be everyone who could be reached via mass media.

In today's social marketing era, more effort needs to be spent identifying who your target viewers should be. They are the opinion leaders who discover new videos on a daily basis and then decide to share some of them with others a few times a week using social media.

However, you learned in Chapter 2 that you can often identify opinion leaders by their behavior. As Figure 3.2 illustrates humorously, opinion leaders like Chad Vader, Day Shift Manager, are more likely to have either rated an online video or posted comments after seeing a video online.

Figure 3.2 "Chad Vader - Day Shift Manager #1"

As Figure 3.3 illustrates musically, opinion leaders like Miley Cyrus and Mandy Jiroux are more likely to have uploaded a video file online for others to watch, such as their "M&M CRU" dance battle videos.

Figure 3.3 "M&M CRU FINAL DANCE BATTLE - Cyrus Blaine Seacrest Tatum"

And as you will see in Chapter 7, opinion leaders are more likely to share links with others by posting them to a website or blog.

Using these visible signs, it is possible to identify the opinion leaders on YouTube. They are who your target viewers should be. Here's how:

Monday: Visit YouTube's home page

Tuesday: Click the Videos tab

Wednesday: Click the Channels tab

Thursday: Click the Community tab

Friday: Visit You Choose '08

Monday: Visit YouTube's Home Page

To begin, let's visit YouTube's home page: www.youtube.com. Now, if you already have a YouTube Account, please log out. I want you to see YouTube's home page the way visitors without accounts would see it.

Everyone signed out?

Entrepreneur: "Before we begin today's lesson, should I turn off my cell phone, beeper, and iPod, too?"

No, that won't be necessary.

As Figure 3.4 illustrates, tabs for Home, Videos, Shows, Channels, and Community appear across the very top of the YouTube home page. To the right of these tabs is a search box. We'll explore these areas in more detail over this coming week.

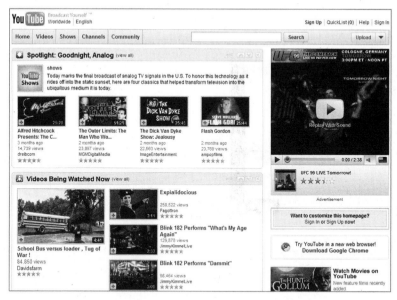

Figure 3.4 YouTube - Broadcast Yourself

Spotlight videos are prominently displayed at the top of the home page. Although they don't appear every day, when they do, Spotlight videos are organized around a theme like the final broadcast of analog TV signals in the U.S.

Lower down, thumbnails of four videos being watched now appear. On days without spotlight videos, videos being watched now appear at the top of the home page. Underneath these are thumbnails of four Featured Videos.

Scroll down and there are the most popular videos in eight categories, as well as the overall most viewed and top favorited video. And over on the right side are advertisements, which YouTube calls "Promoted Videos." If some of these monikers seem new, they are. YouTube renamed a few modules in March 2009 and made other changes to the homepage in April 2009

In June 2008, YouTube introduced a personalized home page. The customizable home page featured new interactive modules that could be moved around, removed, and replaced to create a more personal video discovery experience.

The new home page included the latest videos from subscriptions, personalized recommendations (an algorithmically selected set of videos based on past views and favorites), and an easier way to see what friends were uploading, favoriting, and rating as well as home page regulars like featured videos and videos being watched now.

In addition, the new personalized home page featured a dashboard that included stats about the user's Inbox. This is significant because it means veteran Tubers and new YouTubers are probably getting very different answers to the question, "What should I watch today?"

YouTube Director: "How do you get featured on YouTube?"

That's a good question. Featured Videos are primarily populated with videos from YouTube's thousands of partners, but they might also include select user videos that are currently popular or that YouTube has previously showcased in Spotlight Videos. YouTube automatically rotates these videos throughout the day to keep them fresh.

"How do you get featured on YouTube" is also the title of an animated short that is also called "The Birds and the Biz" from Jantze studios. As the thumbnail in Figure 3.5 illustrates, it finally explains the secret behind getting your work featured by YouTube.

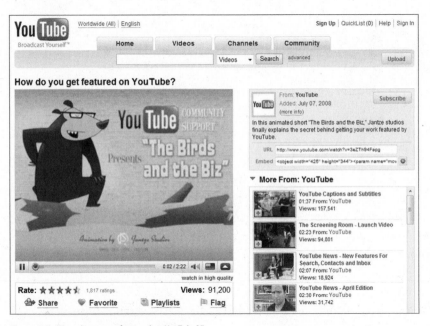

Figure 3.5 "How do you get featured on YouTube?"

According to Papa Bear, "YouTubers have a better chance of having their films featured on the site by not only creating original work but also by becoming a fully vested member of the YouTube community."

YouTube Director: "And how do you become a fully vested member of the YouTube community?"

Well, according to pops, "It all starts with creating a channel and uploading a video. If you want to increase your presence, you make playlists, join groups, subscribe to other videos, and get involved just like you would with any other community."

He adds, "By joining groups, replying to other videos, even making more videos, you'll build a following and have a better chance of catching the eye of one of those busy YouTube bees."

YouTube Director: "Those busy YouTube bees sound like an anthropomorphic version of opinion leaders, if you ask me."

I agree. As we'll discuss later in this chapter, opinion leaders have greater social participation than their followers.

YouTube Director: "Do only the most-viewed videos get picked?"

No. According to pops, "YouTube only pays attention to what the community is doing and they never really know what crazy new thing will be next." Go to www .youtube.com/watch?v=3eZTh94Fapg to watch the entire animated film. It's one of the favorites in YouTubeHelp's channel.

YouTube Director: "How do you get spotlighted on YouTube?"

That's another good question. According to YouTube, "The YouTube Team likes to highlight videos they think users want to watch; videos that hopefully inform, inspire, and entertain."

As of this writing, YouTube is planning to take a more thematic approach to showcasing some of the best videos the YouTube community and partners produce. When you see these videos, they will have top billing on the page—a true spotlight.

Tuesday: Click the Videos Tab

Now, click the Videos tab (http://www.youtube.com/browse) at the top of the YouTube home page. As you can see in Figure 3.6, this will take you to the Videos page, where you'll see some new elements.

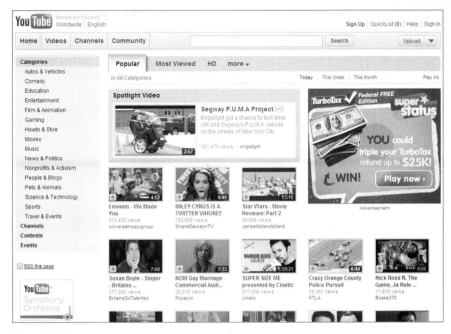

Figure 3.6 Videos

For starters, there is a link at the top that says Spotlight Video. Selected by the YouTube Editors, it's a "cool video you might be interested in" feature. Yes, the YouTube Editors can be opinion leaders too.

Underneath are 23 Popular videos in all categories. And other tabs across the top of the page are Most Viewed, and HD, and more. These are called Honors and are given to videos by the YouTube community.

Down the left side of the Videos page are 16 Categories:

- Autos & Vehicles
- Comedy
- Education
- Entertainment
- Film & Animation
- Gaming
- Howto & Style
- Movies
- Music
- News & Politics
- Nonprofits & Activism
- People & Blogs
- Pets & Animals
- Science & Technology
- Sports
- Travel & Events

These categories are selected by YouTubers when they upload a new video.

Click the Most Viewed tab and then the All Time link, as you can see in Figure 3.7.

Underneath that are the most viewed videos of all time: "Avril Lavigne - Girlfriend" (with over 118 million views as of April 2009) and "Evolution of Dance" (with over 117 million views). We looked at the music video from RCA Records in Chapter 2, so click "Evolution of Dance" to see Judson Laipply's dancing comedy in Figure 3.8.

Added on April 6, 2006, Jud says his video is "the funniest 6 minutes you will ever see!" His video amassed over 10 millions views in under two weeks and has been featured on *Good Morning America*, *The Today Show*, and countless others. So, the public and the press agree.

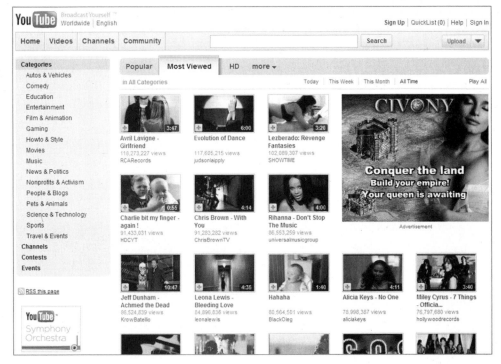

Figure 3.7 All — Most Viewed (All Time)

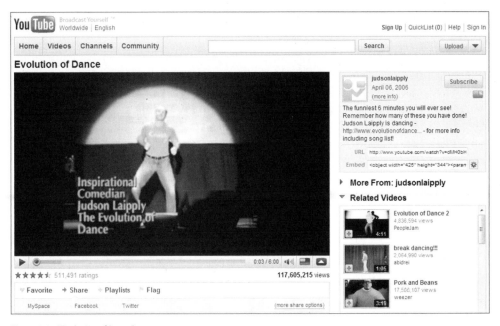

Figure 3.8 "Evolution of Dance"

As Figure 3.9 shows, when you scroll down, you'll see Statistics & Data. Click on the triangle on the left and you will see this video not only had more than 117 million views, it also had over 511,000 ratings, 1,775 responses, and more than 323,000 comments. In addition, it had been favorited more than 697,000 times and received eight honors, including #1 Top Favorited (all time), #7 Most Discussed (all time), and #15 Most Responded (all time).

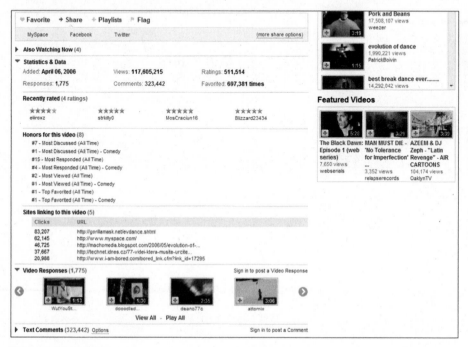

Figure 3.9 Statistics & Data

Underneath this, you'll see the top five sites linking to this video—ranked by which ones sent the most clicks to "Evolution of Dance." That's a qualified list of opinion leaders from outside the YouTube community.

Next, you'll see 1,775 video responses to "Evolution of Dance." Click on the "View All" link and you'll see how many of these are an homage by an opinion leader in the comedy category.

Underneath this, you'll see more than 323,000 text comments. Read a sample of these comments and you'll see that some are spam, but many are by opinion leaders.

How can you tell if a comment is spam? As Justice Potter Stewart once said about obscenity, "I know it when I see it."

Wednesday: Click the Channels Tab

Now, click the Channels tab (http://www.youtube.com/members) at the top of the YouTube home page. As Figure 3.11 illustrates, this will take you to the Channels page, where you'll see some more new elements.

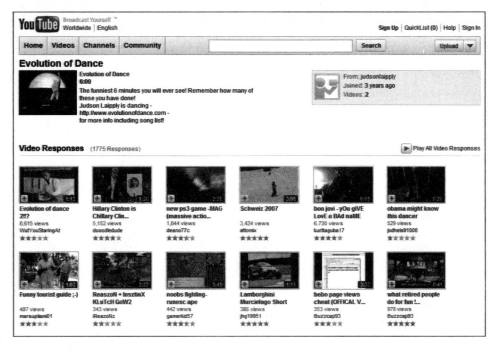

Figure 3.10 Video Responses

Figure 3.11 Channels

To begin with, there are two links across the top: Most Subscribed and Most Viewed. Again, these honors are given to channels by the YouTube community.

Down the left side of the Channels page are 15 categories (as of this writing, Movies wasn't listed on the Channels page). Underneath are nine different account types, which are selected when a new brand channel is created on YouTube, and links to You Choose 08 (which we'll look at on Friday):

- Comedians
- Directors
- Gurus
- Musicians
- Non-Profit
- Partners
- Politicians
- Reporters
- Sponsors
- You Choose 08

Finally, at the bottom of the list are links to Contests, Events, and the YouTube Screening Room.

As you see in Figure 3.12, click the All Time link and the most viewed channels are Universal Music Group (with over 3.8 billion views as of April 2009) and Sony BMG (with over 610 million views). With almost 9,458 videos, we have to take a look at Universal Music Group's VLogging channel.

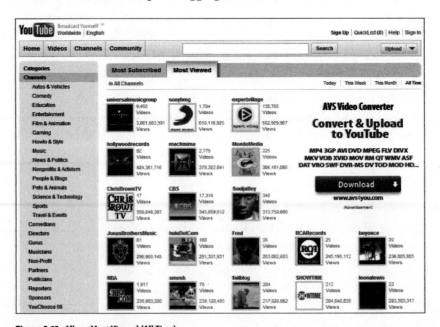

Figure 3.12 All — Most Viewed (All Time)

In Figure 3.13 is the Universal Music Group (UMG) Music Video Channel. Launched on August 23, 2006, it had almost 665,000 subscribers as of April 2009, making it the #4 most subscribed channel of all time.

Figure 3.13 Universal Music Group's channel

This means close to 665,000 subscribers get notified each time UMG uploads a new video, dramatically accelerating the "time-to-take-off" for Universal Music Group's dozens of record labels as well as a multitude of record labels owned or distributed by its record company subsidiaries around the world. However, UMG doesn't display its subscribers, so we can't see who their opinion leaders are.

UMG's channel also had over 25 million channel views as of April 2009. Channel views are the number of times YouTubers look at a user's page, which contains a user's profile information, videos, and other features. This means YouTubers have visited UMG's brand channel more than 25 million times to look for videos, playlists, and groups. This kind of brand loyalty also helps to accelerate the "time-to-take-off" for a new video from UMG.

Thursday: Click the Community Tab

Now, click the Community tab to go to the Community page (http://www.youtube.com/community), where you'll see additional new elements (Figure 3.14). This includes Contests, Events, Groups, and Community Help Forums.

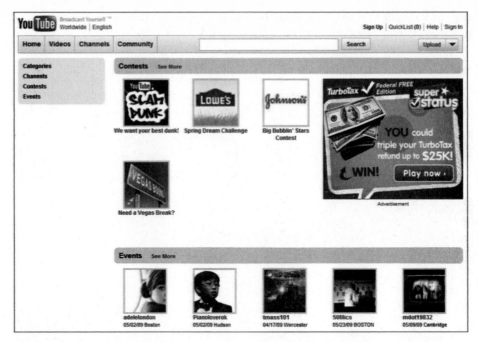

Figure 3.14 Community

Contests

A contest is a competition where users can submit videos and other users can vote on them. The official YouTube Contests section is for paid advertisers only. Each contest is different so you'll have to check out the particular contest page you're interested in to find out more details about it.

Non-official contests can be created by anyone in any number of ways ranging from the creation of groups to simple video responses.

For example, on August 18, 2008, Better Homes and Gardens magazine's BetterRecipes.com site launched an online video contest to find "America's Next Cooking Celebrity." To enter, all participants had to do was upload a video of them preparing an original recipe to BetterRecipes's YouTube channel, which appears in Figure 3.15.

A panel of judges selected two semifinalists, who were flown to Des Moines, Iowa, for a cook-off in the famous Better Homes and Gardens Test Kitchen. The cook-off aired on the Better Today television show in 30 markets around the country. The winner would also have their very own cookbook published by Better Homes and Gardens.

At that time, an ad on the YouTube home page cost $175,000 a day, plus a commitment to spend $50,000 more in ads on Google or YouTube. For a small fraction of that cost, Better Homes and Gardens hired my company to conduct an outreach program to opinion leaders with cooking blogs or cooking channels on YouTube. We also wrote an optimized press release to promote the contest.

Figure 3.15 Enter Now! America's Next Cooking Celebrity

Participants from across the country embraced the challenge in creative ways. The first to respond was Jolene Sugarbaker, "The Trailer Park Queen" and a YouTube guru. She commented on the BetterRecipes's channel, "What a great contest! Jumping into my kitchen now!"

Jolene Sugarbaker's channel had 161 videos, over 6,000 subscribers, and more than 138,000 channel views at the time. She also has an official site, a MySpace page, and a vlog. She was the first opinion leader to adopt the contest.

By the time the contest ended in early October, the introductory video had 21,661 views and there were 75 video responses, making it the #13 most responded video that month in the Howto & Style category, as well as the #40 most responded video of all time in that category.

The two finalists were Rob Barrett, who has the cooking4dads channel on YouTube and the Cooking for Dads website, and Kristina Vanni, who has the kristina-vanni channel on YouTube and the Recipe Souvenirs website.

"Hundreds of talented people entered our cooking contest—but Kristina and Rob really stood out from the rest," said Heather Morgan Shott, senior food editor of BHG.com. "They dazzled us with their creativity, cooking chops, and, ultimately, their delicious dishes."

The panel of judges then selected Rob as the winner based on his personality, ability to communicate the creation of his dish to the audience, final presentation, and taste. Rob is not a professional chef, just a dad who has learned to cook fun meals for the whole family.

"Rob is a natural," said Jennifer Darling, executive food editor for Meredith Special Interest Media. "Anyone can follow his directions and his recipes were yummy— great family food. We're all excited to see his Tastebook recipe collection that he's putting together."

Groups

Joining a group is one way to become a fully vested member of the YouTube community and build relationships with opinion leaders. If you have some interesting videos and thoughts to contribute, and like participating in conversations with others, you might want to join a group:

- From the group's main page, click the Join This Group link in the upper-right corner.
- If the group owner allows anyone to join the group, you'll automatically become a member. Otherwise, you'll have to wait until the group owner gives you permission before you can post videos or topics for discussion.
- Once you've joined a group, it's easy to post new topics for discussion or add comments to other topics.

Forums

The YouTube Community Help Forums are unmoderated. But you will often find opinion leaders helping other YouTubers, and occasionally a YouTube representative will post tips and clarifications.

Friday: Visit You Choose 08

YouTube launched You Choose 08 on March 1, 2007. As Figure 3.16 illustrates, the platform featured videos from the presidential campaigns, the news media, and other contributors.

The first presidential candidate in the spotlight was Mitt Romney, who posted a video on April 11, 2007, asking the YouTube community a question, monitored response videos for a week, and then posted another video reflecting on what he'd seen.

Romney was followed by John Edwards on April 18, John McCain on April 25, Dennis Kucinich on May 1, Duncan Hunter on May 9, Hillary Clinton on May 16, Mike Huckabee on May 23, Joe Biden on May 30, Tom Trancredo on June 7, Barack Obama on June 17, Sam Brownback on June 20, Chris Dodd on June 28, Jim Gilmore on July 5, Bill Richardson on July 11, Rudy Giuliani on July 18, Mike Gravel on July 28, and Ron Paul on August 5. Millions of people checked out the candidates' YouTube channels, and thousands communicated directly with those running for president via ratings, comments, and video responses.

Figure 3.16 You Choose 08

On June 14, 2007, YouTube announced another way of bringing that dialogue to national television: the CNN/YouTube debates. The Democratic debate on July 23 and the Republican debate on November 28 featured questions from YouTube videos.

Eight Democratic presidential candidates faced 39 questions about the war in Iraq, the environment, health care, education (sex and otherwise), gay marriage, and lots more. The questions were direct, heartfelt, and even brought some levity to politics. For example, as Figure 3.17 illustrates, Billiam the Snowman from kotasHQ asked the Democratic candidates about global warming.

People submitted almost 5,000 questions to the GOP hopefuls right on YouTube, 2,000 more than the Democrats got. And the eight Republican candidates sparred on 34 of these important issues, including the economy, Iraq, and immigration.

In other words, the "invisible caucus" of opinion leaders in YouTube's News & Politics category that I mentioned in Chapter 2 was very visible. Did it impact the real caucuses and primaries held in 2008?

That's the question that politicians seeking office in 2010, 2012, and beyond need to ask.

Figure 3.17 "CNN/YouTube Debate: Global Warming"

As I mentioned earlier, the Pew Internet & American Life Project reported in June 2008, that 35 percent of Americans had watched online political videos—a figure that nearly tripled the reading Pew got in the 2004 race. And 51 percent of wired Democrats and Independents had watched some type of political campaign video, compared with 42 percent of wired Republicans. In addition, Obama supporters outpaced McCain supporters in their usage of online video.

Aaron Smith, a research specialists, and Lee Rainie, director of the Pew Internet Project, said, "The punch-counterpunch rhythms of the campaign are now usually played out online in emails and videos rather than in faxed press releases and 30-second ads."

What impact did online video have on the outcome of the 2008 presidential election?

As Figure 3.18 illustrates, BarackObamadotcom's channel on YouTube, which had been launched on September 5, 2006, had just over 113,000 subscribers and 18+ million channel views as of November 1, 2008. The 1,760 videos on the channel had 93,929,314 views all time.

And as you can see in Figure 3.19, clicking the subscriber's link showed you the photos and names of the opinion leaders who followed the Obama campaign.

Figure 3.18 The Obama Biden page

Figure 3.19 Obama Biden's subscribers

JohnMcCaindotcom's channel on YouTube, which had been launched on February 23, 2007, had 28,000 subscribers and over 2 million channel views on that date. And the 327 videos on the channel had over 24 million views all time. But the McCain campaign didn't display the photos and names of their subscribers, so we don't know who the opinion leaders who followed the McCain campaign were.

Overall, Obama's videos on YouTube had almost a 4-to-1 lead over McCain's videos in total views and a 4-to-1 lead and a 9-to-1 lead in channel views the Saturday before Tuesday's presidential election.

In the previous month, Obama's videos had 16+ million views compared to almost 4 million views for McCain's. In the previous week, Obama's videos had over 4 million views compared to 633,000 views for McCain's. Although on Election Day, McCain's videos had almost 140,000 views compared to 91,000 views for Obama's, it was of course too little too late.

Week 2: Find Opinion Leaders on Other Online Video Sites

Based on its market share, I believe YouTube should be the center, but not the circumference, of your video marketing strategy. So let's take a serious look some of the other online video sites to see if we can find opinion leaders there as well. But which other online video sites merit a serious look?

It's difficult to identify opinion leaders who use Google Video or blinkx because video search engines don't invite users to post comments.

Although there are scores of video sharing sites, only a handful have a market share that's greater than 1 percent. For example, TubeMogul took a sample of 200,000 videos on July 17, 2008. It then compared average cumulative views for the following sites: Crackle, Dailymotion, Metacafe, MySpace, Revver, Stupid Videos, Veoh, Yahoo! Video, and YouTube.

As Figure 3.20 illustrates, although YouTube dominated in cumulative views, the seven other online video sites still reach a great deal of the audience out there.

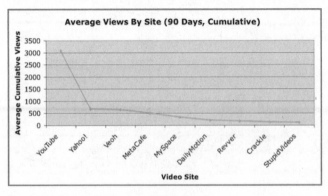

Figure 3.20 Average views for several online video sites

Adding up the video sharing site averages, veteran marketers and new YouTubers can almost double their audiences by distributing their videos to Yahoo! Video, Veoh, Metacafe, MySpace, and Dailymotion as well as YouTube.

Let's explore these video sharing sites and see what happens if we say, "Take me to your opinion leaders":

Monday: Start with Yahoo! Video

Tuesday: Check out Veoh

Wednesday: Look at Metacafe

Thursday: Watch MySpace Video

Friday: View Dailymotion

Monday: Start with Yahoo! Video

Let's start at Yahoo! Video (`http://video.yahoo.com`), where 45.4 million unique viewers watched an average of 7.8 videos per viewer in April 2009 according to comScore Video Metrix. That's a total of 355.2 million videos—or a 2.1 percent share of all the videos viewed in the United States that month.

In Canada, comScore Video Metrix reported that Yahoo! Video was the #3 video property in February 2009. And TubeMogul reported in July 2008 that Yahoo! Video was #2 in average views by site, behind only YouTube. This is one of the places to look for opinion leaders.

As you can see in Figure 3.21, Yahoo! Video is a pop-culture mashup. It has unicorns, chipmunks, ninjas, cats, and robots. It also has music videos and news, sports, autos, comedy, TV clips, and movie previews.

Figure 3.21 Yahoo! Video

The people at Yahoo! Video handpick the most original and up-to-date videos for your viewing pleasure, from user-created content to exclusive Web shows. So, they are some of the opinion leaders that you will want to get to know.

In addition, uploading your videos to Yahoo! Video will help them show up in the blended results in Yahoo! Search.

To get started, create a personal profile. Then view, rate, and review videos. Demonstrate your good taste by programming and sharing your own personal play-lists. And check out the Yahoo! Video Blog to find out what the people behind Yahoo! Video have to say about the world of online video.

If you dig deeper, you'll see that Yahoo! Video displays comments from other viewers. Many of these comments were made by opinion leaders in the Yahoo! Community.

Tuesday: Check Out Veoh

Today, let's check out Veoh (http://www.veoh.com), an Internet TV service that gives viewers the power to easily discover, watch, and personalize their online viewing experience. It ranked #3 in TubeMogul's research.

As you can see in Figure 3.22, Veoh gives you free access to a wide variety of TV and film studio content, independent productions, and user-generated videos on the Web. This includes hit CBS, NBC, FOX, and Comedy Central shows as well as YouTube clips.

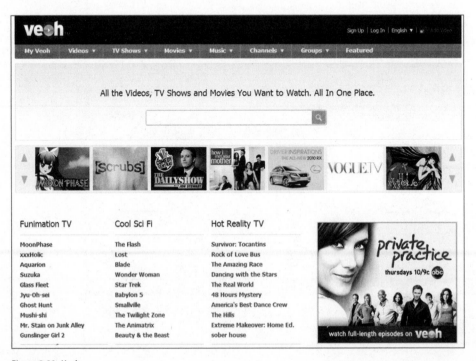

Figure 3.22 Veoh

Veoh is an open platform for content publishers of all sizes and sophistication. As of October 2008, more than 100,000 content publishers—from CBS, Viacom's MTV Networks, ABC, Warner Bros. Television Group, ESPN, and Lions Gate to thousands of independent filmmakers and content producers—used Veoh to connect with an audience of more than 28 million unique users per month worldwide.

In addition, Veoh offers a unique publisher optimization program that gives marketers tools to help them raise awareness of their content and cultivate loyal viewing audiences.

Veoh also displays the comments of viewers underneath individual videos, enabling you to identify the most engaged, influential viewers. According to Veoh, about 6 million of its U.S. viewers are considered "engaged viewers" who watch more than an hour of online video a week.

You might also want to check out "Watching The Web: How Online Video Engages Audiences," a study entitled commissioned by Veoh Networks and conducted by Forrester Consulting that found in October 2008, "not all online video viewers are created equal."

The study found "engaged viewers" make up nearly 40 percent of all online video viewers and watch nearly 75 percent of all online video. Engaged viewers who spend the most time watching and sharing long-form content have certain characteristics:

- They are more likely to watch videos all the way through.
- They pay more attention to online video than they do TV.
- They interact with and rate the videos they watch more frequently.
- They are twice as likely to recall in-video ads and post-rolls than nonengaged viewers.
- They agree more readily that advertising is fair and helps pay for their free experience.
- They consider banner ads and ads that come in between videos (mid-rolls) most effective.

Wednesday: Look at Metacafe

Today, let's take a look at Metacafe (http://www.metacafe.com/), a video entertainment site that attracted more than 44 million unique viewers worldwide in December 2008, according to comScore Media Metrix. More than 11 million of these unique viewers are in the United States.

As you can see in Figure 3.23, Metacafe is focused exclusively on short-form entertainment from new, emerging talents and established Hollywood heavyweights alike.

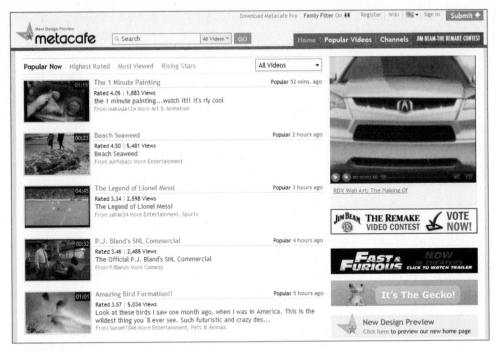

Figure 3.23 Metacafe

Metacafe is not a video sharing site that allows any and every video to be posted. Instead, Metacafe focuses on two key initiatives launched in 2008:

- Teaming with content partners in key short-form entertainment categories including TV clips, movie trailers, music videos, sports highlights, video game trailers, comedy sketches, news, and animated videos;

- Growing usage of Wikicafe, which empowers the Metacafe community to add and edit the tags, titles, descriptions and more for any of the millions of videos on the site, helping improve video search results and recommendations.

Recent Metacafe initiatives include:

- A new NBA channel, which features game highlights, top plays and weekly recaps.

- A new Music channel, which features established artists and up-and-coming acts in the genres of Pop, Rock, R&B, Hip Hop, Country and Latin.

- The addition of more than 30 featured channels from best-of-the-web content partners and boutique production firms making short-form videos.

- The MetaFest online-offline film festival, which honored 26 short films by 23 filmmakers from 10 countries and awarded more than $10,000 in prizes.

Pay particular attention to three features of Metacafe that can help you to identify the opinion leaders in this community:

Community Auditions A community review panel of more than 80,000 volunteers takes a first look at each of the thousands of videos submitted to the site every day.

Community Rankings The VideoRank system identifies and exposes the most popular videos by automatically gauging every interaction each viewer has with a video.

Community Rewards The Producer Rewards program pays video creators for their best original work, as determined by the viewers.

Thursday: Watch MySpace Video

Today, let's watch MySpaceVideo (http://vids.myspace.com/). According to comScore Video Metrix, 49 million viewers in the United States watched an average of 7.9 videos per viewer on MySpace in April 2009. That's a total of 387 million videos—or a 2.3 percent share of all the videos viewed in the United States that month.

And TubeMogul reported on July 17, 2008, that MySpace Video was #5 in average views by site, behind YouTube, Yahoo! Video, Veoh, and Metacafe. So this is another one of the places to look for opinion leaders.

As you can see in Figure 3.24, MySpace Video is similar to the YouTube video sharing site. MySpace introduced MySpaceTV in early 2007 and it is still in beta mode.

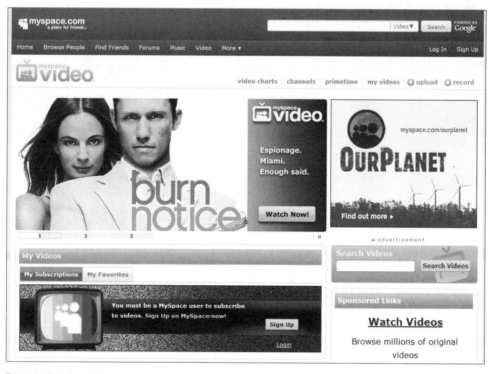

Figure 3.24 MySpaceVideo

Friday: View Dailymotion

Finally, let's view Dailymotion (http://www.dailymotion.com/us). According to com-Score, Dailymotion attracted over 44.2 million unique monthly viewers worldwide in January 2009.

As you can see in Figure 3.25, Dailymotion is a video entertainment site. Every day, over 15,000 new videos are uploaded into Dailymotion's global network of 18 localized video entertainment sites. In January 2009, Dailymotion delivered over 914 million videos to users including "curated content" from premium and Motionmaker creative contributors.

Figure 3.25 Dailymotion

In March 2009, Dailymotion announced a distribution agreement with Hulu. The agreement with Hulu will give Dailymotion's audience access to an additional 40,000 premium videos from Hulu's extensive online video library, including full-length episodes from major television studios, full-length feature films from major film studios, as well as news and other content from more than 130 content providers.

As you saw with the previous video sharing sites, you can find opinion leaders on Dailymotion by looking for visible signs like posted comments on videos.

Obviously, there are lots of other online video sites. TubeMogul also looked at Revver, Crackle, and Stupid Videos. Hitwise data suggests MegaVideo should be added to the list. We'll look at Google Video and other video search engines in Chapter 4.

But at some point, you will need to draw a line. Because YouTube dominates the online video market and every other online video site has a market share in the single digits—or lower—your video marketing strategy doesn't need to extend too far beyond the ones we've looked at.

There may a few opinion leaders in other places, but not enough to create a critical mass.

Week 3: Reverse the Old Map of Mass Media

Now that we've identified *who* our target viewers are, let's get an overview of *what* they are seeking; *when*, *where*, and *why* they seek it; and *how* to inform, persuade, or entertain them.

To map out your video marketing strategy, it helps to have a map—an accurate, up-to-date map of social media and the video sharing process.

Finding such a map may seem like an impossible dream, but it is a quest that requires all of the imagination, passion, and discipline of Don Quixote plus the practicality, realism, and cleverness of Sancho Panza.

Monday: Re-examine the old map

Tuesday: Identify the opinion leaders

Wednesday: Learn how to optimize video for YouTube

Thursday: Create compelling video content

Friday: Customize your YouTube channel

Monday: Re-examine the Old Map

Most veteran marketers already have an old map of how communication works. It's probably in their old marketing textbooks—it's definitely in both *Marketing Management* by Philip Kotler and *Principles of Marketing* by Kotler and Gary Armstrong.

The earliest version of this map was drawn by Harold Lasswell in 1939, when he was director of war communications research at the U.S. Library of Congress. It was declassified in 1948. It asked the question, Who says what in which channel to whom with what effect?

As Figure 3.26 illustrates, Lasswell's map has been redrawn over the years to include nine elements in the communication process.

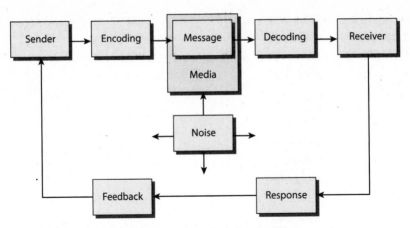

Figure 3.26 Elements in the communication process in the broadcast TV era

According to Kotler, these elements are defined as follows:

Sender The party sending the message to another party

Encoding The process of putting thought into symbolic form

Message The set of symbols that the sender transmits

Media The communication channels through which the message moves from sender to receiver

Decoding The process by which the receiver assigns meaning to the symbols encoded by the sender

Receiver The party receiving the message sent by another party

Response The reactions of the receiver after being exposed to the message

Feedback The part of the receiver's response communicated back to the sender

Noise The unplanned static or distortion during the communication process, resulting in the receiver receiving a different message than the sender sent

There are just two problems with this map.

First, it's old. It dates back to the mass media era of broadcast TV. But, as we've already observed in Chapter 2, YouTube doesn't work like mass media; it works like other social media.

Social media are primarily Internet-based tools for sharing and discussing information among human beings. Or, as Suzie Reider shared, "It's all about the dialogue/conversation."

In other words, a social medium like YouTube is a two-way street. But if you look closely at Diagram 3.1, you'll see that the arrows between the elements in the communication process are all pointing one way.

This brings me to the second problem with this map. It starts on the left with the sender instead of on the right with the target viewers.

So, maybe we need to reverse Lasswell's old model and ask, "Who seeks what in which channel from whom with what effect?"

To illustrate what an up-to-date, customer-oriented map of the communications process looks like, check out Figure 3.27.

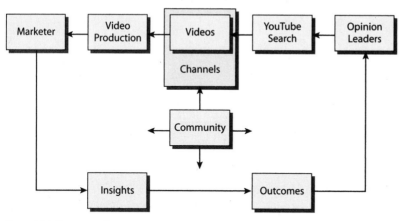

Figure 3.27 Elements in the communication process in the video sharing era

These may appear to be minor edits, but they represent a major paradigm shift. Let me explain by sharing a quick story.

I'm an American, who graduated from the University of Michigan. But I spent my junior year at the University of Edinburgh. I remember flying into the capital of Scotland for the first time. I looked out my window at the city from 30,000 feet and then down at a map in my lap.

My map showed me the main streets, but it didn't tell me people drove on the wrong side of the road. And it didn't begin prepare me for the George Bernard Shaw observation, "England and America are two countries separated by a common language."

For example, the first time I asked a Scottish lass for a *date*, she said she didn't have any *dried figs*. When I explained I wanted to take her to the *movies*, she said, "Oh, you mean the *cinema*." When I said I'd meet her in front of her *apartment*, she said, "You mean my *flat*." Then she asked who else was going, and it was my turn to say, "Just you and me." She looked puzzled and asked, "Did the film get bad reviews?"

Later, I learned social networks on that side of the pond worked differently than boy-meets-girl worked on this side. Over there, a group of college students would meet at a pub and then go to the theatre together. This enabled people to get to know each other before pairing up years later. And, when we traveled, we walked or took a double-decker bus. None of the students who became my friends owned a car. The petrol was too dear.

So, to help you map out your video marketing strategy, let me begin on the right side of Kotler's diagram—with the element he called "Receiver." I'd strongly recommend that we call the person who should drive your video marketing strategy "opinion leader."

Finally, an important safety tip: Before you cross the street, look in the opposite direction. Remember, they don't just drive on the wrong side of the road over in YouTube Nation, they also put their steering wheels on the wrong side of the car.

This is not your father's Oldsmobile.

Tuesday: Identify the Opinion Leaders

Today, you will learn how to use the techniques covered earlier to identify the specific opinion leaders you want to reach.

According to Rogers, an opinion leader is an individual who "is able to influence other individuals' attitudes or overt behavior informally in a desired way with relative frequency."

How do opinion leaders differ from their followers? Rogers made several generalizations based on four decades of research.

Opinion leaders have greater exposure to mass media than their followers. "Opinion leaders gain their perceived competency by serving as an avenue for the entrance of new ideas into their system," he wrote.

Opinion leaders are "more cosmopolite" than their followers. Rogers described opinion leaders as "people on the edge" who "carry information across the boundaries between groups. They are not people at the top of things so much as people at the edge of things, not leaders within groups so much as brokers between groups."

Opinion leaders have greater contact with change agents than their followers.

Opinion leaders have greater social participation than their followers. "In order for opinion leaders to spread messages about an innovation, they must have extensive interpersonal network links with their followers. Opinion leaders must be socially accessible," he said.

Opinion leaders have higher socioeconomic status than their followers. "We expect that a follower typically seeks an opinion leader of somewhat higher socioeconomic status," Rogers observed. And more formal education.

Opinion leaders are more innovative than their followers. "If opinion leaders are to be recognized by their peers as competent and trustworthy experts about innovations, the opinion leaders should adopt new ideas before their followers," he concluded.

Rogers also identified four methods for identifying opinion leaders: (1) sociometric techniques, (2) informants' ratings, (3) self-designating techniques, and (4) observation. He added that all four methods are about equally valid, so your choice can be based on convenience.

I covered how to identify opinion leaders on YouTube and other online video sites in the first half of this chapter. Take some time to look for opinion leaders in your specific category. Start by looking for them in the sites linking to a video, video responses, and text comments.

Wednesday: Learn How to Optimize Video for YouTube

The next element in this reverse road map isn't Decoding. That's too passive a description for the active process of discovering new videos. I'd call it Video Optimization.

As I mentioned in Chapter 1, comScore qSearch reports that Americans conduct almost 2.6 billion expanded search queries on YouTube a month.

I estimate that followers who have heard about new videos from opinion leaders are conducting about two-thirds of these search queries. But opinion leaders who are searching for new videos are conducting the other third.

So how do you get your new video discovered when most people haven't heard about it yet?

The answer is to use video optimization to improve your search result rankings in YouTube as well as video search engine optimization, or VSEO, to improve your search results rankings in Google Video results. These can also increase the odds that your videos will get blended into Google universal search results.

As I mentioned in Chapter 1, there are a lots of urban legends about how to optimize video for Singingfish or other video search engines. Let's begin our discussion of video optimization by reading what the YouTube Help Center says about search result rankings:

> We believe strongly in allowing the democracy of the Web to determine the inclusion and ranking of videos in our search results. After determining the content of the video using our spidering technology, YouTube combines sophisticated text-matching techniques to find videos that are both important and relevant to your search. Our technology examines dozens of aspects of the video's content (including number of hits and rating) to determine if it's a good match for your query.
>
> We're continually working to improve our algorithms to provide the most relevant results for your query.

YouTube also provides this general information in its video toolbox about making your video easy to find:

> When you upload your video, we require you to choose at least one category and enter at least one tag to describe the content in your video. Adding this information helps other YouTube members find your video, so if you want an audience, help them out! The more accurate the tags are on each video, the easier it is for everyone to find cool videos to watch.
>
> Make your tags as descriptive as you can—if you took a video of your friends at the beach, you might want to tag it like this: party beach surfing. Each tag is separated from the others by a space.

If you don't get the kind of YouTube search results that you expected, there are a number of things you can do to improve performance:

- Make sure your keywords are really relevant to your video or channel content, and try removing those keywords that might be too generic.

- A two-word keyword should work pretty well, but single word keywords may be too general, especially for a really broad topic with a lot of other videos running on the same or similar keywords.

- Check to be sure that your video's thumbnail image is the most engaging of your image options. Your thumbnail is the first thing people see in YouTube search results.

I'll cover how to optimize video for YouTube in Chapter 4.

Thursday: Create Compelling Video Content

The next element in my reverse road map could be called Message. But I call it Video. Why? Because I agree with Marshall McLuhan, who observed back in 1964, "The medium is the message."

In his best-known book, *Understanding Media: The Extensions of Man*, McLuhan describes the "content" of a medium as a juicy piece of meat carried by a burglar to distract the watchdog of the mind. In other words, we tend to focus on the content, which can provide information, education, or entertainment, but in the process, people largely miss the structural changes in our affairs that are introduced subtly, or over long periods of time.

For example, many viral marketing strategies focus on creating funny videos—because they assume that jokes, bloopers, and humorous clips are the only content opinion leaders will share with their followers.

Not that there's anything wrong with that.

But as you saw in Chapter 2, *Comedy* isn't the most popular genre of video. *News* is. And the 2007 YouTube Awards had 12 categories of popular videos. In addition to Comedy, there were awards for Adorable, Creative, Eyewitness, Inspirational, and Instructional videos as well as ones for Commentary, Music, Politics, Series, Short Film, and Sports.

"Allen's Listening Tour" isn't funny. The most viewed video all time—"Avril Lavigne - Girlfriend"—isn't humorous either.

So, Comedy is just one of the types of content that can go viral. Newsworthy, entertaining, and useful content can go viral too.

What is critical, no matter what type or category of content you create, is whether it is worth watching. Will an opinion leader tell their followers, "You gotta check this out!"

Or, as Rogers explained about "the two-step flow model," the first step involves a transfer of *information*, but the second step also involves the spread of interpersonal *influence*.

These are the structural changes in our affairs that are introduced subtly, or over long periods of time, that McLuhan was talking about.

I'll cover how to create compelling video content in Chapter 5.

Friday: Customize Your YouTube Channel

The next element in my reverse road map could be called Media. But I call it Channel.

Why? Lasswell used the term *Channel*. And Rogers says, "A *communication channel* is the means by which messages get from one individual to another."

Some of these communication channels are *mass media channels*, which enable one or a few individuals to reach an audience of many. But other channels of communication are *interpersonal channels*, which involve an exchange between two or more individuals.

A YouTube channel page serves both roles. On your channel page, other YouTube users can see your public videos, favorite videos, bulletins, and subscribers. Your channel page also displays several links that let other people connect with you (or your brand) by sending you a message, sharing your channel with friends, or adding comments to your channel.

But as I mentioned earlier in this chapter, YouTube should be the center but not the circumference of your video marketing strategy.

According to comScore Video Metrix, YouTube has a 40 percent share of videos viewed in the United States. According to Hitwise, YouTube accounts for 79 percent of all U.S. visits to online video sites. Although different methodologies produce different figures, both firms recognize that YouTube has a dominant market share. Nevertheless, there's no reason to stop there. Even the TubeMogul data indicated that you can almost double your views by distributing your video content to additional online video sites.

In addition to distributing their videos to the top online video sites, veteran marketers and new YouTubers will also want to use word-of-mouth marketing best practices and ethical guidelines to make it simpler for friends to tell friends about stuff they like as well as to empower and amplify the voice of the consumer.

I'll cover how to create both kinds of channels in Chapter 6.

Week 4: New Map

Yogi Berra once observed, "If you don't know where you are going, you might not get there." But if you already know that you want more than half of your videos get over 100 views, then you need to follow the new map through all nine steps of the video sharing process.

Let continue down that path by looking at the central element of our social media model: Community.

Monday: Engage the YouTube community

Tuesday: Learn how to produce a video

Wednesday: Become a YouTube partner and video advertiser

Thursday: Trust but verify YouTube insight

Friday: Measure outcomes vs. outputs

Monday: Engage the YouTube Community

The central element in the mass media era may have been Noise. But I think the central element in the social media era is Community.

In Fact, the YouTube Fact Sheet in the company's press room uses *community* 14 times in 1,144 words. Here are just half a dozen of the most important examples:

> *Founded in February 2005, YouTube is the world's most popular online video* community, *allowing millions of people to discover, watch and share originally-created videos....*

> *YouTube is building a* community *that is highly motivated to watch and share videos....*

> *YouTube offers a* community *for everyone, including personal video creators such as cooking, beauty, health, and fitness experts; aspiring and professional musicians; amateur and established filmmakers; comedians; and professional content owners....*

> *The* community *is truly in control on YouTube and they determine what is popular on the site....*

> *YouTube will always be an open* community *and we encourage users to send in their thoughts and comments about their experiences on the site....*

> *At the end of the day, it's all about the* community *and we will continue to do what we can to make the user experience a prosperous one.*

Now, communities can be noisy. I'm a former chairman of the Acton Board of Selectmen, and I've heard members of the community speak at public hearings and presented my share of controversial articles at New England town meetings.

So I understand what pops the bear meant in the video "How do you get featured on YouTube?" As I mentioned earlier in this chapter, pops said, "YouTubers have a better chance of having their films featured on the site...by becoming a fully vested member of the YouTube community." And according to pops, this involves "joining groups, replying to other videos, even making more videos."

You also have to respect the YouTube community. I'm not asking you to give it the kind of respect reserved for the lady in the DMV, people that remember jingles from tons of old commercials and, uh, people that support local music and seek out independent film. I mean don't abuse the site. Every cool new community feature on YouTube involves a certain level of trust. Please don't abuse that trust.

YouTube staff reviews flagged videos 24 hours a day, seven days a week to determine whether they violate their Community Guidelines. When they do, YouTube removes them. Accounts are penalized for Community Guidelines violations and serious or repeated violations can lead to account termination. If your account is terminated, you won't be allowed to create any new accounts.

I'll cover how communities work in Chapter 7.

Tuesday: Learn How to Produce a Video

The next element in my reverse road map can be called Encoding. But I call it Video Production.

According to the Pew Internet Project I mentioned in Chapter 2, 62 percent of online video viewers said their favorite videos were "professionally produced," while 19 percent of online video viewers expressed a preference for content "produced by amateurs." Another 11 percent said they enjoy both professionally produced video and amateur online video equally.

With over 15 hours of video uploaded to YouTube every minute, it's important to learn how to produce a video. This includes tips about shooting, editing, uploading to YouTube, and even creating some special effects.

I will also cover why it makes sense to keep videos two to three minutes long. For example, TubeMogul posted the results of a study in December 2008 that found most videos steadily lose viewers once "play" is clicked.

TubeMogul measured viewed-seconds for a sample of 188,055 videos, totaling 22,724,606 streams, on six top video sites for a two-week period. The study found that 10.4 percent of online video viewers click away after watching a video 10 seconds and 53.6 percent leave after a minute.

I'll cover tips and tricks for making "professionally produced" videos that are two to three minutes long in Chapter 8.

Wednesday: Become a YouTube Partner and Video Advertiser

The next element in my reverse road map can be called Sender. But I call it Marketer.

YouTube is exploring a variety of ways to help the community to monetize content. For example, its User-Partner Program gives original content creators the chance to generate revenue from their work and receive the same promotional benefits afforded to YouTube's other professional content partners.

YouTube has partnership deals with thousands of content providers. These partnerships and the wide range of content they represent provide appropriate environments for brand marketers and countless opportunities for high-profile placements. Here are half a dozen examples:

Education *Carnegie Mellon University* joined November 16, 2007. The university's channel features the last lecture by Professor Randy Pausch. Its 102 videos had over 11.7 million views as of April 2009. Its channel had over 7,600 subscribers and 191,000 views.

Entertainment *CBS* joined September 21, 2006. The broadcast network's channel features entertainment, news, and sports. Its 17,316 videos had over 345 million views as of April 2009. Its channel had over 110,000 subscribers and 5.7 million views.

Film & Animation *Mondo Media* joined January 22, 2007. The director features mini shows—short, viral, and funny videos twice a week. Its 225 videos had over 366 million views as of April 2009. Its channel had over 223,000 subscribers and 7.9 million views.

Gaming *EA* joined September 27, 2005. The channel features a variety of videos about the company's video games. Its 727 videos had over 76 million views as of April 2009. Its channel had over 73,000 subscribers and 2.2 million views.

Pets & Animals *National Geographic* joined May 7, 2006. The channel features shows about animals and the planet. Its 1,005 videos had over 147 million views as of April 2009. Its channel had over 133,000 subscribers and 3.3 million views.

Sports *NBA* joined November 20, 2005. The channel features NBA highlights. Its 1,917 videos had over 230 million views as of April 2009. Its channel had over 112,000 subscribers and 9 million views.

Whether an Ad Age 100 advertiser or a local retailer, everyone can launch their ad campaign on YouTube. So, we'll also take a look at some of the YouTube Ad Opportunities to discover how your brand can converse with this vibrant community. This includes YouTube InVideo Ads, YouTube Video Ads, and YouTube Contests.

And we'll look at some of the newer options. For example, in October 2008, the YouTube Blog announced that the video sharing site was starting to test full-length programming. Apparently, YouTubers had been asking "to be beamed up with Scotty, to devise a world-saving weapon using only gum and paperclips, and to get your grub on at 'The Peach Pit.'"

Hey, I'm not making this up.

Through a deal with CBS, YouTube started offering *Star Trek*, *MacGyver*, and *Beverly Hills, 90210* to YouTube Nation in the new Theater View style that YouTube rolled out earlier that week.

The YouTube Blog added, "As we test this new format, we also want to ensure that our partners have more options when it comes to advertising on their full-length

TV shows. You may see in-stream video ads (including pre-, mid-, and post-rolls) embedded in some of these episodes; this advertising format will only appear on premium content where you are most comfortable seeing such ads."

In October 2008, YouTube also added "click-to-buy" links to the watch pages of thousands of YouTube partner videos. Click-to-buy links are non-obtrusive retail links, placed on the watch page beneath the video with the other community features.

Just as YouTube users can share, favorite, comment on, and respond to videos quickly and easily, now users can click-to-buy products—like songs, books, and movies—related to the content they're watching on the site. YouTube got started by embedding iTunes and Amazon.com links on videos from companies like EMI Music, and providing Amazon.com product links to the newly released video game Spore on videos from Electronic Arts.

And in November 2008, YouTube announced Sponsored Videos, a new advertising program that enables all video creators— from the everyday user to a Fortune 500 advertiser— to reach people who are interested in their content, products, or services, with relevant videos. Anyone can use Sponsored Videos to make sure their videos find a larger audience, whether you're a start-up band trying to break out with a new single, a film studio seeking to promote an exciting movie trailer, or even a first-time uploader trying to quickly build a following on the site.

I'll cover how to become a YouTube Partners as well as how to create video advertising in Chapter 9.

Thursday: Trust but Verify YouTube Insight

The next element in my reverse road map can be called Feedback. But I call it Insight.

Whether a YouTube video has 10 views or 10 million, people always want to know the same thing: Who's watching this? Where do viewers come from? How did they find my video?

On March 26, 2008, we started getting some answers. That was the day when YouTube released YouTube Insight, a free tool that enables anyone with a YouTube account to view detailed statistics about the videos they upload to the site.

This tool helps anyone who uploads videos to YouTube better understand and serve their audiences. For example, users might use Insight to tailor upload strategies to increase their videos' view counts and improve their popularity on the site. And *partners* who increase their videos' popularity also increase the number of monetizable views their videos get and, as a result, generate more revenue.

Advertisers had also been asking YouTube for a tool like Insight for quite some time, in an effort to look for metrics that help them determine the marketing return on investment (ROI) of their campaigns, both online and off. With YouTube Insight, the company turned YouTube into one of the world's largest focus groups. Insight helps advertisers optimize their marketing efforts, determine how successful they were, and discover previously unknown marketing opportunities. I'll cover how YouTube Insight works in Chapter 10.

But as Ronald Reagan often said, "Trust, but verify." That's why we will also examine other measures of success as well.

For example, TubeMogul serves online video producers, advertisers, and the online video industry by providing independent information about online video performance. It also offers a universal upload feature to the Web's top video sharing sites.

TubeMogul's analytic technology aggregates video-viewing data from multiple sources to give veteran marketers and new YouTubers an improved understanding of when, where, and how often their videos are watched. It lets them track and compare what's hot and what's not, measure the impact of marketing campaigns, gather competitive intelligence, and share the data with colleagues or friends.

An alternative is Visible Measures, an independent third-party measurement firm for Internet video publishers, advertisers and viral marketers. The company's patented approach has been designed from the ground up to meet the unique challenges of measuring digital video reach and engagement.

Visible Measures provides its customers and partners with unprecedented visibility into their online video audiences and how they engage with both content assets and advertising placements. Visible Measures is a member of the Interactive Advertising Bureau's (IAB) Digital Video Committee and the Advertising Research Foundation (ARF).

I'll cover how YouTube Insight, TubeMogul, Visible Measures, and other measurement tools work in Chapter 10 as well.

Friday: Measure Outcomes vs. Outputs

The final element in my reverse road map can be called Response. But I call it Outcome.

At the end of the day, somebody somewhere in your organization will want to know what your insight is worth in cold, hard cash.

I learned this lesson the hard way back in 1986, when I was the director of corporate communications for Lotus Development Corp., which was then the largest independent software company. Shortly after I got the position, I was told by one of my managers that I was her 13th boss in the past four-and-a-half years. I soon discovered why my 12 predecessors had lost their jobs after holding the position for an average of four months.

After my first month on the job, I took a very thick stack of news clippings to Jim Manzi, the chairman, president, and CEO of Lotus. Manzi took one look at it and said, "If I could deposit these clips in a bank, they'd be worth something. Until you can measure the value of PR in cold, hard cash, don't waste my time with these reports."

I'd never heard it put that bluntly before, but Manzi was right.

So over the next two decades, I pioneered new ways to measure results in business outcomes instead of media outputs. In the 1990s, Jeffrey Tarter, the editor of

Softletter, called me "the guru of lead tracking." A few years later, Katie Delahaye Paine, the publisher of *The Measurement Standard*, called me a "measurement maven."

In 2005, Southwest Airlines and my company won an award for excellence in public relations measurement and evaluation from the Institute for Public Relations and *PR News* for our case study, which was entitled, "You Are Now Free to Link PR and Sales."

So, as I started writing this book, I also started looking for case studies of videos, channels, advertising, and contests that had accomplished more than going viral. I started looking for veteran marketers and new YouTubers who had discovered new ways of measuring marketing ROI.

That's why I interviewed the following people for this book:

- Arun Chaudhary, the New Media Road Director for the Barack Obama 2008 Presidential Campaign. The 1,839 videos on BarackObamadotcom's channel on YouTube had 132 million views as of April 2009. But that's not as impressive as the 69.5 million votes and 365 electoral votes that Democrat Barack Obama won in the election, becoming the first American-American elected President.

- John Goldstone, the Producer of Monty Python & the Holy Grail, Life of Brian and The Meaning of Life. MontyPython's Channel on YouTube has 54 videos and over 85,000 subscribers as of April 2009. But when Monty Python launched their channel in November, I was more impressed that their YouTube videos shoot to the top of the most viewed lists, their DVDs also quickly climbed to No. 2 on Amazon's Movies & TV bestsellers list, and their sales increased 23,000 percent.

- George Wright, the first marketing director of Blendtec. Yes, yes, it is impressive that the 84 "Will it Blend?" videos on the Blendtec channel on YouTube had a total of over 73 million views as of April 2009. But I'm more impressed that the company's sales are up 700 percent.

- Michael Buckley, best known for his vlog, What the Buck? In October 2007, Buckley "broke all records" of YouTube ratings when four of his shows ended up on the week's 10 top-rated videos. However, I was more impressed when he told The New York Times in an interview that he was earning over $100,000 from YouTube advertisements.

I'll share more details about their success stories as well as some other YouTube and video marketing case studies in Chapter 11.

Month 2: Optimize Your Video

4

Americans conducted more than 2.9 billion "expanded search queries" on YouTube during January 2009. This makes optimizing your content for YouTube Search an important step to take before uploading your video. In this chapter, you will learn how to research keywords, how to optimize video for YouTube and the Web, and what to do when someone asks, "Have you tried searching under 'fruitless'?"

What Is Video Optimization?

Veteran marketers are often surprised to learn that YouTube accounts for more than 99 percent of all videos viewed at Google Sites (according to comScore Video Metrix), which means Google Video accounts for less than 1 percent. And they are frequently shocked to discover YouTube does not crawl the Web, which means videos on their own sites are not found when Americans conduct more than 3.2 billion expanded search queries a month on YouTube (according to comScore qSearch 2.0).

I can't tell you how many times I've been asked to speak about "video search engine optimization" at SEO conferences, despite the fact that YouTube accounted for 79 percent of all U.S. visits to online video sites in February 2009, according to Hitwise, and Google Video received the second highest percentage of visits with 4.6 percent.

These market share percentages differ because comScore includes sites with video content, such as Viacom Digital's Comedy Central, while Hitwise only looks at 60 of the leading online video-specific websites. Their sample sizes and methodologies also differ. Nevertheless, both comScore and Hitwise show YouTube is dominant and video search engines have a collective market share in the single digits.

Now, I'm not trying to embarrass some of my friends and colleagues in the search engine industry who are still focusing more than 90 percent of their efforts on optimizing website video for video search engines, which have less than 10 percent share of market. Instead, let me just observe diplomatically that Singingfish is dead, Yahoo! Video doesn't crawl websites anymore, Google Video has a market share in the low single digits, and other video search engines have even less.

It's like no one got the memo: The horse race is over. YouTube won. So it may be helpful to define a few more terms:

- *Video optimization* means optimizing video for both types of online video sites.
- *YouTube optimization* means optimizing video for YouTube Search.
- *Video search engine optimization* means optimizing website video for Google Video and other video search engines.

This is also as good a place as any to explain what video optimization is not. It is *not* about the best formats for uploading. I'll talk about video format, aspect ratio, resolution, audio format, frames per second, maximum length, and maximum file size in Chapter 8, which is about *video production*. High-quality video production is important when people *watch* a video, but it won't help them *discover* it.

So when I talk about *video optimization*, I'm talking about editing a video's metadata and content in order to improve its search result rankings. For videos on YouTube, this means editing the title, description, and tags as well as increasing its views and improving its ratings. These video optimization techniques are important to help people *discover* a video, which is what this chapter is all about.

Now, I don't mean to pick on veteran marketers only. New YouTubers are often surprised to learn the Discovery tab in YouTube Insight will show them which keywords viewers used to find their video. And they are frequently shocked to discover YouTube Search and Google Search are such significant sources of views.

I can't tell you how many times I've been asked what this means:

> *After determining the content of the video using our spidering technology, YouTube combines sophisticated text-matching techniques to find videos that are both important and relevant to your search. Our technology examines dozens of aspects of the video's content (including number of hits and rating) to determine if it's a good match for your query.*

Some of my friends and colleagues in the YouTube community don't realize that, depending on site traffic, changes to video information—including changes to tags and comments—can take six to eight hours to show up in the YouTube search index.

Plus, there are a lot of other questions about YouTube processes that you can't find answers to in the Help Center. And as Figure 4.1 illustrates, all of us want to know what to tell a friend or colleague if they ask, "Have you tried searching under 'fruitless'?"

"Have you tried searching under 'fruitless'?"

Figure 4.1 "Have you tried searching under 'fruitless'?" (Cartoon by Danny Shanahan in *The New Yorker*, December 24, 2001.)

So this chapter will teach you how to research keywords, how to optimize video for YouTube and the Web, and what to do on the numerous occasions when you have to think outside the search box.

Week 1: Research Keywords

Keywords—which are also called search terms—are the specific phrases that a searcher might type into a search field.

According to Jennifer Grappone and Gradiva Couzin, the authors of *Search Engine Optimization: An Hour A Day* (Sybex, second edition 2008), "The keywords you choose *this week* will be the focus of your entire optimization process." I agree.

Although some of the tools and techniques used to research keywords for video optimization are similar to the ones used for search engine optimization, others are different.

Why? There are several reasons. For starters, people searching for video content are more likely to be looking for topics that entertain them and less likely to be looking for something to buy than they would using a web search engine. So, let's go through the process for finding video keywords step by step. Your tasks for this week are as follows:

Monday: Brainstorm keyword suggestions

Tuesday: Use the Google AdWords Keyword Tool

Wednesday: Check out query suggestions

Thursday: Examine other keyword tools

Friday: Analyze keyword effectiveness

Monday: Brainstorm Keyword Suggestions

The first step in keyword research is to get into the mind of your viewer. Think about the words people would type to find your video.

I find it useful to put keywords in categories. In the next step of this process, you will need to make sure that your title, description, and tags actually include these words.

So, as I brainstorm keywords, I think again about the Kipling poem I mentioned in Chapter 2:

I keep six honest serving-men

(They taught me all I knew);

Their names are What and Why and When

And How and Where and Who.

For example, some of the most relevant keywords and keyword phrases will fall into the category *Who*. People often search for videos about celebrities, so some of the most popular keywords are their names. There is also a growing multitude of YouTube celebrities like Tay Zonday (Chocolate Rain), Lauren Caitlin Upton (Junior Miss

South Carolina), and Judson Laipply (Evolution of Dance) whose names have become YouTube keywords. Even if you don't think the CEO of your company, governor of your state, or president of your university is a "celebrity," their names are likely to be keywords.

Many of the top YouTube search terms fall into the category *What*. People search for topics related to what entertains them, so choose your keywords accordingly: from song titles and movie titles to the objects in a video in YouTube categories like Autos & Vehicles or Pets & Animals.

As Table 4.1 illustrates, Compete's monthly compilation of the top 40 searches made on YouTube shows that most of the top 10 search terms in October 2008 fell into either the Who or What categories.

▶ **Table 4.1** Top 10 YouTube Search Terms (October 2008)

Rank	Term	Category	% of All Searches
1	Lil Wayne	Music (Artist)	0.122%
2	Fred	Comedy	0.120%
3	Sex	Adult	0.082%
4	Beyonce	Music (Artist)	0.076%
5	Whatever You Like	Music (Song Title)	0.072%
6	Womanizer	Music (Artist)	0.072%
7	Chris Brown	Music (Artist)	0.067%
8	Porn	Adult	0.059%
9	Jonas Brothers	Music (Artist)	0.059%
10	Disturbia	Music (Song Title)	0.058%

Nevertheless, *When* can be useful category on occasion. You'll find that holidays—New Year's Day, Martin Luther King, Jr. Day (MLK Day), Groundhog Day, Valentine's Day, Presidents Day, St Patrick's Day, Good Friday, Easter, April Fools' Day, Tax Day, Earth Day, Mother's Day, Memorial Day, Flag Day, Father's Day, Independence Day, Labor Day, Rosh Hashanah, Yom Kippur, Columbus Day, United Nations Day, Halloween, Election Day, Veterans Day, Thanksgiving, Black Friday, Cyber Monday, Hanukkah, Christmas, and Kwanzaa—are all part of search phrases.

Where is also useful, particularly in the Sports and Travel & Events categories. For example, conduct a YouTube search for "Where the Hell is Matt?" The 22 videos on MattHarding2718's YouTube channel took more than a year to make and star Matt, age 32, dancing in 42 countries with a cast of thousands. As of April 2009, Matt's videos had over 44 million views and his channel had over 40,000 subscribers. Do you think Stride, "The Ridiculously Long Lasting Gum," that sponsored Matt's dancing is still dancing too? Stride's continued sponsorship of follow-up videos indicates that it is.

Why is an often overlooked category. But you'll find that adjectives like funny and hilarious are the root of YouTube search terms. So are *adorable* and *cute*, which are often used as adjectives when searching for such nouns as *animals*, *babies*, *kittens*, and *puppies*. Or think about trends in online video overall—like hot topics, political awareness, celebrity gossip, and popular videos—when choosing your keywords.

Finally, *How* is a category killer in online video, and how-to videos have gone mainstream. The most viewed YouTube channel in the Howto & Style category is illumistream's channel, which offers the largest library of health, pregnancy, and sex education videos on the web. Its 742 videos had more than 89 million views as of April, 2009 and the channel had over 36,000 **subscribers and 3.4 million channel views.**

And popular YouTube keywords include How to be emo, how to be gangster, how to be ninja, how to save a life, and how to tie a tie. In fact, "How to Tie a Tie - Expert Instructions on How to Tie a Tie" from GeorDorn's channel had over 2.4 million views as of April 2009.

Use these six honest serving-men as you generate keywords. You'll probably use Who and What when writing your title, description, and tags, and you may be able to squeeze in When, Where, Why, or How.

Tuesday: Use the Google AdWords Keyword Tool

When researching keywords, many veteran marketers use the Google AdWords Keyword Tool. There are three ways to access the AdWords Keyword Tool: from within one of your ad groups; from your AdWords account's Tools menu; and from the following external URL:

```
https://adwords.google.com/select/KeywordToolExternal
```

The Keyword Tool allows you to build extensive, relevant keyword lists—even if you aren't an advertiser. This tool includes the following features:

Two ways to search for keywords Use keywords you enter or any URL for your search.

Keyword performance statistics See Google's performance data for keyword search volume, search volume trends, and estimated average cost per click.

Easy keyword manipulation Select a few keywords here and there, or add them all at once. You can also download your keyword list as a CSV file.

Keyword results based on regularly updated data Google's advanced search engine technology provides information on potential keywords from last month and the past year.

Here are some advanced tips for using the Keyword Tool:

Find keywords based on channel content. Instead of entering your own keywords, try using the Website Content option. It lets you enter the URL of any site related to your business— including a YouTube channel. The AdWords system will scan the video channel and then suggest relevant keywords. Don't hesitate to enter the URLs of your competitors' channels to learn what keywords they might be using.

Find synonyms. The Use Synonyms box in the Descriptive Words or Phrases option is always checked by default. This means it might suggest *bed and breakfast* as a synonym for the keyword *hotel*.

Get specific. The default option for the tool is Broad Match. But I recommend using Exact Match. This is the most targeted option. Although you're likely to see a lower approximate search volume with exact match, you're also likely to a more accurate picture of organic (unpaid) searches.

Still, it's important to remember that this is a web search tool, not a video search tool. And as I mentioned earlier, people using a web search engine are more likely to be looking for something to buy and less likely to be looking for topics that entertain them than they would when searching for video content.

Wednesday: Check Out Query Suggestions

When researching keywords, many new YouTubers use the auto-fill suggestion drop-down menu on YouTube. Added in May 2008, this new feature was designed to help Tubers searching for videos.

As you type in your search terms, a menu will appear with suggested results to choose from to help you more quickly find the videos you're looking for. On the search results page, you'll also get an additional list of recommended searches by clicking on any of the terms listed next to the new Also Try menu.

Query suggestions are enabled by default now, although you can opt out by clicking the Advanced Options link next to the Search button. Then uncheck the Display Query Suggestions As I Type box in the settings.

As Figure 4.2 illustrates, as you type in *funny* you'll see funny video, funny cats, funny accidents, funny pranks, funny stuff, funny animals, funny babies, funny dogs, funny football, and funny commercials. These suggestions might help you tap into the search intent of millions of YouTube searchers.

But be careful: Many of the query suggestions will be for the top YouTube search terms used by followers to find the most popular videos. These followers have already heard about a video from opinion leaders but aren't sure they know its exact title. In other words, the query suggestions option is less likely to be used by opinion leaders, who want to discover new videos before the rest of the world has beaten a well-worn path to their door.

For example, do you really want to optimize your video for the following query suggestions: battle at Kruger, Boeheim, Brookers, chocolate rain, Chris Crocker, daft punk hands, digital soul, evolution of dance, Jake Coco, Judson Laipply, Junior Miss South Carolina, Justin Timberlake, Kimberleigh, Lauren Caitlin Upton, leave Britney alone, Lisa Nova, LonelyGirl15, LucyInLA, Mentos and Coke, me singing what goes around, MyNameIsMeghan, Nora the piano playing cat, Numa Numa guy, Obama girl, Ok Go, otters holding hands, Paris in jail the music video, Renetto, Soulja Boy tell em how to crank that, surprised chipmunk, Tay Zonday, Terra Naomi, TheHill88, TheSilentPatriot, or UFO Haiti?

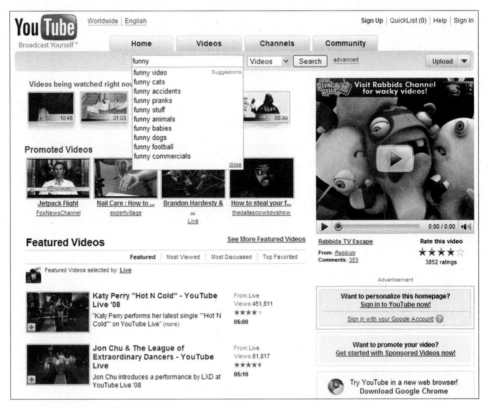

Figure 4.2 Query suggestions for *funny*

So, take query suggestions with a grain of salt. There will be times when it is smart to use them, but more often than not it will be wiser to ignore the suggested results.

Thursday: Examine Other Keyword Tools

There are other keyword tools that new YouTubers and veteran marketers may want to check out. I recommend the following tools:

Google Trends, which lets you enter up to five topics and see how often they've been searched on Google and Google News over time. It also shows which geographic regions searched most for your topics. Go to http://www.google.com/trends to see it.

KeywordDiscovery.com's free search term suggestion tool, an introductory version of its advanced keyword research tool. Its keyword data is compiled from a number of search engines. Go to http://www.keyworddiscovery.com/search.html to check it out.

Microsoft's adCenter Labs keyword forecast, which forecasts the impressions and predicts demographic distributions of keywords. Enter keywords separated by semicolons and click the Submit button. Go to http://adlab.msn.com/Keyword-Forecast/ to see it.

And Wordtracker offers Keyword Questions, a free tool that lets you find the specific questions that people type into search engines. The answers look like they were generated by Kipling's six honest serving-men.

As Figure 4.3 illustrates, the tool works by pairing a keyword like *video* with one of six question words: *who, what, where, when, why,* and *how.* It then conducts a broad match from Wordtracker's database and gives you up to 100 questions that people have asked in the last 140 days.

Find the questions that people are asking in your market	

Enter a single or short keyword:

video [Search]

Results for: *video*   Download

Question	Times asked
1 where can i get the paris hilton video free	1,259
2 sedu hair how to video	654
3 who invented video games	449
4 what was the first video game	130
5 why are video games addictive	114

Figure 4.3 Find the questions that people are asking in your market.

Go to http://labs.wordtracker.com/keyword-questions to check it out.

Search Engine Marketer: "What if I had a coffee channel?"

You could enter *coffee* and find questions like "who invented the coffee maker," "why use cold water when brewing coffee," "how to make iced coffee," and "how to clean a coffee pot."

YouTube Director: "What if I had a flower shop channel?"

You could enter *sorry* and find questions like "how to say sorry to your girlfriend" or "how to say sorry after huge argument."

Navin R. Johnson: "What if I had a channel on UFOs?"

You might be interested to know that the most popular questions on UFOs include "how to fake UFO photographs" and "how to build a UFO." Sorry, the tool doesn't suggest, "Where is Area 51?"

Friday: Analyze Keyword Effectiveness

Keyword research involves much more than generating a long list of potential search terms and then using keyword tools to discover which ones are the most popular. Generally, the most popular keywords are already being used by the most popular videos.

You also need to factor in competition when conducting your keyword analysis. Although there are no tools (yet) that help you do this for YouTube, there is an approach that was pioneered for web search that can be adapted for this purpose.

It's called the keyword effectiveness index (KEI) and it was created by Sumantra Roy, a respected search engine positioning specialist from 1stSearchRanking. KEI divides the number of times a keyword has appeared in searches performed by users by the number of competing web pages to identify which keywords are most effective for a campaign.

The commercial versions of both KeywordDiscovery.com and Wordtracker use KEI as part of their keyword analysis tools. As Wordtracker explains, "The higher the KEI, the more popular your keywords are, and the less competition they have. Which means you have a better chance of getting to the top."

The best use of KEI that I've seen comes from SEO Research Labs. Although its reports include the KEI analysis scores generated by Wordtracker, it uses this for comparison only because it is based on the total number of matches for a given search phrase, which overstates the competition your keywords face. As Figure 4.4 illustrates, SEO Research Labs also shows you how many pages use your keywords in their title as well as the number of pages with the search term in both the title and incoming link text, which are more accurate measures of the level of competition for your keywords.

Search Term	Count	Exact	In Title	Title+Anchor	KEI1	KEI2	KEI3
dedicated hosting	401	1,500,000	29,500	3,630	2.34120	31.26486	57.54134
dedicated server	452	1,980,000	38,600	7,010	1.95431	27.59823	35.54600

Figure 4.4 KEI Analysis Report

You can also create your own version of KEI by exporting data from the Google AdWords Keyword Tool into Microsoft Excel and then creating a new column that divides the Approximate Average Search Volume (using Exact Match) by Advertiser Competition. Again, this uses data on web searches instead of video searches as well as an indication of advertiser competition instead of video competition.

Nevertheless, with about 83.4 million videos already on YouTube, you can't ignore competition when you research keywords.

Week 2: Optimize Video for YouTube

After you think about the words people would type to find your videos, you need to make sure your title, description, and tags actually include those words within them.

This may appear obvious, but it comes as a surprise to many veteran marketers and new YouTubers.

They are shocked, shocked to find that changing their title, description, and tags needs to be done.

Now, most of them know that video optimization involves changing metadata, the data about your data. But many don't realize that for videos on YouTube, metadata is the title, description, and tags.

So, to help them understand that optimization is just a fancy name for copyediting, I show them the information in the YouTube Help Center about search result rankings. It says, "YouTube combines sophisticated text-matching techniques to find videos that are both important and relevant to your search." Then I ask, "What text can YouTube's technology use to determine if a video is a good match for a query?" That's when the light bulb goes on: the only text that YouTube's algorithms can use to provide the most relevant results for a query is a video's title, description, and tags.

To provide the most important results, YouTube also says, "Our technology examines dozens of aspects of the video's content (including number of hits and rating) to determine if it's a good match for your query."

Now, you don't control the number of hits (views) or rating your video gets. The YouTube community does. And, as pops said in "How do you get featured on YouTube?," you have a better chance of having your videos get more views and better ratings by "creating original work" and "becoming a fully vested member of the YouTube community."

So, to optimize video for YouTube, you need to include your keywords in your title, description, and tags. Then, you also need to produce compelling content that the YouTube community will watch and share in order to increase the number of hits to and improve the rating of your originally created videos.

Let's look at all five factors:

Monday: Write an optimized title

Tuesday: Write an optimized description

Wednesday: Add optimized tags

Thursday: Get views the right way

Friday: Allow and ask for ratings

Monday: Write an Optimized Title

The most important text to optimize is the title of your video. Think of your title as a headline.

YouTube limits titles on video watch pages to 120 characters (including spaces). Since the average word is five characters long (plus a sixth character for the space), this means most titles are limited to about 20 words.

And the typical search term is now about three words long. So it's now possible to optimize your title for up to six search terms instead of just three. Still, as the Knight Templar told Indiana Jones, "You must choose, but choose wisely."

As a former news editor of the *Beverly Times*, I learned to use Kipling's six honest serving-men to write front page headlines on deadline. I'd ask, "*Who* said *what*?" Or, "*What* happened to *whom*?" On occasion, I might ask, "*Why* did *who* say *what*?" Or, "*How* did *what* happen to *whom*?"

(Because the *Beverly Times* was a local daily newspaper, I rarely needed to ask, "*When* or *where* did a story occur?" The obvious answers were yesterday in Beverly.)

Feel free to ask Kipling's famous questions when writing the title of your video. And, if you've organized your keyword research into the six categories that Kipling once used, you'll discover that you can write optimized titles almost as quickly as unoptimized ones.

Let me share another tip for optimizing your title. I call this optimization technique "Russian nesting dolls." Russian nesting dolls, like the ones in Figure 4.5, are a set of dolls of decreasing sizes placed one inside the other. I look for popular keywords nested within longer search terms. For example, *nesting dolls* is a popular keyword and *Russian nesting dolls* is a longer search term.

Figure 4.5 Russian nesting dolls

By using the longer search term, my video will get found when someone is searching for *nesting dolls* or *Russian nesting dolls*. However, if I used the popular keyword, then my video will get found if someone searches for *nesting dolls*. It may not get found when someone else searches for *Russian nesting dolls*, because I hadn't included *Russian* in my title.

If you choose the longer search term, you have chosen wisely.

On any page other than the watch page, only the first 32 characters of the title will be displayed followed by an ellipsis (really, three periods). So the first five words in your title will do double duty. If you want to include your brand name in the title, it should always go last.

Tuesday: Write an Optimized Description

The next important text to optimize is the description of your video. It can be up to 1,000 characters long. That's about 166 words.

YouTube encourages you to be as detailed as possible—short of offering an entire transcript: "The more information you include, the easier it is for users to find your video!" But, only the first 120 characters of the description are displayed in YouTube Search results, so it's useful to include your search terms in the first 20 words of your description because they'll appear in bold.

Your description should include URLs to a relevant channel or playlist or to another website. Your links only become clickable if they are preceded by http://—so www.yoursite.com won't make the URL clickable but http://www.yoursite.com will.

Putting links into the first 120 characters of your description is the best way to drive traffic to a non-YouTube site. Offsite links aren't allowed *anywhere* but in the description, so use them.

Unfortunately, the limit on how much text gets displayed has led some people to mistakenly conclude that longer descriptions don't impact YouTube search result rankings. But they do, particularly for long tail search phrases that are typically longer and more detailed than normal.

The bad habit of writing shorter descriptions is often reinforced by the logical fallacy that people watch a video, they don't read its description. This ignores the stubborn fact that people need to discover a video before they can watch it. And a longer description can often help them discover it.

David Ogilvy wrote about the importance of long copy in his classic book *Ogilvy on Advertising*. He said, "A blind pig can sometimes find truffles, but it helps to know that they are found in oak forests."

YouTube provides some advice on writing your video description. It says, "To best promote your video, you'll want its description to be both accurate and interesting." Here are a few tips to help you get started:

Make your description clear and specific. Your video should stand out from the crowd. Try to determine what content it contains that will help users find it and distinguish it from other videos. Using descriptive language in complete sentences is a good idea. In addition, many people will read the description while watching a video, especially if it starts slowly. So, if you use opening credits or a lengthy exposition, then make sure your description tells as good a story as your video does. And, if your video has a "surprise ending," don't spoil it by revealing "the butler did it" in your written description.

Give credit when appropriate. If people don't know the exact title or other keywords associated with your video, they might search the name of a participant or another website where it's featured. Be sure to include as much information as you feel comfortable including, but be careful not to include anything that shouldn't be publicly displayed. Also, if you use Creative Commons material or copyrighted material that you have permission to use, the lower half of the description is a good place to put all the attribution information. Then it's technically attached to the video, but it doesn't consume valuable screen real estate.

Categorize correctly. The category into which you place your video is part of its description as well. People are more likely to rate your video highly and watch it more frequently if it's placed in a relevant category. Now, some videos could go in one of several categories. And all categories are *not* created equal. Some categories are much more popular than others, but videos in popular categories often face more competition. A good way to check is to go to www.youtube.com/browse and examine the individual browse pages for relevant categories. Then select the category that seems "best." If that doesn't work, then you can always change the category of your video later by following these steps:

1. Go to the My Videos page.
2. Click the Edit Video Info button next to your video.
3. Choose the radio button for your new category within the Video Category section.
4. Click the Update Video Info button to save your video information.

Wednesday: Add Optimized Tags

The final text to be optimized is your tags. You can use up to 120 characters in your tags. This means you can have as many as 20 tags. Tags are the keywords that describe your videos. YouTube says, "Enter as many tags as you'd like into the Tags field." For example, a surfing video might be tagged with *surfing*, *water*, and *waves*. Users who enjoy watching surfing videos can then search for any of those terms and that video will show up in their search results.

YouTube provides this general information in its video toolbox about making your video easy to find:

> *When you upload your video, we require you to choose at least one category and enter at least one tag to describe the content in your video. Adding this information helps other YouTube members find your video,*

so if you want an audience, help them out! The more accurate the tags are on each video, the easier it is for everyone to find cool videos to watch.

Make your tags as descriptive as you can—if you took a video of your friends at the beach, you might want to tag it like this: party beach surfing. *Each tag is separated from the others by a space.*

Tags help you label videos you upload so that other people can find them more easily. However, YouTube tags are currently based on single words rather than phrases. This means that keywords are a little more specific than video tags. For example, the tag *orange* might refer to the fruit or the color, and this lack of semantic distinction can lead to inappropriate connections between items.

In 2003, Delicious, the social bookmarking site, enabled its users to add "tags" to their bookmarks as a way to help find them later. Flickr also allowed its users to add tags to each of their pictures, constructing flexible and easy metadata that made the pictures highly searchable. The influence of Delicious and the success of Flickr popularized the concept, and other Web 2.0 sites—including YouTube, Technorati, and other social media—also implemented tagging.

The main difference between keywords and video tags is that keywords should be more than one word long. An effective keyword consists of multiple words to form a single phrase that's relevant to your video. Using multiple words helps you be a little more specific.

Just as you can change your category, you can also change your tags. Brad O'Farrell, the technical editor of this book, says you can see an example of this at `http://www.youtube.com/watch?v=JpBGRA6HHtY`. "Mario: Game Over" from comedy group POYKPAC was nominated for Best Comedy Video of 2007 in the YouTube Awards. While views "peaked" that year, POYKPAC has continued to increase the views of their Super Mario sketch video (now up to 12 million views) by constantly updating it with newly relevant tags.

For example, POYKPAC added *Galaxy* when Mario Galaxy was released and *Super Smash Brothers Brawl* when it was released and got millions of views from people searching for gameplay footage. They even added tags that made it relevant to "Super Mario Rescues the Princess: Seth MacFarlane's Cavalcade," when it went viral in September 2008.

Thursday: Get Views the Right Way

As the "Mario: Game Over" example illustrates, making sure your keywords are actually included in your title, description, and tags helps the YouTube algorithm know that your video is relevant to a search. But its technology examines dozens of aspects of the video's content to determine if it's important—including number of views.

This has been the subject of a good deal of controversy over the viewing figures of some YouTube videos. There have been claims that automated systems—including robots, spiders, and offline readers—have been used to inflate the amount of views received. Use of any automated system that "sends more request messages to the YouTube servers in a given period of time than a human can reasonably produce in the same period" is forbidden by YouTube's terms of service.

For example, a YouTube video featuring the anime franchise Evangelion had a view count of around 98 million as of October 2008, but it has been barred from the YouTube charts due to automated viewing.

And "Avril Lavigne - Girlfriend" has also been accused of having an exaggerated number of views due to the use of a link with an auto-refresh mechanism posted by AvrilBandAids, a fansite devoted to Avril Lavigne. Clicking on the link will automatically reload the YouTube video of "Girlfriend" every 15 seconds. Fans of Avril Lavigne are encouraged to "Keep this page open while you browse the internet, study for exams, or even sleep. For extra viewing power, open up two or more browser windows at this page!"

Finally, an unofficial video of the song "Music Is My Hot Hot Sex" by the Brazilian band Cansei De Ser Sexy briefly held the #1 slot for the all-time most viewed video, with around 114 million views in March 2008. However, it was temporarily removed from YouTube after allegations of automated viewing before being deleted by the uploader.

Italian writer Clarus Bartel, who had uploaded the video, denied attempting to boost its ranking, stating, "These gimmicks do not belong to me. I've got nothing to do with it."

A spokesperson for YouTube said, "We are developing safeguards to secure the statistics on YouTube. Although it is somewhat difficult to track how often this happens, it is not rampant. As soon as it comes to our attention that someone has rigged their numbers to gain placement on the top pages, we remove the video or channel from public view."

So, avoid using tricks to inflate the number of hits your video gets. A good rule of thumb is whether you'd feel comfortable explaining what you've done to a reporter for the *New York Times*.

To get views the right way, don't forget the thumbnail! According to eye tracking studies conducted by Enquiro Research, the thumbnail images are the first things that attract a searcher's eyes. People look at the thumbnail and title before they click on a video, and it's beneficial if the two make sense together and create a compelling image/text combo.

There are other tactics to get views the right way. For example, many people check out the "rising videos," "most discussed," "recent videos," "most responded," "top favorited," and "top rated" videos today, this week, and this month. As your video gets on these lists, it gets more views, both through people browsing the lists and through automated internal promotion.

This means getting more views quickly is ultimately more beneficial than getting many views over a long period of time because they would also get bonus views from being on lists. So any promotional efforts—done through purchasing promotion from YouTube, getting a video featured by YouTube, or promoting it on your own channel—should be focused on getting a sharp spike at first rather than a steady stream.

O'Farrell, who is the syndication manager at My Damn Channel as well as the technical editor of this book, shared with me a personal example of this tactic working. He uploaded "Shelly Two" with David Wain and Elizabeth Banks (`http://www.youtube.com/watch?v=jbV1_2jJ0Ow`) to MyDamnChannel's channel, and it became the most viewed video of the day on YouTube for two days in a row, due to a focused effort of simultaneously posting it, getting it featured by a YouTube editor, promoting it on the channel, and tagging it with recently released movies with Wain and Banks in them.

There are other legitimate ways to easily boost your view count. Anyone can apply to be a partner at http://www.youtube.com/partners, and user partners get more promotional options than regular users. One of these is that the video featured on your channel page will "auto-play," meaning that when anyone visits your channel, it also counts as a view for your video. Not only is this not against the rules, you actually can't disable the auto-play feature.

Another thing that's different for user partners is that the most recent videos on their video watch pages are their own by default—whereas, for non-partner users, the "related videos" displayed on their watch pages are from non-partners by default. For example, check out "STELLA - Birthday" at `http://www.youtube.com/watch?v=xdby-GkQ1g0` and you'll see "More From: MyDamnChannel" in the right column.

The "more from this user" box shows the latest videos created by the user, but users can make a "top videos list" that will show up at the top of the "more from this user" list, meaning the first video in your top videos will continue to get more views. In addition to that, the "top videos" will also appear on the channel page. So basically, the "top videos" and featuring a video on your channel page are two legit ways to increase a video's views.

Two other techniques to drive traffic from one video to another—as opposed to just general promotion across your channel—are annotations and video responses. Annotations can be used to embed clickable text boxes within a video frame itself. If you have one video that is currently popular and another video that you want to promote, you can create annotations in the popular video that link to the other one.

In addition, if you post a popular video as a video response to an unpopular video, it'll slightly increase the unpopular video's views. However, this doesn't really work the other way around. In other words, posting your video as a response to a random popular video isn't helpful because the *many* videos that could be posted as responses to a popular video aren't as prominently linked to as the *one* video to which a popular video is posted as a response.

Friday: Allow and Ask for Ratings

One of the other aspects that YouTube's algorithm uses to determine if your video's content is important is its rating. The community is truly in control on YouTube, and they determine the rating of your video. But you need to enable them to do that by selecting "Yes, allow this video to be rated by others" in the Ratings section of your sharing options. This is the default option and you should select it.

Now, you also have the option of selecting "No, don't allow this video to be rated." But you are then eliminating one of the signals that YouTube uses to determine if your video is a good match for a query. And if you *ever* disable ratings, your video can never be on the "top rated" lists.

If you want millions of people to discover, watch, and share your originally created videos, then you need to allow the YouTube community to rate them. And you don't need to be afraid that you'll be graded on a bell curve.

Amanda Watlington, the owner of Searching for Profit, and I have been teaching a workshop since April 2007 that was initially entitled "Getting Found in All the Right Places" and was later retitled "Optimizing for Universal Search." During the workshop, Watlington presented the findings of a paper that looked at the ratings of YouTube videos along with a number of other issues.

The paper was written by a team of computer scientists from the United States, Canada, and India. According to their paper:

> *An important part of Web 2.0 is user interaction. One of the interactive features of YouTube is a video rating system where users may rate videos on a scale of 0–5 stars (0 being low and 5 being high). The average rating of a video provides insight into how well liked it is by users.*

> "YouTube Traffic Characterization: A View From the Edge,"
> by Phillipa Gill, Martin Arlitt, Zongpeng Li, and Anirban Mahanti

The paper examined whether users enjoyed the content they were watching. The answer was generally "Yes." The paper reported, "For all sets of videos we observed, the average rating is 3 or higher over 80% of the time. The mean rating of videos in the most popular lists is consistently near 4 with very little variation."

So, you should allow ratings. But should you ask for them too?

"What the Buck" is one of the most viewed entertainment shows on YouTube with over 101 million views and 400,000 subscribers as of April 2009. Michael Buckley, the host/writer/producer of the show, creates it in the second bedroom of his home.

"WhatTheBuckShow" won a YouTube Award in 2007 in the Commentary category for "LonelyGirl15 is Dead!" As Figure 4.6 illustrates, it was a video response to his "OMG!!! Jonas Brothers and Fred Join Cast of Lonelygirl15!"

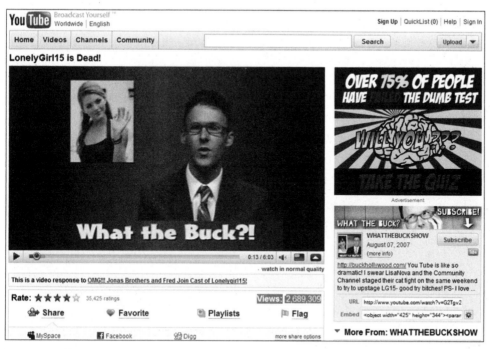

Figure 4.6 "LonelyGirl15 is Dead!"

Buck frequently "breaks the fourth wall" and specifically *asks* his audience to rate his video 5 stars to help him out.

The need to get good ratings in order to get high search result rankings also puts a premium on "creating original work," which we will examine in Chapter 5. And it puts a premium on "becoming a fully vested member of the YouTube community," which we will tackle in Chapter 7.

Week 3: Optimize Video for the Web

Now, I'm fairly confident that somebody in your organization will want to know if there is an alternative to putting the YouTube community in control and letting them determine if your video is popular.

There is: You can add online video to your website, set up a video feed, and optimize it for video search engines.

The upside of this approach is obvious: You control the search results rankings on your website and you determine which videos are relevant and important.

The downside is also obvious: Your videos won't be found when Americans conduct more than 3.2 billion expanded search queries a month, according to comScore qSearch 2.0, and it won't be discovered other ways by the 107.1 million viewers who watched 63.5 videos per viewer on YouTube.com in April 2009, according to comScore Video Metrix.

Either way, your organization faces the trade-offs that the Genie faced in *Aladdin*, "Phenomenal cosmic powers! Itty-bitty living space!"

The good news is you have it both ways. You can optimize video for YouTube and optimize video for the web at the same time. And video optimization best practices for YouTube and the web don't conflict.

So here's what we'll do this week:

Monday: Research Google Video

Tuesday: Investigate blinkx

Wednesday: Study Truveo

Thursday: Examine Live Search Video

Friday: Explore Brightcove

Monday: Research Google Video

Although YouTube has struck numerous partnership deals with content providers such as the BBC, CBS, the NBA, the Sundance Channel, and many music labels, let's imagine that your top management doesn't want to just *give away* your original content to YouTube.

Disney made a similar decision in the late 1970s when cable television was often divided between basic and premium channels. Disney went the premium route, only to watch Nickelodeon capture the larger basic cable market for TV shows for kids. In the 1990s, an executive at Disney told me that this was one of their biggest strategic mistakes.

But, for argument's sake, let's say you don't shape the strategy for your organization. You just implement it. So your only option is to optimize video for the Web. What should you do?

Jennifer Grappone and Gradiva Couzin, the authors of *Search Engine Optimization: An Hour A Day*, offer some sound advice:

On-page text and links to the video First and foremost, make sure all the videos on your site are presented on individual URLs. Text surrounding the video file, and links pointing to it, give contextual help to search engines, so include keywords there.

Video filename Just like search-friendly URLs for HTML pages, video filenames should contain descriptive terms, separated by dashes.

Video file metadata Many video-production/encoding tools allow the input of metadata in the video file itself. This can include content-specific elements such as title, description, or even a text transcript, and it can also include technical information such as format/encoding quality. If you have control over these elements, be sure to include keywords.

Media RSS enclosures Of particular usefulness in SEO are the `<title>`, `<description>`, `<keyword>`, and `<text>` enclosures in your MRSS feed.

When the second edition of their book was published in April 2008, Jennifer and Gradiva had already spotted the importance of Google Video Sitemaps, which had only been introduced a few months earlier. They wrote, "With Video Sitemaps, Google is setting a new course—away from the media RSS feed format that has been accepted for years. But we all know that when Google shows up at a party sporting a new fashion, the whole school will be wearing it the next day." I agree, so add submitting a Google Video Sitemap to your to-do list. You can get more information about creating a Video Sitemap at:

```
http://www.google.com/support/webmasters/bin/answer.py?answer=
80472&ctx=sibling#2
```

Google Video Sitemaps is an extension of the Sitemap protocol that enables you to publish and syndicate online video content and its relevant metadata to Google in order to make it searchable in the Google Video index. You can use a Video Sitemap to add descriptive information—such as a video's title, description, duration, and so on—to make it easier for users to find a particular piece of content. When a user finds your video through Google, they'll be linked to your hosted environments for the full playback.

When you submit a Video Sitemap, Google will make the included video URLs searchable on Google Video. Search results will contain a thumbnail image (provided by you or autogenerated by Google) of your video content as well as information contained in your Video Sitemap.

A Video Sitemap uses the additional video-specific tags in Table 4.2. In its simplest form, a Video Sitemap can include a single tag to let Google know there is a video playable at a specific landing page URL. Optional fields let you specify other attributes of the video available on that page. The more information you provide in the Sitemap extension, the less Google will have to do to try to discover and extract that information. Google may use text available on your video's page rather than the text you supply in the Video Sitemap, if it differs.

Once you have created your Video Sitemap, you can submit it to Google using Webmaster Tools.

Tag	Required?	Description
`<loc>`	Yes	The `<loc>` tag specifies the landing page (aka play page, referrer page) for the video. When a user clicks on a video result on a search results page, they will be sent to this landing page.
`<video:video>`	Yes	
`<video:content_loc>`	Optional	The URL of the actual video content. Note: Although this element is optional, you must provide *one* of either the `<video:content_loc>` or `<video:player_loc>`.
`<video:player_loc>`	Optional	A URL pointing to a player for the video. The most common case for this is with Flash video. The URL of the SWF file that plays your video should be specified in `<video:player_loc>` and the URL of the FLV (actual video file) would be specified in `<video:content_loc>`. The required attribute `allow_embed` specifies whether Google can embed the video in search results. Allowed values are Yes and No.
`<video:thumbnail_loc>`	Optional	A URL pointing to the URL for the video thumbnail image file. This allows you to suggest the thumbnail you want displayed in search results. If you provide a `<video:content_loc>` tag, Google will attempt to generate a set of representative thumbnail images from your actual video content. However, Google Video strongly recommends that you provide a thumbnail URL to increase the likelihood of your video being included in the video index.
`<video:title>`	Optional	The title of the video. Limited to 100 characters.
`<video:description>`	Optional	The description of the video. Descriptions longer than 2,048 characters will be truncated.
`<video:rating>`	Optional	The rating of the video. The value must be float number in the range 0.0–5.0.
`<video:view_count>`	Optional	The number of times the video has been viewed
`<video:publication_date>`	Optional	The date the video was first published, in W3C format. Acceptable values are complete date (YYYY-MM-DD) and complete date plus hours, minutes, and seconds (YYYY-MM-DDThh:mm:ss). Fraction and time zone suffixes are optional. For example, `2007-07-16T19:20:30+08:00`.

Tag	Required?	Description
`<video:tag>`	Optional	A tag associated with the video. Tags are generally very short descriptions of key concepts associated with a video or piece of content. A single video could have several tags, although it might belong to only one category. For example, a video about grilling food may belong in the Grilling category but could be tagged *steak*, *meat*, *summer*, and *outdoor*. Create a new `<video:tag>` element for each tag associated with a video. A maximum of 32 tags is permitted.
`<video:category>`	Optional	The video's category. For example, cooking. The value should be a string no longer than 256 characters. In general, categories are broad groupings of content by subject. Usually a video will belong to a single category. For example, a site about cooking could have categories for Broiling, Baking, and Grilling
`<video:family_friendly>`	Optional	Whether the video is suitable for viewing by children. Allowed values are Yes and No.
`<video:duration>`	Optional	The duration of the video in seconds. Value must be between 0 and 28800 (8 hours). Non-digit characters are disallowed.

Tuesday: Investigate blinkx

You should also optimize video for blinkx. As I just mentioned, blinkx had almost 1.4 million unique visitors in February 2009. Shown in Figure 4.7, blinkx is the world's largest and most advanced video search engine with an index of over 32 million hours of searchable video.

Figure 4.7 blinkx

To help marketers maximize traffic to online video, blinkx offers a white paper on video search engine optimization. It covers the following topics:

- Cleaning and conversion of metadata
- Optimizing titles, description, and filenames
- Leveraging sitemaps
- Utilizing Media RSS
- Content management
- Where to submit
- What to avoid

Go to http://www.blinkx.com/whitepapers to download the video SEO white paper. It is a dozen pages long and provides very ecumenical advice.

For example, it covers first-generation video search solutions, like Singingfish, which depended entirely on metadata. It also outlines what you should do to optimize your content for second-generation video search engines that aim to understand and extract meaning from the video itself as well as spider textual metadata.

The blinkx SEO white paper also covers optimizing your title, description, and tags, which we've already covered, as well as optimizing other metadata, the filename, the sitemap, RSS and Media RSS, the format, in-format metadata, and content management, which are factors in video search engine rankings.

The good news is that none of these recommendations contradict what you need to do to optimize a video for YouTube. Video search engines just look at some things like metadata that YouTube ignores, while YouTube looks at some things like views that video search engines ignore.

For example, just because YouTube ignores the great metadata stored in your MOV file is no reason not to add it for video search engines. The blinkx SEO white paper recommends using tools like Sorenson Squeeze, Autodesk Cleaner, and CastFire to help you ensure that you maintain metadata between conversions and help you keep your metadata profile clean.

The blinkx SEO white paper also provides some guidelines to follow when optimizing your metadata:

- Make sure your tags are relevant to your content. This seems obvious, but it takes some thought as well as some keyword research to get into the minds of users.
- Use as many tags as you can. There is no penalty for using all of your available tag space.
- Spread your tags out among your clips. Adding more tags can help snag some long tail terms.
- Use adjectives. Remember that lots of folks are browsing and they'll use adjectives to find what they are in the mood to view.

- Have some category descriptor tags. It's important to remember YouTube's default search settings are Videos, Relevance, and All Categories.

- Match your title and description with your most important tags. SEO best practices apply here as well.

- Don't use stop words or waste tag space on noise words like *and* and *to*.

In other words, optimizing video for video search engines is similar to optimizing video for YouTube. You just optimize different things.

Wednesday: Study Truveo

You will also want to optimize your video for Truveo, which had almost 2.5 million unique visitors in February 2009 according to Compete. Founded in 2004, Truveo launched its first commercial video search service in 2005. It was acquired by AOL in January 2006 and currently operates as a wholly owned subsidiary of AOL, LLC.

Shown in Figure 4.8, Truveo powers video search for AOL, Microsoft Corporation, CNET's Search.com, Brightcove, and hundreds of other video destinations worldwide. Across the network of websites it powers, Truveo reaches an audience of over 40 million users every month.

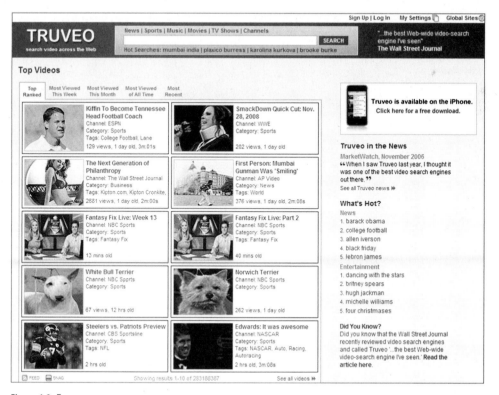

Figure 4.8 Truveo

Truveo opened up its search engine to the online video community in 2006, and hundreds of content producers use its Director Account program to make their video searchable by the millions of users across the Truveo network. The Truveo Director Account program uses a Media RSS feed to get your video content into Truveo's video search index in near real time. To learn more about the free program, go to:

`http://developer.truveo.com/DirectorAccountsOverview.php`

Thursday: Examine Live Search Video

Today, we'll try to figure out what Microsoft is doing in the online video market. But it won't be easy.

First, examine Live Search Video (http://search.live.com/video/). As Figure 4.9 illustrates, it is Microsoft's video search engine.

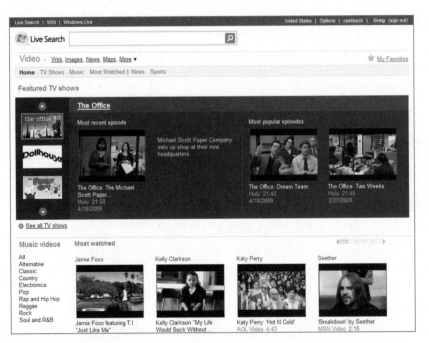

Figure 4.9 Live Search Video

Live Search Video includes featured TV shows like "The Office,"music videos (including some of the most watched on MSN Video), recent news videos, recent sports videos, and most watch videos (including ones on YouTube).

Next, go to MSN Video (http://video.msn.com/video.aspx?mkt=en-us). As Figure 4.10 illustrates, it is Microsoft's video sharing site.

It features "What's Hot" (40 videos). It also has categories for News, Money, Sports, Celebrity, Movies, Music, TV, Life, Autos, and Soapbox User Videos.

Figure 4.10 MSN Video

Confused? As Winston Churchill once said in a radio broadcast October 1939, "I cannot forecast to you the action of Russia. It is a riddle, wrapped in a mystery, inside an enigma; but perhaps there is a key. That key is Russian national interest."

So, if Microsoft today is like Russia back then, then the key to understanding what it will do is figuring out what is in its best interest.

Right now, it seems to be a little of this, a little of that.

But as you try to guess where Microsoft is going, keep this in mind:

- According to comScore Video Metrix, Americans watched 6.8 billion videos on YouTube in April 2009. By comparison, Americans watched less than 32 million on Google Video that month.

- According to Hitwise, YouTube accounted for 79 percent of all U.S. visits to 60 of the leading online video-specific websites in February 2009. By comparison, Google Video accounted for 4.6 percent that month.

Although their methodologies and samples differ, both of these firms paint a similar picture. The online video market resembles a penny-farthing bicycle. The big front wheel is the video sharing site and the little back wheel is the video search engine.

What do you think Microsoft sees?

Friday: Explore Brightcove

If you work for one of the world's largest broadcast, print, music, or brand publishers, then you might want to consider using Brightcove. It is an online video platform designed for professional websites. Its latest version, Brightcove 3, is more search engine friendly than earlier ones.

Founded in 2004 as an Internet distribution channel, Brightcove is now a Software-as-a-Service (SaaS) business.

Brightcove is used by leading media companies, including Dow Jones, Showtime (Dexter, The Tudors), Lifetime, AMC (Mad Men), *Time* magazine, and the *New York Times*. It is also used by big corporations like Sun Microsystems, universities like NYU, and political organizations like the Obama campaign.

In December 2008, Brightcove announced the formation of the Brightcove Alliance, a global network of technology and distribution partners who have integrated with the Brightcove online video platform, as well as solution providers building customer websites and video applications using Brightcove. The Brightcove Alliance launched with more than 90 partners, including AOL Video, Metacafe, Veoh Networks, Blinkx, TubeMogul, and Visible Measures.

Brightcovealso offers a Video SEO Playbook that provides practical strategies and tactics that you can use today. This includes:

- De-mystifying video SEO
- Contextual publishing
- Inbound links
- Video feeds and sitemaps
- Metadata
- Site architecture
- Emerging techniques

To download it, just go to:

http://www.brightcove.com/resources/video-seo-playbook/

Week 4: Think outside the Search Box

Now that you've learned how to research keywords as well as how video optimization works, let me share some case studies that required a little imagination and a lot of perspiration in order to get results.

Monday: Optimize video for news stories

Tuesday: Optimize video for product introductions

Wednesday: Optimize video of key leaders

Thursday: Optimize video of major celebrities

Friday: Optimize video of speakers and exhibitors

Monday: Optimize Video for News Stories

On January 7, 2006, Jill Carroll became an international cause célèbre when she was kidnapped in Baghdad while reporting in Iraq for the *Christian Science Monitor*. She was freed on March 30, 2006.

On August 7, 2006, Robin Antonick, the *Monitor*'s chief web officer, asked me to provide some "SEO guidance." The *Monitor* was preparing to publish Jill's story about her 82 days of captivity in Iraq. In an 11-part multimedia series, Jill would reveal how she survived, her thwarted escape plan, her highs and lows, and the details of her final release. The first part of the multimedia series was scheduled to appear on Sunday evening, August 13—less than a week later.

The *Monitor* had already negotiated a broadcast deal with ABC News. Robin asked if there were other, measurable ways to help promote "Hostage: The Jill Carroll Story." I told him that online video, press release optimization, blogger outreach, and media relations could help generate publicity and increase website traffic.

I recommended focusing media relations efforts on Yahoo! News, MSNBC, CNN, and AOL News. According to Nielsen//NetRatings, these are the top online current events and global news destinations. I also recommended blog outreach to Boing Boing and The Huffington Post. According to Technorati, these blogs have a lot of authority.

And I recommend distributing an optimized press release in Canada and the United Kingdom as well as the United States. I also recommended adding a video clip to the release, because 90 percent of journalists say visuals are important. The video clip could also be uploaded to YouTube.

The series featured online videos, image galleries, and podcasts, but there was some reluctance to just give away original content to YouTube. So I reminded them that Hollywood found it useful to give away movie trailers to promote original content. And I recommended the folks at the *Monitor* create a 43-second YouTube video to promote their 11-part multimedia series. They did.

But, when I conducted keyword research, Google Trends showed me that *Jill Carroll* hadn't been a popular search query since she had been freed. So I had to make an educated guess that these were the words people would type to find our video and press release. I guessed right.

On Thursday, August 10, we started sending emails to top bloggers and pitched "Hostage: The Jill Carroll Story" to the editors of Yahoo! News, AOL News, and CNN.com. One of the first questions they asked us was, "Do you have video?" We had video.

As Figure 4.11 illustrates, we uploaded a video clip promoting the upcoming series to YouTube and optimized it for *Jill Carroll*. We also attached the video to a Business Wire Smart News Release, which was distributed in the United States, Canada, and the United Kingdom on Friday, August 11.

Figure 4.11 "The Jill Carroll story"

With a compelling story and a broadcast deal with ABC News, the *Monitor*'s editors knew "Hostage: The Jill Carroll Story" would get a lot of website traffic. But, they were surprised by exactly how many visitors our integrated marketing program helped them generate.

While ABC News covered Jill's story on Sunday evening, August 13, so did Yahoo! News, MSNBC, CNN, AOL News, The Huffington Post, and Boing Boing. Within the first 24 hours, there were 247 news stories and 1,014 blog posts about "Jill Carroll." By September 7, there were 1,710 stories and 4,685 posts.

Within the first 24 hours, more than 450,000 unique visitors flooded CSMonitor.com, seven times its daily average in July. And page views for the first day broke through the 1 million mark, a massive increase from the site's July average of 121,247 page views per day.

Although almost 90 percent of these visitors were Americans, Canadians and the British also showed strong interest in Carroll's story. Now, credit for the quality of the story belongs to Carroll and the editors of the *Monitor*, however our team was given the lion's share of the credit for getting publicity and increasing website traffic.

Why? From August 13 to 28, CNN.com, Yahoo! News, AOL News, The Huffington Post, Boing Boing, and MSNBC generated almost 300 times more visitors to CSMonitor.com than ABC News had.

So, what's the moral of this story?

A survey conducted in May 2007 by *PR News* and Medialink revealed that PR pros weren't using online video as often as they were watching it. As I reported on the Search Engine Watch Blog at the time, 69 percent of the nearly 300 people who responded to the survey said they'd watched online video footage for business purposes within the last 10 days, but only half had video posted on their corporate websites.

So, what gives? "Video is still an underutilized resource among PR pros—especially those in B2B communications," Larry Thomas, COO of Medialink, told *PR News* at the time. "Execs are watching video themselves, but they're not taking advantage of these cost-effective distribution tools."

The main excuses respondents cited for not using online video were the inability to measure impact/ROI (30 percent) and financial feasibility (28 percent). But, Thomas added, not enough public relations professionals were "taking existing video assets and repurposing (them) in addition to creating content from scratch."

When it comes to online video, Thomas concluded, "PR execs can't stand on the sidelines anymore. They must accelerate their evolution by experimenting. It's scary, but it's even scarier to know that people are talking about you whether you're there or not. We're in a media 2.0 world, and video is the currency of the marketplace."

So, when you are finished reading this book, share it with your PR people. They need to learn how to optimize video too.

Tuesday: Optimize Video for Product Introductions

In December 2007, my business partner, Jamie O'Donnell, produced, optimized, and uploaded three videos for Marvell Technology, a leader in the development of storage, communications, and consumer silicon solutions. He did this in conjunction with three announcements that Marvell made at the International CES 2008 trade show in January 2008:

- Introduction of the Marvell TopDog 11n-450, the industry's first 802.11n chip operating at 450 megabits per second (Mbps)
- Demonstration of Marvell's latest in smart digital green technology, its digital power factor correction (PFC) controllers
- Announcement that Marvell's award-winning Qdeo video processing was a featured technology of the Onida 42″ Xaria LCD-TV

Needless to say, Marvell is a technology-driven company. Founded in 1995, Marvell has more than 5,000 employees and continues to grow. Focusing on investment in research and development has brought some of the industry's finest engineers to Marvell.

There was some skepticism within Marvell about whether to put much energy into online video—even optimized online video—for such ultra-techie product demonstrations. Many people at the company thought that YouTube was where you went to watch funny cat videos.

To set expectations appropriately, Jamie shared the Rubber Republic research that found 70 percent of videos get at least 20 views, 50 percent get at least 100 views, and fewer than 20 percent get more than 500 views.

Figure 4.12 MarvellTechnologyLtd's Channel

But as Figure 4.12 illustrates, "Green technology initiative: Marvell's digital PFC chips" had over 1,000 views as of November 2008, "802.11n Wifi by Marvell" had just over 2,700 views, and "High-Definition Video Processing with Marvell's Qdeo" had more than 3,000 views.

If you're optimizing videos for keywords like *802.11n*, *PFC*, and *Qdeo*, you don't face a lot of competition. And sometimes you get better results by using keywords with a high KEI instead of more popular ones with a big approximate average search volume.

And as for the "it's too technical for an online video" argument, YouTube has a Science & Technology category. And, yes, if you want to watch funny cat videos, YouTube has a Pets & Animals category too.

Wednesday: Optimize Video of Key Leaders

The next video optimization tip comes from YouTube: "Use the YouTube Insight Discovery tab to see which keywords and referrers are driving traffic to your video for more keyword ideas."

We had produced and optimized a video that featured Penn President Amy Gutmann talking with students from the Village Academy High School during their visit to the University of Pennsylvania on May 8, 2008.

But using YouTube Insight, we saw that some of the search queries used on YouTube Search and Google Search to discover the video were for Dr Amy Gutmann. As Figure 4.13 illustrates, it isn't difficult to squeeze "Dr." into the title, even with the (at that time) 60-character limit.

Figure 4.13 "Dr. Amy Gutmann, Penn's President, on increasing access"

We suggested that the title, description, and tags be edited to include "Dr." As of December 1, 2008, "Dr. Amy Gutmann, Penn's President, on increasing access" had almost 2,000 views, making it the second most viewed video on UnivPennsylvania's channel on YouTube.

Thursday: Optimize Video for Major Celebrities

The next video optimization tip also comes from YouTube: "Consider using your current tags (or other user's tags) as keywords."

In 2008, we optimized and uploaded more than 170 videos to YouTube for STACK Media, a leading media company focused on serving active young males. The company's STACKVids, STACK Football, STACK Baseball, and STACK Basketball channels present expert sport workout tips and inside stories from the world's premier athletes.

For STACK, John Mulligan of my firm and Joe Christopher of Blast Advanced Media codeveloped a YouTube batch uploader that enabled us to lay out multiple videos on a grid so we could organize our best keywords and structure our video optimization program.

But John also used tags for related videos as keywords for STACK's YouTube videos showing "Allen Iverson training" and "Peyton Manning working out." As Figure 4.14 illustrates, the combination of tips, tools, and techniques boosted daily views across all four STACK channels.

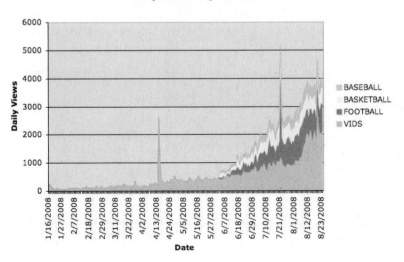

Figure 4.14 Daily Views by Channel

"Related videos" are now based on converging viewer histories more than keywords. In other words, if several users watch one video and then later watch another, they show up as related, regardless of metadata. So, things change and a technique that worked well in 2008 may not work in 2009.

Friday: Optimize Video of Speakers and Exhibitors

In 2008, we also produced, optimized, and uploaded more than 185 videos for Incisive Media's Search Engine Strategies (SES), a leading global conference and training series focused on search engine optimization and search engine marketing.

The most viewed video on the SESConferenceExpo's channel was "The Big Switch by Nicholas Carr." It featured an interview of Nicholas Carr, author of The Big Switch: Rewiring the World, from Edison to Google." He was also the keynote speaker at both SES London and SES New York. Added on February 4, 2008, this video interview had 3,310 views by December 1.

But as Figure 4.15 illustrates, when we used the YouTube Insight Discovery tab, we saw that 60 percent of our total views had come from the embedded player, while 11 percent had come from Google Search and 10 percent had come from YouTube Search.

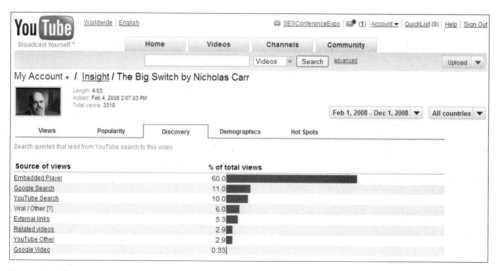

Figure 4.15 *"The Big Switch by Nicholas Carr"*

However, the number of hits coming from being embedded in an optimized press release that we'd used PRWeb to distribute or from being embedded in Rough Type, Nicholas Carr's blog, had helped the video to get high ranking in Google universal search for search queries like *The Big* Switch, as Figure 4.16 illustrates.

And the number of hits from the embedded player had helped the video to get high ranking in YouTube Search results for search queries like Nicholas Carr, as Figure 4.17 illustrates.

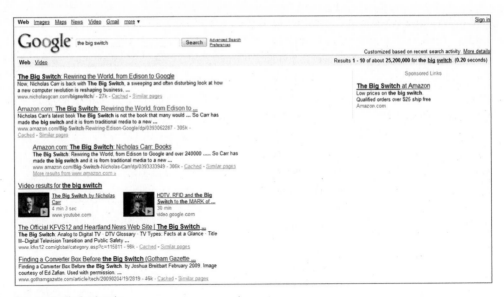

Figure 4.16 The Big Switch

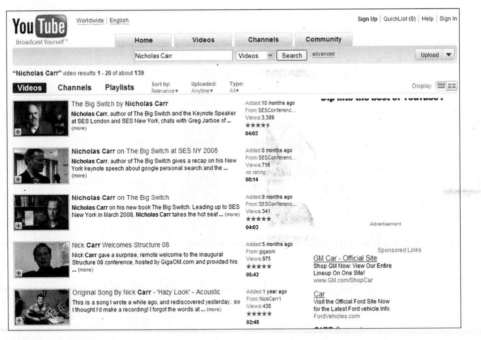

Figure 4.17 Nicholas Carr

That's why we had John and Joe codevelop an automated email notifier for SES that let us individually contact people we had interviewed to let them know when their video interview had been uploaded to YouTube—in case they wanted to embed it on their website or blog. John and Joe also codeveloped an SES video player widget that encouraged bloggers to embed multiple SES videos on their blogs by allowing the header, playlist content, and format to be customized for their viewers.

As of December 2008, the 185 videos from SES London, SES New York, SES Toronto, and SES San Jose 2008 had over 47,000 views, a significant accomplishment for a business-to-business event marketer. That's about three times more views than the number of people who attended these four conferences and expos.

Although more than 90 percent of the video interviews conducted for SES were with conference speakers, one of the more creative elements of the integrated online campaign from an exhibitor relations perspective was the "escalator pitch" at SES New York.

The escalator pitch was like an elevator pitch for SES exhibitors—except the escalators at the Hilton New York moved much faster than the elevators. It was so popular that 14 exhibitors lined up for their 46 seconds of fame. And it was equally popular with viewers.

For example, the "Sendori Escalator Pitch, SES NY 2008" was added on March 20, 2008. As Figure 4.18 illustrates, less than nine months later it had been viewed 1,131 times. And 65 percent of those views had come from the embedded player.

Figure 4.18 "Sendori Escalator Pitch, SES NY 2008"

What's the net net? Sometimes you need to think outside the search box to get results from your video optimization efforts.

In the next chapter, we'll look at "creating original work," which you also need to get good ratings, which are in turn necessary to get high search result rankings.

Month 3: Create Viral Video Content

5

Yogi Berra said, "You can observe a lot just by watching." If you want to learn how to make a viral video, then what he said actually makes sense. In this chapter, you'll watch the best viral videos of 2007 and 2008 to learn how to make original content worth watching and compelling content worth sharing. After you've learned how to create a viral video, you can tell your close friends, "I can't wait to see what you're like online."

Chapter Contents:

See the Power of "The Last Lecture"

YouTube's slogan is "Broadcast Yourself." And millions of people are broadcasting themselves to the YouTube community, including: amateur and professional and established filmmakers; aspiring and professional musicians; comedians; personal video creators such as cooking, beauty, health, and fitness experts; and professional content owners.

Although optimizing a new video's title, description, and tags can help opinion leaders discover it when conducting a relevant query, it is the content of the new video that determines whether it is worth watching—and, more importantly, worth sharing with their followers.

So, opinion leaders don't judge a video by its title. Although discovery is mainly a transfer of *information*, the decision to share a video also involves using their interpersonal *influence*. As Figure 5.1 illustrates, that's why an opinion leader says, "I can't wait to see what you're like online."

"I can't wait to see what you're like online."

Figure 5.1 "I can't wait to see what you're like online." (Cartoon by Paul Noth in *The New Yorker,* July 4, 2005.)

Let me give you an example to make this two-step process clear.

My wife, Nancy, read *The Last Lecture*, the *New York Times* best-selling book written by Randy Pausch, a professor at Carnegie Mellon University. The book was born out of a lecture Pausch gave in September 2007 entitled "Really Achieving Your Childhood Dreams."

After reading the book, which is 224 pages long, Nancy decided to buy copies to give as Christmas presents to all three of our kids in 2008. Although I hadn't read the book, I discovered a video of Pausch's last lecture on the CarnegieMellonU channel on YouTube.

I wasn't the first to discover the video. As Figure 5.2 illustrates, "Randy Pausch Last Lecture: Achieving Your Childhood Dreams" had more than 8 million views on YouTube as of January 1, 2009.

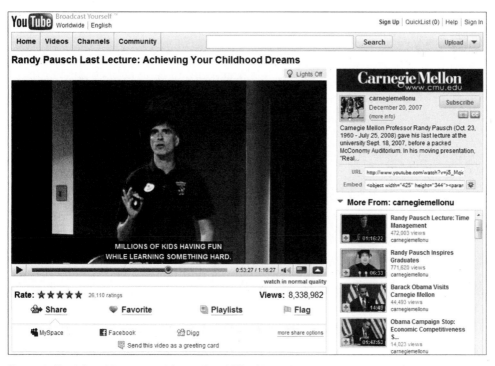

Figure 5.2 "Randy Pausch Last Lecture: Achieving Your Childhood Dreams"

But if you look closely, you'll also notice that the video is 1 hour, 16 minutes, and 27 seconds long. So the decision to watch it wasn't trivial. And the view count in YouTube doesn't mean someone watched more than half of the video, which is how Dailymotion counts a "view." But, I figured that I could watch the video in less time than I could read the book. And I could click away at any time if the video turned out to be boring.

Pausch's moving presentation wasn't boring. His talk was modeled after an ongoing series of lectures where top academics were asked to think deeply about the question, What wisdom would you try to impart to the world if you knew it was your last chance?

A month before giving the lecture, Pausch had received a prognosis that the pancreatic cancer with which he had been diagnosed a year earlier was terminal. Before speaking, Pausch received a long standing ovation from a large crowd of over 400 colleagues and students. When he motioned them to sit down, saying, "Make me earn it," some in the audience shouted back, "You did!"

During the lecture Pausch was upbeat and humorous, shrugging off the pity often given to those diagnosed with a terminal illness. At one point, to prove his own vitality, Pausch dropped down and did push-ups on stage.

He offered insights on computer science and engineering education, multidisciplinary collaborations, and working in groups and interacting with other people. Pausch also offered his listeners inspirational life advice that can be applied to one's professional and personal life.

At the end of 1:16:27, I was in tears. On New Year's Day, I shared a link to the video with my kids, just in case they hadn't read the book yet. Although there's no substitute for reading the book, not everyone has the time. And once you've seen the video, you make time to read the book.

Week 1: Watch the Best Viral Videos of 2007

Before you learn how to make a viral video, let me define what one is.

According to Wikipedia, "A viral video is a video clip that gains widespread popularity through the process of Internet sharing, typically through email or Instant messaging, blogs and other media sharing websites." It adds, "Viral videos are often humorous in nature."

Wikipedia gives some examples of viral videos, including televised comedy sketches such as Saturday Night Live's "Lazy Sunday" from 2005; amateur video clips like Judson Laipply's "Evolution of Dance" from 2006; and Web-only productions such as Obama Girl's "I Got a Crush...On Obama" from 2007. Some "eyewitness" events have also been caught on video and have gone viral, including the "Battle at Kruger" from 2007.

You'll get a better idea of what a viral video is by watching some. But before we start, are there any questions?

Search Engine Marketer: "What is the best digital camcorder?"

YouTube Director: "What is the best video editing software?"

Small Businessperson: "What is the worst that can happen?"

Those are all good questions and I'll tackle them in Chapter 8, which is about video production. But this chapter is about video content. Good production is important, but it won't save bad content.

If you need a professional example, compare *Star Wars Episode IV: A New Hope* from the original trilogy with *Star Wars Episode I: The Phantom Menace* from the prequel trilogy. Although the production quality had improved two decades later, the content hadn't.

If you want an amateur example, watch "Star Wars according to a 3 year old." Fans of the film can go on for hours discussing the plot, but this sweet-faced little lady sums it up in less than two minutes. If not the most detailed description of *Star Wars* ever, it's arguably the most adorable. As Figure 5.3 illustrates, it had about 10 million views as of January 1, 2009.

Figure 5.3 "Star Wars according to a 3 year old."

If a three-year-old can become a YouTube sensation just by retelling the original *Star Wars* story, then don't underestimate the Force of content. With that in mind, let's check out some of the best viral videos of 2007:

Monday: Observe "Jeff Dunham - Achmed the Dead Terrorist"

Tuesday: See "Charlie bit my finger—again!"

Wednesday: Check out "Potter Puppet Pals in 'The Mysterious Ticking Noise'"

Thursday: Look at "Battle at Kruger"

Friday: View "Soulja Boy Tellem - How to Crank That - INSTRUCTIONAL VIDEO"

Monday: Observe "Jeff Dunham - Achmed the Dead Terrorist"

One of the best viral videos of 2007 is "Jeff Dunham - Achmed the Dead Terrorist." As Figure 5.4 illustrates, it had more than 78 million views on YouTube as of January 1, 2009, making it the #6 most viewed video of all time in any category.

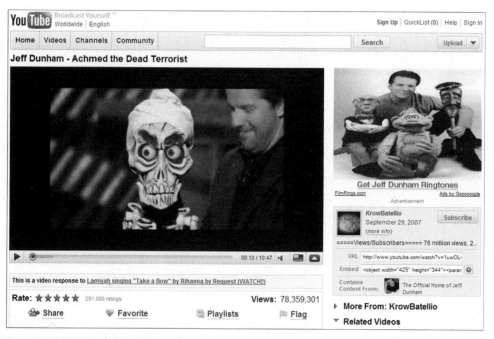

Figure 5.4 "Jeff Dunham - Achmed the Dead Terrorist"

If you look at the statistics and data for this video, you will also see that it has six honors:

- #28 - Most Discussed (All Time)
- #3 - Most Discussed (All Time - Entertainment
- #6 - Most Viewed (All Time)
- #1 - Most Viewed (All Time - Entertainment
- #2 - Top Favorited (All Time)
- #1 - Top Favorited (All Time - Entertainment

Dunham is an American ventriloquist and stand-up comedian. He has performed at comedy clubs across the United States since the late 1980s and has also appeared on numerous television shows, including *Late Show with David Letterman* and *The Tonight Show*. In January 2008, Dunham was voted the top comedian in Comedy Central's "Stand-Up Showdown."

Dunham's act includes seven puppets, known by his fans as the Suitcase Posse. They include Achmed the Dead Terrorist, Bubba J, José Jalapeño on a Stick, Melvin the Superhero, Peanut, Sweet Daddy D, and Walter. Although each puppet has a backstory and Dunham brings them all to life, the one that's gone viral is Achmed.

The skeletal corpse of an incompetent suicide bomber, Achmed is used by Dunham to perform comedy based on the contemporary issue of terrorism. Achmed is known for yelling, "Silence! I kill you!" to people in the audience who laugh at his customs. The dead terrorist first appeared in "Spark of Insanity" and made an appearance in the "Very Special Christmas Special," singing a song called "Jingle Bombs." The special's November 2008, premiere was the highest rated telecast in Comedy Central's history.

A TV commercial for a ringtone featuring Dunham's character Achmed the Dead Terrorist was banned by the South African Advertising Standards Authority in 2008 after a complaint was filed by a citizen stating that the ad was offensive and portrayed all Muslims as terrorists. The ban angered Dunham, who issued a statement that read, "Achmed makes it clear in my act that he is not Muslim." In fact, the puppet jokes when asked about this that a label on him says, "Made in China."

In October 2008, Dunham told Fox News, "I've skewered whites, blacks, Hispanics, Christians, Jews, Muslims, gays, straights, rednecks, addicts, the elderly, and my wife. As a stand-up comic, it is my job to make the majority of people laugh, and I believe that comedy is the last true form of free speech."

There are a couple of serious lessons to learn from this funny video.

First, "characters" like Achmed are above average in their ability to change brand preference. And research by Mapes & Ross has found that people who register a change in brand preference after seeing a commercial or video are three times more likely to buy a product or idea.

Second, if you want to avoid your video being misunderstood, then you had better make it crystal clear. A study of TV commercials by Purdue University found *all* of them were miscomprehended, some by as many as 40 percent of viewers, none by fewer than 19 percent.

Tuesday: See "Charlie bit my finger - again!"

Fionn Downhill, the CEO and president of Elixir Systems, suggested the next viral video from 2007: "Charlie bit my finger - again!" As Figure 5.5 illustrates, it had over 72 million views on YouTube as of January 1, 2009.

Harry and Charlie's father, Howard, says, "Even had I thought of trying to get my boys to do this I probably couldn't have, neither were coerced into any of this and neither were hurt (for very long anyway). This was just one of those moments where I had the video camera out because the boys were being fun, and they provided something really very funny."

Figure 5.5 "Charlie bit my finger – again!"

Look at the statistics and data for this video. It has 19 honors:

- #12 - Featured - Hong Kong
- #7 - Featured - Comedy - Hong Kong
- #3 - Most Discussed (All Time) - United Kingdom
- #24 - Most Discussed (All Time)
- #1 - Most Discussed (All Time) - Comedy - United Kingdom
- #4 - Most Discussed (All Time) - Comedy
- #35 - Most Responded (This Month) - Comedy - United Kingdom
- #29 - Most Responded (All Time) - United Kingdom
- #3 - Most Responded (All Time) - Comedy - United Kingdom
- #37 - Most Responded (All Time) - Comedy
- #2 - Most Viewed (All Time) - United Kingdom
- #9 - Most Viewed (All Time)
- #1 - Most Viewed (All Time) - Comedy - United Kingdom
- #2 - Most Viewed (All Time) - Comedy
- #1 - Top Favorited (All Time) - United Kingdom
- #3 - Top Favorited (All Time)
- #1 - Top Favorited (All Time) - Comedy - United Kingdom
- #2 - Top Favorited (All Time) - Comedy
- #51 - Top Rated (All Time) - Comedy - United Kingdom

What lesson can we learn from this viral video? "Slice of life" videos have been found to be above average in their ability to change people's brand preference. Copywriters detest them because most of them are so corny—and don't require scripts. But realistic and charming slices can also be effective at the cash register.

Wednesday: Check Out "Potter Puppet Pals in 'The Mysterious Ticking Noise'"

Another one of the best viral videos of 2007 is "Potter Puppet Pals in 'The Mysterious Ticking Noise.'" As Figure 5.27 illustrates, it had more than 56 million YouTube views as of January 1, 2009.

Figure 5.6 "Potter Puppet Pals in 'The Mysterious Ticking Noise'"

According to the statistics and data for this video, it had six honors:

- #19 - Most Discussed (All Time)
- #3 - Most Discussed (All Time) - Comedy
- #16 - Most Viewed (All Time)
- #4 - Most Viewed (All Time) - Comedy
- #4 - Top Favorited (All Time)
- #3 - Top Favorited (All Time) - Comedy

"Potter Puppet Pals in 'The Mysterious Ticking Noise'" was created by Neil Stephen Cicierega, an American comedian, filmmaker, and musician. He is also the creator of a genre of Flash animation known as animutation. And he lives near me, in Kingston, Massachusetts.

Cicierega's *Potter Puppet Pals* is a comedy series that is a parody of Harry Potter. It originated in 2003 as a pair of Flash animations on Newgrounds.com and later resurfaced in the form of a series of live-action puppet shows released in 2006 on YouTube and Potterpuppetpals.com.

"The Mysterious Ticking Noise," added on March 23, 2007, was nominated for and won the 2007 YouTube Award in the Comedy category with 33.6 percent of the votes in the category.

Cicierega has worked on videos with fellow Massachusetts Internet filmmakers and close friends Kevin James, Ryan Murphy, Max Pacheco, and J.L. Carrozza. In 2008, Neil, Ryan, and Kevin were commissioned to make a series of "webisodes" for Plymouth Rock Studios. The series, called *New Kids on the Rock*, is a tongue-in-cheek comedy series about the trio's attempts to make webisodes for Plymouth Rock Studios.

Several of Cicierega's short films have been featured on television shows such as G4's *Attack of the Show!*, The CW's *Online Nation*, and CBBC's *Chute!* In addition to *Potter Puppet Pals*, the director adds regular video content to the NeilCicierega channel on YouTube.

Although Cicierega is just 23 years old, he has been Internet-notable for a while. Back in 2000, when he was only 14, he formed the band Lemon Demon. The band's song/video "Ultimate Showdown of Ultimate Destiny" (in which several unrelated fictional characters fight) "went viral" on New Grounds in 2005.

A recurring theme in a lot of Cicierega's work is to play off of preexisting intellectual property and distort it in a way that is often disturbingly incompatible with the tone of source—for example, Mr. Rogers murdering people in "Ultimate Showdown of Ultimate Destiny," or Dumbledor being a sexual predator in *Potter Puppet Pals*. "Ultimate Showdown" and "Potter Puppets" are similar in that they became massively popular by having content that the viewer was already invested in.

Unlike the creators of other videos from this week, Cicierega is someone who is very much aware of Internet memes and was actively pursuing mass Internet appeal via an established method of remixing pop culture rather than accidentally stumbling into it.

What other lesson can we learn from this award-winning video? Sound effects can make a positive impact on brand preference. On the other hand, research has found that using background music is neither a positive nor a negative factor.

Thursday: Look at "Battle at Kruger"

This *National Geographic*-worthy footage was shot and uploaded to YouTube by a regular guy on safari with his family. The unbelievable confrontation between a herd of water buffalo, a pride of lions, and a couple of crocodiles—along with the surprise ending—has kept people at edge of their seats since it was uploaded on May 3, 2007.

Clearly this viral video captured the world's attention. As Figure 5.7 illustrates, "Battle at Kruger" had 40 million views on YouTube as of January 1, 2009.

Figure 5.7 "Battle at Kruger"

According to the statistics and data for this video, it had six honors:

- #2 - Most Discussed (All Time) - Pets & Animals
- #31 - Most Viewed (All Time)
- #1 - Most Viewed (All Time) - Pets & Animals
- #32 - Top Favorited (All Time)
- #2 - Top Favorited (All Time) - Pets & Animals
- #17 - Top Rated (All Time) - Pets & Animals

The amateur wildlife video that was shot in September 2004 at a watering hole in Kruger National Park, South Africa, during a safari guided by Frank Watts. It was filmed by videographer David Budzinski and photographer Jason Schlosberg.

Taken from a vehicle on the opposite side of the watering hole with a digital camcorder, the video begins with the herd of buffalo approaching the water. The lions charge and disperse the herd, picking off a young buffalo and unintentionally knocking it into the water while attempting to make a kill. While the lions try to drag the buffalo out of the water, it is grabbed by a crocodile, which fights for it before giving up and leaving it to the lions. The lions sit down and prepare to eat but are quickly surrounded by the massively reorganized buffalo, who move in and begin charging and kicking at the lions. After a battle that sees one lion being tossed into the air by a buffalo, the baby buffalo—still alive, to the astonishment of the onlookers—escapes into the herd. The emboldened buffalo then proceed to chase the remaining lions away.

"Battle at Kruger" won the 2007 YouTube Award in the Eyewitness category. A *National Geographic* documentary on the video debuted on the National Geographic channel on May 11, 2008.

What other lesson can we learn from this award-winning video? Avoid visual banality. If you want viewers to pay attention to your video, show them something they have never seen before.

Friday: View "Soulja Boy Tell'em - How to Crank That - INSTRUCTIONAL VIDEO!"

There hasn't been a dance craze like the Soulja Boy since the Macarena. Soulja Boy Tell'em, a breakout rap artist, made a video in his parents' garage featuring a dance he created for one of his songs. He was only 16 at the time his video went viral.

Interest in the dance exploded, so he created a follow-up instructional video on how to do it. Now everyone from college football teams to cartoon characters are "cranking that" like Soulja Boy.

As Figure 5.8 illustrates, "Soulja Boy Tell'em - How to Crank That - INSTRUCTIONAL VIDEO!" had nearly 40 million views on YouTube as of January 1, 2009.

Figure 5.8 "Soulja Boy Tell'em - How to Crank That - INSTRUCTIONAL VIDEO!"

According to the statistics and data for this video, it had 10 honors:

- #6 - Most Discussed (All Time) - Howto & Style
- #52 - Most Responded (Today) - Howto & Style
- #13 - Most Responded (This Week) - Howto & Style
- #18 - Most Responded (This Month) - Howto & Style
- #95 - Most Responded (All Time)
- #2 - Most Responded (All Time) - Howto & Style
- #34 - Most Viewed (All Time)
- #1 - Most Viewed (All Time) - Howto & Style
- #39 - Top Favorited (All Time)
- #1 - Top Favorited (All Time) - Howto & Style

Soulja Boy Tell'em was born DeAndre Ramone Way, but he is better known as Soulja Boy. Soulja Boy posted his songs on the website SoundClick in November 2005. Following positive reviews on the site, Soulja Boy then established his own web pages on YouTube and MySpace.

In September 2007, his single "Crank That (Soulja Boy)" reached number one on the Billboard Hot 100. The single was initially self-published on the Internet, and it became a #1 hit in the United States for seven nonconsecutive weeks starting in September 2007.

His YouTube video, "Soulja Boy Tell'em - Crank That (Soulja Boy)," had almost 45 million views as of January 11, 2009.

What other lesson can we learn from this how-to video? "Demonstrations" that show how well your product or idea performs are above average in their ability to persuade. And demonstrations don't have to be *dull*.

Week 2: Make Original Content Worth Watching

Now that you've watched some of the best viral videos of 2007, do you see a pattern? They fall into a variety of categories, including Comedy, Entertainment, and Pets & Animals as well as Howto & Style. Although three are "humorous in nature," two are not.

So what do the viral videos we've watched so far have in common? In addition to being among the most viewed, they are also among the most discussed and top favorited. I imagine that they are also ones that made their way into conversations both at work and at home because they tell stories.

This is the key to making original content worth watching.

Of course, I'm not the only one who understands the importance of storytelling. As Figure 5.9 illustrates, Sony's Backstage 101 online learning center has an article entitled "Tell a Story with Video."

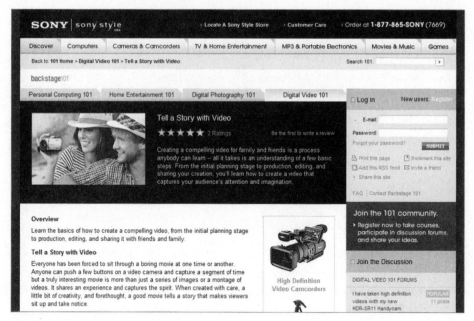

Figure 5.9 Tell a Story with Video

According to Sony, "Before you shoot a single frame, you should understand exactly how you want your story to be told and what you want the audience to take away from it. No matter what kind of story you choose to tell, the best place to start isn't with a camera and microphone—it's with a pen and paper." Sony advises that you ask a few key questions:

Who is your audience? Is this video for a business audience, or is it for your family and friends?

What point of view will you take? Will you tell it from your own perspective, from that of one of your subjects, or will a third-person narrator do the talking?

Where does the story take place?

When do the key events that propel the story take place?

Why is this story worth telling?

How will you tell the story? How will your video connect emotionally with the audience?

There's also a language to storytelling. If you don't know how to speak it, you've watched enough movies and TV programs to understand it. Start wide to give the audience an idea of where you are. Cut to medium to learn more about your subject. Get tight to capture the emotion.

With this in mind, let's watch some more viral videos from 2007. Although they don't tell stories like the videos you saw in week 1 did, several have backstories. The dramatic revelation of secrets from a backstory is a useful technique for developing a story; it was first recognized as a literary device by Aristotle.

Monday: Observe "'Chocolate Rain' Original Song by Tay Zonday"

Tuesday: See "PARIS IN JAIL" and "LEAVE BRITNEY ALONE!"

Wednesday: Check out "me singing 'what goes around' Justin Timberlake"

Thursday: Look at "'I Got a Crush...On Obama' by Obama Girl"

Friday: View "Otters holding hands" and NORA the piano-playing cat

Monday: Observe "'Chocolate Rain' Original Song by Tay Zonday"

Tay Zonday's "Chocolate Rain" was the underdog smash hit of the summer of 2007. The song, with its unconventional lyrics and delivery, struck a chord with the YouTube community and sparked imitations from everyday people and celebrities alike. Even Green Day's Tre Cool got in the mix!

It was clear that Zonday and his tune had pop culture a-buzz when he appeared as a guest on both *Jimmy Kimmel Live* and VH1's *Best Week Ever*. Now Zonday's popping up in Internet commercials like the one for Dr. Pepper's new Cherry Chocolate beverage, and his breathe-away-from-the-mic move has become a meme of our time.

As Figure 5.10 illustrates, "'Chocolate Rain' Original Song by Tay Zonday" had almost 33 million views on YouTube as of January 1, 2009.

Figure 5.10 "'Chocolate Rain' Original Song by Tay Zonday"

According to the statistics and data for this video, it had 14 honors:

- #8 - Most Discussed (All Time)
- #3 - Most Discussed (All Time) - Music
- #70 - Most Responded (Today)
- #23 - Most Responded (Today) - Music
- #59 - Most Responded (This Week)
- #13 - Most Responded (This Week) - Music
- #38 - Most Responded (This Month)
- #8 - Most Responded (This Month) - Music
- #10 - Most Responded (All Time)
- #3 - Most Responded (All Time) - Music
- #46 - Most Viewed (All Time)
- #33 - Most Viewed (All Time) - Music
- #52 - Top Favorited (All Time)
- #33 - Top Favorited (All Time) - Music

"Chocolate Rain" was the winner in the Music category in the 2007 YouTube Awards.

Now, here's the backstory on "Chocolate Rain": Zonday's real name is Adam Nyerere Bahner. The video was originally posted on 4chan.org, an extremely popular, graphic, trend-setting message board. However, the discussion on 4chan was focused on mocking Tay rather than an earnest appreciation of his video. In fact, tons of parody videos were made in response, including ones by non-4chan users.

Although the video was posted on April 22, 2007, it didn't really go viral until July 26, 2007, when YouTube simultaneously featured all of the parody and response videos on its home page.

So, the opinion leaders who turned "Chocolate Rain" into a viral video were the 4chan community and a few members of the YouTube staff. Nevertheless, the history behind Zonday's "success" makes a fun backstory to tell as opinion leaders share his video with their followers.

There is another lesson to be learned here: "When you have nothing to say, sing it." The lyrics are cryptic: "Zoom the camera out and see the lie." But the piano riff and drum loop are hypnotic. Zonday has said, "I don't know what causes people to listen to my music. If I could speak it, there would be no reason to write songs."

Tuesday: See "PARIS IN JAIL" and "LEAVE BRITNEY ALONE!"

Uploaded on the heels of Paris Hilton's jail sentence, this reggae-lite music video pokes fun at the heiress in a delightfully cheeky way. As Figure 5.11 illustrates, "PARIS IN JAIL: The Music Video" had over 25.5 million views on YouTube as of January 1, 2009.

PARIS IN JAIL: The Music Video

1:16 / 2:48

watch in normal quality

This is a video response to HARRY POTTER IN THE HOOD is the HALF BLOOD PRINCE OF BEL-AIR

Rate: ★★★★☆ 46,415 ratings   Views: 25,625,215

👣 Share   💚 Favorite   📋 Playlists   🏴 Flag

Advertisement

omovies
June 06, 2007
(more info)   Subscribe

Stalk us now on http://www.Twitter.com/oMovies
.... Visit the crib: website:
http://www.OMOVIES.COM Be our friend with
benefits on MYSPACE website:
http://www.myspace.com/O...

URL   http://www.youtube.com/watch?v=k66epn
Embed   <object width="425" height="344"><parar ⚙

▼ **More From: omovies**

Figure 5.11 "PARIS IN JAIL: The Music Video"

According to the statistics and data for this video, it had six honors:

- #96 - Featured - Czech Republic
- #84 - Featured - Sweden
- #45 - Most Discussed (All Time) - Comedy
- #94 - Most Viewed (All Time)
- #7 - Most Viewed (All Time) - Comedy
- #89 - Top Favorited (All Time) - Comedy.

Contrast "PARIS IN JAIL" with "LEAVE BRITNEY ALONE!" Chris Crocker's raw, melodramatic emotion captured the attention of YouTubers. Whether people despised, sympathized, or were confused by him, nobody could look away and Crocker became an instant YouTube star when he uploaded "LEAVE BRITNEY ALONE!" on September 10, 2007.

It became one of the Most Responded videos of all time, with 2,252 video responses as of January 1, 2009. Even actor Seth Green created a spoof of it.

Crocker, who is 21, was actually pulling in millions of views before the media started reporting on his "LEAVE BRITNEY ALONE!" video. If you look at his YouTube channel, his first video, "Chris Crocker - This & that," has over 3.9 million views, close to 17,000 ratings, and more than 30,000 comments and has been favorited over 10,000 times.

Crocker has gone on to make several television appearances and has even signed a development deal to star in his own TV show. As Figure 5.12 illustrates, "Chris Crocker - LEAVE BRITNEY ALONE!" had nearly 24 million views on YouTube as of January 1, 2009.

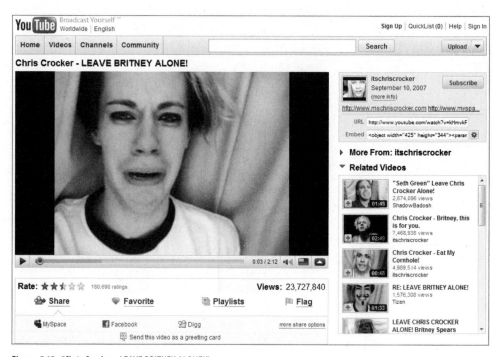

Figure 5.12 "Chris Crocker - LEAVE BRITNEY ALONE!"

According to the statistics and data, this video had five honors:

- #4 - Most Discussed (All Time)
- #1 - Most Discussed (All Time) - Entertainment
- #86 - Most Responded (This Month)
- #21 - Most Responded (This Month) - Entertainment
- #21 - Top Favorited (All Time) - Entertainment

Now, it may appear that "PARIS IN JAIL" and "LEAVE BRITNEY ALONE!" have nothing in common. But they do. Both of these viral videos use "news" as their backstories. And videos that contain news are above average in their ability to change people's brand preference as well as to capture the attention of the media.

Wednesday: Check Out "me singing 'what goes around' Justin Timberlake"

Esmee Denters rose to fame singing songs from her bedroom in Osterbeke, Netherlands. Her beautiful voice captivated everyone who heard it and she became one of the top musicians on YouTube.

Then, in May 2007, she shocked fans when she uploaded a video of her singing a Justin Timberlake song and the pop star appeared at the end playing the piano. Denters then signed on as the first artist on Timberlake's record label and she has since released her debut album.

As Figure 5.13 illustrates, "me singing 'what goes around' Justin Timberlake" had just over 19 million views on YouTube as of January 1, 2009.

Figure 5.13 "me singing '"what goes around' Justin Timberlake"

According to the statistics and data, this video had nine honors:

- #96 - Featured - Sweden
- #49 - Most Discussed (All Time)
- #1 - Most Discussed (All Time) - Netherlands
- #23 - Most Discussed (All Time) - Music
- #1 - Most Discussed (All Time) - Music - Netherlands
- #1 - Most Viewed (All Time) - Netherlands
- #1 - Most Viewed (All Time) - Music - Netherlands
- #5 - Top Favorited (All Time) - Netherlands
- #3 - Top Favorited (All Time) - Music - Netherlands

Timberlake first heard Denters on YouTube singing cover versions of popular songs. He tracked her down and signed her to his label, Tennman Records.

At the same time, Tennman Records announced that she would be opening for Timberlake at 10 venues during his 2007 European tour, making Denters the first amateur singer in history to go directly from a personal YouTube posting to commercially performing on a major stage.

She has appeared on *The Oprah Winfrey Show* on an episode that was dedicated to YouTube stars. Her first album with Tennman Records was released in March of 2009.

What's the lesson here? No, don't rush out and get "testimonials by celebrities." These are below average in their ability to change brand preference. Viewers guess that the celebrity is only doing it for the money, and they are right.

Besides, viewers have a way of remembering the celebrity while forgetting the singer-songwriter. That's why it was smart to limit Timberlake's cameo appearance until the very end of the video.

Thursday: Look at "'I Got a Crush…On Obama' by Obama Girl"

This catchy video showcases an attractive young woman who feels quite, ah, strongly about a certain presidential candidate. Created by the political satire group Barely Political, founded by Ben Relles and Leah Kauffman, the video not only notched millions of views, it also caught the attention of bloggers, mainstream media, and even those running for office.

As Figure 5.14 illustrates, "'I Got a Crush…On Obama' By Obama Girl" had 12,546,852 views on YouTube as of January 1, 2009.

Figure 5.14 "'I Got a Crush…On Obama' By Obama Girl"

According to the statistics and data, this video had three honors:

- #75 - Most Discussed (All Time)
- #14 - Most Discussed (All Time) - Comedy
- #55 - Most Viewed (All Time) - Comedy

It's worth noting that this is one of the few videos to go viral without being among the top favorited in its category. I wonder if the controversial "Call Me" TV ad—run by the Republican Party in 2006 to attack Democratic candidate Harold Ford, Jr., in the Tennessee U.S. Senate election—hurt Obama Girl's ratings by the politically savvy YouTube community in 2007.

Brad O'Farrell, the technical editor of this book, tells me that getting views without being favorited may sometimes be caused by "thumbnail gaming." Barely Political and its new spin-off, Barely Digital, both feature videos containing attractive, scantily clad women. Then, they make sure their cleavage is in the thumbnail. This artificially inflates their views because thousands of teenage boys click on the video only to be disappointed by its "content." In other words, no one is favoriting it because it is the ol' bait and switch.

O'Farrell also points out that Congressman Ford's real-life girlfriend, who was being alluded to in the "Call Me" ad, was Julia Allison, a columnist for *Time Out New York* and creator of the group blog NonSociety.com. So, the backstory behind this video may have contributed to its success despite the lack of favorable YouTube ratings.

Since the advent of blogs, journalistic backstories have become much more visible and interesting to the general public. Blogs often focus on the backstory both before and after the standard news story is covered in the media. This is beginning to change the lines between story and backstory and alter the definitions of journalism.

This may also explain why Ettinger's performance in "I Got a Crush…On Obama" earned her scores of media appearances, from a part in a *Saturday Night Live* sketch to an appearance in a video for *The Onion News Network*. Barely Political's most popular video was also named one of 2007's 10 best videos by *Newsweek*, *People* magazine, Associated Press, and YouTube.

In October 2007, Barely Political was bought by Next New Networks for an unknown amount. Herb Scannell, cofounder and CEO of Next New Networks, said, "With Barely Political, we've added a team that can grow our reach to a very important audience—one that likes their politics with a healthy serving of humor—timed perfectly with the upcoming 2008 election season."

On May 7, 2008, Barely Political posted a YouTube video entitled "Senator Gravel Lobbies Obama Girl! The music video!" In the video, Presidential candidate Mike Gravel tries to persuade Obama Girl to switch her support from Obama to him. Her response near the end of the video is, "I'll think about it."

Is there a lesson to be learned from "'I Got a Crush...On Obama' By Obama Girl"? There is: avoid "thumbnail gaming." These gimmicks generally hurt more than they help.

Friday: View "Otters holding hands" and NORA the Piano-Playing Cat

What is cuter than otters? Otters holding hands, of course! This YouTube video rocketed to fame on the strength of its sheer adorableness.

As Figure 5.15 illustrates, "Otters holding hands" had almost 12 million views on YouTube as of January 1, 2009.

Figure 5.15 "Otters holding hands"

According to the statistics and data, this video had four honors:

- #21 - Most Discussed (All Time) - Pets & Animals
- #11 - Most Viewed (All Time) - Pets & Animals
- #7 - Top Favorited (All Time) - Pets & Animals
- #69 - Top Rated (All Time) - Pets & Animals

Compare "Otters holding hands" with NORA the piano-playing cat. Nora the cat proves that paws work just as well as fingers when it comes to banging the ivories. (And she should! One of her "masters" is a musician/composer/teacher.)

As Figure 5.16 illustrates, "'NORA: Practice Makes Purr-fect' - Check the sequel too" had almost 12 million views on YouTube as of January 1, 2009. (By the way, I did check "Nora: The Sequel - Better than the original!" It had 3.5 million views.)

Figure 5.16 "'NORA: Practice Makes Purr-fect' – Check the sequel too."

According to the statistics and data, this video had five honors:

- #11 - Featured - Hong Kong
- #2 - Featured - Pets & Animals - Hong Kong
- #10 - Most Discussed (All Time) - Pets & Animals
- #12 - Most Viewed (All Time) - Pets & Animals
- #15 - Top Favorited (All Time) - Pets & Animals

What is the lesson learned from watching "Otters holding hands" and NORA the piano-playing cat? It is about "emotion." Researchers have not yet found a way to quantify the effectiveness of emotion, but I have come to believe that video content that is nostalgic, charming, and even sentimental can be enormously effective. And emotion can be just as effective as any rational appeal, especially when there is nothing unique to say about pets and animals.

Week 3: Observe the Top Viral Videos of 2008

Now that you've seen some videos worth watching, let's ask, What types of content makes a new video so worth sharing that it goes viral?

Back in 2006, many people created videos that consisted of jokes, bloopers, and funny clips because it appeared humorous videos like "Evolution of Dance" were the most likely to go viral.

During 2007, YouTube went mainstream, with an audience that closely mirrored the demographics of the U.S. online population. And the categories of online video content that went viral expanded to include Entertainment, Howto & Style, Music, Pets & Animals, and Comedy.

By 2008, the content that YouTubers were watching and talking about had expanded again to include News & Politics, People & Blogs, plus Travel & Events. You could see this diversity reflected in the YouTube Year-End Video Roundup for 2008, which featured the most popular videos on YouTube's home page on January 1, 2009.

YouTube's list highlighted just some of the videos that had gone viral using a formula that includes view counts, most shared, most discussed, top rated, and general popularity or influence on popular culture. These viral videos came from regular users, emerging online studios, and the largest of media companies, indicating YouTube had truly leveled the playing field for all content creators.

Or, as Figure 5.17 illustrates, you could get a second opinion by looking at the chart of the top 20 viral videos compiled by Unruly Media.

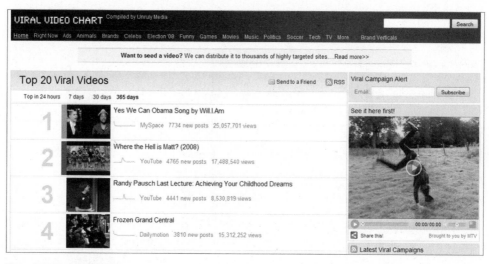

Figure 5.17 Top 20 Viral Videos

Based in London, Unruly Media scans several million blogs a day to see which online videos people are talking about the most. The viral video seeding specialist counts the number of times each video is linked to and the number of times each video is embedded.

As this was written, Unruly Media looked for references to videos on only three of the most influential video sharing sites: YouTube, MySpace, and Google Video. However, they plan to add more soon.

Using both YouTube's and Unruly Media's lists, let's check out the top viral videos of 2008. Why are we looking at more videos? The types of original content that millions of people were discovering, watching, and sharing wasn't consolidating in 2008; it was diversifying. How do I know? As Yogi Berra once said, "You can observe a lot just by watching."

> Monday: Watch "Miley Cyrus - 7 Things - Official Music Video (HQ)"

> Tuesday: Look at "christian the lion"

> Wednesday: Check out "Pork and Beans"

> Thursday: See "Where the Hell is Matt? (2008)"

> Friday: View "Yes We Can - Barack Obama Music Video"

Monday: Watch "Miley Cyrus - 7 Things - Official Music Video (HQ)"

Now, I'm not the target demographic for this first YouTube video, but it became a cultural phenomenon in 2008. As Figure 5.18 illustrates, "Miley Cyrus - 7 Things - Official Music Video (HQ)" had almost 57.5 million views on YouTube as of January 1, 2009.

Figure 5.18 "Miley Cyrus - 7 Things - Official Music Video (HQ)"

> According to the statistics and data, this video had nine honors:

- #9 - Featured - India
- #11 - Featured
- #2 - Featured - Music - India
- #4 - Most Discussed (All Time)
- #2 - Most Discussed (All Time) - Music

- #14 - Most Viewed (All Time)
- #9 - Most Viewed (All Time) - Music
- #94 - Top Favorited (All Time)
- #67 - Top Favorited (All Time) - Music

7 Things was uploaded to the HollywoodRecord channel on June 28, 2008. The music video also appeared on ABC and the Disney Channel the same day.

It rocketed to the #14 most viewed video of all time in just six months. At that rate, it could overtake "Avril Lavigne - Girlfriend" as the #1 most viewed video of all time by the end of 2009.

According to People.com, the song "combines Avril Lavigne-style angst with dad Billy Ray Cyrus' country twang." And the *Village Voice* also made comparisons of Miley with Avril, stating that Cyrus "guns for full-on vintage-Avril territory" but adding that the song was "boring."

In the music video, Cyrus describes the pain of a recent breakup by listing seven things that she hates about her ex-boyfriend. Near the end of the video, Miley holds a picture of Nick Jonas with scribbles on his face.

Although I won't comment on the rumors that the ex-boyfriend is Jonas, I do want to observe that 7 Things was the #4 most discussed video of all time as of January 1, 2009. So, a little rumor can go a long way.

This music video also inspired several user-generated parodies—and one of them, by VenetianPrincess, was as popular as some of the other top viral videos of 2008. As Figure 5.19 illustrates, "Miley Cyrus - 7 Things - Spoof" had over 12 million views on YouTube as of January 1, 2009.

Figure 5.19 "Miley Cyrus - 7 Things - Spoof"

According to the statistics and data, this video had six honors:

- #8 - Featured - India
- #45 - Most Discussed (All Time)
- #10 - Most Discussed (All Time) - Comedy
- #52 - Most Viewed (All Time) - Comedy
- #86 - Top Favorited (All Time)
- #17 - Top Favorited (All Time) - Comedy

It's also worth noting that there are more than 360,000 subscribers to Venetian-Princess's channel, which helped "Miley Cyrus - 7 Things - Spoof" go viral virtually the minute it was uploaded. Another 17 of VenetionPrincess's videos also have more than a million views, and her videos have been featured on MSNBC, CNN, FOX, G4TV, ABC, CBS, and *USA Today*.

The *Hannah Montana* star also launched her own YouTube channel, miley-mandy, with her best friend Mandy Jiroux. The girls have used their channel to vlog and generally horse around for their audience of over 292,000 subscribers, and it's also where they post their "M&M Cru" dance battle videos, which together have notched nearly 15 million views and have taken the world's "biggest online dance battle" to a whole new level.

Mileymandy's "M&M CRU FINAL DANCE BATTLE - Cyrus Blaine Seacrest Tatum" squeezes more than 50 celebrities into a 9-minute, 59-second video that has more than 6 million views. Their closest competitor is WHATTHEBUCKSHOW'S "Biggest Online Dance Battle in The History of Mankind!," which squeezes more than 130 YouTube celebrities into a 3-minute, 57-second video that has 3.2 million views.

Are there any lessons to be learned here? Yes, there are two.

The first is about "changes of scene." "M&M CRU FINAL DANCE BATTLE - Cyrus Blaine Seacrest Tatum" uses a great many changes of scene without confusing people, but I can't say the same for "Biggest Online Dance Battle in The History of Mankind!"

The second lesson is about "supers." In "M&M CRU FINAL DANCE BATTLE - Cyrus Blaine Seacrest Tatum," the names of all the people in the video are set in type and superimposed over their first appearance. Although everyone who stars is listed in the description of "Biggest Online Dance Battle in The History of Mankind!," the video doesn't use supers. Even people in the video would be hard pressed to tell you when they appear, especially when they appear in a four-quadrant grid.

Tuesday: Look at "christian the lion"

This video about an unbreakable bond between man and beast was one of the most talked about in 2008. It briefly chronicles the true story of a lion being reunited with the two men who raised him, years after he'd been released back into the wild and become the leader of his own pride.

Christian was a lion originally purchased by Australians John Rendall and Anthony "Ace" Bourke from Harrods department store of London in 1969 and ultimately reintroduced to the wild. The actual reunion took place in 1972, but this archive footage was rediscovered and posted to YouTube in early 2008.

Rendall and Bourke, with their girlfriends, Jennifer Mary and Unity Jones, cared for the lion where they lived in London—until it was a year old. Christian's increasing size and the increasing cost of his care led Rendall and Bourke to understand they could not keep him in London.

When Bill Travers and Virginia McKenna, stars of the film *Born Free*, visited Rendall and Bourke's furniture shop and met Christian, they suggested that Bourke and Rendall ask for the assistance of George Adamson, the Kenyan conservationist who, together with his wife, Joy, was the subject of their movie. Adamson agreed to help reintegrate Christian into the wild at his compound at Kora National Reserve.

When Rendall and Bourke were informed by Adamson of Christian's successful reintroduction to the wild, they traveled to Kenya to visit Christian and were filmed in the documentary *Christian, The Lion at World's End*.

According to the documentary, Adamson advised Rendall and Bourke that Christian may not remember them. The film shows the lion at first cautiously approach and then quickly leap gently onto the two men, standing on his hind legs and wrapping his front legs around their shoulders, nuzzling their faces. The documentary also shows the female lions, Mona and Lisa, and a foster cub named Supercub welcoming the two men.

The viral video of this reunion received worldwide attention more than 30 years after the event. As Figure 5.20 illustrates, "christian the lion" had more than 11 million views on YouTube as of March 30, 2009.

Figure 5.20 "christian the lion"

According to the statistics and data, this video had nine honors:

- #2 - Featured
- #6 - Most Discussed (All Time) - Pets & Animals
- #3 - Most Responded (Today) - Pets & Animals
- #12 - Most Responded (This Week) - Pets & Animals
- #22 - Most Responded (This Month) - Pets & Animals
- #12 - Most Responded (All Time) - Pets & Animals
- #2 - Most Viewed (All Time) - Pets & Animals
- #5 - Top Favorited (All Time) - Pets & Animals
- #2 - Top Rated (All Time) - Pets & Animals

As of March 2009, the versions of this video had more than 20 million views on YouTube, MySpace, and Google Video.

What is the lesson to be learned here? It is a combination of "emotion" with a "reason why." Viewers also need a rational excuse to justify their emotional decisions. So, always include one—if you can.

Wednesday: Check Out "Pork and Beans"

Weezer's "Pork and Beans" video debuted on YouTube on May 23, 2008. Drawing on more than 20 YouTube stars, the video saluted some of the more memorable moments and people in YouTube's history.

The video had over 1.2 million views in its first 24 hours up on YouTube. As of May 29, it has reached 4 million views. The video quickly became the most-watched video on the Internet the weekend following its release.

It was the most popular video of the month in June, reaching 7.3 million views by June 16. And as Figure 5.21 illustrates, "Pork and Beans" had almost 16 million views on YouTube as of January 1, 2009.

According to the statistics and data, this video had 11 honors:

- #1 - Featured
- #73 - Most Discussed (All Time)
- #37 - Most Discussed (All Time) - Music
- #95 - Most Responded (Today)
- #28 - Most Responded (Today) - Music
- #37 - Most Responded (This Week) - Music
- #69 - Most Responded (This Month) - Music
- #41 - Most Responded (All Time)
- #11 - Most Responded (All Time) - Music
- #33 - Top Favorited (All Time)
- #19 - Top Favorited (All Time) - Music

Figure 5.21 "Pork and Beans"

The song from the alternative rock band's 2008 album, *Weezer*, was written by Rivers Cuomo as a reaction to a meeting with Geffen executives where the band was told they needed to record more commercial material. The music video for "Pork and Beans" was directed by Mathew Cullen (R.E.M., Beck, Modest Mouse) of Motion Theory.

"It was mayhem making the video," said Weezer guitarist Brian Bell said in a press release distributed by YouTube. "We were performing with all these amazing YouTube celebrities, and I felt like I had walked into my own computer."

As Nicholas Carlson of Vallywag observed on May 23, 2008, "The band gets the geeks. So it's no surprise that they understand one of the easiest ways to go viral on YouTube and across the Web is to make multiple references to videos gone viral before."

This is the first time a major label band had featured such a multitude of YouTube celebrities in its video. The following YouTube stars made cameos:

- Connor Berge ("One Man Band")

- Gary Brolsma ("Numa Numa")

- Dramatic Prairie Dog ("Dramatic Look")

- magnum9er ("How the Dramatic Prairie Dog was Born")

- Mark Allen Hicks ("Afro Ninja")

- Fritz Grobe and Stephen Voltz ("Diet Coke + Mentos")

- Leal55 ("G.I. Joe Gay")

- Matt McAllister ("Guiness World Record for most T-Shirts worn at one time.")
- Chris Crocker ("Chris Crocker - LEAVE BRITNEY ALONE!")
- Zuchini ("All Your Base Are Belong to Us")
- Lauren Caitlin Upton ("Miss Teen USA 2007 - South Carolina answers a question")
- Raze7ds ("Star Wars Kid")
- Psychotic Kids ("Crank That Soldier Boy")
- Judson Laipply ("Evolution of Dance")
- Tay Zonday ("'Chocolate Rain' Original Song by Tay Zonday");
- Kevin Federline ("K-Fed Popozao")
- **pecari1988** ("Daft Hands - Technologic")
- **imalibubarbiei** ("Daft Bodies - Harder, Better, Faster, Stonger")
- Liam Kyle Sullivan ("Shoes the Full Version")
- **gswanson17** "Charlie the Unicorn"
- Dancing Banana ("It's Peanut Butter Jelly Time!!!")
- Blendtec ("Will It Blend?")

As of January 15, 2009, the versions of this video had 20,271,085 views on YouTube, MySpace, and Google Video.

Is there a lesson here? There is and it's about "testimonials." The most effective testimonial videos are those that show loyal users of your product or idea testifying to its virtues—when they don't know they are being filmed.

When you pick loyal users to testify, avoid those who would give such polished performances that viewers would think they were professional actors. The more amateurish the performance, the better.

> **Note:** Of course, if you are Weezer, you can be the exception to this rule. Or, as Brad O'Farrell informs me, you can "covertly" post a remix of "Pork and Beans" on your alternate account, PBJT1927's channel, and retitle it "Re: Pork and Beens." Then, you could dirty it up with VHS recording artifacts, screen capture artifacts, and digital video compression artifacts. And you could include memes that were left out from the original, such as the Potter Puppet Pals. And, as of March 30, 2009, you'd have more than 226,000 views.

Thursday: See "Where the Hell is Matt? (2008)"

Matt Harding is best known as the goofy guy who danced his way around the world—first in 2006, when he danced solo, and then again in 2008, when Harding re-created his hit video, this time dancing with residents of the places he visited.

Harding was known by his friends for a particular dance, and while videotaping each other on vacation in Vietnam, his travel companion suggested he add the dance. The video was uploaded to his site, wherethehellismatt.com, for friends and family to enjoy. The video was passed around by email and eventually went "viral," with his server getting 20,000 or more hits a day as it was discovered country by country in 2005.

When Stride, "The Ridiculously Long Lasting Gum," offered to sponsor a second trip, Harding created a second version of the video, called "Dancing 2006." Harding's video clips have appeared on numerous television shows:

- MSNBC's *Countdown with Keith Olbermann* (August 18, 2005)
- *Inside Edition* (August 19, 2005)
- *The Ellen DeGeneres Show* (October 10, 2005)
- *40 Greatest Internet Superstars on VH1* (March 23, 2007)
- *Jimmy Kimmel Live* (August 6, 2008)
- *The Daily Show* (November 6, 2008)

In 2007, Jawed Karim, one of the founders of YouTube, stated that Harding's video is his favorite video posted to YouTube.

Harding's silly jigs have brought inspiration and joy to millions of people. As Figure 5.22 illustrates, "Where the Hell is Matt? (2008)" had more than 15 million views on YouTube as of January 2009.

Figure 5.22 "Where the Hell is Matt? (2008)"

According to the statistics and data, this video had 34 honors:

- #1 - Featured - India
- #5 - Featured
- #93 - Featured - Brazil
- #26 - Featured - Travel & Events - Germany
- #26 - Featured - Travel & Events - Australia
- #22 - Featured - Travel & Events - Canada
- #26 - Featured - Travel & Events - United Kingdom
- #26 - Featured - Travel & Events - Ireland
- #45 - Featured - Travel & Events - India
- #25 - Featured - Travel & Events - New Zealand
- #22 - Featured - Travel & Events - Israel
- #41 - Featured - Travel & Events
- #24 - Featured - Travel & Events - Spain
- #35 - Featured - Travel & Events - Mexico
- #27 - Featured - Travel & Events - France
- #32 - Featured - Travel & Events - Italy
- #51 - Featured - Travel & Events - Japan
- #24 - Featured - Travel & Events - South Korea
- #22 - Featured - Travel & Events - Netherlands
- #31 - Featured - Travel & Events - Poland
- #24 - Featured - Travel & Events - Brazil
- #26 - Featured - Travel & Events - Russia
- #39 - Featured - Travel & Events - Hong Kong
- #28 - Featured - Travel & Events - Taiwan
- #25 - Featured - Travel & Events - Czech Republic
- #24 - Featured - Travel & Events - Sweden
- #1 - Most Discussed (All Time) - Travel & Events
- #92 - Most Responded (Today) - Travel & Events
- #37 - Most Responded (This Week) - Travel & Events
- #19 - Most Responded (This Month) - Travel & Events
- #7 - Most Responded (All Time) - Travel & Events
- #2 - Most Viewed (All Time) - Travel & Events
- #1 - Top Favorited (All Time) - Travel & Events
- #2 - Top Rated (All Time) - Travel & Events

The various versions of this video had totaled about 17.5 million views on YouTube, MySpace, and Google Video. As one observant user said, "It shows that no matter how different we are on the outside, inside we all just want to dance, laugh, and have fun."

However, Amanda Watlington (of Searching for Profit) and I have been showing Harding's "Where the Hell is Matt" videos at Search Engine Strategies workshops since April 2007. And unless we point it out, no one notices the mention of Stride in the closing credits.

Is there a lesson to be learned here? There is, and it's "brand identification." Research has demonstrated that a shocking percentage of viewers remember a video but forget the name of its sponsor. And many marketers think it is crass to belabor the name of a sponsor.

So, for the benefit of those who are more interested in selling than entertaining, there is a nonintrusive way to register your brand name: watermark your video content.

Friday: View "Yes We Can - Barack Obama Music Video"

When Barack Obama delivered his concession speech after the New Hampshire primary, little did he know he was providing the script—and the inspiration—for the most-watched political video of 2008. Will.i.am's "Yes We Can" music video, a celebrity-studded mash-up of Obama's speech, became an instant viral sensation upon its release in early February and had a massive influence on Election 2008 and popular culture.

As Figure 5.23 illustrates, "Yes We Can - Barack Obama Music Video" had close to 15 million views on YouTube as of January 1, 2009. The video has inspired voters, young people, and satirists alike.

Figure 5.23 "Yes We Can - Barack Obama Music Video"

According to the statistics and data, this video had four honors:

- #41 - Most Discussed (All Time)
- #5 - Most Discussed (All Time) - News & Politics
- #2 - Most Viewed (All Time) - News & Politics
- #2 - Top Favorited (All Time) - News & Politics

The music video was produced by will.i.am and Mike Jurkovac; it was directed by Jesse Dylan, the son of singer Bob Dylan. Although the lyrics are entirely quotations from Senator Obama, the Obama presidential campaign had no involvement in its production. "Yes We Can" was honored with the first-ever Emmy Award for Best New Approaches in Daytime Entertainment. Joe Klein of *Time* characterized it as "brilliant."

The viral music video, shot in sparse black and white, features Barack Obama's image in collage fashion; the performers—celebrities including musicians, singers, and actors—echo his words in a hip-hop call-and-response manner as his voice plays in the background. Will.i.am and John Legend performed the song on the final day of the 2008 Democratic National Convention at INVESCO Field in Denver.

Since the original posting on YouTube, the video has been reposted a number of times by other users. It also inspired the spoof songs "john.he.is" and "No You Can't," satirizing the Republican candidate John McCain. As of January 15, 2009, the versions of this video had just over 25 million views on YouTube, MySpace, and Google Video.

What is the lesson here? It's about "talking heads." This is the derisive name given to videos that consist of a pitchman extolling the virtues of a product or idea. Agency people find them noncreative and are sick of them, but several marketers use them because they are above average in changing brand preference.

Talking heads are particularly appropriate for announcing new products or introducing new ideas. Of course, it doesn't hurt if one of your talking heads is Barack Obama.

And it also helps if your talking heads include Will.i.am, Scarlett Johansson, Kareem Abdul-Jabbar, Common, John Legend, and 40 other celebrities.

Week 4: Create Compelling Content Worth Sharing

So, how do you create video content that's so compelling even prudent opinion leaders will decide its worth sharing with their followers?

First, as you've observed, your video needs to tell a story. Although this story can be humorous in nature, it can also be serious.

We've already uncovered the quirky and unusual, seen first-hand accounts of current events, and found videos about people's hobbies and interests. As the types of video content uploaded to YouTube continue to diversify, I expect to see videos from new artists and filmmakers as well as people's favorite TV moments go viral too.

Second, the most viewed viral videos are also among the most discussed and top favorited. In other words, the stories they tell made their way into conversations because opinion leaders liked retelling them.

These stories can be adorable, creative, funny, inspirational, or instructional. But they enable people to inform, educate, and entertain others at home, around the office, or across the globe.

Third, viral videos can come from original content creators large and small. For example, the most viewed videos of all time as of April 2009 were created by professionals as well as amateurs:

"Avril Lavigne - Girlfriend" with over 118.7 million views (RCA Records);

"Evolution of Dance" with over 118.6 million views (Judson Laipply);

"Lezberado: Revenge Fantasies" with over 103.5 million views (Showtime);

"Charlie bit my finger - again!" with over 93.8 million views (HDCYT);

YouTube says it offers "a community for everyone," including comedians, aspiring and professional musicians, amateur and established filmmakers, professional content owners, and personal video creators such as cooking, beauty, health, and fitness experts. I think that YouTube offers communities for each of these segments and a dozen more.

This increasing complexity makes creating viral video content that much harder with each passing year. It reminds me of Gene Kelly and Stanley Donen's musical *Singin' in the Rain*, the comic story of Hollywood's transition from silent films to the "talkies." It also reminds me of Ken Auletta's book *Three Blind Mice*, the tragic story of how the TV networks lost their way in the 1980s as cable television started taking more than half of their audience.

The changes in viral video content from "Diet Coke + Mentos" to "Pork and Beans" may seem evolutionary, but since they occurred in the space of just three years, from 2005 to 2008, they are revolutionary.

What should veteran marketers and new YouTubers do? You have two options. First, you can enroll in a course like Sony's "Video Storytelling 201: Story Structure and Shooting Techniques," illustrated in Figure 5.24.

The instructor is Don Freidkin, a writer with a background in film and video writing, producing, and directing. One of his favorite projects was producing, directing, and cowriting *The Sea Above*, a series of 26 half-hour shows on popular astronomy for KERA-TV in Dallas. He's also done live coverage of events ranging from state political conventions to San Antonio's series of Fiesta parades.

I like Freidkin's approach: he helps you "pursue your directorial hunches." He assigns situations where "you have less control!" And he recognizes you'll be held to "a standard of objectivity."

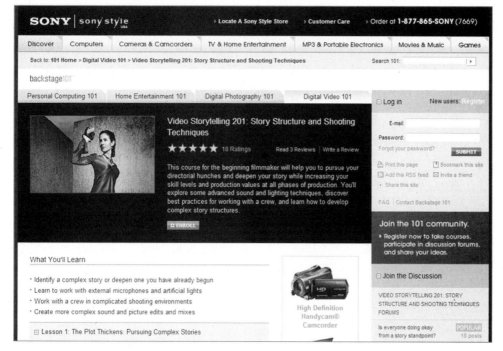

Figure 5.24 "Video Storytelling 201: Story Structure and Shooting Techniques"

He says, "You should consider looking for stories with conflict, high emotional stakes, and very different consequences depending on how things turn out. These are some important elements of good storytelling. They help you establish empathy with your characters and demonstrate that the story matters."

He adds, "Good documentaries range dramatically in topic, so make sure you follow your passions and interests, even when it comes to breaking news. The point here is to get you out shooting in public, learn to expect the unexpected, and incorporate it into your film!"

And he observes, "All of your filmmaking choices negate any notion of objectivity: what event you'll shoot, what you frame and how, when you roll, what questions you ask, and so on. All of these are subjective choices that frame 'reality' according to your interest. There is nothing objective about that process. The thing to do, then, is not to attempt to be objective, but to accept your subjective approach and try to remain open and interested to new information and points of view."

Second, "You can observe a lot just by watching." This may appear to be funny advice, but in a rapidly changing field, it's the best way I know to discover what works, what doesn't, and what's promising.

And knowing how to make a funny video doesn't mean you know how to make a music video any more than knowing how to create *The Dueling Cavalier* meant

Monumental Pictures knew how to create *The Dancing Cavalier*. And we're all still learning how to make a viral video in other categories. So, let's watch some more of the top viral videos of 2008:

> Monday: Watch "Frozen Grand Central"
>
> Tuesday: Look at "Rick Astley - Never Gonna Give You Up"
>
> Wednesday: Check Out "Fred Loses His Meds"
>
> Thursday: See "Super Mario Rescues The Princess: Seth MacFarlane's Cavalcade"
>
> Friday: View "Test Your Awareness: Do The Test"

Monday: Watch "Frozen Grand Central"

The New York–based collective Improv Everywhere has become a firm favorite on YouTube, thanks to its unique public hijinks. Videos like "No Pants Subway Ride" and "Food Court Musical" offer good examples of its large-scale pranks, but the elaborate public performance "Frozen Grand Central" was especially popular with viewers.

The video features more than 200 people simultaneously freezing in place at Grand Central Station in New York City; the reactions of onlookers are as striking as the stunt itself. As Figure 5.25 illustrates, "Frozen Grand Central" had over 14.5 million views on YouTube as of January 1, 2009.

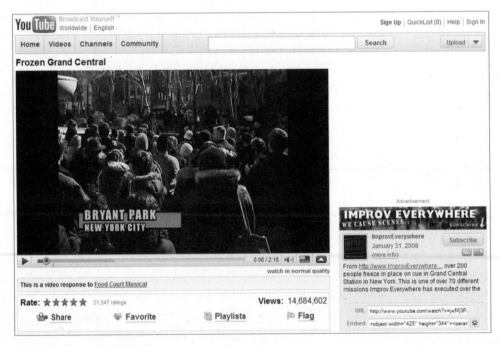

Figure 5.25 "Frozen Grand Central"

According to the statistics and data, this video had four honors:

- #3 - Featured
- #30 - Most Viewed (All Time) - Comedy
- #40 - Top Favorited (All Time) - Comedy
- #84 - Top Rated (All Time) - Comedy

The Improv Everywhere comedic performance art group was formed in 2001 by Charlie Todd. Its slogan is "We Cause Scenes."

Members of the group, called agents, carry out nonthreatening pranks, called missions, in public places. The stated goal of these benevolent missions is to cause scenes of "chaos and joy."

Some of the group's events are similar to flash mobs, but the group's website insists it has nothing to do with flash mobbing and that Improv Everywhere was created years before flash mobbing gained popularity.

Although Improv Everywhere's missions often include its longtime members, many are open to the public. The group has organized and carried out over 80 missions, including synchronized swimming in a park fountain, repeating a five-minute sequence of events in a Starbucks coffee shop over and over again for an hour, and flooding a Best Buy store with members dressed exactly like the staff.

Improv Everywhere has been profiled by many national and international media outlets including the *New York Times*, the *Today Show*, and ABC's *Nightline*.

As of January 15, 2009, the versions of this video had about 15.3 million views on YouTube, MySpace, and Google Video.

Is there another lesson to be learned here? Yes, it is "show the product in use." It pays to show a product or idea being used and, if possible, the end result of using it. Would an opinion leader's followers believe Improv Everywhere had pulled off the "Frozen Grand Central" stunt if they couldn't show it to them?

Tuesday: Look at "Rick Astley - Never Gonna Give You Up"

Chances are that at some point in 2008, you or someone you know experienced a "Rick Roll"—a bait-and-switch prank that dupes you into watching the video for Rick Astley's 1980s hit "Never Gonna Give You Up." The joke even transcended the Internet, where it was born, with organizers of football games, parades, and rallies Rick Rolling unsuspecting attendees.

But perhaps the ultimate Rick Roll occurred on April Fool's Day in 2008, when YouTube rigged up every feature video on the home page to play Astley's infamous clip. As Figure 5.26 illustrates, "Rick Astley - Never Gonna Give You Up" had over 13.7 million views on YouTube as of January 1, 2009.

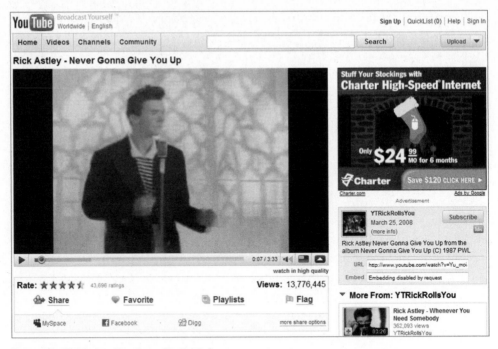

Figure 5.26 "Rick Astley - Never Gonna Give You Up"

According to the statistics and data, this video had five honors:

- #2 - Featured - India
- #6 - Featured #1 - Featured - Music - India
- #65 - Most Discussed (All Time)
- #31 - Most Discussed (All Time) - Music

If you haven't been Rick Rolled yet, here's how it works: A person provides a Web link that they claim is relevant to the topic at hand, but the link actually takes the user to the Astley video. The URL can be masked or obfuscated in some manner so that the user cannot determine the true source of the link without clicking. When a person clicks on the link and is led to the web page, they are said to have been Rick Rolled.

As Rick Rolling has spread, it has extended beyond Web links to playing the video or song disruptively in other situations, including in public places. This culminated when Astley and the song made a surprise appearance in the 2008 Macy's Thanksgiving Day Parade, a televised event with tens of millions of viewers.

Similar to "Chocolate Rain," Rick Rolling is a joke that started with opinion leaders on 4chan and then took off when members of the YouTube staff adopted it as their April Fool's Day joke.

What's the lesson here, you may ask. It's about "humor."

Conventional wisdom has always preached that people buy products or adopt ideas because they believe them to be labor-saving or good value for the money—not because a vendor tells jokes about them in videos. Claude Hopkins, the father of modern advertising, proclaimed, "People don't buy from clowns."

But humor can sell. And it can persuade opinion leaders to Rick Roll their followers.

Now, I must warn you that very, very few marketers can create funny videos that *are* funny. Unless you are one of the few, don't try.

Wednesday: Check Out "Fred Loses His Meds"

Who says you can't become an overnight success on YouTube? Fifteen-year-old Lucas Cruikshank, or Fred Figglehorn as he is known to fans, created a Web series in which he plays a hyperactive six-year-old with anger management issues.

Fred's hyperkinetic videos quickly caught people's attention and helped make him the fastest-rising star in YouTube history. "Fred Loses His Meds" (his second video) was Fred's first to break a million views, jump-starting his meteoric rise to his position at the end of 2008 as the #1 Most Subscribed Channel on YouTube with almost 743,000 subscribers.

As Figure 5.27 illustrates, "Fred Loses His Meds" had over 12.6 million views on YouTube as of January 1, 2009.

Figure 5.27 "Fred Loses His Meds"

According to the statistics and data, this video had eight honors:

- #5 - Featured - India
- #8 - Featured
- #1 - Featured - Comedy - India
- #54 - Most Discussed (All Time)
- #12 - Most Discussed (All Time) - Comedy
- #99 - Most Responded (All Time) - Comedy
- #51 - Most Viewed (All Time) - Comedy
- #22 - Top Favorited (All Time) - Comedy

"Fred" has been sponsored since its inception by Zipit, which has several cameos in various videos posted to the Fred channel. Though, for the most part, the collaboration has been kept low key, Fred now has a separate website promoting the Zipit Wireless Messenger and has also starred in a Zipit commercial.

Are there lessons to be learned here? Yes, there are two.

The first is "open with the fire." If you can grab attention in the first 30 seconds, you stand a better chance of holding the viewer. Or, as David Obilvy wrote in *Ogilvy on Advertising*, "When you advertise fire-extinguishers, open with the fire."

The second is about "close-ups." It's a good thing to use close-ups when a person or a product is the hero of your video.

Thursday: See "Super Mario Rescues The Princess: Seth MacFarlane's Cavalcade"

As the creator of *Family Guy* and *American Dad*, Seth MacFarlane has had a tremendous impact on envelope-pushing animated entertainment. In 2008, MacFarlane decided to bring his talents to the Internet, launching "Seth MacFarlane's Cavalcade of Cartoon Comedy" exclusively on Google and YouTube.

Not only was this a groundbreaking event for online video, it also opened up new opportunities for advertisers, as content creators started to generate revenue from their videos both on and off YouTube. As Figure 5.28 illustrates, "Super Mario Rescues The Princess: Seth MacFarlane's Cavalcade" had 5.7 million views on YouTube as of January 1, 2009.

According to the Statistics and Data, this video had 10 honors:

- #10 - Featured - India
- #12 - Featured
- #2 - Featured - Comedy - India
- #22 - Most Responded (Today)
- #5 - Most Responded (Today) - Comedy
- #63 - Most Responded (This Week)
- #10 - Most Responded (This Week) - Comedy
- #19 - Most Responded (This Month) - Comedy

- #21 - Most Responded (All Time) - Comedy
- #27 - Top Favorited (All Time) - Comedy

Figure 5.28 *"Super Mario Rescues The Princess: Seth MacFarlane's Cavalcade"*

Seth MacFarlane's "Cavalcade" is a web series, which consists of comic cartoon shorts unrelated to each other. It is distributed by Burger King, with new episodes released weekly. There will be 50 altogether.

It has seen a successful launch on MacFarlane's YouTube channel, SethComedy, becoming the most watched YouTube channel of the week by obtaining over 3 million video views only two days after the first episode was released. The series is similar to the "cutaway gags" of MacFarlane's TV series *Family Guy*, which deliberately break continuity for comic effect. Starting with the 12th episode, the introduction was shortened and the profanity was uncensored.

What's the lesson here? My editor, Pete Gaughan, thinks it is to hire a "professional entertainer" and get a "big-bucks sponsor." And he's right. Amateurs today are competing with professionals more frequently.

But that's like Captain Renault telling Rick in the movie *Casablanca*, "I'm shocked, *shocked* to find that gambling is going on in here!"

Yes, amateurs are competing with professionals on YouTube—and some amateurs are competing quite successfully. Why? The professionals have learned to spend big bucks creating a 30-second spot or a 30-minute episode. Does this give them an advantage creating a 3-minute video?

Sometimes it does and sometimes it doesn't. I have no research to prove it, but I suspect that there is a negative correlation between the money spent on producing videos and their power to sell products or ideas.

Friday: View "Test Your Awareness: Do The Test"

Finally, Transport for London (TFL) is running a campaign to reduce the number of cyclists that are hurt on the roads because of what they call "change blindness." TFL notes that only a portion of what people see actually enters their consciousness—and people often fail to see a change in their surroundings because their attention is focused elsewhere.

So, they created a video to warn people to look out for cyclists. It starts wide: How many passes did the team in white make? It asks you to cut to medium: Did you see the Moonwalking bear? And it ends tight on TFL's key message, "It's easy to miss something you're not looking for."

As Figure 5.29 illustrates, "Test Your Awareness: Do The Test," had just over 5.5 million views on YouTube as of January 1, 2009.

Figure 5.29 "Test Your Awareness: Do The Test"

According to the statistics and data, this video had eight honors:

- #7 - Most Discussed (All Time) - Howto & Style - United Kingdom
- #2 - Most Viewed (All Time) - Howto & Style - United Kingdom
- #17 - Most Viewed (All Time) - Howto & Style

- #3 - Top Favorited (All Time) - Howto & Style - United Kingdom
- #9 - Top Favorited (All Time) - Howto & Style
- #91 - Top Rated (All Time) - United Kingdom
- #1 - Top Rated (All Time) - Howto & Style - United Kingdom
- #8 - Top Rated (All Time) - Howto & Style

As of January 14, 2009, the versions of this video had been viewed almost 7 million times on YouTube, MySpace, and Google Video.

What's the last lesson to be learned here? Yes, it's about "problem solution." This technique is as old as television. You show viewers a problem that they are familiar with, and then you show how your product or idea can solve it.

Now that you've learned how to create a viral video, the next chapter will teach you how to customize your YouTube channel.

Month 4: Create a Channel

YouTube accounted for 79 percent of all U.S. visits to online video sites in February 2009. This means YouTube should be the center, but not the circumference, of your video marketing strategy. In this chapter, you will learn how to set up a basic YouTube channel, how to create and customize a brand channel, and how to distribute videos to other sites—although this may not stop some people from making comments like, "When I was a boy, I had to walk five miles through the snow to change the channel."

Chapter Contents:

Center vs. Circumference

According to Hitwise, 79 percent of all U.S. visits to online video sites in February 2009 were to YouTube. Google Video received the second highest percentage of visits with 4.6 percent followed by MySpaceTV with almost 4.0 percent. The top 10 online video sites in this custom category appear in Table 6.1, from Hitwise.

▶ **Table 6.1** Top Ten Online Video Websites, Ranked by Market Share of U.S. Visits, February 2009

Rank	Sites	Domain	Visits
1	YouTube	www.youtube.com	79.03%
2	Google Video	video.google.com	4.55%
3	MySpace video	vids.myspace.com	3.95%
4	Hulu	www.hulu.com	2.52%
5	Yahoo! Video	video.search.yahoo.com	1.56%
6	Metacafe	www.metacafe.com	1.40%
7	Dailymotion	www.dailymotion.com	1.05%
8	Megavideo	www.megavideo.com	0.77%
9	MSN Video	video.msn.com	0.73%
10	Veoh	www.veoh.com	0.72%

The Hitwise data means that creating a YouTube channel should be the center, but not the circumference, of your video marketing strategy.

A channel is a YouTube user's page. It contains a user's profile information, videos, and favorites. But veteran marketers and new YouTubers will want to consider creating and customizing a YouTube brand channel as well as distributing videos beyond YouTube. We'll look at your options in these areas and I'll make some recommendations.

However, I can't promise that any of this will prevent some people from wishing we didn't have this technology, making comments like the one in Figure 6.1, "When I was a boy, I had to walk five miles through the snow to change the channel."

This is a new world and some people haven't explored it yet. So we will also spend some time looking at the emerging best practices being used by a few of the best-known brands.

Week 1: Set Up a YouTube Channel

A YouTube channel page serves as a profile page for a veteran marketer or new YouTuber. On your channel page, other YouTube users can see your public videos, your favorite videos, and your bulletins and subscribers. Your channel page also displays several links that let other people connect with you (or your brand) by sending you a message, sharing your channel with friends, or adding comments to your channel.

"When I was a boy, I had to walk five miles through the snow to change the channel."

Figure 6.1 "When I was a boy, I had to walk five miles through the snow to change the channel." (Cartoon by Mick Stevens in *The New Yorker,* October 2, 2006.)

Figure 6.2 shows SageRock's Channel, which contains the personal and business videos of Sage Lewis. He is a 37-year-old web marketing expert in Akron, OH, who does a daily web marketing video show at http://www.webmarketingwatch.com/video/.

Figure 6.2 SageRock's channel

YouTube provides a lot of helpful information for getting started in its Help Center. Let's go through the process of creating a YouTube channel step by step:

Monday: Create your YouTube account

Tuesday: Upload channel background

Wednesday: Customize your home page

Thursday: Customize channel design

Friday: Customize your YouTube channel

Monday: Create Your YouTube Account

The first step in setting up a YouTube channel is creating your YouTube account. Go to www.youtube.com/signup and complete the form that appears in Figure 6.3 to create a new account.

Figure 6.3 Create your YouTube account

The form allows you to specify the following information:

The Account Type field specifies the type of user account that you want to create. YouTube offers several different types of user accounts, including YouTuber, which is the standard account type. I've included some information about the differences between other account types later.

The Email Address field specifies the email address associated with your account. This address will not be displayed on your channel page, meaning people will not be able to see your email address. However, YouTube will use it to notify you of new subscribers, comments, or other events, depending on the email options that you set for your account. For example, if you allow it, people can find your account based on your email.

The Username field specifies the permanent identification of your account in the YouTube community. Your username will be publicly displayed and will also appear in the URL for your channel page. Once you've created your account, you cannot change the username associated with it. Make sure the name you select represents your brand well. User names can be up to 20 characters long and you may use only alphanumeric characters (A–Z, a–z, and 0–9).

The Password and Re-type Password fields specify the password that you will use to log in to your account. To maintain the integrity of your account, I recommend that you choose a password that has strong password strength, which is the highest level.

The Location and Postal Code fields are both required. Enter the values that correspond to the location of your headquarters.

The Gender field specifies the gender associated with your account. Although this field is required to get demographic data for YouTube Insight, your YouTube channel doesn't display it.

The Date of Birth field lets YouTube calculate the age of a YouTube account's owner. YouTube does display this age on your channel page, so make sure you set a reasonable age. You must be over 13 to register. Although you can hide it by modifying your account settings, you can not change it.

The Word Verification field requires you to enter the text that appears in the CAPTCHA image to complete your account creation. I find this to be the hardest part of creating a YouTube account.

There are several types of YouTube accounts, including Director, Musician, Comedian, Guru, and Reporter. They all share the basic YouTube features like uploading, commenting, sharing, and video responses. But each specialized account type also offers different customization options:

Comedian Allows custom logo, style, and show date information, and CD purchase links on your profile page.

Director Allows customized "Performer Info" to be displayed on your profile page, describing yourself, your influences, and your style. Some Directors from YouTube's early days have been grandfathered in, so they can post videos over 10 minutes long. However, all new Directors have a 10-minute limit.

Guru Allows custom logo, genre, and links on your profile page.

Musician Allows custom logo, genre and tour date information, and CD purchase links on your profile page.

Non-Profit A status obtained by 501(c)(3) nonprofit organizations accepted into YouTube's nonprofit program.

Politician Only available to one who is running for office or currently involved with the politics of government.

Reporter Allows you to describe your beat, your influences, and your favorite news sources.

Sometimes, people will change their account type to get higher ranking on the account-type lists. For example, there are more Directors than Gurus. According to Brad O'Farrell, the technical editor of this book, this has prompted the YouTube community to joke that Gurus are just people who are desperate to get to the top of a list, any list.

Tuesday: Upload Channel Background

You now have the ability to upload background images hosted on YouTube. This will enable you to display a customized background image. Here are the steps to do this:

1. Log in and click My Account in the upper-right corner.
2. In the Channel Settings section, click the Channel Design link.
3. Scroll down to the Advance Customization Setting section.
4. In the Background Image field, click the browse button to upload an image that you'd like to use as your background. The image size must be less than 256K.
5. Decide whether you'd like your image to repeat across your channel or appear only once. Choose Yes or No next to the Repeat Background Image field.
6. Click the Update Channel button.

The Channel Preview area to the right of the customization fields should update as you make changes. This will give you a basic idea of how your channel will appear once you've updated it. The image you've uploaded should be viewable within 6 hours.

If you don't tile your wallpaper, it will be perfectly centered behind your channel page. Also, depending on the viewer's screen size, the edges of the background image will be surrounded by a solid background color—except for the top, which is aligned to the top of the page.

You can change the background color in the Channel Design page. A common technique is to make a tall background image that faces to the solid color symmetrically on the left and right, then gradually fades to the same background color—as a gradient—as it goes down.

To see an example of this technique, look at MinisodeNetwork's channel at www.youtube.com/minisodenetwork.

I recommend that you select a background image that mirrors the look and feel of your other online branding. For example, your background image can feature unique logos, images, and celebrities associated with your brand. Selecting the right background image provides a consistent and seamless branding experience to your brand enthusiasts.

Image specifications Your background image can fill the entire site background. The image should have a maximum size of 200KB.

- If you set the Repeat Background Image option to No, the image will in the background of your page directly below the YouTube header. The area of the page that is not covered by the background image will be filled in with the custom colors that you specified for your channel. The total size of the image should be 1,200 pixels by 1,200 pixels.

- If you set the Repeat Background Image option to Yes, your background image will be tiled horizontally and vertically to fill the page. If you elect to tile your image, the edges of the graphic should blend off to a solid color to ensure that the tiles blend together nicely.

Hosting your background image YouTube does not host your background image. You will need to host the image on your own server, or you can upload it to another site such as Google Pages. To upload an image to Google Pages, you must have a Gmail account. I recommend that you create a separate Gmail account rather than using a personal account.

The following four steps explain how to upload an image to Google Pages:

1. Log in to your account at http://pages.google.com.

2. The Uploaded Stuff module displays on the right side of the Google Page Creator page. Click the upload link in that module.

3. Browse to the image that you want to upload.

4. After you upload your image, it will appear in your list of uploaded stuff.

Wednesday: Customize Your Home Page

Your personalized home page shows 10 modules by default and allows you to choose them and move them around:

- Latest from Subscriptions
- Recommended for You
- Spotlight Videos
- Friend Activity
- Rising Videos
- Insight Map
- Insight Chart
- Videos Near You
- Inbox
- About You

There's also a Promoted Videos bar that you *cannot* remove.

You will see this page only when you are signed into your account. To select the modules you want to display, click the Add/Remove Modules link under the search box on the top of YouTube's home page. To move the modules around, click the arrow buttons (move up or down) in the upper-right corner of each module's section. To choose how many videos you want to see and the layout of the module, click the Edit link next to the arrow buttons.

Thursday: Customize Channel Design

Although some of these tasks appear to be straightforward, Pete Gaughan, the editor of this book, says I should issue the following warning: If you care deeply about design, today's lesson will take more than an hour! There, you've been warned.

Now, go to your account and under My Channel, click the Channel Design link.

This is where you get to show off your artistic talent. You can choose to use one of four basic color themes, create your own color schemes for everything from the background to the fonts, and even link to a URL that has an image you'd like to display as your background.

I've mentioned uploading a background on Tuesday. It can be done via a URL or by uploading a file, but it's the same feature.

For an image to be used as your background image, it needs to be hosted on the Web. You should see the URL in your browser's address bar when you're looking at the full-sized image. The URL should end with .jpg, .jpeg, .png, .gif, or a similar image filename extension. You can also right-click the full-sized image and select Copy Image Location. Paste this URL in the Background Image field.

In addition, you can reposition the channel sections you'd like to appear on your page and hide those you don't need. This is also where you can select the particular video you'd like to have featured on your channel. Remember to click the Update Channel button at the top or bottom of the page and wait a few minutes to see your changes take effect.

If you want to see examples of customized channel designs, look at these channels:

- machinima's channel: www.youtube.com/machinima

- mileymandy's channel: www.youtube.com/mileymandy

- SouljaBoy's channel: www.youtube.com/SouljaBoy

- Fred's channel: www.youtube.com/Fred

- SethComedy's channel: www.youtube.com/SethComedy

Friday: Customize Your YouTube Channel

Several links under Channel Settings on your account page will help you show your personality through your channel:

Channel Info Log in to your account and under My Channel, click the Channel Info link. This is where you can edit all your channel's basic settings and the information about yourself that you choose to make public. You have two options to create a profile picture: you can display the last video you uploaded or select a more permanent picture from My Videos. If you'd like a specific picture to serve as your channel profile, I recommend you upload a short (5 seconds or so) video of only that picture. Once that video is uploaded, you can select it for your profile picture. This is also the page where you can choose whether you'd like to display comments and bulletins on your channel. You can also switch your channel type between Comedian, Director, Guru, Musician, and YouTuber. Fill in whatever personal information you're comfortable with in the provided fields—none are mandatory.

Personal Info Log in to your account and under My Channel, click the Personal Info link. From this page you can fill out your personal, professional, and educational information as well as your interests and hobbies. In addition, this is the page where you may choose to hide or display your age. Simply edit the information and then click the Update Channel button.

Location Info Log in to your account and under My Channel, click the Location Info link. Here you can fill out where you currently live and your hometown. Again, you only have to fill out the information as you choose and then click the Update Location button.

Organize Videos You have the option to choose nine videos to feature in the Videos section of your channel page. To organize your videos, follow these four steps:

1. Sign in to your account and click Account in the top right.

2. Under My Channel, click the Organize Videos link.

3. Check the Add box below the videos you'd like to have featured on your channel page. You can see the order of the videos in the Preview of Channel Videos section on the right side.

4. Click the Update Channel button when you finish.

Recent Activity The recent activity box is located on your YouTube channel. This box provides your channel viewers with a summary of recent updates to your channel, making your channel more dynamic, fresh, and timely. For example, if you recently added a new favorite to your channel, your channel's visitors can find this favorite in the new recent activity box (as well as in the usual favorites box). The recent activity box also consolidates My Recent Ratings and My Recent Comments boxes into this single activity window. Additionally, the recent activity box enables you to incorporate bulletins into your activity alerts, updating other users of your current status.

In addition to these basic options, if your channel type is switched to be any other kind besides YouTuber, you will be given options for such things as external URLs, event dates, performer information, and more.

Week 2: Create a YouTube Brand Channel

The next part of this step-by-step guide explains how to create a YouTube brand channel. Figure 6.4 shows Oprah's brand channel.

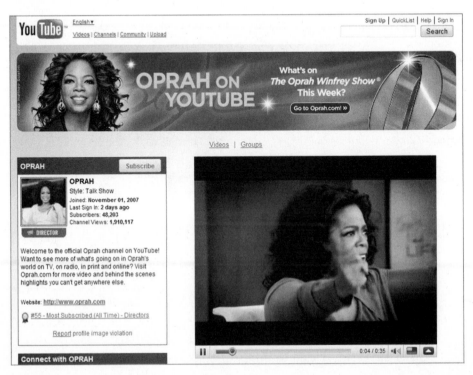

Figure 6.4 Oprah's channel

Brand channels provide you with a number of features that aren't available on standard user channels:

A channel page banner image of your choosing displays at the top of your brand channel. You can provide a link for the banner or an image map that specifies where different areas of the banner should link. Additional images provide additional branding opportunities on the watch page.

A branding box provides additional communication or promotional space as well as an opportunity to embed links on your channel page. This box contains only text.

The featured video plays automatically when users visit your channel page.

The More from this User module on the watch page is customized to drive additional traffic to your other brand channel content. Although this feature is available on all channels, it's "expanded" by default on brand channels to display up to the first nine videos that you select in your Organize Videos page.

What'll we do this week?

Monday: Set up a brand channel account

Tuesday: Design your channel page

Wednesday: Customize the channel page

Thursday: Customize the video page

Friday: Modify the channel colors

Monday: Set Up a Brand Channel Account

After creating your account, fill out the YouTube Partner Program application form at www.youtube.com/partners. As you do, it will conduct an automated review of your account and let you know if you are unlikely to qualify for the YouTube Partner Program.

Applications are reviewed for a variety of criteria, including but not limited to the size of your audience, country of residence, quality of content, and consistency with YouTube's community guidelines and terms of use.

If you do qualify, request to have your account converted to a brand channel two weeks before the launch of any campaign.

Then, set the email preferences for your account. To do so, log in to your account and navigate to the Email Options page. Choose the types of events for which you would like to receive email notifications or specify that you do not want to receive any emails for the listed events, and then click the button to save your email options.

You are now ready to begin uploading dummy video content. However, do not yet upload the videos that you want to appear on your channel page. Once you receive confirmation that your account has been converted to a brand channel, you can complete the additional customizations that are exclusively available to brand channels.

The day before your campaign begins, upload the videos that you want to be visible on your channel page. Only relatively new videos are eligible to be among the "Most Viewed" videos of the day. I also recommend that you remove any dummy videos that you uploaded while designing your channel.

Tuesday: Design Your Channel Page

Now let's look at designing your brand channel page, which includes several extra display elements that allow you to customize your channel to reinforce your brand identity.

The wireframe image in Figure 6.5 illustrates the general layout of a brand channel page. The image shows a two-column display beneath a channel banner. The columns are separated by 23 pixels of space. In addition, 15 pixels of vertical space separate modules within a column. The dotted blue line indicates where the fold would appear in a typical browser window at 1024′768 resolution.

The figure does not display several additional modules that could be included on a channel page, such as a subscribers box, a friends box, or a comments box, because brand advertisers rarely use these modules. We'll cover all of the modules that can appear on your channel page on Thursday of next week.

The numbered modules in the wireframe image contain the following content:

The channel banner appears at the top of a brand channel page. This header is available only for brand channels. Upload an 875-by-150-pixel image that is 20KB or smaller for the banner.

The channel info module contains content that describes your channel. This module appears on all channel pages. The module displays a channel icon, statistics for your channel, and some public information from your YouTube profile, such as your country, website, and age. (You can choose to hide the age associated with your brand channel account.) The rankings section of the channel info module only appears if your channel has achieved a notable ranking, such as being one of the most viewed channels or most subscribed-to channels. The rankings section displays up to three rankings and, if there are more than three rankings, will display a link to view them. YouTube automatically generates the content for this part of the channel info module.

The connect box contains content that allows YouTube users to interact with your channel. This module appears on all channel pages. The module displays links to send a message to the channel owner, share the channel with a friend, and add the channel owner as a friend. The module also displays your video page icon, a 55-by-55-pixel thumbnail image that you select, and the URL for your channel page.

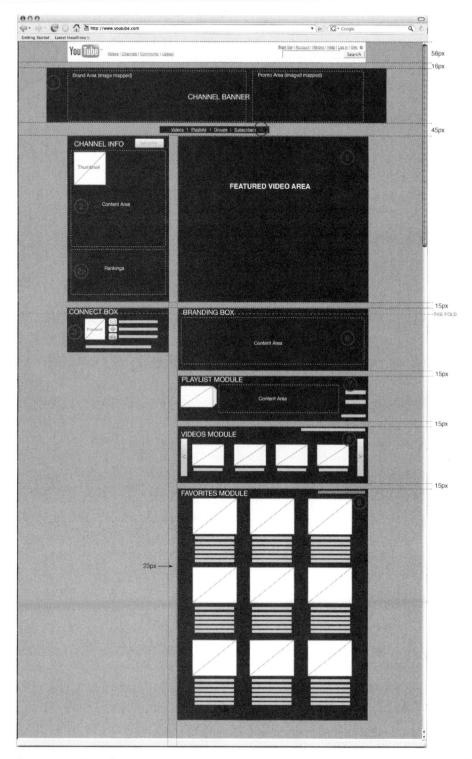

Figure 6.5 Wireframe of brand channel page

The channel links display a standard set of links that appear on all channel pages. The links point to different types of content associated with your channel, including a list of your videos, favorite videos, playlists, groups, friends, subscribers, and subscriptions. The link to a list of your favorite videos will display only if your channel page displays the favorite videos module. Similarly, other links display only if your page also displays the modules related to them.

The featured video module is a 560-by-465-pixel area that displays the featured video for your channel. The video will play automatically when a user visits your brand channel page. (On standard channel pages, users need to click the video or the play control to initiate the playback.) The featured video information box below the video displays the video title, the channel name, the number of views for the video, and the number of comments on the video.

In addition to the featured video module, YouTube offers several other options for displaying featured content on your brand channel page:

Partners can create gadgets to customize the content that appears within the video module. Gadgets can, but do not need to, show videos. Contact your account executive for information about creating a custom gadget.

Partners can run contests to encourage users to interact with their brand. Go to www.youtube.com/community to find links to YouTube contests. Partners that create contests can customize a contest module that can appear instead of or in addition to the featured video module. The contest module can also be customized to include content about the contest. Contact your account executive for information about running contests on YouTube.

The optional branding box lets you specify promotional text and links related to your brand. This module is available only for brand channels. The branding box title may be up to 100 characters long, and the branding box text may be up to 4,500 characters long. The branding box text may not contain HTML markup, though you can use line breaks to create paragraphs of text. Even though you cannot insert HTML hyperlinks in the branding box text, YouTube will also automatically convert any URLs in your text to links.

The optional playlist module lets you feature one or more playlists that contain content related to your brand. Your featured playlists could contain your own videos or YouTube videos related to your brand. For each playlist, the module will display a thumbnail image for the first video in the playlist, a link to play the playlist, a link to subscribe to the playlist, and a link to share the playlist. The module also displays a link to all of the brand channel's playlists.

The optional videos module displays thumbnail images for videos that you have uploaded directly to your account. Each thumbnail links to its associated video, and you can choose whether to display the thumbnails in a scroller or a grid. In a scroller, the box will display four thumbnail images with buttons to scroll to the next (or previous) set of four images. In a grid, the videos box displays up to nine thumbnail images as well as a link to see all of your videos.

The optional favorites module displays thumbnail images for your favorite videos. Favorite videos are videos that you have explicitly tagged as favorites, similar to the way you would bookmark a web page. As with the videos module, each thumbnail links to its associated video and you can choose whether to display thumbnails in a scroller or a grid.

Wednesday: Customize the Channel Page Layout

There are a couple of ways to customize your channel page layout.

Channel Banner

The channel banner is an 875-by-150-pixel JPEG image that appears at the top of your channel page. I recommend that you choose an image that is 20KB or smaller. The option to upload a channel banner is available only to brand channels.

The following are best practices for your brand channel banner:

- Use the channel banner to feature unique branding, images, and celebrities. By including images of logos, products, or celebrity spokespeople, you help visitors to your channel page quickly associate the channel with your brand.

- Integrate your YouTube brand channel with your other online properties to create a seamless brand experience. For example, you could link the whole channel banner area to your website or use an image map to link to different areas of your website.

- Incorporate the channel banner graphic in your custom background image, then upload an 875-by-150-pixel transparent GIF image for your channel banner. You can use the image map to link different parts of the channel banner area to different URLs. Because YouTube displays a search box and several other links at the top of the page, the space allocated to the channel banner is centered 60 pixels below the top of the page.

To upload your channel banner, log in to your account and navigate to the Branding Options page in the Edit Channel menu. In the Channel Banner field, select the locally saved image that you would like to use.

If you want your entire channel banner to link to the same URL, enter that URL in the Channel Banner Link field. If your channel banner links to multiple locations, enter your image map code in the Image Map Code field.

Profile Icon

The profile icon is an 88-by-88-pixel image that appears on your channel page in the channel information box and in the video details box on the video watch page for your uploaded content. I recommend that you upload an image of a product, logo, or spokesperson closely associated with your brand.

Here's how to select the profile icon for your channel:

1. Log in to your account and navigate to the Personal Profile page in the Edit Channel menu.

2. Click the Choose an Image link next to the Profile Picture header.

3. Browse to the image that you want to use for your profile icon and select it.

4. Click the Update Channel button to upload your image.

Thursday: Customize the Video Page

There are also a couple of ways to customize your video page layout.

Video Page Banner

The video page banner is a 400-by-55-pixel image that appears on the pages where users watch your channel's videos. The video page banner is available only for brand channel partners.

The banner presents an additional opportunity to promote your brand. As Figure 6.6 illustrates, the banner will link to your channel page when displayed on your video pages.

Figure 6.6 Kraft Cooking Video Challenge

To set the video page banner for your channel, log in to your account and navigate to the Branding Options page in the Edit Channel menu. In the Video Page Banner field, select the locally saved image that you would like to use for your video page banner and then click the Save Branding Options button at the bottom of the page to upload the image to YouTube.

Video Page Icon

The video page icon is a 55-by-55-pixel image that appears on your channel page in the Connect with CHANNEL_NAME box. I recommend that you use this image to reinforce your brand image by displaying a secondary logo or personality associated with your brand.

For example, a sports team might use the profile icon to display the team logo and the video icon to display the team mascot. Because the icon appears next to links related to user interaction, an icon that features a celebrity or personality associated with your brand may be preferable if that fits within the context of your brand image.

To set the video page icon for your channel, log in to your account and navigate to the Branding Options page in the Edit Channel menu. In the Video Page Icon field, select the locally saved image that you would like to use for your video page icon and then click the Save Branding Options button at the bottom of the page to upload the image to YouTube. I recommend that you choose an image that is 10KB or smaller.

Friday: Modify the Channel Colors

YouTube offers several basic color schemes, which are displayed near the top of the Channel Design page. However, to ensure that your channel truly reflects your brand identity, I recommend that you modify the colors in the Advanced Design Customization section of the page. As Figure 6.7 illustrates, that section allows you to match the colors on your channel page exactly to your brand colors. After setting the colors for your channel, click the Update Channel button to save your settings.

The settings described in the following sections are customizable.

General Settings

Background Color A solid color will be used as the background color of the page.

Link Color Links appear in the channel information, connect, subscriptions, video log, and comments boxes.

Label Color Labels appear in the video log box and comments box.

Transparency Level This figure lets you adjust the transparency of the modules on your page.

Font You can choose between Arial, Times New Roman, Verdana, and Georgia.

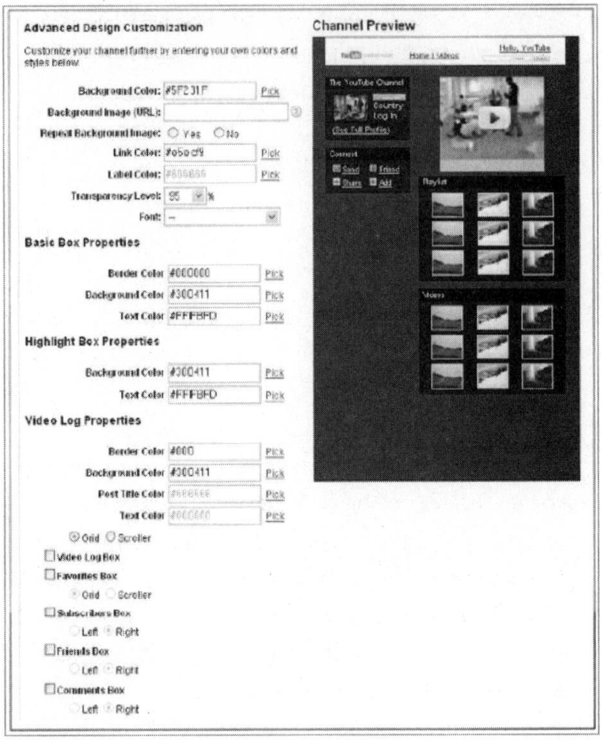

Figure 6.7 Advanced Design Customization

Basic Box Properties

Border Color This setting defines the border color for all content modules except for the video log box.

Background Color This setting defines the background color for all content modules except for the channel information, branding, contests, and bulletins boxes.

Text Color This setting defines the color for text in all modules except the channel information, branding, contests, and bulletins boxes.

Highlight Box Properties

Background Color This setting defines the background color for the channel information, branding, contests, and bulletins boxes.

Text Color This setting defines the color for text in the channel information, branding, contests, and bulletins boxes.

Video Log Properties

This section lets you customize the border color and background color of the video log box. You can also customize the color for the titles of video log posts and the text color in the box. To see some examples, go to SouljaBoy's Channel at `http://www.youtube.com/SouljaBoy`, nigahiga's Channel at `http://www.youtube.com/nigahiga`, or hotforword's Channel at `http://www.youtube.com/hotforwords`.

Week 3: Customize Your Brand Channel Page Content

The Layout Properties section of the Channel Design page lets you select the different sections that you want your channel to display. For example, you might choose to display the subscribers box but not the friends box.

In addition, you can choose whether certain modules will display on the right or left side of the channel page. Finally, you can choose the format—grid or scrolling box—of the Videos and Favorites sections.

Monday: Select featured video

Tuesday: Edit channel information box

Wednesday: Choose channel page boxes

Thursday: Select other channel page boxes

Friday: Use other customization options

Monday: Select Featured Video

The first option in the Layout Properties section lets you choose whether to display a featured video on your channel page. Typically, brand channel partners opt to show a featured video unless they are displaying a custom gadget or contest module that also plays video.

If you display a featured video, you have the option of either automatically setting it to your most recently updated video or specifying the video that will be featured. For brand channels, the featured video plays automatically when users visit your channel page. I recommend that you update your featured video frequently to keep fresh content on your channel page.

For example, Disney Media Networks and YouTube announced the launch of multiple ad-supported channels on March 30, 2009, featuring short-form content from ESPN and the Disney/ABC Television Group. However, channel rollout wasn't scheduled to begin until early May for the Disney/ABC Television Group channels.

Previews of what will be available upon official launch can be viewed at `www.YouTube.com/ABC` and `www.YouTube.com/ESPN`.

As Figure 6.8 illustrates, Lindsay Mayer of ABC.com appeared in the featured video on the ABC channel page. She told viewers that their favorite programming from the ABC primetime, late night, and daytime lineup would soon be available on YouTube.

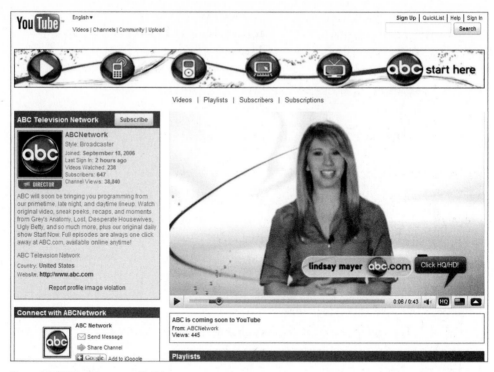

Figure 6.8 ABC is coming soon to YouTube.

You can also set your latest video to be automatically displayed as your featured video, which keeps your channel fresh and drives the views up for your video, which is currently eligible for the "most viewed today/this week/this month" lists.

Because your featured video is the first thing users will see when they visit your channel page, it's important to engage them with videos that capture your brand image. Here are ways to do that:

Talk directly to users about your brand.

Provide information that will help users to navigate through your channel's content.

Encourage users to share their experiences with your brand by posting comments on your channel page.

Highlight news, brand or product updates, and other information that your brand enthusiasts value.

Promote your brand and encourage visits to other brand properties, including your website.

Update users about new products or contests.

Music, movie, and TV brands can feature previews, trailers, music videos, and behind-the-scenes footage.

It's also important to remember that your channel page usually *isn't* the first thing that most viewers will see. They will see one of your videos first, so you need to make sure that every one of your videos and your watch page banner makes people *want* to go to your channel page next.

Some YouTubers even go so far as directly telling people to check out their channel. You can also use video annotations to put a link to your channel from each of your videos.

Tuesday: Edit Channel Information Box

The channel information box appears on the left side of your channel page below the channel banner. If your brand is identified with a specific person or group of people, I recommend that you enter personal profile or location information about the brand.

On the other hand, if your brand is associated with an actual product, personal profile information could confuse users who visit your channel page. I recommend that you use the channel information box to highlight key products or personalities associated with your brand.

For example, go to the vlogbrothers's channel (www.youtube.com/vlogbrothers) and read the channel information box. As Figure 6.9 illustrates, it explains that Hank and John Green, who are brothers, decided not to write to each other during all of 2007 and instead make daily video blogs.

Figure 6.9 Brotherhood 2.0.0.9

The channel information box also explains that they decided to keep updating the YouTube channel at least once a week after the initial "Brotherhood 2.0" project ended. In addition, it explains that the community of nerdfighters that they helped create is now stronger than ever and lives at www.nerdfighters.com.

The following list explains where to enter the information. (If your brand channel is not a standard YouTube account—other channel types are Directors, Musicians, Comedians, and Gurus—some of these fields may not be displayed. To change the channel type for your account, log in to your account and navigate to the Channel Info page in the Edit Channel menu. Then change the channel type for your account.)

- To edit the box's title, log in to your account and navigate to the Channel Info page in the Edit Channel menu. Update the Title field and then click the Update Channel button.

- The icon that appears in the module displays a frame from one of your videos. To select your channel icon, log in to your account and navigate to your My Videos page, which lists all of your videos. Click the Make Profile Icon button next to the video still that you want to use for your channel icon. Your video must be publicly visible to use a still from it as your channel icon. I recommend that you upload a video of your logo or another still image closely associated with your brand, such as a picture of a product or spokesperson, and then use that video for your profile icon.

- The channel information box also displays several pieces of information about your YouTube account, including the date your account was created, your last login time, the number of videos that you have watched, the number of people who subscribe to your account, and the number of times your channel page has been viewed. YouTube automatically determines the values of the fields in this section of the module.

- Your channel description appears below your profile icon. To edit the description title, log in to your account and navigate to the Channel Info page in the Edit Channel menu. Update the Description field and then click the Update Channel button.

- Your name, age, and personal description appear below your channel description. To update these fields, log in to your account and navigate to the Personal Profile page in the Edit Channel menu. I recommend that you hide the age associated with your account unless the brand is actually associated with a specific person. For example, a brand associated with a particular entertainer or athlete might display that person's age. However, a brand associated with an entertainment company or sports league would not display an age. After updating the appropriate fields, click the Update Channel button near the bottom of the page to save your settings.

- To update the Hometown or Country fields, log in to your account and navigate to the Location Info page in the Edit Channel menu. After updating the appropriate fields, click the Update Location button near the bottom of the page to save your settings. The channel information box will not display your zip/postal code but does display any other location fields for which you enter information.

- To update any of the remaining fields that appear in the channel information box, log in to your account and navigate to the Personal Profile page in the Edit Channel menu. The channel information box does not currently display the gender, relationship status, or student information associated with your account. However, if you enter information for these fields, it will be accessible to developers who use the YouTube APIs to retrieve your public profile. So, if your brand does not represent a specific person, I recommend that you leave the Gender and Relationship Status fields blank.

Wednesday: Choose Channel Page Boxes

Today, I'll explain how to set up the branding box, playlist box, videos box, and video log box.

Branding Box

The branding box, which is available only for brand channel partners, provides an opportunity to communicate information about your brand, products, or services to people who visit your channel page. This module is optional and will appear only if you enter a branding box title and branding box text on the Branding Options page. If you opt to display this module, it will appear on the right side of your channel page below your featured video.

As Figure 6.10 illustrates, the branding box for smosh's channel (www.youtube.com/smosh) contains "Smosh Links" to their new website, bloopers, posters, MySpace profile, and Twitter feed.

Figure 6.10 Smosh Links

To set your branding box content, click the Edit Channel button on your channel page and then click the Branding Options link on the left side of the page. After modifying your branding box content, click the Save Branding Options button to save your settings.

There are a couple of factors to keep in mind:

- The branding box title may be up to 100 characters long.

- The branding box text may be up to 4,500 characters long. YouTube will display an error message if you try to submit branding box text that contains HTML. However, you can use line breaks to create paragraphs of text. In addition, YouTube will automatically convert any URLs in your text to links but will not convert email addresses to links. If your text contains any URLs that are longer than 60 characters, they will link to the correct locations but the displayed URLs will be truncated after the 57th character and appended with ellipses (...).

I recommend that you use the branding box to convey a message that explains the purpose of your brand, channel, or content. The branding box can also include links to online fan forums and communities. Encourage users to share their own videos and use comments to relay their own experiences with your brand. Finally, update the branding box content periodically to keep your channel page content fresh.

The following list contains branding box suggestions for partners in specific industries:

- Music, movie, or TV partners might use this area or the channel information box to highlight information about events, such as tour dates and locations, premiere dates, or showtimes for important episodes.

- Consumer products companies might use the branding box to promote new products or encourage users to provide feedback about existing or potential products.

- Automobile companies might use the branding box to feature news about popular vehicles, auto shows, press conferences, and vehicle premieres.

Playlist Box

The playlist box provides a way to highlight sets of related videos that users can view serially. By grouping similar videos, playlists can help users to navigate your channel. Users can also subscribe to your playlists to be automatically notified when you add new videos. The playlist box can link to up to three playlists, which you select on the Channel Design page in the Edit Channel menu.

As Figure 6.11 illustrates, CBS's channel (www.youtube.com/CBS) features five playlists. The order of the playlists depends on the order they are added on the channel design page. You can also choose which video's icon represents an entire playlist in the playlist options.

Figure 6.11 CBS's playlists

The following list identifies several other best practices for creating and selecting playlists for your channel page:

- Create playlists that contain multiple videos related to specific aspects of your brand. For example, a sports team might create one playlist for videos showing game highlights and another playlist for videos showing postgame interviews.

- Encourage users to share their experiences with your brand. By creating playlists of user-submitted videos that promote your brand image, you can engage users with fresh content while also building a community around your brand channel.

- Keep your channel page content fresh by periodically creating new playlists and displaying them in the playlists box.

Videos Box

The videos box displays thumbnail images and information for videos that you uploaded to your YouTube account and that you would like to feature on your channel page. The box links to each video but does not play videos directly.

By default, the videos box displays your most recent videos. For example, sonybmg's channel (www.youtube.com/sonybmg) includes "Willie Nelson—Naked Willie EPK" and eight other videos in its videos box, as Figure 6.12 illustrates.

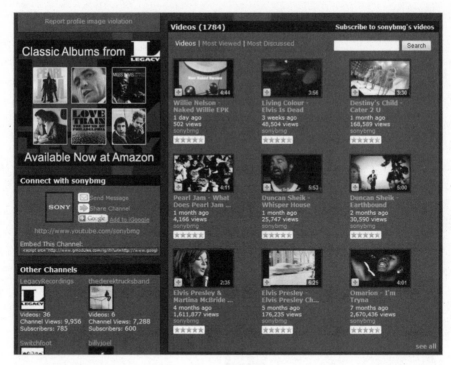

Figure 6.12 sonybmg's videos

To display the videos box, log in to your account and navigate to the Channel Design page in the Edit Channel menu. Verify that the Videos Box option is checked and also select whether the box should display a grid or a scroller. If the box displays a grid, it will show up to three rows of three videos. If the box displays as a scroller, it will show one row of up to four videos as well as arrows to scroll to additional featured videos.

To select the videos that appear in the videos box, navigate to the Organize Videos page in the Edit Channel menu. To set the order in which your videos will display in the videos box, click the Remove link below any video that appears in the preview pane. Then, in the select pane, check the Add check box below each video that will display in the videos box. The videos you select will also be the first videos to appear at the top of the More from This User box on your video watch pages.

Begin by checking the first video that should be displayed, then the second video, and so forth. If you do not select enough videos to fill the box, YouTube will display your most recently submitted videos after the videos you explicitly select.

Video Log Box

Video logs represent a form of blogging in which the medium is video. The video log box gives you an opportunity to add to your channel page more videos that will engage visitors.

The box displays up to two entries from a playlist that you have designated as your video log. Each video log entry that appears on your channel page can be played directly on the page by clicking on the video. The video log box displays some details about the video as well as a link to view all posts to the video log.

The contents of your "vlog" playlist will go in this box. As Figure 6.13 illustrates, nigahiga's channel (www.youtube.com/nigahiga) uses a vlog box to display videos as a series of embedded players rather than thumbnails.

Figure 6.13 nigahiga's vlog

I recommend that you use the video log box only if your video content actually lends itself to a blogging format. For example, a sports team could use a video log to track the exploits of a fan who follows the team on a road trip. However, the team would not use a video log to display normal game highlights.

Similarly, a music artist might use a video log to showcase videos from a concert tour, including behind-the-scenes videos from concerts or tour buses. However, the artist would not use a video log for music videos.

Thursday: Select Other Channel Page Boxes

Today, I'll explain how to set up the favorites, subscriptions, subscribers, and comments boxes as well as discuss best practices for your design.

As Figure 6.14 illustrates, boburnham's channel uses all of these channel page boxes (www.youtube.com/boburnham).

Figure 6.14 boburnham's favorites

Favorites Box

Like the videos box, the favorites box displays thumbnail images and information for videos that you want to feature on your channel page. However, whereas the videos box can contain only your videos, the favorites box can contain other people's videos that you have designated as favorite videos.

Use the favorites box to build a sense of community by featuring videos that show people sharing their experiences with your brand. This approach encourages users to interact with your brand and also enables your brand enthusiasts to interact with each other.

Although you can mark your own videos as favorites, I recommend that you avoid doing so. This will send a clear message that the favorites box real estate on your channel page is intended for videos that your brand enthusiasts submit.

To display the favorites box, log in to your account and navigate to the Channel Design page in the Edit Channel menu. Verify that the Favorites Box option is checked and also select whether the box should display a grid or a scroller.

To select the content for the favorites box, follow the instructions for selecting content for the videos box. However, after linking to the Organize Videos page, click the My Favorites link above the preview pane.

Subscriptions Box

The subscriptions box identifies other channels to which your brand channel account has subscribed. The module displays the profile icon for each channel.

By displaying the subscriptions box, you can promote a family of associated brands. For a branded channel, you can simply use the Other Channels module located on the branding page to do this.

You can add several channels this way. Although your subscriptions box can display six of your own associated brands, it's a good idea to use this area to pay homage to other channels in the YouTube community.

For example, a TV station might maintain brand channels for several programs. The station could use the subscriptions box to let users easily navigate from one program's brand channel to another.

You could also use the subscriptions box to highlight other channels that are related to your brand but that you do not maintain.

For example, a snowboarding equipment company might have a brand channel that links to channels maintained by popular snowboarders who use that company's equipment.

To display the subscriptions box, choose the Subscriptions Box option and choose whether it will display on the right or left side of your channel page. When you are finished, click the Update Channel button near the bottom of the page to save your settings.

Subscribers Box

The subscribers box identifies YouTube users who have subscribed to your brand channel. The module displays the profile icon for each subscribed user.

By displaying the subscribers box, you can showcase your channel's popularity. To specify whether your channel page will display the subscribers box, follow the instructions for the subscriptions box but choose the Subscribers Box option.

Comments Box

Enabling users to post comments on your channel and video pages encourages people to interact with your brand and fosters a sense of community. By empowering users to share opinions and feedback about your brand or products, you can obtain valuable, direct insight into your brand that can improve your programming and marketing decisions.

However, enabling users to post comments also bears a certain degree of risk because comments might contain inappropriate language or display inappropriate profile icons. For this reason, most advertiser brand channels choose to hide comments.

If you do choose to display comments, you can mitigate the associated risk by assigning someone to review and remove inappropriate comments promptly. You can also set comments to appear only after you've approved them.

To specify whether users can post comments on your channel page, log in to your channel and click the Edit Channel button. Then click the Channel Design link on the left side of the page.

If users can post comments, then under the Layout Properties header, opt to display the comments box and choose whether it will display on the right or left side of your channel page. Then click the Update Channel button to save your settings. If users cannot post comments, make sure the comments box option is not displayed.

After indicating whether you want the comments box to display, click the Channel Info link on the left side of the page. If you opted to display the comments box, then make sure the Display Comments on Your Channel option is checked beneath the Channel Comments header.

Friday: Use Other Customization Options

There are additional content modules and other options for customizing your brand channel.

Contests Box

I recommend that you hide the contests box on your brand channel page.

Contest Module

You should display the contest module on your site if you are running a YouTube contest or if you have developed a custom gadget to display featured content. Otherwise, you should hide this module on your brand channel page.

Contact your account executive if you would like more information about contests and gadgets.

Bulletins Box

The bulletins box shows a list of messages that you have broadcast to all of your YouTube friends. However, the box could also show bulletins that your YouTube friends have broadcast to you.

For this reason, many brand channel partners opt to hide the bulletins box on their channel pages. If you do show the bulletins box, be very cautious about which YouTube users you allow to designate you as a friend because bulletins from those users could appear on your channel page.

Recent Activity Box

There's also now a recent activity box that shows when you subscribe to channels or add friends.

Videos Rated Box

The videos rated box displays a list of the five videos that you rated most recently. For each video, the box displays a thumbnail image, the video title, and your rating.

Typically, brand channel partners opt to hide this module on their channel pages. However, if you do opt to show this module, I recommend that you use it to encourage user interaction with your brand by rating user-submitted videos related to your brand. In this case, however, you may decide to rate only videos that positively represent your brand image in order to avoid having negatively rated videos appear on your channel page.

Recent Comments Box

The recent comments box displays a list of the five videos for which you most recently added text comments. For each video, the box displays a thumbnail image, the video title, and your comment.

Typically, brand channel partners opt to hide this module on their channel pages. If you do opt to show this module, use it to encourage user interaction with your brand by posting positive comments on videos that positively represent your brand. In addition, you may decide to only post comments on videos that do positively represent your brands so that negative comments do not appear on your channel page.

Even though the box displays five videos, it may display more than five comments if you submit multiple comments on one video before submitting comments on any other videos. In addition, the box may display the same video multiple times if you submit multiple comments on that video but also comment on other videos in between.

The following sequence illustrates both of these behaviors: (1) You submit a comment on video ABC, (2) you submit a comment on video XYZ, (3) you submit a second comment on video XYZ, and (4) you submit a second comment on video ABC.

In this scenario, the recent comments box would display three thumbnail images. The first thumbnail would be of video ABC and the second comment that you submitted on that video would appear next to the image. The second thumbnail would be of video XYZ and both of your comments on that video would appear next to the image, with the most recent comment appearing first. The third thumbnail would be of video ABC and the first comment you posted on that video would appear next to the image.

Friends Box

The friends box displays the profile icons of users you have added as friends or users from whom you accepted invitations to be friends.

Typically, brand channel partners choose to hide this module on their channel pages to prevent their channels from displaying any inappropriate images in their "friends" profile icons. Some brand channel partners that display the module choose to add only associated brand channels as friends.

Events Box

The events box displays only on the channel page of Comedians or Musicians who've added event dates to their channel.

The events box displays up to five events and a link to all events if you have entered more than five. The module provides the date, time, and location of each event as well as an event description and a link to buy tickets if you provided one. If your channel page displays the events box, I recommend that you delete events after they occur to ensure that your page displays an up-to-date event list.

Branding Options

The Branding Options page in the Edit Channel menu displays several other options for customizing your brand channel:

- The Tracking Image URL field lets you specify the URL for a 1-by-1-pixel tracking image that you use to collect statistics for views of your channel or video pages.
- The Google Analytics Account ID field lets you specify a Google Analytics account you use to track usage and performance of your brand channel account.

Week 4: Distribute Your Videos to Other Sites

If YouTube accounts for almost four out of five U.S. visits to online video sites, then it makes sense to spend most of your time learning how to set up a YouTube channel as well as how to create and customize a brand channel. You will, however, also want to distribute your videos beyond YouTube because nobody wants to ignore 21 percent of the online video market.

But there are 68 online video sites in Hitwise's custom category, and nobody can afford the time and money required to distribute their videos to scores of sites with less than 1 percent market share. So we'll look at the online video distribution options that make the most sense.

Nevertheless, I'm sure there's someone you know who remembers the "good old days" when a record number of Americans watched Super Bowl XLII. In fact, data from Nielsen Media Research found that on February 3, 2008, 97.5 million U.S. viewers saw the New York Giants beat the New England Patriots 17 to 14.

That made it the most-watched Super Bowl in history, leaving it behind only the series finale of M*A*S*H in 1983 for viewership. Advertisers who paid an average of $2.7 million for a 30-second spot could reach this audience all at once. As Figure 6.15 illustrates, you can browse the 2008 Super Bowl commercials by quarter at AOL Sports.

But according to comScore Video Metrix, more than 147 million U.S. Internet users watched an average of 100.7 videos per viewer in January 2009. This means 77 percent of the total U.S. Internet audience viewed a total of 14.8 billion online videos during the month. The duration of the average online video was 3.5 minutes, so the average online video viewer watched 356 minutes of video during the month.

That's about the length of the Super Bowl—if you include the pregame and half-time shows.

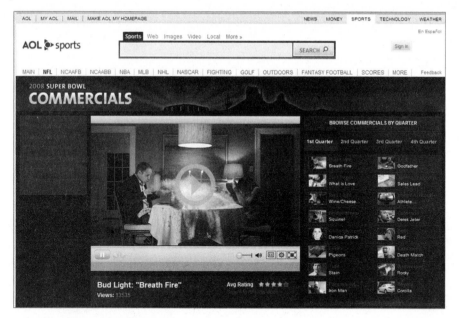

Figure 6.15 2008 Super Bowl commercials

Mention these facts the next time grandpa reminisces about the "good old days" of broadcast TV. It may not prevent him from saying, "When I was a boy, I had to walk five miles through the snow to change the channel." But, it may help explain why it makes sense for you to distribute online videos to multiple sites.

Now, Hitwise says YouTube has a 79 percent share of U.S. visits to online video sites, but comScore says YouTube has a 40 percent share of the online video market. Although they use different methodologies, both sources indicate that there is intelligent life beyond YouTube. The only question is whether distributing your content to other online video sites should be a major or minor part of your marketing strategy.

Monday: Use TubeMogul

Tuesday: Use Visible Measures

Wednesday: Submit to Blinkx

Thursday: Get a Truveo Director Account

Friday: Use press release distribution

Monday: Use TubeMogul

Start by going to TubeMogul (www.tubemogul.com). Founded in 2006 by online video buffs who met while in graduate school at UC Berkeley, TubeMogul lets you upload videos once and distribute them to more than 20 video sharing sites. As Figure 6.16 illustrates, TubeMogul distributes videos to YouTube, MySpace, Google Video, Dailymotion, Crackle, Yahoo! Video, Metacafe, and Break.com.

Figure 6.16 Video sites supported

TubeMogul's free beta service has been live since November 2006. In January 2008, TubeMogul announced the launch of its Premium Products, which include a host of new professional features. Through its acquisition of Illumenix in October 2008, TubeMogul is also able to offer rich engagement and performance metrics. I'll talk about TubeMogul's online video analytics in Chapter 10.

Using TubeMogul provides a number of benefits:

Save time Uploading videos to each site in your distribution is no longer necessary. Upload to TubeMogul and let its Universal Upload tool do the rest. Then you can log in to understand your viewership across online video sites in one place.

Increase your reach With your videos on more sites at no extra effort, your opportunity to gain viewers multiplies. Users of Universal Upload have almost doubled their views per video.

Improve your understanding of viewer base Getting a better understanding of your customer base helps you to create more targeted and relevant content or products and services.

Track trends and buzz Tracking online video analytics across multiple sites helps you see spikes in viewership, identify trends, and monitor the pulse of online video viewers.

Assess marketing efforts Analyzing spikes and trends in viewership across any range of time lets you assess the effectiveness of your marketing efforts.

Gain competitive intelligence Seeing what's working for your counterparts and competition helps you compare and contrast their viewership trends with your own.

Share the intelligence Sending and sharing data and charts with colleagues or friends builds support for your campaigns.

Brad O'Farrell, the technical editor of this book, has a counter-argument against using TubeMogul. The TubeMogul system is often out-of-date with YouTube and other online video sites and still requires manual tweaking after uploading a video. This can mean some features, such as enabling video responses or geotagging, do not work they way they normally do in YouTube until they are manually readjusted.

In addition, errors in TubeMogul's system can cause your video to get stuck in limbo—sometimes for days at a time. Although this can also happen on individual video sites, O'Farrell thinks using TubeMogul can actually add more steps to the process of uploading a video to multiple sites than it is subtracting.

With YouTube dwarfing the other online video sites in market share, the online video market resembles Snow White and (to be politically correct) the seven vertically challenged men. So, I would recommend that you upload to YouTube manually and use TubeMogul to distribute to other online video sites.

Tuesday: Use Visible Measures

An alternative to using TubeMogul is using Visible Measures. As Figure 6.17 illustrates, you can find it at www.visiblemeasures.com.

Figure 6.17 Measure viral video and audience engagement with Visible Measures.

Visible Measures has a Video Placement Multiplier tool that distributes your video content to over 40 of the top video sharing sites—from the leading video sharing sites to tightly targeted niche destinations. Video Placement Multiplier allows you to match your brand messaging with your target audience while giving you maximum control over brand placement. You provide Visible Measures with the videos and Video Placement Multiplier does the rest.

The first step in its automated video placement process involves providing Visible Measures with your video assets and metadata by filling out a simple form about the metatags, titles, descriptions, and categories you want to use for your videos. This allows them to prepare your videos for distribution and gives you control over brand placement.

Video Placement Multiplier classifies and categorizes every video sharing site Visible Measure supports. This approach is designed to help give you power over where and how your brand is seen, helping it reach your target audience while staying clear of undesirable content.

To distribute your video content to audiences across the Internet, Video Placement Multiplier uses an automated viral seeding technique that targets the most visited video destination sites. These video sharing sites—regardless of size—are continuously monitored to ensure functionality and compatibility with your video content.

Visible Measures has access to over 40 of the top video sharing sites, which enables them to distribute your video assets where they will have the most reach and the largest impact for your target audience.

Video Placement Multiplier is integrated with the Visible Measures Viral Reach Database, their measurement solution showing the true reach and audience engagement of online videos. This means that after your video content is seeded, you can immediately begin tracking how the community responds, no matter where it goes or how it changes.

Wednesday: Submit to Blinkx

Next, head over to blinkx (blinkx.com). The video search engine has an index of more than 32 million hours of video and audio content, including favorite TV moments, news clips, short documentaries, music videos, video blogs, and more. And blinkx processes over 7 million searches per day.

As Figure 6.18 illustrates, blinkx has over 420 media partnerships and powers the video search for many of the world's most frequented sites, including national broadcasters, commercial media companies, and private video libraries. This enables blinkx to reach over 63 million unique visitors and generates over 667 million page views per month.

Go to www.blinkx.com/rssupload to submit your video to blinkx. Currently, blinkx only allows submission using RSS. The video search engine accepts the Media RSS and RSS 2.0 specifications. Your feed must contain media enclosures so that blinkx can ascertain and process the video content itself.

Figure 6.18 Blinkx media partners

Thursday: Get a Truveo Director Account

As Figure 6.19 illustrates, you will also want to head over to Truveo (www.truveo.com).

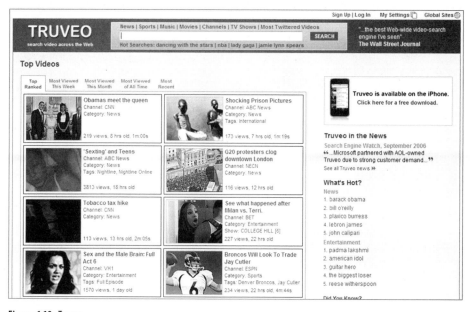

Figure 6.19 Truveo

The Truveo search engine powers video search on some of the most popular destinations on the Web, including AOL Video, AOL Search, Brightcove, CBS RADIO's sites, Clevver, CSTV, Excite, Flock, InfoSpace, Kosmix, Microsoft Corporation, Pageflakes, PureVideo, Qwest, CNET's Search.com, Sportingo, Sports Illustrated, Widgetbox, and YourMinis, reaching an audience of over 75 million users a month.

You'll want to sign up for the Truveo Director program, which is a free feature for site owners or content publishers. It's a quick and easy way to get your content into Truveo's video search index. Upon successful registration, Directors will receive the following benefits:

- Ability to upload RSS feeds of your content

- Instant validation of your RSS feed

- Near real-time indexing of your video assets in their search engine

- Status monitoring, error reporting, and statistics for your feeds

Friday: Use Press Release Distribution

Finally, I recommend that you—or your one of your PR people—visit one of the leading press release distribution services: Business Wire, GlobeNewswire, Marketwire, PR Newswire, or PRWeb.

All of these offer some flavor of service that allows you to embed online video content into your press releases. As Figure 6.20 illustrates, I embedded a YouTube video into a PRWeb press release for BHG.com, the interactive companion to *Better Homes and Gardens* magazine.

Figure 6.20 BHG.com holds straw poll for Halloween pumpkin carving stencils of Barack Obama, Joe Biden, John McCain, and Sarah Palin

Here's the backstory: On October 4, 2008, BHG.com announced a straw poll for Halloween pumpkin carving stencils of Barack Obama, Joe Biden, John McCain, and Sarah Palin. BHG.com Senior Holidays Editor Debra Steilen made my day when she forwarded an email from Amanda Cortese, senior publicity manager at Meredith, who let us know that CNN had used pieces of our Presidential Pumpkin Picks video as part of a story on election tactics.

More importantly, the press release and publicity helped to increase searches for "Better Homes and Gardens" and other promoted brands by 38.9 percent year over year. And they also helped to increase visits to BHG.com 14.5 percent year over year.

Month 5: Engage the YouTube Community

7

YouTube began as a video sharing site and has quickly grown into the world's leading online video community. In this chapter, I'll teach you how to become a fully vested member of the YouTube community. You'll study the most discussed YouTube Live highlights, find out why you should add YouTube to your site and share videos, and learn the latest lessons of viral marketing. You'll also discover the comic irony of one sheep saying to another, "Sure, I follow the herd—not out of brainless obedience, mind you, but out of a deep and abiding respect for the concept of community."

Chapter Contents:
Paul Revere's Ride
Week 1: Become a Member of the YouTube Community
Week 2: Study the Most Discussed YouTube Live Highlights
Week 3: Add YouTube to Your Site and Share Videos
Week 4: Learn the Latest Lessons of Viral Marketing

Paul Revere's Ride

Although YouTube began as a video sharing site, it has quickly grown into the world's leading online video community.

According to Wikipedia, a "community" has been traditionally defined as "a group of interacting people living in a common location." With the advent of the Internet, the concept has expanded because people can now gather virtually in an online community and share common interests.

The key to becoming an opinion leader in a community is to continually look over your shoulder and consider where the rest of the social system is regarding new ideas.

As I mentioned in Chapter 2, Everett Rogers, author of *Diffusion of Innovations*, noted, "The interpersonal relationships between opinion leaders and their followers hang in a delicate balance. If an opinion leader becomes too innovative, or adopts a new idea too quickly, followers may begin to doubt his or her judgment."

This delicate balance between opinion leaders and their followers explains the comic irony in Figure 7.1, where one sheep says to another, "Sure, I follow the herd—not out of brainless obedience, mind you, but out of a deep and abiding respect for the concept of community."

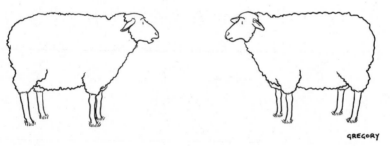

GREGORY

"Sure, I follow the herd—not out of brainless obedience, mind you, but out of a deep and abiding respect for the concept of community."

Figure 7.1 "Sure, I follow the herd—not out of brainless obedience, mind you, but out of a deep and abiding respect for the concept of community." (Cartoon by Alex Gregory in *The New Yorker*, June 30, 2003.)

So, how do you become an individual who is able to informally influence other individuals' attitudes or overt behavior in a desired way with relative frequency? In other words, how do you become an opinion leader in the YouTube community or any other community?

As Harold Lasswell observed, the key is analyzing *who* says *what* in which *channel* to *whom* with what *effect*. Before we tackle how to engage the YouTube community, let's look at the how the interpersonal communication behavior of opinion leaders drives the diffusion process—and how it was able to create a critical mass of adopters long before the Internet was invented.

My favorite example of how this works is Paul Revere's ride. It demonstrates that opinion leaders and diffusion networks existed 230 years before YouTube was founded in 2005. That story also resonates for me, in part, because I live in Acton, Massachusetts, home of the Acton Minutemen (Figure 7.2). Actonians like to say, "The battle of Lexington was fought in Concord by the men of Acton."

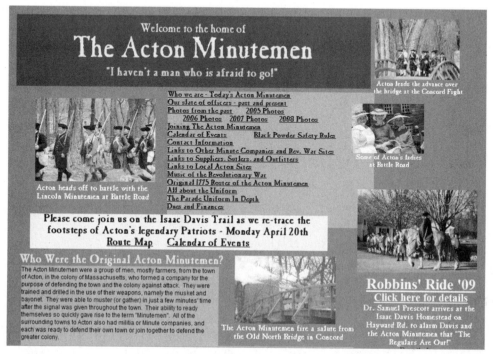

Figure 7.2 Welcome to the home of the Acton Minutemen

And I recommend reading *Paul Revere's Ride* (Oxford University Press, 1994) by David Hackett Fischer, which tells a more compelling story than Henry Wadsworth Longfellow's famous poem tells. According to Fischer, Paul Revere was able to spread the alarm so effectively because he had played a key role earlier in the Boston Tea Party. He was also a member of several clubs in the Boston area, including the London Enemies List, the North Caucus, and the Long Room Club. He also networked socially at two taverns, Cromwell's Head and Bunch of Grapes. The other members of these clubs and people who gathered at taverns were the political leaders who ended up starting the American Revolutionary War in 1775.

It's also worth noting that Fischer's map of the Middlesex alarm is cited by Rogers to illustrate how opinion leaders and diffusion networks work. As Figure 7.3 illustrates, as many as 40 riders carried news of the British expedition throughout Middlesex County—a 750-square-mile area—from 11:00 p.m. on April 18 to 9:30 a.m. on April 19, 1775.

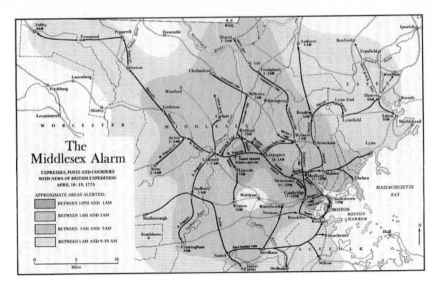

Figure 7.3 The Middlesex Alarm

Notice that the Waltham militia didn't join in the fighting, even though Lexington is next door. What happened?

Although Henry Wadsworth Longfellow made it sound like Revere was the only rider that night, there was another: William Dawes, Jr. And Waltham, which was on Dawes's route, never received an effective alarm.

Rogers explained, "Revere knew exactly which doors to pound on during his ride on Brown Beauty that April night. As a result, he awakened key individuals, who then rallied their neighbors to take up arms against the British."

He added, "In comparison, Dawes did not know the territory as well as Revere. As he rode through rural Massachusetts on the night of April 18, he simply knocked on random doors. The occupants in most cases simply turned over and went back to sleep."

Table 7.1 outlines why the midnight ride of William Dawes failed to raise the alarm in Waltham. He didn't know the anti-British opinion leaders.

▶ Table 7.1 Similarities and Differences of Alarm Riders

Who	Paul Revere	William Dawes
Says what	"The regulars are out!"	"The regulars are out!"
In which channel	Word of mouth on a fast horse	Word of mouth on a fast horse
To whom	Opinion leaders	Random doors
With what effect	Rallied their neighbors to take up arms	Turned over and went back to sleep

It's also worth noting that neither Revere nor Dawes rode through Acton. On their ride from Lexington to Concord, they met Dr. Samuel Prescott at 1:00 p.m. When the three arrived near Hartwell's tavern in Lincoln, they were attacked by four British officers from a scouting party. Revere and Dawes were taken prisoner, but Prescott succeeded in escaping by jumping his horse over a wall. He was the only one of the three men to reach Concord and warn the town.

Prescott then proceeded farther west to warn Acton. He arrived at the Isaac Davis homestead between 2:00 and 3:00 a.m. to alarm the captain of the Acton Minutemen that "the regulars are out!"

In other words, Revere didn't broadcast his message to every Middlesex village and farm. The message that "the regulars are out" went viral from Revere to Prescott to Davis. And the midnight ride of William Dawes didn't have the same impact because he didn't know the opinion leaders in Waltham and they wouldn't have known him.

In this chapter, I'll show you what Revere did that you should do today, what Dawes did wrong that you shouldn't do, and why help from people like Prescott is unpredictable but not unexpected when you engage the community.

Week 1: Become a Member of the YouTube Community

The first thing you need to do to become a fully vested member of the YouTube community is follow the YouTube Community Guidelines. Here are some common-sense rules that will help you steer clear of trouble:

- Respect copyrights and don't violate YouTube's terms of use. Only upload videos that you made or that you are authorized to use. This means don't upload videos you didn't make and don't use content in your videos that someone else owns the copyright to, such as music tracks, snippets of copyrighted programs, or videos made by other users, without necessary authorizations.

- YouTube isn't for pornography or sexually explicit content. If your video is sexually explicit, even if it's a video of yourself, don't upload it to YouTube.

- Don't post videos showing animal abuse, drug abuse, under-age drinking and smoking, or bomb making.

- Graphic or gratuitous violence isn't allowed. If your video shows someone being physically hurt, attacked, or humiliated, don't post it.

- YouTube isn't a shock site. Don't post gross-out videos of accidents, dead bodies, or similar things intended to shock or disgust.

- YouTube encourages free speech and defends everyone's right to express unpopular points of view. But YouTube doesn't permit hate speech.

- Things like predatory behavior, stalking, threats, harassment, intimidation, invading privacy, revealing other people's personal information, and inciting others to commit violent acts are taken very seriously. Anyone caught doing these things may be permanently banned from YouTube.

- Everyone hates spam. Don't create misleading descriptions, tags, titles, or thumbnails in order to increase views. It's not okay to post large amounts of untargeted, unwanted, or repetitive content, including comments and private messages.

Members of the YouTube community can flag a video if they believe it doesn't belong on the site. As Figure 7.4 illustrates, you can learn about flagging by watching a video that YouTube provides. The YouTube staff reviews flagged videos 24 hours a day, seven days a week to determine whether they violate YouTube Community Guidelines. If they do, the staff removes them.

Monday: Comment on videos

Tuesday: Post video responses

Wednesday: Create contests

Thursday: Join or create YouTube groups

Friday: Interact with the YouTube team

Figure 7.4 "Flagging on YouTube: The Basics"

Monday: Comment on Videos

You can start the process of becoming a fully vested member of the YouTube community by commenting on your favorite videos.

To post a text comment for a video, start typing in the Comment on This Video field or click the Post a Text Comment link below the video player. Then, enter your comment and click the Post Comment button. Keep your comments respectful and relevant, so they can be enjoyed by the full YouTube community.

Here are some tips on commenting on videos:

- Decide on the kind of image you want to convey. With the exception of Internet trolls, it's generally a good idea to be nice to people when making text comments to their videos. Just keep in mind that everything you're saying is public and archived.

- Think about whether you're talking to the content creator, the other commenters, or just yourself. If your comment is clearly addressed to the person who made the video ("Nice job on the effect at 1:20! How did you do that?"), then you're more likely to solicit a reply from the content creator, which could lead them to investigate your own channel and become a subscriber.

- Don't spam other people's video or channel comments with your videos. In the words of my technical editor, Brad O'Farrell, "It's lame and ineffective." Rather, you should participate in their discussions in an interesting way, which can encourage people to check out your own channel.

- On your *own* videos, it's nice to reply to as many comments as possible. Not only does it show you care, it will facilitate more discussion (people replying to your replies) which can raise your ranking on the most discussed list.

- Put offsite contact information in your profile. Sometimes discussions in the comments can lead to users clicking through to your profile to figure out how to get in touch with you, which can lead to a continued relationship. A lot of the YouTube community happens outside of YouTube itself. Be prepared to interact with the YouTube community through email, blogs, Facebook, Twitter, GChat, MSN, AIM, and RSS.

For example, if you posted a text comment to "Boston Red Sox - 'Greatest Day' - Yankees Choke," it's much nicer to ask a question like, "What font is the *New York Post* headline using at 0:51?" As Figure 7.5 illustrates, there's no need for Boston Red Sox fans to be mean-spirited and scurrilous. That's the job of Gotham's tabloids.

Figure 7.5 "Boston Red Sox – 'Greatest Day' – Yankees Choke

Tuesday: Post Video Responses

The next step toward becoming a fully vested member of the YouTube community is to post responses to other videos.

If the owner of a video has allowed video responses, you can post one by clicking the Post a Video Response button, located under the video on its watch page. You will then be given three options for choosing your response video:

Record a Video YouTube will automatically attempt to detect your computer's settings if you choose to respond via QuickCapture. Click the Allow button in the window that pops up so that YouTube can access your camera and microphone. Before you can begin recording your web cam response, be sure to enter information into all the fields on the left side of the screen.

Choose a Video The drop-down here allows you to respond with any video you've already posted. However, your video can be used as a response only once. If you've used a video as a response in the past and want to use it for a new response, it will no longer be listed as the earlier response.

Upload a Video This works pretty similarly to the normal upload process. Click the Upload a Video link. Enter all of your video's information, then click either Go Upload a File to upload a file or Use QuickCapture if you decide to use your web cam after all.

Although text comments should be respectful and relevant, video responses can also be funny or interesting. Let me give you an example.

On August 30, 2007, Bryan Levi, a 21-year-old film and video student at Penn State who goes by the handle Levinator25 on YouTube, posted "Tiger Woods PGA Tour 08 Jesus Shot." As Figure 7.6 illustrates, Levi's Jesus Shot video showed a glitch in the world's #1 selling golf video game from EA Sports.

Figure 7.6 "Tiger Woods PGA Tour 08 Jesus Shot"

On August 19, 2008, Tiger Woods and EA Sports posted a video response to "Tiger Woods PGA Tour 08 Jesus Shot." They demonstrated that the "glitch" Levinator25 thought he found in the game was not a glitch at all. As Figure 7.7 illustrates, "It's not a glitch. He's just that good."

Figure 7.7 "Tiger Woods 09 – Walk on Water"

Both Levi and EA Sports president Peter Moore told David Sarno of the *Los Angeles Times* they thought the whole situation was very funny.

O'Farrell also says using video responses to your own videos is "one of the easiest-to-control ways to get traffic to flow from one video to the next" by creating a prominent link at the bottom of the popular video. For example, "Play him off, keyboard cat" (www.youtube.com/watch?v=2ndx_Id1UQU) was getting a huge surge in traffic from embedded players as this was written. So he made it a video response to "Jill," a new episode of Wainy Days. From May 15 to May 20, 2009, "Jill" got over 30,000 views.

Wednesday: Create Contests

Another way to become a fully vested member of the YouTube community is to create a contest. As I mentioned in Chapter 3, you can create your own, or a paid advertiser can spend $500,000 or more to create a YouTube contest on its brand channel page.

A contest is a competition where users can submit videos and other users can vote on them. Nonofficial contests can be created by anyone in any number of ways, ranging from the creation of groups to simple video responses.

Since we looked at a nonofficial contest in Chapter 3, let's check out one of the official contests that have been created by paid advertisers.

On April 18, 2007, Heinz spun the bottle and gave consumers a chance to create their own TV commercials celebrating their love affair with the thick, rich taste of America's favorite ketchup. Consumers could submit their 30-second TV commercials to TopThisTV.com, which was powered by YouTube.

How did the YouTube community respond? Members submitted more than 4,000 qualified contest entries, which got 5.2 million online views. This means consumers spent more than 43,000 hours watching submissions, and even more time interacting with the brand.

Who was hungry for fame? Andrew Dodson of Wheelersburg, Ohio, won $57,000 and a well-earned place in the 130-year history of a bona fide cultural icon when his winning commercial titled "Heinz: The Kissable Ketchup" aired during "Primetime Emmys" that September.

What was the business outcome? On June 1, 2007, Teresa F. Lindeman of the *Pittsburgh Post-Gazette* wrote an article entitled, "Heinz's marketing blitz paying off." She quoted David Moran, president and chief executive officer of Heinz North America, who said, "We've already seen a pickup in the (ketchup) business."

How do we know the pickup was significant? As Figure 7.8 illustrates, Heinz announced Top This TV Challenge Take Two on December 14, 2007.

Heinz received more than 2,000 qualified video entries for the sequel to its hugely successful Top This contest. The winner was Matt Cozza of Chicago.

Figure 7.8 Hungry For More?

A personal experience served as the inspiration for his entry, "Now We Can Eat," making him the winner of $57,000 and a 30-second spot on national TV.

In Cozza's winning video, a man and woman sit down in a restaurant and realize there's no Heinz ketchup on the table. The pair is dismayed as they look around for an extra bottle. Finally, a server swings by their table, dropping off a bottle of Heinz ketchup and the tagline "Now we can eat" flashes on the screen.

Thursday: Join or Create YouTube Groups

Although technology has changed dramatically since 1775, people's social behavior hasn't. So, engage in the twenty-first-century version of joining groups like the London Enemies List, North Caucus, and Long Room Club.

Joining groups allows you to share videos and have discussions on a common theme. You can find groups the quickest by visiting the Community tab located near the top of every page.

See a group full of interesting videos and conversations? Have some thoughts to contribute, and like hearing the thoughts of others? If so, you might want to join that group. To join a group, follow these steps:

- From the group's main page, click the Join This Group link in the upper-right corner.

- If the group owner allows anyone to join the group, you'll automatically become a member. Otherwise, you'll have to wait until the group owner gives you permission before you can post videos or topics for discussion.

Once you've joined a group, it's easy to post new topics for discussion and add comments to other topics. If you've got something to say to a large group, you might want to post a new topic so other members can respond to your thoughts. To post topics to a group follow these steps:

1. Go to the Group's main page:

    ```
    http://www.youtube.com/group/[GROUP NAME]
    ```

2. Scroll down until you see an empty text field under the words *Add New Topic*.

3. Type in the text you'd like to use to describe the topic you'd like to discuss with other group members.

4. Click the Add Topic button.

If you'd like to offer more information to a topic you or someone else created, adding comments is the way to go. Here's how to add comments to a topic:

1. First, join the group to which you'd like to post a comment.

2. On the group's main page, the discussion topics will be listed under Discussions. Click the topic to which you'd like to add your comment.

3. Enter the comment into the Add New Comment field.

4. Click the Post Comment button.

You'll then see your comment written under the topic. Alternatively, if you'd like to directly reply to someone else's topic or join in on an existing subthread, follow steps 1 and 2, then click the Reply button on someone's comment. Type your reply and click the Post Comment button.

You can also create your own group—with you as the owner/moderator—by clicking the Account link, located at the upper-right portion of any page, and then clicking the Groups link located within the More section.

If you've got a topic or group of topics that calls for a discussion with a larger group of people, you may want to consider creating a group. Groups allow multiple people to discuss things publicly and post videos that apply to the discussion. As a creator or member of a group, you can choose to add videos, invite other members, begin conversations, and offer comments to the videos and topics that other members have added.

If you're creating a group, you can have as little or as much control over the topics and flow of conversation as you want. To create a group, follow these steps:

1. Either from your account page or the Groups main page, click the Create a Group button.

2. Enter all the relevant information about the group you'd like to create, including title, tags, and description. Many people like to use the description to help define what sorts of conversations and videos their group is intended to have.

3. Choose a group name URL. Make sure the URL you choose is one you'll continue to be satisfied with because it can't be changed in the future.

4. Select the permissions regarding who can see your group, how uploads and postings will occur, and how your group icon will be created.

5. Click the Create Group button.

Joining or creating groups is a great way to become a fully vested member of the YouTube community. And groups are a good way to ask the YouTube community for feedback on a contest or ideas for a sequel.

As Figure 7.9 illustrates, there were 806 videos, 3,736 members, and two discussions in the Freshburst Surprise group page as of April 2009. The makers of Freshburst Listerine Pocketpaks were asking the YouTube community, "What would you like to try again for the second time?"

Friday: Interact with the YouTube Team

Back in 1775, social networking in places like Cromwell's Head and Bunch of Grapes helped Revere to become a fully vested member of the Sons of Liberty. Today, there are places like the YouTube Blog and TestTube where you can become a fully vested member of the YouTube Community.

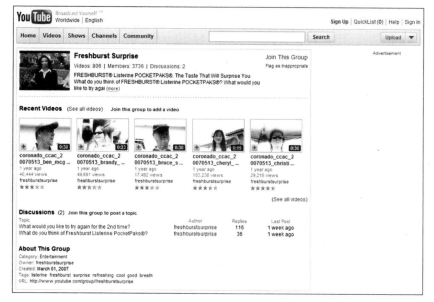

Figure 7.9 Freshburst Surprise

You can't rub elbows with Samuel Adams, John Hancock, or Dr. Joseph Warren anymore. However, by commenting on the posts in the YouTube Blog, you can interact with the following members of the YouTube team:

- Andrew Bangs, YouTube Sports
- Tracy Chan, Product Manager
- Nikhil Chandhok, Product Manager
- Stanley Chen, Engineer, Gmail
- Mark Day, YouTube Comedy
- Michele Flannery, YouTube Music
- Brian Glick, Product Manager
- Obadiah Greenberg, Strategic Partnerships Team
- Steve Grove, YouTube News & Politics
- Sadia Harper, Community Manager, YouTube Howto & Style
- Michele K-Tel, YouTube Music
- Ryan Junee, Product Manager
- Curtis Lee, Product Marketing Manager
- Olivia M., YouTube News & Politics
- Chris Maxcy, Partnerships Director
- David McMillan, YouTube Entertainment

- Nick Mehra, Strategic Partner Development
- Sara Pollack, Entertainment Marketing Manager, YouTube Film
- Mia Quagliarello, Sr. Community Manager
- Ramya Raghavan, YouTube News & Politics
- Shiva Rajaraman, Product Manager
- Michelle Schlachta, Community Manager
- Umang Sharan, Engineer
- David Stewart, Product Marketing
- Kenny Stoltz, Product Manager
- Hiroto Tokusei, Senior Product Manager
- Thai Tran, Product Manager
- Colin W., Help Center Guru
- Hunter Walk, Director, Product Management
- Patrick Walker, Director of Video Partnerships, Europe, Middle East and Africa
- Nate Weinstein, YouTube Film

Why would you want to interact with these members of the YouTube team? Well, some of them play a role in selecting spotlight videos. Although YouTube's members rate videos they like, the YouTube team plucks out some interesting and timely content from the community and partners to showcase on the Categories page. Spotlight videos are not advertisements and are not based on any commercial relationship.

However, the more important question is why would these members of the YouTube team want to interact with you? Who wants to engage in a conversation with "nattering nabobs of negativism" or self-seeking sycophants of servility?

So, instead of becoming a troll or a sockpuppet, I recommend you be yourself and share input and feedback that communicate your experience, talent, and expertise. That's why the YouTube Blog was created in the first place.

Another way to interact with the YouTube team is to participate when they invite you to enter the YouTube Slam Dunk Contest, test YouTube RealTime, or ask Secretary of State Hillary Clinton a question.

For example, Hunter Walk, YouTube's director of product management, posted an item to the YouTube Blog on March 3, 2009, asking members of the YouTube community to "Adopt a Feature." SteveDutzy responded by making a video that let the rest of the community in on a fun (if perverse) game he plays with Insight (Figure 7.10).

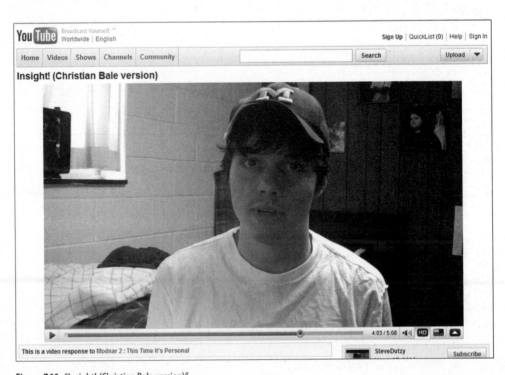

Figure 7.10 "Insight! (Christian Bale version)"

Petercoffin broadcast from space to explain how Insight can contribute to inspiration, monetization, and, um, you'll see (Figure 7.11).

Figure 7.11 "Insight... IN SPACE!"

Two weeks later, Walk mentioned—and linked to—both of these videos in the YouTube Community Help Forums. SteveDutzy and Petercoffin gave the Insight feature some TLC by making videos explaining how it works. And their mixture of straightforward instruction and comedy is "something that never looks bad on your permanent record," as Greg Marmalard said in *Animal House* (1978).

If you are able to interact with the YouTube team on a technical level, then go to TestTube, their ideas incubator. That is where YouTube engineers and developers test out recipes and concoctions that aren't quite fully baked and invite you to tell them how they're coming along. In April 2009, the mixtures they were working on included Caption Tube, Video Annotations, Active Sharing, Warp, and Streams.

O'Farrell adds, "The best way to interact with the YouTube team is to volunteer for anything you can, report any bug you can, send a video to the editors anytime you find something good and unseen. They will appreciate the help, and it will put you on their radar. But don't treat the YouTube staff as a means to an end; just try to be genuinely helpful. If you can't do this, it's best to just not bother them."

Week 2: Study the Most Discussed YouTube Live Highlights

Just as Revere participated in events like the Boston Tea Party to become a fully vested member of the Sons of Liberty, you should participate in events like YouTube Live to become a fully vested member of the YouTube community.

YouTube's first official live community celebration took place on November 22, 2008, at the Herbst Pavillion at the Fort Mason Center in San Francisco. Part concert, part variety show, and part party, the event brought to life many of the amazing videos and talent that YouTube viewers had already made popular.

As a sponsor for the event, Flip Video gave away a free Flip Video Mino to all of the audience members to record any of YouTube Live. A station to upload videos to YouTube from the Mino was also provided, promoted, and sponsored by Flip.

As Figure 7.12 illustrates, the event was also streamed live on YouTube at the same time, enabling millions from around the globe to partake in the festivities.

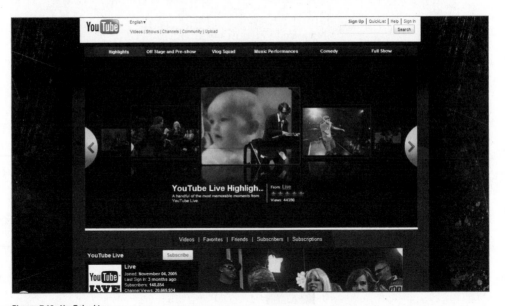

Figure 7.12 YouTube Live

On November 23, 2008, the second YouTube Live was held in Tokyo, Japan. The next two annual events will take place in late 2009 and late 2010.

Although YouTube users have been gathering informally for years, YouTube Live '08 was the first time that the YouTube community leaped off the screen and onto a stage. Since you are interested in how to become a fully vested member of this community, let's study the most discussed YouTube Live highlights to see who are already fully vested members and hear their backstories.

There were 30 special guests and performers at YouTube Live '08, including Will.i.am, Esmee Denters, Fred, Soulja Boy, and Tay Zonday. Since they were profiled in Chapter 5, let's profile five others: Katy Perry (the opening act), Joe Satriani and Funtwo, MythBusters, Bo Burnham, and Akon (the closing act).

Videos of their performances are among the top 10 most viewed and most discussed from YouTube Live '08.

Monday: Check out Katy Perry

Tuesday: Listen to Bo Burnham

Wednesday: Rock with Joe Satriani and Funtwo

Thursday: Watch MythBusters

Friday: Examine Akon

Monday: Check Out Katy Perry

The opening act at YouTube Live '08 was Katy Perry, who performed her latest single "Hot N Cold." As Figure 7.13 illustrates, this had more than 5.4 million views as of April 2009, making it the most viewed video of the event.

Figure 7.13 "Katy Perry 'Hot N Cold' – YouTube Live '08"

If you look at the statistics and data, you'll see "Katy Perry 'Hot N Cold' - YouTube Live '08" was also the most discussed video, with over 20,000 text comments. With 231 video responses, it was also the #41 most responded video of all time in the music category as of April 2009.

As you study this video, check out how Perry engages her audience through shout-outs and comments and by reaching out to the man with the Flip Video Mino at 3:05. So, the right questions to ask are as follows:

Who Katy Perry was born Katheryn Elizabeth Hudson on October 25, 1984. She changed her surname to Perry, her mother's maiden name, because Katy Hudson was too close to Kate Hudson, the film actress.

What The three most viewed videos on CapitolMusic's channel are "Katy Perry - I Kissed a Girl (Official Video)" with more than 16.4 million views, "Katie Perry - Hot N Cold" with over 11.7 million views, and "Katy Perry - Ur So Gay" with almost 3.7 million views. They are also the three most discussed videos on the channel.

When You could say it all started in April 2008 when Madonna told Ryan Seacrest that Perry's "Ur So Gay" was her favorite song. "It may have been a small comment on her behalf, but it was a large comment in my world," Perry says on her official website.

Where Born in Santa Barbara, California, Perry is the middle child of two pastors. She grew up singing in church. Fans seem to respond to her approachable girl-next-door quality—if the girl next door is a self-described "glamour ninja"—because it's not an act.

Why Why does Perry think she's connected with a mass audience when the road to stardom is littered with failed wannabes? "Because I'm just myself," she says on her website, "and that's all people want. People want to hear artists who are themselves, but who do interesting things and sing about them in an interesting way that maybe they have tried to conceive but couldn't." She adds, "Plus, anybody can meet me. I'm not distant. I'm very much the same person I was before the hit singles. I just have a schedule for breakfast, lunch, and dinner."

How Perry's song "I Kissed a Girl" reached #1 in the United States as well as in 20 countries across the globe. A hit in its own right, the song became a YouTube sensation by spawning hundreds of parody videos created by users around the world.

Tuesday: Listen to Bo Burnham

Introduced by Perry, Bo Burnham performed his new song "Welcome to YouTube" on YouTube Live '08. As Figure 7.14 illustrates, this had over 1.7 million views as of April 2009, making it the second most-viewed video of the event.

If you look at the statistics and data, you'll see that "Bo Burnham 'Welcome to YouTube' performed on YouTube Live '08" was also the second most discussed video, with more than 9,800 text comments.

Figure 7.14 "Bo Burnham 'Welcome to YouTube' performed on YouTube Live '08"

As you study this video, listen to how Burnham encourages comments by making unpredictable but not unexpected remarks. The right questions to ask are as follows:

Who Bo Burnham was born Robert Burnham in August 1990.

What The 17 videos on boburnham's channel had over 43.4 million views as of April 2009, making it the #20 most viewed of all time in the Comedians category. The channel also had more than 210,000 subscribers, making it the #28 most subscribed of all time. His most viewed video is "I'm bo yo." with over 8.2 million views. It's also the most discussed video, more than 30,000 text comments.

When According to Burnham, 2006 was the beginning of what would become his musical comedy career. Rehearsing a play at an all-boys' Catholic high school that summer, he began writing songs about teenage angst and playing them to his fellow thespians. He then videotaped himself performing two songs and posted them to YouTube in December so his older brother Pete could watch them from college.

Where All of Burnham's home-released videos are self-recorded in and around his family's home in Hamilton, Massachusetts, most in his bedroom. He rarely changes camera angles while performing—simply setting the video camera on a stack of books.

Why One of YouTube's most talented young performers, Bo's original and craftily worded songs are funny, but they also make you think. The 19-year-old comedian has also released a best-selling EP, taped an upcoming HBO comedy special, and signed a deal to write a feature-length movie musical for producer Judd Apatow. Another reason why "Welcome to YouTube" generated so many comments as well as views on Live's channel was because it was the world premiere of a new song in a medium that values originality and freshness, with just a dash of self-deprecating humor.

How While response to his first two videos on YouTube, "My Whole Family..." and "My 'little secret...'", was initially unexceptional, they became an overnight sensation when they were copied to Break.com, with traffic to his videos multiplying over 111 times.

Wednesday: Rock with Joe Satriani and Funtwo

Freddie Wong, who first gained notoriety through a video he posted on YouTube titled "Guitar Hero 2 Rush YYZ on Expert," played *Guitar Hero* before two real guitar heroes, guitar legend Joe Satriani and "Canon Rock" virtuoso Funtwo, rocked out at YouTube Live '08 (Figure 7.15). "Guitar Hero–Joe Satriani & Funtwo–YouTube Live" was the third most viewed video of the event, with over 1.5 million views as of April 2009.

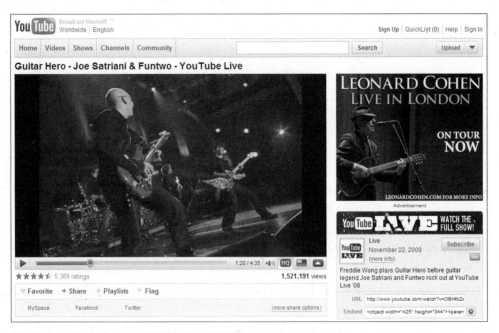

Figure 7.15 "Guitar Hero - Joe Satriani & Funtwo - YouTube Live"

If you look at the statistics and data, you'll see that "Guitar Hero - Joe Satriani & Funtwo - YouTube Live" was also the third most discussed video, with more than 7,300 text comments. It also had 66 video responses.

As you study this video, scroll down to see that it has more than 70 video responses. It seems that the Guitar Hero "cultural phenomenon" inspires others to rock with the legend and virtuoso. So, the right questions to ask are as follows:

Who Joseph "Satch" Satriani was born July 15, 1956. Lim Jeong-hyun, also known by the online alias funtwo, was born July 5, 1984.

What Satriani has 15 Grammy Award nominations, the most of any artist without winning. In addition to his own material, he has recorded and toured with acts such as Mick Jagger, Deep Purple, Alice Cooper, and Spinal Tap. Lim played and recorded his cover of "Canon Rock" during 2005. He uploaded his video to a Korean music site, Mule.co.kr. It was then uploaded to YouTube by a viewer nicknamed guitar90, under the title "guitar." As the video gained in popularity, viewers speculated on who was beneath the baseball cap. As of April 2009, the video was the #20 most viewed video of all time on YouTube with over 58.5 million views, the #10 most discussed video of all time with over 266,000 text comments, the #13 most responded video of all time with over 2,000 video responses, and the #6 top favorited video of all time.

When In 1988, Satriani was recruited by Paul McCartney of The Beatles as lead guitarist for Lennon's second solo tour. On August 27, 2006, Virginia Heffernan of the *New York Times* identified Lim as the real funtwo in an article entitled "Web Guitar Wizard Revealed at Last."

Where Satriani was born in Westbury, New York and now resides in the Bay Area. Lim was born in Seoul, Korea.

Why YouTube is a haven for aspiring guitar aficionados hoping to glean techniques from the masters. Few can rival Satriani's skill, but millions continue to try as videos of the guitar legend rank among the site's most popular and most commented.

How "Someone else called guitar90...grabbed the video and put it on YouTube where it became a sensation," Lim said in a TV interview.

Thursday: Watch MythBusters

Next, Adam Savage of Discovery Channel's *MythBusters* blasted Jamie Hyneman with 20,000 paintballs using Leonardo 2.0 at YouTube Live. Shown in Figure 7.16, this was the #7 most viewed video of the event, with over 1.1 million views as of April 2009.

If you look at the statistics and data, you'll see "MythBusters YouTube Live" was also the #6 most discussed video of YouTube Live, with more than 2,600 text comments. And it had 59 video responses, making it the #22 most responded video of all time in the Science & Technology category.

Figure 7.16 "MythBusters YouTube Live"

As you study this video, watch how Savage and Hyneman promote the giant robot they designed to shoot paint at a canvas. So, here are the right questions to ask:

Who Adam Whitney Savage was born July 15, 1967. James Earl "Jamie" Hyneman was born September 25, 1956.

What *MythBusters* is a popular science television program produced by Australian Peter Rees of Beyond Television Productions for the Discovery Channel in the United States and Canada. Its most viewed video on DiscoveryNetworks's channel on YouTube is "MythBusters - Ask a Ninja!" with close to 1.7 million views.

When Initial pilots for the show were first created by Rees in 2002 for the Discovery Channel under the title *Tall Tales or True*. Discovery then commissioned three additional pilot specials. Hyneman came to the show through Rees, who had previously worked with him on *BattleBots*. Savage was asked to cohost the show by Hyneman, who had previously worked with him in commercials.

Where Savage was born in New York City and was raised in Sleepy Hollow, New York. Hyneman was born in Marshall, Michigan, but raised in Columbus, Indiana. Filming for *MythBusters* is based in San Francisco, though some elements of production are done in Artarmon, Australia.

Why The series stars special effects experts Savage and Hyneman, who use basic elements of the scientific method to test the validity of various rumors, urban legends, myths, movie scenes, and news stories in popular culture. Hyneman plays the straight man and Savage is the comic relief.

How In August 2008, Hyneman and Savage demonstrated the power of the graphics procession unit versus a central processing unit at an event sponsored by NVIDIA. They did this by creating an image of the Mona Lisa with a giant parallel processing paintball gun. An encore of the demo was given at YouTube Live '08 featuring Hyneman standing in the path of the paintballs wearing a suit of armor.

Friday: Examine Akon

Finally, Akon's music medley of "I'm So Paid" and "Right Now" was the closing act on YouTube Live '08. Shown in Figure 7.17, this was the #10 most viewed video of the event, with over 668,000 views as of April 2009.

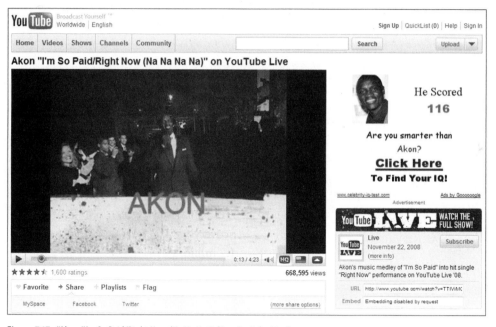

Figure 7.17 "Akon 'I'm So Paid/Right Now (Na Na Na Na)' on YouTube Live"

If you look at the statistics and data, you'll see "Akon 'I'm So Paid/Right Now (Na Na Na Na)' on YouTube Live" was also the #7 most discussed video, with more than 2,400 text comments. It also had 25 video responses.

As you study this video, examine how Akon enters through the audience, shakes hands with people, and encourages them "to make some noise out there" before he goes stage diving and crowd surfing. The right questions to ask are as follows:

Who Aliaune Damala Bouga Time Puru Nacka Lu Lu Lu Badara Akon Thiam was born April 30, 1973. His stage name is Akon.

What "Akon - 'Don't Matter'" had more than 64 million views as of April 2009, making it the #14 most viewed YouTube Video of all time.

When Akon began writing and recording tracks in his home studio. The tapes found their way to SRC/Universal, which released Akon's debut LP *Trouble* in June 2004. He rose to prominence following the release of "Locked Up," the first single from his debut album.

Where Akon was born in St. Louis, Missouri, and moved between America and Senegal until he was 15; then he moved to Jersey City, New Jersey.

Why On April 16, 2008, an article in the Smoking Gun entitled "Akon's Con Job" said, "Akon's ad nauseum claims about his criminal career and resulting prison time have been, to an overwhelming extent, exaggerated, embellished, or wholly fabricated, an investigation by The Smoking Gun has revealed. Police, court, and corrections records reveal that the entertainer has created a fictionalized backstory that serves as the narrative anchor for his recorded tales of isolation, violence, woe, and regret. Akon has overdubbed his biography with the kind of grit and menace that he apparently believes music consumers desire from their hip-hop stars." On May 16, 2008, Akon told Chris Harris of MTV News, "It's not something I was trying to glorify or turn back to. It was something I was trying to forget."

How Akon's unique blend of West African style and his skills, and moves caught the ears of executives at SRC/Universal.

As all five of these backstories indicate, these fully vested members of the YouTube community have talent, but each one got their big break with a little help from someone else. Is this just a coincidence, or is this the way that diffusion networks work? Or, to ask a related question, do opinion leaders matter?

And at a live event, all five demonstrated that they know how to engage the YouTube community.

Week 3: Add YouTube to Your Site and Share Videos

This week, you'll find out why you should add YouTube videos to your website, blog, or social network page. You'll also find out why you should share videos with your friends and colleagues.

The reasons are as straightforward as the routes of the British Expedition and the Patriot Messengers on April 18 and 19, 1775. As Figure 7.18 illustrates, these routes were relatively straightforward, at least for colonial New England.

You should add YouTube to your site and share videos because you want to be more like Revere and less like Dawes. In his book *The Tipping Point: How Little Things Can Make a Big Difference* (Back Bay Books, 2002), Malcolm Gladwell compares the two alarm riders.

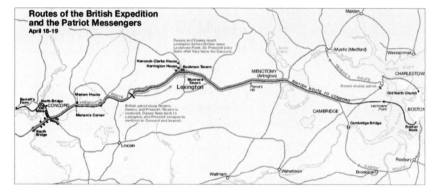

Figure 7.18 Routes of the British Expedition and the Patriot Messengers (Source: nps.gov)

Revere was able to galvanize the colonial minutemen so effectively in part because he was what Gladwell calls a "Connector." Revere was "the man with the biggest Rolodex in colonial Boston." He knew just about everybody, particularly the revolutionary leaders in each of the towns that he rode through.

In contrast, Gladwell calls Dawes an "ordinary man." He wasn't a "maven" who gathered extensive information about the British, he didn't know what was going on, and he didn't know exactly whom to tell.

This analogy also explains why you need to network socially beyond the larger community like Boston (or YouTube) and into the smaller villages like Waltham (or MySpace). If you're ever called upon to knock on doors (or promote videos) in the middle of the night (or on short notice), you want to rally your neighbors (or potential viewers) to take action; you don't want them to simply turn over and go back to sleep.

So, whatever presence you have on the Internet—a large website, a blog, or a social network page—you should find a way to integrate YouTube into it. You should also use email marketing best practices to send truly personal notes to your friends and colleagues notifying them when you have posted new videos that they might want to watch and share.

Monday: Add videos to your blog or website

Tuesday: Add videos to your social network page

Wednesday: Add videos to your eBay auction

Thursday: Use email marketing best practices

Friday: Read social media marketing tips

Monday: Add Videos to Your Blog or Website

Entrepreneur: "How do you add a video to your blog or web page?'

Well, you'll need to edit the HTML of your blog entry or page—this should be relatively straightforward. In Blogger, for example, just click the Edit HTML tab.

Next, go to the video that you want, and look for the Embed box in the About This Video section. Copying the HTML code that's there into your website will create an embedded player. The video will play within your site when the user clicks the Play button.

You can resize the player by editing the object `width="425"` and `height="350"` fields at both the beginning and end of the embedded player code. Make sure the sizes you choose have the same ratio as the default numbers so the video doesn't get stretched—just multiply the width by 0.8235 to get the height.

O'Farrell adds that you can customize things like color and autoplay by editing the code. Or, you can use "wizards" that edit the code for you, like the YouTube Embed Code Customizer (`http://screencastprofits.com/youtube`).

YouTube Director: "Should I add a playlist to my blog or web page?"

If you want to show a selection of videos, then embed a playlist. When you update the playlist on YouTube, the playlist on your site will update as well. This is a good way of creating longer stories through a series of videos or simply giving your readers more preselected content to watch.

Another way to embed a playlist is to create a custom player. Go to your YouTube account and click Custom Video Players, then Create Custom Player. Select a color and format for your player, and then choose what is going to play in it—you can choose a playlist, your own uploaded content, or your favorites—and then click the Generate Code button.

Copy and paste the code into your blog entry or web page, just as you did with the embedded video earlier.

Search Engine Marketer: "I work for a large blog. How can video increase user engagement on our site?"

Video is much more engaging than text. It draws more users and keeps them on your site for longer. YouTube has a large repository of Internet video content along with the search, playback, and API tools to make adding video easier for you. It's also a good way to get other sites to create relevant links to yours.

When looking to increase engagement, try using video as a way to start discussion or get links by creating more context for your users. PerezHilton.com, "Hollywood's most hated website," frequently embeds YouTube videos to generate comments and inbound links (Figure 7.19).

YouTube Director: "How do I post videos on our site using YouTube?"

All you need to do is upload the videos to YouTube first. There's no charge and YouTube will cover hosting and streaming costs. It's not only a great way to increase user engagement on your site, it's also very easy, and free as well.

Figure 7.19 *"Twilight - with Cheeseburgers!"*

Once you've uploaded the videos to YouTube, you can pull them back to your site dynamically by creating a feed of your most recently uploaded videos. You can export feeds of your most recently uploaded videos, your favorites, and playlists. So if you want to be able to choose which videos the feed displays on your site easily, you can just favorite them on your YouTube channel or add them to a playlist.

Search Engine Marketer: "Can visitors search YouTube videos from my website?"

You can use the YouTube application programming interfaces (APIs) to let users search YouTube directly from your site, pulling up results that can viewed without having to go to YouTube. Using APIs in combination, you can limit searches by category, tag, or user. You can also control the number of results returned and whether they're ranked by number of views or the relevance.

For example, if you have content on your own YouTube channel, you can build an application that allows users to search only through your own videos and then watch them without leaving your site. For more information (Figure 7.20), go to `http://code.google.com/apis/youtube/overview.html`.

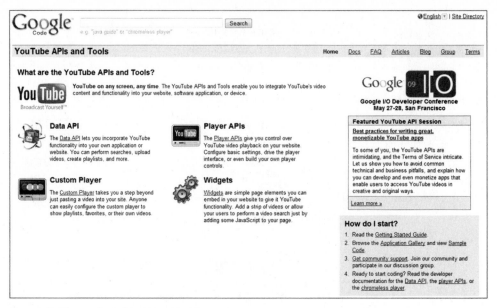

Figure 7.20 What are the YouTube APIs and Tools?

Entrepreneur: "How can I make money with embedded videos?"

If you have an AdSense account, you can add video units to your site. Video units are embedded, customizable video players featuring content from categories, individual content providers, or automatic keyword-based targeting. Here's how to set up your player, assuming you've already signed up for AdSense and linked your accounts (`https://www.google.com/adsense/login/en_US`):

1. Go to `www.youtube.com/adsense_learn`, fill out the information required, and choose the theme and layout.

2. Choose the content options. If you choose Automated Content, Google will fill the player with videos based on the content of your site. You can add keywords to target further.

3. Click the Generate Code button to get your HTML code and save the player.

4. Copy the code from the Embed Code section and paste it into your website or blog where you would like the player to appear.

Tuesday: Add Videos to Your Social Network Page

If you have one, you should also add videos to your social network page.

Adding videos to your profiles on social networks like MySpace and Facebook is a great way to share your videos or favorites with friends. Or, if you're promoting something like your band on MySpace, videos will help attract visitors to your page, who can then share the link with their friends. The social network sites have similar ways to add videos, so I'll use MySpace as an example.

Sign in to your MySpace profile and then click the Edit Profile button.

Next, go to the video that you want, and look for the Embed box in the About This Video section. Copying the HTML code that's there into your social network page will create an embedded player.

As you've just learned, you can resize the player by editing the object width="425" and height="350" fields at both the beginning and end of the embedded player code. Once again, make sure the sizes you choose have the same ratio as the default numbers so the video doesn't get stretched—just multiply the width by 0.8235 to get the height.

Click Preview, and then Submit.

YouTube also has an official presence on Facebook and Twitter. As Figure 7.21 illustrates, you can sign up for these groups to receive the latest company news, product updates, and hot video alerts.

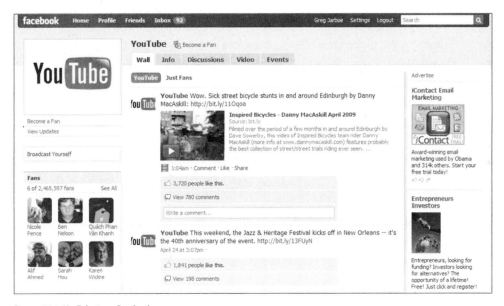

Figure 7.21 YouTube is on Facebook

Here's how to become a YouTube Facebook fan:

1. Create a Facebook account (www.facebook.com) if you have not already.

2. Sign in to your account.

3. Go to www.facebook.com/youtube.

4. Once you are on the YouTube page, you will see the option Become a Fan in the upper-right corner of the page. Click it to join.

Here's how to become a YouTube Twitter follower:

1. Create a Twitter account (http://twitter.com) if you have not already.

2. Sign in to your account.

3.   Go to http://twitter.com/youtube.

4.   Click the Follow button under the YouTube logo to start getting tweets every day.

Wednesday: Add Videos to Your eBay Auction

You can even add videos to an eBay auction.

Filming an item to post on eBay is perfect for creating extra interest, especially for more expensive objects where the buyer will want to know more about the item before bidding. Here's how to do it:

1.   Film your item. How you do this is up to you. Then upload the video to your YouTube account in the normal way.

2.   Sign in to eBay, click Sell, and select Advanced Sell.

3.   Choose a category and move on to the Create Your Listing page.

4.   When you get to the Describe the Item You're Listing area, click the HTML tab.

5.   Go to your video on YouTube.com, and copy the embed code from the gray box to the right of the video player. Paste this into the HTML box in the eBay listing. You should still add all the text for your eBay posting as normal.

6.   As I mentioned earlier, you can resize the player by editing the object width="425" and height="350" fields at both the beginning and end of the embedded player code. Once again, make sure the sizes you choose have the same ratio as the default numbers so the video doesn't get stretched—just multiply the width by 0.8235 to get the height.

7.   Complete the posting as usual.

Davd Nehrig started using YouTube videos in some of his eBay auctions back in late 2007. As Figure 7.22 illustrates, Nehrig, who is also known as 720sports, said:

> *I started using video primarily because I find some of our items extremely difficult to photograph, and even if you can get a good pic of the item, it's difficult to describe what it does or how it works. Take snowboard bags for instance. Very difficult to photograph to begin with. But how do you show all the pockets, compartments and features of the bag? With video you can physically demonstrate how it works and what sets it apart from other like items. On top of that you've truly put a face, a voice and a personality with your company. I think it makes buyers feel a bit more at ease seeing a live person on the other end. You become a virtual salesperson. So hows it working you ask? VERY well. We've seen a dramatic increase in sales of items with video vs a side by side listing of the same item without video. We absolutely plan on using more video and I think it's a trend you'll see more often.*

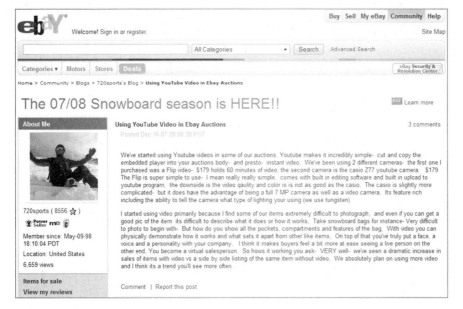

Figure 7.22 The 07/08 Snowboard season is HERE!!

Thursday: Use Email Marketing Best Practices

You should also use email marketing best practices to notify your friends and colleagues—or people you've interacted with—when you have posted new videos specifically of interest to them.

Now, email isn't the latest and greatest social media marketing tool or channel. But it still works. Or at least it can work if you use the best practices described by Seth Godin is his classic book *Permission Marketing: Turning Strangers into Friends and Friends into Customers* (Simon & Schuster, 1999).

In Chapter 4, I mentioned that "The Big Switch by Nicholas Carr" was the most viewed video on SESConferenceExpo's channel. I also pointed out that more than half of the views came from the embedded player. And many of the views from this source had come from Nicholas Carr's blog, Rough Type.

What I didn't mention was how the video ended up in Rough Type. We uploaded the video to YouTube on February 4, 2008. Then I sent a personal email to Carr, who happens to be a neighbor, letting him know that our video interview was now on YouTube. On February 7, he embedded the video in a post entitled, "lonelyauthor15."

He wrote, "We all deserve our four minutes of YouTube fame, and mine arrives today with this video, in which I discuss some of the themes of *The Big Switch* with Greg Jarboe of Search Engine Strategies." He added, "Now that I've boiled the book down for YouTube, my next challenge will be to Twitter it."

What was the secret ingredient in this success story? I sent him an email.

But wait! There's more!

Let's look at the second most viewed video on SESConferenceExpo's channel. It's entitled "Matt Cutts, Google, discusses mobile search at SES San Jose 2008." It was uploaded on November 18, 2008, and had more than 4,000 views as of April 2009.

Views of the video spiked on December 3, 2008—more than two weeks after it was uploaded. And the source of over 79 percent of the total views came from the embedded player. And 55 percent came from Matt Cutts: Gadgets, Google and SEO. As Figure 7.23 illustrates, that's his blog.

Figure 7.23 SES San Jose video interview

In his post, Cutts writes, "Another day, another video interview. This one was with Greg Jarboe at SES San Jose. You can watch it on the Search Engine Strategies channel on YouTube, or I'll embed it below."

What's the backstory? Around Thanksgiving, we sent Cutts an email.

Friday: Read Social Media Marketing Tips

Of course, YouTube provides a number of Share options beyond email. As of April 2009, there were eight buttons under the Share options:

MySpace Founded in 2003, MySpace is a social networking website owned by Fox Interactive Media, which is owned by News Corp. We explored MySpace in Chapter 3. According to Compete, MySpace.com had close to 56 million unique visitors in the United States in March 2009, down more than 11 percent from the previous year.

Facebook Founded in 2004, Facebook is a social networking website that is privately owned. Users can add friends and send them messages and update their personal profiles. According to Compete, Facebook.com had more than 91 million unique visitors in the United States in March 2009, up 195 percent over the previous year.

Twitter Founded in 2006, Twitter is a social networking and micro-blogging service that enables users to send and read text-based posts of up to 140 characters in length that are known as tweets. According to Compete, Twitter.com had more than 14 million unique visitors in the United States in March 2009, up 1,200 percent over the previous year.

Digg Founded in 2004, Digg is a social news website. Users submit links and stories, and voting stories up and down, called digging and burying, is the site's cornerstone function. According to Compete, Digg.com had more than 36 million unique visitors in the United States in March 2009, up 71 percent over the previous year.

Orkut Launched in 2004, Orkut is a social networking service that is run by Google. The majority of its users are in Brazil and India. According to Compete, Orkut.com had only 502,000 unique visitors in the United States in March 2009, up 13 percent over the previous year.

Live Spaces Released in 2004, Windows Live Spaces is Microsoft's blogging and social networking platform. According to Compete, Spaces.live.com had more than 3.3 million unique visitors in the United States in March 2009, down over 30 percent from the previous year.

Bebo Founded in 2005, Bebo is a social networking website. It was bought by AOL on March 13, 2008, for $850 million. According to Compete, Bebo.com had close to 4.7 million unique visitors in the United States in March 2009, up 34 percent over the previous year.

Hi5 Launched in 2003, Hi5 is a social networking website. According to Compete, Hi5.com had more than 2.7 million unique visitors in the United States in March 2009, up 17 percent over the previous year.

This list of Share options has changed over the years and is likely to continue to change as the relative popularity of different social media shifts.

It would take a whole other book to teach you how to prepare, launch, and measure a social media marketing campaign to cross-promote your video content. Fortunately, as Figure 7.24 illustrates, there is such a book: *Social Media Marketing: An Hour a Day* by Dave Evans (Sybex, 2008).

Evans is an expert in social media marketing. He cofounded Digital Voodoo in 1994 and has developed interactive communication programs for Southwest Airlines, Meredith Publishing, and many other clients. In 2005, he cofounded HearThis.com, a podcasting service firm focused on social media and marketing. He is a ClickZ columnist and a frequent conference speaker and has served on the advisory board for ad:tech as well as the Measurement and Metrics Council for the Word of Mouth Marketing Association (WOMMA).

Figure 7.24 *Social Media Marketing: An Hour A Day*

Social Media Marketing: An Hour a Day is a practical, hands-on guide to implementing and measuring social media as part of an integrated marketing program. It will introduce you to the basics, demonstrate how to manage details, and describe how you can track results. In addition, it will teach you how to leverage blogs, MySpace, Facebook, and Twitter as well as YouTube.

Since the book is 432 pages long, you can't read it all in an hour today. So, go to

www.toprankblog.com/2009/04/social-media-marketing-tips/

and read Lee Odden's post on April 27, 2009, entitled "25 Must Read Social Marketing Tips," in the Online Marketing Blog. That you can read in an hour.

Odden asks a mix of in-house social media marketers as well as social media marketing consultants and agencies to provide specific advice about justifying investment in social media, strategy, tactics, and measuring success. For example, Nick Ayres, the interactive marketing manager of The Home Depot, says this:

> *You really have to start with who your customers are and what their expectations and desires are from you in the space. Based on what you learn, you can much more easily lay out your objectives, strategies and tactics to meet those wants and needs. If you aren't already doing so, one of the first things you need to do before even thinking about a tactic is to just start listening to what's already being said about you. Whether it's on blogs or on Twitter or in existing online communities—wherever your customers are already talking about your brand—you can learn a lot by just paying attention to what's already being said.*

> *If you look at what we've done with Twitter or with our video syndication efforts—posting our how-to videos on YouTube and other video sites—we've had the most success when we've approached the spaces from (our customers and their expectations) rather than a "hey this is cool so let's do it" mindset.*

Week 4: Learn the Latest Lessons of Viral Marketing

This brings us to five of the latest lessons of viral marketing, which is also called social media marketing, buzz marketing, and word-of-mouth advertising.

Although YouTube's slogan, "Broadcast Yourself," makes it sound like a television network, YouTube acts like a video sharing site. And video marketing has weaker links to mass marketing and broadcast advertising and stronger links to viral marketing and word-of-mouth advertising. That's why the central element of the social media and video sharing process isn't "noise." It's "community."

The mass media model defines "noise" as "static or distortion." The social media model sees "community" as a communication network of interconnected individuals who are linked by patterned flows of information. Although there are unplanned aspects of the communication process in both models, the key to understanding how communication flows through these interpersonal networks, according to Rogers, is analyzing "who relays messages to whom."

Perhaps the best example of this can be seen when Revere and Dawes relayed their message to Prescott at 1 a.m. on April 19, 1775.

Dr. Warren in Boston had dispatched Revere and Dawes as alarm riders to warn Hancock and Adams in Lexington that the British army was coming to arrest them and then march on Concord to seize the patriots' store of arms. So, the "sender" and "receivers" in this model of the communication process are clear.

But Prescott was on the road at that hour after an evening with his fiancée, Lydia Mulliken. He joined Revere and Dawes on their ride from Lexington to Concord. And the key is that Prescott joined them as an unplanned alarm rider.

When the three had arrived near Hartwell's tavern in the lower bounds of Lincoln, they were attacked by four British officers of a scouting party. Revere and Dawes were taken prisoner. Prescott had the reins of his horse's bridle cut but succeeded in making his escape by jumping his horse over a wall. Taking a circuitous route through Lincoln, he pushed on with the utmost speed to Concord. He was the only one of the three men to reach Concord and warn the town.

Prescott then proceeded further west to warn Acton. Although his midnight ride to this community was unplanned, I wouldn't call Prescott's alarm "noise." As Figure 7.25 illustrates, he reached Captain Davis in time to muster the Acton Minutemen, march to Concord, and engage the British army at the "rude bridge that arched the flood." In Acton, Prescott's ride is reenacted on Patriots Day eve.

Monday: Watch Susan Boyle go viral

Tuesday: Observe "Twouble with Twitter"

Wednesday: Don't look at "Disgusting Dominos People"

Thursday: Keep an eye on Hulu Tube

Friday: See Magical Trevor

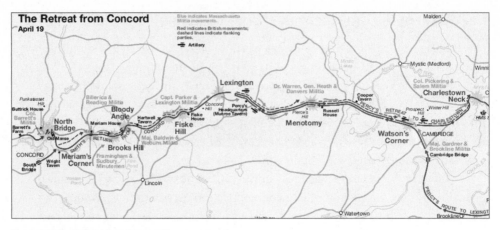

Figure 7.25 The Retreat from Concord (Source nps.gov)

Monday: Watch Susan Boyle Go Viral

One of the latest lessons of viral marketing was the unplanned "noise" created by Susan Boyle, age 47, of Blackburn, Scotland. Her appearance on *Britain's Got Talent* and a clip of her performance on YouTube set off a frenzy of attention.

The Viral Video Chart compiled by Unruly Media on April 30, 2009, showed that the video "Susan Boyle Stuns Crowd with Epic Singing" was the top viral video of the previous 365 days with more than 125 million views.

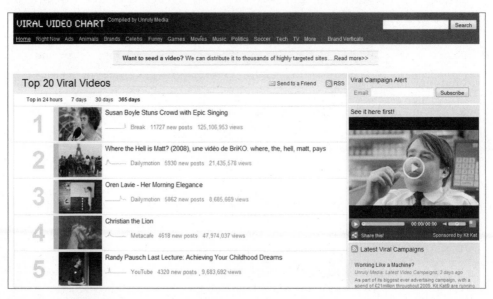

Figure 7.26 Top 20 Viral Videos

As Figure 7.27 illustrates, the video was discovered on April 11, 2009, and blog posts about it probably peaked a week later. As the number of blog posts declined, the video was also being shared less often. Nevertheless, the 165 duplicate videos of Susan Boyle had already generated close to 12,000 blog posts and over 435,000 comments in less than three weeks.

Figure 7.27 "Susan Boyle Stuns Crowd with Epic Singing"

On April 20, 2009, Maria Puente wrote an article in *USA Today* entitled "Why Susan Boyle inspires us: A story like 'a Disney movie.'" She asked, "After a week of unabashed hysteria about Scottish chanteuse Susan Boyle, it's time to pause and ask: What's *that* all about?"

Maybe it was the compelling content of the video: The 47-year-old Boyle, who Puente calls "unglamorous, unfashionable, unknown," takes on a skeptical British audience and sneering panel of judges on *Britain's Got Talent*, including the unsparingly blunt Simon Cowell. "Then, in an instant, she turned jeers to cheers with her rendition of one of the weepier numbers from *Les Misérables*," wrote Puente.

Maybe it's Boyle's Cinderella backstory: "Youngest of nine, learning disabled and bullied as a child, caretaker for her dying mother, never been kissed, singer in the choir, possessor of big dreams," she wrote.

Maybe it's because people tend to root for the underdog. "Or maybe it's just a new reminder of an old truism: You can't judge a book by its cover," Puente concluded.

I think I've discovered the Prescotts that helped a middle-aged woman with frizzy hair from a Scottish village outside Edinburgh go viral. According to TweetStats (http://tweetstats.com/trends), a service that monitors recurring terms on Twitter, the phrase "Susan Boyle" became one of the top Tweets around April 15, 2009, and has gone on to become one of the top 50 trends of all time—behind Sarah Palin but ahead of American Idol.

Now, I recognize that I'm using circumstantial evidence, but this isn't a criminal case. The video was uploaded to YouTube on April 11, but according to the Viral Video Chart didn't take off until April 15. On April 15, tweets about "Susan Boyle" spiked. IceRocket's trend tool (http://trend.icerocket.com) shows that mentions of "Susan Boyle" in blogs didn't spike until April 16. I rest my case.

Tuesday: Observe "Twouble with Twitter"

Let's observe another video that made it to the Viral Video Chart compiled by Unruly Media. As Figure 7.28 illustrates, "'Twouble with Twitter' sous-titré" had become one of the top 20 viral videos of the previous 30 days with more than 1.5 million views as of April 11, 2009.

Figure 7.28 "'Twouble with Twitter' sous-titré"

The video was discovered on March 17, 2009, and blog posts about it peaked a week later, dropped, and then rebounded again around April Fools' Day. As the number of blog posts went up and down, viral sharing of the video followed. Still, the 13 duplicate videos of "Twouble with Twitter" generated close to 1,500 blog posts and over 4,300 comments in less than a month.

The version of this video with the most views was "Twouble with Twitters: SuperNews!" As Figure 7.29 illustrates, it had more than 1.4 million views, which was about 94 percent of the total views as of April 11, 2009.

In the video, a young man struggles against peer pressure to Twitter his life away. The video was a sneak preview of *SuperNews*, an animated sketch comedy series on Current TV. *SuperNews*, which is intended for an adult audience, is full of political humor and popular culture satire.

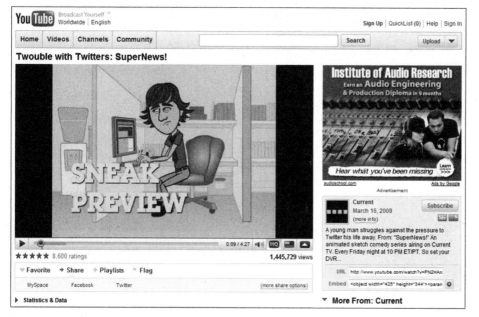

Figure 7.29 "Twouble with Twitters: SuperNews!"

It's worth noting that Al Gore serves as cofounder and chairman of the board of Current, a cross-platform media company that creates and distributes a variety of content. Current's channel on YouTube says "it's like a mini-mall for your mind...."

According to the statistics and data for the video, it had 8,600 ratings, was favorited more than 17,100 times, and generated more than 4,100 text comments and more than 130 video responses as of April 11, 2009. The video also had 17 honors, including being the #60 most responded video that month, #21 most viewed that month, #12 top favorited that month, and #100 top rated that month.

Who played Prescott in this story? On March 23, LambdaFilms, "a 23 year-old dude from Norwich, Norfolk (UK) who joined Digg on March 3rd, 2009," posted "'Twouble with Twitter' - Hilarious Animation" to Digg, saying, "Even though I'm a big fan of Twitter, this is so damn funny. Please digg and shout." It had over 3,400 Diggs when I read and blogged about it on April 1.

It was also one of the featured videos on the front page of YouTube. Which came first, the feature or the Digg?

Wednesday: Don't Look at "Disgusting Dominos People"

Someday, you may be called upon to prevent a video from going viral. That's virtually impossible to do. It would be like Dr. Warren asking Revere and Dawes to stop the British from marching out of Boston.

What you *can* do is respond more rapidly than Domino's Pizza did when a couple of rogue employees at a North Carolina franchise did disgusting things with food and uploaded a video to YouTube on April 13, 2009.

As Figure 7.30 illustrates, four duplicate videos of "Disgusting Dominos People" had received more than 1.3 million views and had generated over 300 blog posts and 8,500 comments by April 17. And viral sharing of this video was still increasing fast and it was getting more popular.

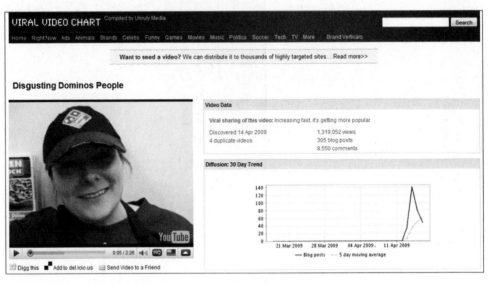

Figure 7.30 "Disgusting Dominos People"

On April 20, Nicole Zerillo of *PRWeek* wrote a front page story entitled, "Crisis forces Domino's to revamp social media plan." She wrote, "Though it announced almost immediately that the employees were fired, Domino's faced criticism that it responded too slowly in the broader online community. A statement on the incident appeared on its corporate site almost a day after the company became aware of the videos, while a video apology from its president went up on YouTube two days later."

As Figure 7.31 illustrates, the video featured company president Patrick Doyle, who responded to the video of (now former) Domino's team members.

Zerillo added, "Strategically, the company initially sought to 'contain' the issue by reaching out solely to audiences who were already aware of the videos." This included GoodAsYou.org, which initially alerted Domino's to the video on the afternoon of April 13, as well as the Consumerist, which also posted news of the incident that day. So, bloggers played the Prescotts in this story.

However, on the night of April 14, the company decided to shift its strategy to include more online outreach, following the advice of its ad agency, Crispin Porter and Bogusky (CPB). Shortly thereafter, staffers began tweeting and leading people to the company's statement on its corporate site, which was also posted that night.

Figure 7.31 "Disgusting Dominos People - Domino's Responds"

The following day, Domino's also created its first corporate Twitter account (http://twitter.com/dpzinfo), pledging to "listen."

Thursday: Keep an Eye on Hulu Tube

As I mentioned earlier, members of the YouTube team are opinion leaders. But even their interpersonal relationships with the YouTube community "hang in a delicate balance."

For example, Shiva Rajaraman, product manager, and Sara Pollack, Entertainment marketing manager of the YouTube Team announced "a new destination for television shows and an improved destination for movies on YouTube" in a post to the YouTube Blog on April 16, 2009.

> To help you navigate through all this great content, we're introducing two new tabs to the YouTube masthead: the Shows tab allows you to browse shows by genre, network, title and popularity, while the Subscriptions tab will grant logged-in users one-click access to fresh content from their favorite creators.

As Figure 7.32 illustrates, one of the spotlight videos on the new Shows tab is "Outer Limits" from MGM Digital Media. The blurb reads, "There is nothing wrong with your YouTube player. Do not attempt to adjust the picture. We are controlling transmission." Apparently, not everyone laughed at the joke.

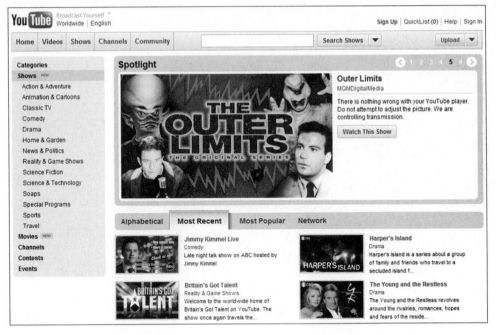

Figure 7.32 The Outer Limits

As of April 30, their post generated more than 400 comments—and Hulu was mentioned more than 100 times. Now, some of the comments were the kind of feedback that Rajaraman and Pollack had requested. But more than 40 of the comments repetitively read as follows:

- "Copy and paste if you agree that corporate companies like Disney and Hulu do not belong on YouTube."

- "Copy and paste if you want YouTube back to the way it was in 2006 / 2007."

These comments didn't communicate anyone's experience, talent, and expertise. They are comment spam. These are tactics Internet trolls would use.

This prompted joltguy, 33, from Canada to write, "Wow. I can't believe some of the complaining in these comments. This is an awesome addition to the site, and because it will be in its own tab you can completely ignore it if you wish. You can't realistically expect any company to just keep eating the cost of bandwidth that YouTube consumes. Gotta pay the bills somehow! Hopefully, Google will move faster on making the commercial content available outside the US than Hulu has. Hulu's been around since 2007 and they still haven't gotten around to it."

In this story, a potential Prescott decided not to join this group on their ride.

Meanwhile, therealweeklynews's channel uploaded a video on April 15, 2009, entitled "HULU TUBE - PHASING YOU OUT OF YOUTUBE." As Figure 7.33 illustrates, the video had more than 324,000 views as of April 30.

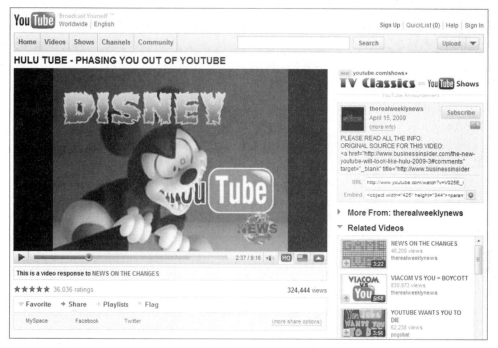

Figure 7.33 "HULU TUBE - PHASING YOU OUT OF YOUTUBE"

The first two-and-a-half minutes of the video attempt to rally the smaller channels on YouTube to fight changes that would cut their total views "in half if not more." The voice-over then asks, "Why is this being done? Because they're bringing on the big boys like Disney."

Now I understand the appeal of the little guy vs. big guy argument and I can see why "HULU TUBE - PHASING YOU OUT OF YOUTUBE" had these statistics:

- Received over 36,000 ratings, making it the #10 top rated that month

- Been favorited more than 18,600 times, making it the #16 top favorited that month

- Generated over 35,600 text comments, making it the #7 most discussed that month

- Generated more than 1,900 video responses, making it the #1 most responded that month and the #14 most responded of all time

But why single out Disney? YouTube had announced on March 31, 2009, that short-form content from the Disney/ABC Television Group, including ABC Entertainment, ABC News, ABC Family and SOAPnet, and ESPN was coming to YouTube. But does the YouTube community feel that threatened by clips of popular prime-time shows like *Lost*, *Desperate Housewives*, and *Grey's Anatomy*?

Or, is there a second explanation?

If you look at the statistics and data for "HULU TUBE - PHASING YOU OUT OF YOUTUBE," you'll see that three of the top five links to this video come from the same site: Alex Jones's www.Infowars.com. And a fourth of the top five links to the video is from Alex Jones's www.PrisonPlanet.com.

Jones is described in Wikipedia as "an American paleoconservative talk radio host, and filmmaker." It adds, "Various observers have referred to him as a conspiracy theorist."

Now, it's not fair to imply that just because "HULU TUBE - PHASING YOU OUT OF YOUTUBE" has three links from Infowars.com and one from PrisonPlanet. com that therealweeklynews is part of some "vast right-wing conspiracy," as Hillary Rodham Clinton would say.

What is fair to ask is, Why single out Disney when YouTube has struck numerous partnership deals with content providers such as CBS, BBC, Universal Music Group, Sony Music Group, NBA, and the Sundance Channel?

And asking the YouTube community to "Copy and paste if you agree that corporate companies like Disney and Hulu do not belong on YouTube" doesn't demonstrate a deep and abiding respect for the concept of community. It smells like "astroturfing," an artificial campaign that seeks to create the impression of being spontaneous.

Who knows what other forces are in play? But, it's worth noting that 7.4 percent more Americans watched 15.2 percent more videos on YouTube during April 2009 than the previous month. It's also worth noting that at least one of the initial protesters, proteanview, uploaded "HULU TUBE Retraction" (http://www.youtube.com/watch?v=ucnosAre1Jc) on April 28, 2009. He wrote in the description of his video, "I'm not too proud to self-correct." So, it appears that another potential Prescott decided to turn around and ride in the other direction.

Friday: See Magical Trevor

Let's conclude with one final lesson from our extended metaphor: Sometimes, it's hard to single out the key opinion leaders in a successful viral marketing campaign. On the night of April 18, 1775, as many as 40 riders carried news of the British expedition throughout Middlesex County from 11:00 p.m. to 9:30 a.m. the next morning. So, is it really fair to mention just three?

In March 2009, Yell, the international directories business, hired my firm to help launch stand-alone TV ads for its U.K. service, based on the signature tune of cult Internet cartoon character Magical Trevor.

Magical Trevor is the creation of animator Jonti Pickering, whose distinctive style and range of animated characters has developed a worldwide following on the Internet. The commercial was produced through Tomboy Films, which represents Jonti's work for commercials.

Yell's public relations department handled the traditional media relations and generated stories in *Marketing Week* and Mad.co.uk and in *Marketing.* The TV campaign, developed by creative communications agency Rapier, broke on March 20 and ran for a month, with two 10-second variants running for a further two months to the end of May across major terrestrial, satellite, and cable channels. It was supported by a 60-second variant on Yell118247's channel on YouTube (www.youtube.com/yell118247; the service's number is 118 24 7) and 40-second radio ads.

There was also a campaign page at www.118247.com where visitors could see the ads, download a ringtone of the theme tune, and participate in a fun poll gauging whether they love or hate the ad.

As Figure 7.34 illustrates, we embedded a YouTube video of the 30-second TV ad into an optimized press release, which was distributed on March 22. We also used PRWeb's TweetIt feature to automatically share the press release through Twitter at the same time it was distributed through PRWeb.

Figure 7.34 Yell Adopts 'Magical Trevor' for First Ever Stand-Alone TV Ads for UK Business Directory Enquiries Service 118 24 7

We also conducted a blog outreach and social media marketing campaign. On March 22, the YouTube video embedded in the press release was also embedded in the blogs Funkadelic Advertising, C64Glen, Welcome to my nightmare, and Your Face is an Advert , and it was embedded in the blog Scrambled eggs and mashed bananas on March 24.

On April 16, Camille Alarcon of *Marketing Week* wrote an article entitled "Yell extends 118 247 campaign following success." She said, "Yell, the international directories business, is extending the advertising campaign for its directory enquiries service 118 24 7, after recording a 70 percent increase in call volumes to its UK call centres."

As Figure 7.35 illustrates, "Yell 118 247 Directory Heaven TV ad by Weebl," the 30-second YouTube video embedded in the press release, tweeted about, and pitched to bloggers, had more than 220,000 views as of April 30, 2009.

Figure 7.35 "Yell 118 247 Directory Heaven TV ad by Weebl"

This 30-second video also had close to 1,200 ratings, was favorited more than 2,250 times, and had six video responses and over 1,300 text comments. It also had nine honors, among them these:

- #2 Most Discussed (This Month) - Film & Animation - United Kingdom
- #10 Most Viewed (This Month) - Film & Animation - United Kingdom
- #4 Top Favorited (This Month) - Film & Animation - United Kingdom
- #7 Top Rated (This Month) - Film & Animation - United Kingdom

As Figure 7.36 illustrates, "118 247 Directory Heaven 'EXTENDED VERSION' TV ad by Weebl," which was embedded in the campaign page at www.118247.com, had more than 29,600 views as of April 30, 2009.

This 60-second video also had only 247 ratings, was favorited just 528 times, and had no video responses and only 214 text comments. It also had four honors:

- #20 Most Discussed (This Month) - Film & Animation - United Kingdom;

- #22 Most Viewed (This Month) - Film & Animation - United Kingdom;

- #11 Top Favorited (This Month) - Film & Animation - United Kingdom;

- #31 Top Rated (This Month) - Film & Animation - United Kingdom.

Figure 7.36 "118 247 Directory Heaven 'EXTENDED VERSION' TV ad by Weebl"

Because there were a lot of riders carrying the news, the whole team deserves credit for the 70 percent increase in call volumes. But it appears that embedding the YouTube video in an optimized press release, using TweetIt, conducting blog outreach, and conducting the social media marketing campaign made a measurable contribution.

Month 6: Learn Video Production

8

It's easy to produce videos on YouTube; some people shoot first and ask questions later. They tell others, "I figure we can blue-screen the kids in later." For those who would rather ask questions first and shoot later, this chapter will help you learn the basics of video production, get video production tips, master video production techniques, and answer frequently asked questions.

Chapter Contents:

Happy Tree #3,079

YouTube is designed to make producing videos as easy as possible. But one of the videos on YouTubeHelp's channel makes it appear too easy. Go to www.youtube.com/watch?v=Apadq9iPNxA and watch "How do I make a video?" As Figure 8.1 illustrates, "Painting with Pictures featuring Rob Boss" quickly covers the basics in just 2 minutes and 22 seconds.

Figure 8.1 Painting with pictures

According to this spoof of Bob Ross, creator and host of *The Joy of Painting*, all you need to make a video is a device that can capture digital movies. This could be your cell phone, a digital camera, or a web cam. You will then copy the digital movies to your computer using a FireWire cable or USB mass storage device.

Next, you can either upload them as is or edit them with software such as Windows Movie Maker or iMovie to add titles and special effects. Or, you can use Adobe Premiere Pro or Apple's Final Cut Pro to edit and improve your videos.

Once you're happy with your final result, you'll need to save the video in a format that YouTube can accept. Unless you're a professional video producer, I recommend that you save your videos as QuickTime MOV, Windows AVI, or MPG files—these are the most common formats and they work well in YouTube.

 Note: Brad O'Farrell, the technical editor of this book, suggests an advanced technical trick to get stereo sound on YouTube, which is usually compressed into mono: Save your video as a Flash Video (FLV) file. Because any format you upload will be converted to FLV anyway, it's possible to get stereo sound this way.

Unfortunately, this spoof video that Rob Boss calls "Happy Tree #3,079" does not cover all the tips and tricks for making better videos. If you have told someone, "I figure we can blue-screen the kids in later," like the guy in Figure 8.2, then you will need to find tips about shooting, editing, uploading to YouTube, and even creating some special effects.

"I figure we can blue-screen the kids in later."

Figure 8.2 "I figure we can blue-screen the kids in later." (Cartoon by Alex Gregory in *The New Yorker*, January 31, 2000.)

This chapter is designed to help you out. It will even give you some tips about using the chroma key technique, which is also referred to as blue-screen, green-screen, and color keying.

Week 1: Learn Video Production Basics

To learn the basics of video production, you should start by reading the YouTube Handbook—especially the tips about camera techniques, lighting techniques, sound, and special effects. As Figure 8.3 illustrates, most of these tips and tricks are provided by *Videomaker* magazine.

Published by York Publishing, Videomaker is the leading consumer magazine for video enthusiasts. If you go to YouTube's Video Toolbox at www.youtube.com/video_toolbox and compare it with the YouTube Handbook, you will see that most of the videos are the same and come from *Videomaker* too.

To take your videos to the next level, visit Videomaker's channel at www.youtube.com/videomaker. Finally, to get more advice from the pros, go to www.videomaker.com/youtube.

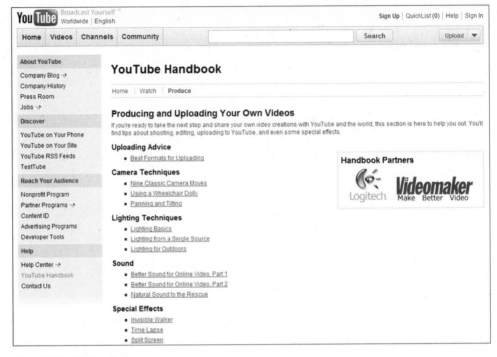

Figure 8.3 YouTube Handbook

If you sign up for Videomaker's free e-newsletter, you'll also get a free tip sheet for videographers.

Monday: Use the best formats for uploading

Tuesday: Use classic camera techniques

Wednesday: Use a single lighting source

Thursday: Use natural sound

Friday: Use special effects

Monday: Use the Best Formats for Uploading

First, read the YouTube Handbook tips about the best formats for uploading. Although YouTube accepts a wide range of video formats for uploading, the video sharing site has found the following settings give the best results:

Video format	H.264, MPEG-2, or MPEG-4 preferred
Aspect ratio	Native aspect ratio without letterboxing (examples: 4:3, 16:9)
Resolution	640×360 (16:9) or 480×360 (4:3) recommended
Audio format	MP3 or AAC preferred
Frames per second	30
Maximum length	10 minutes (2–3 minutes recommended)
Maximum file size	1GB

Of course, I would have provided a different answer before November 24, 2008. As Figure 8.4 illustrates, that was the day YouTube announced that the size of its video player was getting bigger.

Figure 8.4 Bigger Isn't Always Better... But in This Case, We Believe It Is.

The YouTube Team posted this to the YouTube Blog: "We're expanding the width of the page to 960 pixels to better reflect the quality of the videos you create and the screens that you use to watch them. This new, wider player is in a widescreen aspect ratio which we hope will provide you with a cleaner, more powerful viewing experience. And don't worry, your 4:3 aspect ratio videos will play just fine in this new player."

Then on December 16, 2008, YouTube gave everyone a heads-up that it would soon be expanding all standard channels over to the new 960-pixel width. "This is the same change we made with the video watch page a few weeks ago, and will make channels wider and consistent with the rest of the site," said The YouTube Team.

So, it's important to understand that the best video format is a moving target. You will want to read the YouTube Blog regularly to find out what has changed recently.

For example, a common mistake is to output wide-screen videos with horizontal letterboxing and then end up with vertical letterboxing, making the actual video about one-fourth the area of the video player.

Tuesday: Use Classic Camera Techniques

Next, read the YouTube Handbook tip "Nine Classic Camera Moves," which was written by Brian Schaller, a former TV news shooter, reporter, and producer who is now traveling worldwide working on a documentary. Or, you can read his full article at www.videomaker.com/article/10775.

According to Schaller, "Professional videographers usually follow this one rule of thumb: when it comes to camera movement, it must be motivated. 'Because it looks cool' is usually not a valid reason for using tricky camera moves." So, why would you use one of these nine classic camera techniques and how do you execute these shot types? Here are some short summaries of Brian's tips:

Pan This camera technique works great to show the distance between two objects or for a panoramic view from a mountaintop to the valley below. To execute this shot type, use a tripod to smoothly move the camera horizontally from left to right or from right to left.

Tilt This camera technique works best when it is used to show how tall something is or the top and bottom of a stationary object. To execute this shot type, tilt the camera up or down without raising or lowering its position.

Pedestal You use this camera technique to get the proper height for a shot. To execute this shot type, physically move the height of the camera up or down on a tripod.

Dolly You use this camera technique to follow an object smoothly. To execute this shot type, set the camera on tracks or wheels and move it toward or away from a subject.

Floating stabilizer You use this camera technique to follow an object through twists and turns or a person through hallways and doors as well as around rooms. To execute this shot type, strap the stabilizer device to the videographer and mount the camera on a series of metal joints controlled by gyroscopes. Brian adds, "You can also buy or make an inexpensive alternative that uses counterweights to get a similar effect."

Crane or boom This camera technique gives a bird's-eye view as if the camera is swooping down from above. To execute this shot type, use the crane or boom for high sweeping shots or to follow the action of your subject.

Handheld Many news crews and most documentaries use this camera technique because of the spontaneity of the action. To execute this shot type, hold the camera with a tripod. Brian adds, "Professional cameras are large and rest on the user's shoulders. This balances the camera and keeps shaking to a minimum."

Zoom You use this camera technique to bring objects at a distance closer to the lens or to show size and perspective. To execute this shot type, press the lever on the camera to zoom in or out. Adds Brian, "Usually, the harder you press on the lever the quicker the zoom."

Rack focus This camera technique is used to switch from one actor's face to another during conversations or tense moments. It enables you to make a transition similar to an edit by constructing two distinct shots. To execute this shot type, focus on one object, like an actor's face, and then have everything behind him out of focus. Then adjust the focus so that his face becomes blurred and the actress behind him becomes clear.

As Figure 8.5 illustrates, Isaac's "Videomaker's Pans and Tilts 101" demonstrates the first two of the classic camera techniques that Schaller outlined. Isaac shows what a pan and a tilt are and how they can improve the quality of the shots in your videos.

Figure 8.5 "Videomaker's Pans and Tilts 101"

Wednesday: Use a Single Lighting Source

If you need to learn lighting basics, watch "Videomaker's Lighting Techniques 101." As Figure 8.6 illustrates, Isaac gives some helpful hints for better lighting in your videos.

This video accompanies another one of my favorite tips: "Illuminations: One-Light to Cover them All." It was written by Jim Stinson, author of *Video: Digital Communication & Production* (Goodheart-Willcox, 2008). You can his full article at www.videomaker.com/article/11114.

Why work with only a single lighting source? According to Jim, there are three key reasons: "Poverty, portability, and power. You may not have the budget for a full light kit, or the need to do much interior lighting. You may be working out of your trusty Prius, with no room to store a bunch of lights and stands and cables, and no assistant to schlep all that stuff around. Or you may have to light a room with a single household circuit that may also have outlets in other rooms (Oh, how many times I've found this in older buildings). Plug in a second light and... BLOOEY!"

Figure 8.6 "Videomaker's Lighting Techniques 101"

He says you can work with a single light either when the ambient light at a location is feeble or when you want to control the lighting perfectly. How you do this depends on your instrument of choice.

If you use a spotlight, Jim says you'll need something to bounce its light back from the other side of the subject. For head and shoulder shots, a standard reflector may work fine. However, it's often easier to work with a softlight—whether box or umbrella—because this light seems to wrap around the subject to create key and fill at once.

He adds that backgrounds may not be a problem if you have ambient light on location. However, when your lonely unit is the sole source, you have to light carefully.

With a spotlight, Jim suggests you reposition both light and reflector so that the bounce light hits the rear wall as well as the subject. With a softlight, about all you can do is move the subject closer to the wall, move the light farther from the subject, or a bit of both. "Be careful moving the subject closer, it may flatten the look of the shot," he advises.

Finally, if you have any choice in the matter, always use a light-colored background wall when working without ambient light. "That way, the bounce light will have a fighting chance of illuminating your subject," Jim concludes.

Thursday: Use Natural Sound

If you need to learn the basics of sound, watch "Videomaker's Better Sound for Online Video 101." As Figure 8.7 illustrates, Isaac's got a good tip for better sound: use an external microphone.

Figure 8.7 "Videomaker's Better Sound for Online Video 101"

Then read the third of my favorite tips, which is entitled, "Sound Advice: Natural Sound to the Rescue." It was written by Hal Robertson, a contributing editor for *Videomaker* magazine as well as the cinematographer, editor, and entire crew for the independent digital feature, Breaking Ten. You can read his full article at www.videomaker .com/article/12249.

Hal asks, "Remember MacGyver? With his trusty Swiss Army knife, some bubble gum, and duct tape, he could fashion weapons, build flying machines, and repair almost anything—all this, just in time to thwart the bad guys and save the damsel in distress."

He says, "You have a similar tool at your disposal—perfect for defeating the evils of audio editing. No, it's not gaffer's tape, it's Natural Sound or Nat Sot, for short. Natural sound is often misunderstood or, worse, ignored by many video editors, but it works great covering tough edits and creating a real sense of space."

Hal says it's easy to record natural sound from locations. Before the talent arrives (or after they leave), simply roll a minute or two of tape to capture the audio environment. As for microphones, you can use the same mics the talent will use, or use the stereo microphone in your camcorder.

He says you can capture your audio-only clips along with the other video material and remove the video to create your natural soundtrack. Although it's not difficult to do this in most editing software, he recommends using Adobe Audition, which has a feature called Open Audio from Video that simplifies the process. If the edited video goes longer than your recording, just loop it again and trim any excess. To create smooth transitions, apply a fade-in and fade-out to the ends of your audio segments.

Finally, Hal suggests that you always roll the tape before the interviews and create several seconds of material that would serve as audio Band-Aids. Before or after the shoot, have the talent clam up for a minute and keep the tape rolling. Using the same microphone in the same location is the best way.

He adds, "Whether you're shooting a movie, a training video or an infomercial, virtually every production will benefit with natural sound. It's a great mix element to reinforce the action onscreen and will cover you in difficult editing situations."

Friday: Use Special Effects

The how-to video you're looking for is "Green Screen," aka "Videomaker's How to Use Green Screen Paper 101." In 52 seconds, Issac explains how to create and use a green-screen effect using basic store-bought items and computer editing software. As Figure 8.8 illustrates, it had over 56,000 views as of December 27, 2008.

Figure 8.8 "Videomaker's How to Use Green Screen Paper 101"

For more tips, read "The Keys to Chromakey: How To Use A Green Screen" by Ed Driscoll at www.videomaker.com/article/13055/.

For example, Driscoll explains, "In the past, the main color for chromakeying was blue. Beginning in the late 1970s, there was a slow industry flip-over to green-colored screens for chroma. That's because of the detail in the green color channel that digital cameras retain."

He also recommends lighting the background as evenly as possible, with no hot spots. This makes postproduction work much easier.

In addition, Driscoll says, "It helps to stand the subject as far away from the backdrop as possible to separate the two. This helps to reduce spill from the lights illuminating the talent into the lighting on the green screen. It helps to blur the backdrop, which keeps wrinkling and other blemishes from affecting the key."

Week 2: Get Video Production Tips

After you've learned the basics of video production, you'll want to visit YouTube's Help Center to get some video production tips.

YouTube is constantly rolling out new features that let you add multitrack captions and subtitles to your videos, add interactive commentary and links, and use a new 16:9 widescreen player size.

Monday: Keep videos 2 to 3 minutes long

Tuesday: Learn how to upload

Wednesday: Use video annotations

Thursday: Add captions and subtitles

Friday: Use HD widescreen resolution

Monday: Keep Videos 2 to 3 Minutes Long

One of the articles that I recommend you read is "Video Length and Size." It says, "There are two ways to upload your video: by using our Single File Uploader or the YouTube Uploader (for multiple files). With either of these methods, your videos can be up to 1GB in size and 10 minutes long." The article adds, "The longer and/or higher quality your video is, the more compression will be required to fit it into 1GB. You can compress your video using movie editors, like Windows Movie Maker or Apple iMovie."

Over in the Partner Help Center, YouTube says, "Videos must be a minimum of 30 seconds in order to be eligible for revenue sharing." So, videos should be somewhere between 30 seconds and 10 minutes long.

If you look at the lengths of the 20 most viewed videos of all time on YouTube, they range from 0:55 to 12:03, with the median between 3:47 and 4:00. But there are good reasons videos should be only 2 to 3 minutes long.

In December 2008, TubeMogul posted the results of a study that found most videos steadily lose viewers once "play" is clicked, with 10.4 percent clicking away after 10 seconds and 53.6 percent leaving after a minute.

Note: TubeMogul was able to conduct this viewer-engagement study because of its acquisition of Illumenix, a video metrics firm, in October 2008. Illumenix tracks how much of a video is actually watched, when a viewer clicks away, and what the most popular segments of a video are. TubeMogul renamed this Flash-based analytics service InPlay.

For a two-week period, TubeMogul measured viewed seconds for a sample of 188,055 videos, totaling 22,724,606 streams, on six top video sites. The study's findings were dramatic. As Figure 8.9 illustrates, most online video viewers watch mere seconds, rather than minutes, of a video.

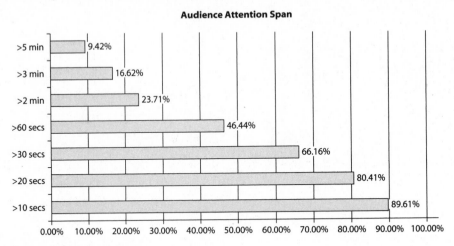

Figure 8.9 Audience Attention Span

According to David Burch, TubeMogul's marketing manager, "Online video viewers' short attention span seems especially relevant to advertisers looking to strategically trim ad budgets as the economy contracts. For starters, it is clear that post-roll ads are of limited effectiveness." For example, the post-roll ad in the final seconds of a 3-minute video will be viewed by only 16.62 percent of the initial audience, on average.

Burch adds, "Another takeaway is that overlay ads should be displayed as early as possible in a video, preferably within the first few seconds." On YouTube, where most overlay ads appear at about 15 seconds into the video, 10.39 percent of the initial viewers are not likely to see the ad.

That's why it makes sense to keep videos 2 to 3 minutes long. Although you can hold an audience's attention longer if your content is more compelling, consider creating two videos if you have more than 4 to 6 minutes of less-compelling content.

Tuesday: Learn How to Upload

Another popular article in YouTube's Help Center that I recommend you read is "How to Upload." As Figure 8.10 illustrates, it is accompanied by a video called "How to Upload A Video to YouTube" by Katie Stiles.

Once you've finished editing your video, make sure it's less than 10 minutes long, smaller than 1GB in size, and in an acceptable format. Then you're ready to upload it. According to YouTube's Help Center, here's how you do that:

1. Click the Upload button in the upper-right corner of any YouTube page.
2. Click the Browse button to browse for the video file you'd like to upload to YouTube. Select the file you want to upload.

Figure 8.10 "How to Upload A Video to YouTube"

3.   Click the Upload Video button to start the uploading process.

4.   As the video file is uploading, enter as much information about it as possible in the relevant fields, including title, description, category, and tags. You're not required to provide specific information, but the more information you include, the easier it is for users to find your video.

5.   Click the Save Changes button to save the updates you've made to the video file.

You can upload up to 10 video files in a single uploading session. To upload multiple videos, follow these steps:

1.   Click the Add Videos To Upload button.

2.   Select the videos you want to upload.

3.   Once you've added all the videos that you want to upload and confirmed that the total file size is less than 1GB, click the Upload Videos button.

It can take 15 to 30 minutes for your video to upload to YouTube if Internet traffic is normal and you have a fast connection. But it can take up to an hour if you are uploading video during a busy conference at an old hotel.

In March 2009, YouTube released a new Flash uploader for all supported browsers. And it came with a long-awaited and much-requested feature: an upload progress bar that lets you know the status of your upload. YouTube's next step will be to provide the estimated video processing time for your upload so you know if you have time to get a cup of coffee.

In April 2009, YouTube added some new options for uploaders. You can now tweak the appearance of your video when played on YouTube or in an embedded player. Just insert some of the hint tags below into the tags field of your video:

yt:crop=16:9	This zooms in on the 16:9 area and removes windowboxing.
yt:stretch=16:9	This fixes anamorphic (widescreen) content by scaling it to 16:9.
yt:stretch=4:3	This fixes 720×480 content that is the wrong aspect ratio by scaling it to 4:3.
yt:quality=high	This sets the default to a high-quality stream, depending on availability.

If you receive an error with your upload, you might want to make sure you're attempting to upload a file that's recognized by YouTube. YouTube accepts video files from most digital cameras, camcorders, and cell phones in the AVI, MOV, WMV, and MPG file formats.

Remember, your video needs to meet YouTube's uploading requirements: it can't be larger than 1GB and can't be more than 10 minutes in length. If your video file doesn't meet these requirements, you will have to re-edit it on your computer and then upload the new file. Do you get the impression that I've learned this particular lesson the hard way? After watching "How to Upload a Video to YouTube," visit BeforeAndAfterTV's channel and watch Katie's other tutorials:

- "Apple iMovie Tutorial - How to Edit Your Video"
- "Flip Video Camera - Transferring from Camera to Computer"
- "Embedding YouTube Videos"

Wednesday: Use Video Annotations

On June 4, 2008, YouTube announced a new way to add interactive commentary to your videos—using video annotations. As the video by Torley in Figure 8.11 illustrates, this feature enables you to add background information, create branching stories, or add links to any YouTube video, channel, or search results page—at any point in your video.

YouTubers have control over creating and editing an unlimited number of annotations on their videos. To start annotating, you need to upload videos to your account first. Then log in and view one of your videos. On the video page, click the blue Edit Annotations button to the right of the video.

In January 2009, YouTube made it easier to add annotations directly to your videos. Simply log in to YouTube, watch your video on the watch page, and then click the video to start adding annotations. You can also change an annotation's color.

It's also easier for your annotations to link to a variety of different YouTube pages. You can link to another video, channel page, playlist, group, or search query. You can even link to a video response page or message window to prompt for feedback from your audience.

However, my technical editor says if you create a new link, it will invalidate the old one. You might consider putting new links in the description of your video to give viewers free reign to add annotations.

Figure 8.11 "Add video annotations – YouTube Help Center"

As you play your video, you can insert commentary by adding speech bubbles, notes, and highlight boxes anywhere you want. You can also use the menu on the left to save a draft, delete commentary, edit start/stop times, or add links to your annotations. Once you save the final version, click Publish to reveal your annotated video to other users.

If you want to see an example, watch the video by Roi Werner in Figure 8.12. Just go to www.youtube.com/watch?v=Uxnopxb0dic.

Figure 8.12 "How to use YouTube annotations"

To set the video page icon for your channel, log in to your account and navigate to the Branding Options page in the Edit Channel menu. In the Video Page Icon field, select the locally saved image that you would like to use for your video page icon and then click the Save Branding Options button at the bottom of the page to upload the image to YouTube. I recommend that you choose an image that is 10KB or smaller.

If you are looking for some creative ways to use annotations, check out "Interactive shell game" on captdeaf's channel, "My 22nd Skydive" on hendrikm82's channel, and "Interactive card trick" on werneroi's channel.

What else should you know?

As this was written, video annotations were available as a beta feature. YouTube says that, once out of beta, annotations will support more languages (not just English) and appear on videos embedded in other websites. Visit the YouTube Blog for updates.

Thursday: Add Captions and Subtitles

On August 28, 2008, YouTube added a new captioning feature that allows you to give viewers a deeper understanding of your video (Figure 8.13). Captions and subtitles can help people who would not otherwise understand the audio track to follow along, especially those who speak other languages or who are deaf and hard of hearing.

Figure 8.13 "YouTube Captions and Subtitles"

You can add captions to one of your videos by uploading a closed caption file using the Captions And Subtitles menu on the editing page. To add several captions to a video, simply upload multiple files.

If you want to include foreign subtitles in multiple languages, upload a separate file for each language. There are over 120 languages to choose from, and you can add any title you want for each caption.

If a video includes captions, you can activate them by clicking the menu button located in the lower-right portion of the video player. Clicking this button will also allow viewers to choose which captions they want to see.

Some of YouTube's partners have already started using captions and subtitles to offer their users a better understanding of their videos—even with the audio turned off:

BBC Worldwide "Top Gear - Richard Hammond toasts Nissan with a jet car - BBC" (www.youtube.com/watch?v=XraeBDMm2PM) provides captions in five different languages.

CNET "Crave: Do You Crave the iPhone 3G" (www.youtube.com/watch?v=u1lmDNjb_ec) uses captions in this tech product review.

UC Berkeley "Opencast Project Open House at UC Berkeley" (www.youtube.com/watch?v=4WJez1XjI88) uses captions in its footage.

Gonzodoga "BLASSREITER Episode 1" (www.youtube.com/watch?v=Iu3usSSQ_74) uses English subtitles in this Japanese animation.

What else should you know about captions? They can be searched for, so accurate captions will help people find your videos.

Friday: Use HD Widescreen Resolution

In December 2008, YouTube began offering users an option to view content in high definition—720-pixel resolution when the source upload supports it. Table 8.1 summarizes the audio and video specifications you need for the best results on YouTube.

▶ **Table 8.1** Video Optimization for YouTube

Video	
Resolution	Recommended: 1290x720 (16x9 HD) and 640x480 (4:3 SD). There is no required minimum resolution; in general, the higher the resolution the better, and HD resolution is preferred. For older content, lower resolution is unavoidable.
Bit rate	Because bit rate is highly dependent on codec, there is no recommended or minimum value. Videos should be optimized for resolution, aspect ratio, and frame rate rather than bit rate.
Frame rate	The frame rate of the original video should be maintained without resampling. In particular, pull-down and other frame rate resampling techniques are strongly discouraged.
Codec	H.264, MPEG-2, or MPEG-4 preferred.
Audio	
Codec	MP3 or AAC preferred.
Sampling rate	44.1 kHz
Channels	Two (stereo)
Container	MPEGTS (MPEG2 transport stream)

As of this writing, YouTube was still experimenting with this feature. Still, here are some general tips for uploading widescreen videos:

Use originals The less a video is re-encoded prior to uploading, the better the resulting YouTube video quality. Upload your videos as close to the original source format as possible, with a minimum of intermediate re-encoding steps. Each re-encoding can generally degrade the quality of your video and create some specific problems too.

Aspect ratio The aspect ratio of the original source video should always be maintained when it's uploaded. Uploaded videos should never include letterboxing or pillarboxing bars. The YouTube player automatically adds black bars so that videos are displayed correctly without cropping or stretching, whatever the size of the video or the player. For example, the player will automatically add vertical bars to 4:3 videos in the new 16:9 widescreen player size. If the player is resized when embedded on another website, the same process takes place, so 16:9 videos are letterboxed when the player is sized to 4:3. Similarly, anamorphic videos will be automatically letterboxed when shown in either 16:9 or 4:3 sized players. The player can only do this if the native aspect ratio of the video is maintained. If letterboxing is added to a video before it is uploaded to create a 4:3 video from a 16:9 master, then the widescreen player will add pillarbox bars too, resulting in black bars all around the video and a bad viewing experience.

Frame rate The video frame rate should be the same as the original where possible— up-sampling from a 24 fps original can cause judder artifacts, for example. For film sources, a 24 fps or 25 fps progressive master yields the best results, but applying a resampling transfer process—such as telecine pull-down—often result in a lower-quality video.

Resolution High-definition videos are the preferred format and, if you can't use HD resolution, then the higher resolution the better. This also means your video should be upgraded as new formats are developed on the site.

Testing Because there is no facility to re-upload videos, it's important to make sure the audio and video quality is satisfactory before you release your video publicly on YouTube. Once a video becomes popular, the number of views, user ratings, user comments, and other community data cannot be transferred if another, higher-quality version of the same video is uploaded. Make sure you get it right!

Week 3: Master Video Production Techniques

Of course, professional videography consists of more than a handful of video production tips. So let's explore some of the places where you can get expert advice to master video production techniques:

Monday: Visit Expert Village

Tuesday: Visit MarkApsolon's channel

Wednesday: Visit TigerDirectBlog

Thursday: Visit Lockergnome's channel

Friday: Visit TestTube

Monday: Visit Expert Village

One of the places that you'll want to visit is Expert Village's channel on YouTube. Go to www.youtube.com/expertvillage to see more than 139,000 how-to videos on a wide range of topics—from aerobics and BMX tricks to Wii cheats and cooking tips.

For budding videographers, the official YouTube channel of Expert Village offers individual videos like "How To Make a Video for YouTube: Using Quick Capture on YouTube" as well as a playlist with 12 videos on video production basics.

Or, visit the ExpertVillage.com website and you will find a 14-part series by Glen Cornish called "How to Make Professional Digital Video." As Figure 8.14 illustrates, this valuable gem is hidden in plain sight at www.expertvillage.com/video-series/4364_computer-video.htm.

Figure 8.14 How to Make Professional Digital Video

In his 14-part video series for Expert Village, Cornish shows you how to make professional digital video. You can learn all about digital video cameras, lighting equipment, mics and audio, editing software, and codecs.

Glen Cornish

Glen Cornish is an award-winning instructor and digital media producer who started his career in sound engineering, receiving kudos from Quincy Jones for his assistance recording the 1984 Olympic theme. Cornish then moved into video production and 3D animation, helping to establish the J. Paul Getty Museum's digital video and animation in-house facilities.

Cornish has since moved into broadcast engineering, working with ABC station affiliates as well as training others in the digital arts at UC Davis and Stanford's Digital Media Academy. He has since received top honors from UC Davis as instructor of the year.

Cornish also gives you expert tips for getting rid of the echo on your audio, using the white balance like a pro, video formats for professional distribution, and much more. His series includes the following videos:

1. "All About Video Codecs & Making Digital Media"
2. "Audio Basics for Making a Digital Video"
3. "Basic Digital Media & Making Videos"
4. "How to Add Graphics and Titles to Video"
5. "How to Edit Using a Digital Video Camera"
6. "How to Organize Video Clips for Editing"
7. "How to Render & Format Digital Video"
8. "How to Storyboard a Video Shoot"
9. "How to Upload Video to Your Computer"
10. "How to Use a Digital Video Camera"
11. "Lighting Basics for Making a Digital Video"
12. "Tips on How to Make a Digital Video"
13. "Tools Needed to Make a Digital Video"
14. "What is the Time Code in Video Editing?"

Tuesday: Visit MarkApsolon's Channel

The next place you will want to visit is MarkApsolon's channel on YouTube (www.youtube.com/markapsolon).

Who is Mark Apsolon? He is a guru of chromakey (green screen), video production, and lighting. He's been helping people make better videos with his free tutorials on YouTube since September 2006. He also offers training DVDs on his website at www.markapsolon.com.

As Figure 8.15 illustrates, his playlists includes "Mark Apsolon's Video: Tips and Tricks," 16 videos on cheap lighting, green screen, video cameras, and other video production techniques.

Figure 8.15 Mark Apsolon, Video Guru

If you take a look around Apsolon's website, you will find tutorials for chromakey (green screen), video lighting, product reviews, and much more. His videos will help you add that extra flare by using chromakey (green or blue screen) or adding that special effect to your videos. Also take a look at Mark's forums to network with other videographers, filmmakers, and businesses.

If you want to see what a green screen and video editor can do, go to Venetian-Princess's channel (www.youtube.com/VenetianPrincess) and watch "The Princess Chronicles," an episodic fantasy series about the princess's mystical journey around the world.

Wednesday: Visit TigerDirectBlog

The next place you will want to visit is TigerDirectBlog's channel, or its website, ComputerTV, which covers technology and gadget news. In 2009, TigerDirectBlog's channel featured the following videos, all reviews of camcorders:

- "Canon VIXIA HF20 Flash"
- "Canon VIXIA HF S10 HD Digital"
- "Canon VIXIA HF S100 HD Digital"
- "KODAK Zi6 Pocket Video Camera"
- "Panasonic Underwater Camcorder - ComputerTV at CES 2009"
- "Pure Digital Flip Video HD Camcorder"
- "Sony HandyCam DCR-SR42 Digital"
- "Sony DCR-SX60 Handycam"
- "Sony Handycam HDRCX100 HD"
- "Sony Handycam HDRXR200V HD"

As you can see in Figure 8.16, TigerDirectBlog's channel also featured coverage of the annual Consumer Electronics Show (CES) back in January. Although CES 2009 was more low key because of the recession, Tiger TV hosts Albert and Bauer still ran loose in Las Vegas with a camera crew, bringing their viewers the latest from the world's largest consumer technology trade show.

Figure 8.16 Com.puter.TV

During the other 51 weeks of the year, Albert and Bauer provide you with the latest tech-related news for the week, so you don't have to even bother reading the blogs. Tech Update is a YouTube exclusive. It's uncensored and sometimes even funny.

Thursday: Visit Lockergnome's Channel

For a different perspective, you should visit Lockergnome's channel on YouTube, or one of Chris Pirillo's many websites:

http://chris.pirillo.com (his personal blog)

http://geeks.pirillo.com (his geeks community)

http://www.lockergnome.com (his technology blog)

http://www.gnomedex.com (his tech conference)

Pirillo has been called a geek, hardware addict, software junkie, technology enthusiast, shameless self-promoter, early adopter, idea evangelist, tech support blogger, bootstrapper, and media personality. And these are just some of the things he's called himself.

As Figure 8.17 illustrates, Pirillo did a funny review called "YouTube vs. Revver vs. Google Video" on November 27, 2006.

Figure 8.17 "YouTube vs. Revver vs. Google Video"

To give you a sense of what you can "learn" from watching videos on this "educational" channel, check out some of Pirillo's recent videos:

- "YouTube Live - Flip HD Video," uploaded on November 22, 2008, (www.youtube.com/watch?v=zQsB3TZOWUE).

- "What YouTube Tools can you Recommend?" uploaded on December 18, 2008 (www.youtube.com/watch?v=WqQZQfD6jsk).

- "Are You a Movie Mash-up Mixmaster with Muvee?" uploaded December 22, 2008 (www.youtube.com/watch?v=6jwY4idN7Pk).

- "How to Download YouTube Videos to an iPod," uploaded January 13, 2009 (www.youtube.com/watch?v=H-x6-TM_zfU).

- "How to Watch YouTube Subscriptions on the iPhone," uploaded February 15, 2009 (www.youtube.com/watch?v=ML2faiokSzE).

- "How to Piss Off a YouTube User," uploaded February 4, 2009 (www.youtube.com/watch?v=wBQXsrRCHzM).

Now, I understand that Pirillo's style and Lockergnome's content are an acquired taste that you might not acquire. But you can learn a lot from geeks and nerds.

Pirillo is a monthly columnist for *CPU* magazine, and also produces weekly video segments for CNN.com Live, where he offers tech advice to a savvy audience. His daily email newsletter goes out to 100,000+ confirmed opt-in subscribers. He launched his blog network in 1996 and started hosting his own tech conference series in 2001. And he has over 40,000 followers on Twitter.

The 2,178 videos on Lockergnome's channel had over 50.9 million views as of May 2009 making it the #7 most viewed Guru of all time. And with more than 67,000 subscribers, Lockergnome's channel was the #22 most subscribed Guru of all time.

So prepare to be astonished.

Friday: Visit TestTube

The final place you will want to visit is TestTube, YouTube's "ideas incubator." This is where YouTube engineers and developers test out recipes and concoctions that aren't quite fully baked and invite you to tell them how they're coming along.

As shown in Figure 8.18, YouTube was working on a number of mixtures on December 28, 2008.

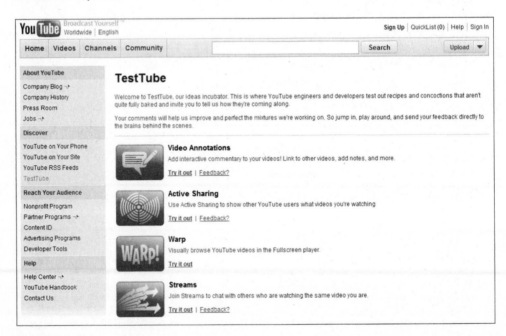

Figure 8.18 TestTube

We've already taken a look at video annotations. So let's take a quick look at CaptionTube, Active Sharing, Warp, and Streams.

CaptionTube lets you add captions and subtitles to your YouTube videos with an interactive caption editor. This enables you to offer viewers a transcript to read, improve discoverability and searching for sales and training videos, create and edit closed captions in multiple languages, and export captions and upload them to your YouTube account.

Active Sharing lets you share what you're watching with other YouTubers. When you start Active Sharing, your username will appear to other users on the videos you watch. A list of videos you've recently watched will also appear on your profile page.

Warp lets you visually browse YouTube videos in a full-screen player. The feedback as of December 28, 2008, wasn't positive. As Comicless observed in the Community Help Forums, "I think the idea of Warp Speed is interesting, but don't exactly understand what it is good for."

Streams lets you create a YouTube room to watch and interact with other users while sharing videos. Everyone in the room can add videos from their Favorites and QuickList, or by pasting in links, and make a running commentary as the videos play.

Week 4: Answer Video Production Questions

Now that you've learned the basics of video production and explored some of the places where you can learn more advanced video production techniques, let's tackle a few of the hardest video production questions:

Monday: What is the best camcorder?

Tuesday: What is the best web cam?

Wednesday: What is the best video editing software?

Thursday: What is the best video converter?

Friday: What is the worst that can happen?

Monday: What Is the Best Camcorder?

I can't tell you how many times I've been asked, What is the best camcorder? No one wants to buy a new camcorder in November only to discover that a better, cheaper model will be introduced in January at CES, the world's largest consumer technology trade show.

As you can see in Figure 8.19, this was one of the open questions at Yahoo! Answers on December 21, 2008.

Figure 8.19 Yahoo! Answers

Because CES is such a key event for camcorder launches, you might want to wait until the second week of January to find out what the best camcorder is.

CES generates more than 5,000 stories about its exhibitors and the industry each year. Try searching for "best camcorder" using Google News or Yahoo! News to get a good answer to the question.

Or, if you can't wait until January, read the latest camcorder reviews:

CamcorderInfo.com: www.camcorderinfo.com

CNET: http://reviews.cnet.com/camcorders

Consumer Reports: www.consumerreports.org

PC Magazine: www.pcmag.com

Videomaker: www.videomaker.com

Or, if you really, really need to know what the best camcorder is as of when this was written, check out the $199 Flip UltraHD video camcorder from Pure Digital Technologies. On April 30, 2009, Jefferson Graham of *USA Today* wrote a review entitled "New Flip Ultra video cameras might flip your switch." He said, "People ask me all the time about purchasing a video camera. For non-pros, the Flip has been my top recommendation, and remains so. It's the top-selling video camera, according to the NPD Group."

The same day, Noah Robischon wrote a review for *Fast Company* entitled "Flip UltraHD Is Pure Digital's Best Pocket Camcorder Yet." He said, "Pure Digital has gone on to sell 2 million camcorders since releasing the original Flip in May 2007, generating an estimated $150 million in revenue. No wonder Cisco bought the company that makes the Flip, Pure Digital, last month for $590 million."

And the technical editor of this book agrees. O'Farrell says, "The Flip video cameras are specifically designed to be the best cameras for YouTube, outputting at exactly the right resolution and quality. And a Flip video camcorder has the technology to help clearly capture situations in low light with true audio. It also holds up to an hour of video on its own internal flash memory and can be transferred to and even edited on any computer with its built-in USB connector and PC/Mac-compatible video editing software. When YouTube introduced HD, the Flip HD also came out. Flip Video is always a great choice for high-quality, low-fi, YouTube-specific content."

Now, you may not need a new Flip video camcorder to start shooting your masterpiece. If you already have a digital camcorder that captures in Digital8, MiniDV, HDV, or any of the DVD formats, then you're ready to go. Your camcorder will need some kind of direct connection to your computer, either to the USB or FireWire ports or by inserting the DVD you've recorded.

If you have an analog camcorder that uses VHS, VHS-C, SVHS-C, 8mm, or Hi8 tape, then you can still get your videos onto YouTube. It will require an extra step and some additional equipment, though, because these camcorders are not usually equipped with computer connections.

You will need to digitize the video with a converter box, which will convert the analog signal from the camcorder to a digital signal that the computer can understand. Maybe this is all that you need instead of the best camcorder.

Tuesday: What Is the Best Web Cam?

I also can't tell you how often I'm asked, What is the best web cam? Because mine was built into my HP Pavilion Entertainment PC, this question generally comes from someone looking for a web cam they can connect to their old laptop or desktop.

Back on July 13, 2006, Logitech, the world's leading manufacturer of web cams, announced a comarketing agreement with YouTube that made it easier for people using Logitech QuickCam web cams to upload their videos. Logitech provided an integrated link to YouTube within its Logitech QuickCam software. In return, YouTube promoted Logitech as its official web cam partner.

Logitech's QuickCam web cams and the Logitech Video Effects software are popular with YouTubers. To find out what the best web cam is these days, you might want to start by visiting the Logitech site, which is illustrated in Figure 8.20.

For example, the Logitech QuickCam Vision Pro web cam for Mac was the first Mac-compatible web cam with premium autofocus technology and Carl Zeiss optics when it was unveiled in June 2008. Focusing is fast and fluid—crisp even in extreme close-ups only 10 centimeters from the camera lens. Logitech's autofocus system compensates for changes in image-edge sharpness and refocuses images in less than 3 seconds.

Its 2-megapixel sensor helps the Logitech web cam capture video images in high resolution. It is assisted by Logitech's RightLight 2 Technology, which enables the web cam to adjust intelligently in dim or harshly backlighted situations.

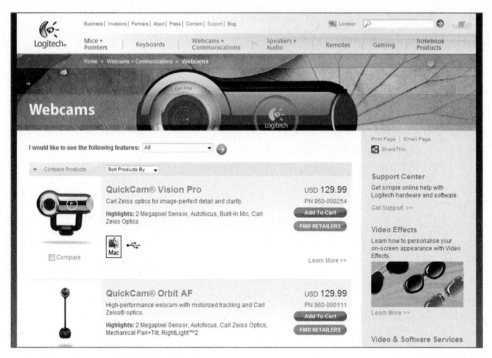

Figure 8.20 The Webcams page on Logitech's site

Of course, that was then and this is now. Ff you want a second opinion or want to see what has been introduced lately, then you can read the latest web cam reviews:

CNET: `http://reviews.cnet.com/4566-6502_7-0.html`

Crunchgear: `www.youtube.com/crunchgear`

Lockergnome: `www.youtube.com/lockergnome`

PC Magazine: `www.pcmag.com`

Webcamworld.com: `www.webcamworld.com/reviews`

Wednesday: What Is the Best Video Editing Software?

Occasionally, I'm asked, What is the best video editing software?

Most new computers come with basic video editing software installed, like Windows Movie Maker or Apple's iMovie. These programs allow you to not only edit the video, but add effects, titles, and music to make your video look and sound more interesting.

However, as Brad O'Farrell notes, "A lot of sounds and packaged special effects in iMovie and Movie Maker are so prevalent on YouTube that they're now clearly visible denotations of amateur content." He advises using plug-ins and original sound effects to avoid homogeneity.

If you want to be a bit more hands-on with your video, check out Adobe Premiere Pro or Apple's Final Cut Pro.

Adobe Premiere Pro is a real-time, timeline-based video editing software application. It is part of the Adobe Creative Suite, a suite of graphic design, video editing, and web development applications, although it can also be purchased separately. Even when purchased separately, it comes bundled with Adobe Encore and Adobe OnLocation. Premiere Pro supports many video editing cards and plug-ins for accelerated processing, additional file format support, and video/audio effects.

Final Cut Pro is a professional nonlinear editing software application developed by Apple Inc. The application is available only for Mac OS X version 10.4 or later and is a module of the Final Cut Studio product. The software logs and captures video onto an internal or external hard drive, where it can be edited and processed.

But, as Figure 8.21 illustrates, CyberLink PowerDirector 7 Ultra won the *PC Magazine* Editors' Choice award in this category in June 2008.

Figure 8.21 PowerDirector 7

But that was then and this is now. So you may want to read the latest video editing software reviews:

CNET: `http://reviews.cnet.com/4566-3670_7-0.html`

PC Magazine: `www.pcmag.com`

Talkingtech: `www.youtube.com/talkingtech`

TopTenREVIEWS: `http://video-editing-software-review.toptenreviews.com`

Videomaker: `http://www.videomaker.com/learn/product-reviews`

Thursday: What Is the Best Video Converter?

The fact that the best video format changes often prompts people to ask, What is the best video converter? So let me start to answer this question by listing all the video files YouTube will accept:

- Windows Media Video (`.avi`)
- 3GP (cell phones)
- AVI (Windows)
- MOV (Mac)
- MP4 (iPod/PSP)
- MPEG
- FLV (Adobe Flash)
- SWF (Shockwave)
- MKV (h.264)

Now, if you think your current video file format isn't recognized by YouTube, you may get the best results from converting your file to MPEG-4 video with MP3 audio. Windows Movie Maker saves projects by default as MSWMM files. These are project files, which only tell Windows Movie Maker the layout of your video but don't contain the final video itself. Because of this, YouTube does not accept MSWMM files. To upload your Windows Movie Maker video to YouTube, select the Save To My Computer option to save and upload the generated file.

To convert almost any other video format to one of the accepted formats listed earlier, I recommend you use FFMPEG. FFMPEG is a command-line tool, so newer users may like to use the free tool, SUPER, which can be found at `www.erightsoft.org`. If these free tools don't produce acceptable results, then try Magic Video Converter. As Figure 8.22 illustrates, you can download and purchase this commercial software at `www.magic-video-software.com/magic_video_converter`.

Keep in mind that each time you convert or "transcode" a video from one type of compression to another, there will be some loss in quality—sort of like making a photocopy of a photocopy. Avoid transcoding a highly compressed video. You'll get poor results. You'll get better results by going back to your original video editing software where you edited the video and re-exporting in a format like MPEG-4 with MP3 audio. Or, if that is unavailable, export it in a RAW, uncompressed video format and then encode it in an external program such as those listed earlier.

Figure 8.22 Magic Video Converter

Friday: What Is the Worst That Can Happen?

Finally, let's tackle the question, What is the worst that can happen? To find out, visit eHow.com, which has a database of over 500,000 articles and videos on how to do just about everything.

For example, as Figure 8.23 illustrates, there is an article by the eHow Arts and Entertainment editor entitled "How to Handle Post-Production Video Emergencies."

The article outlines many of the steps that can help you make the best of the most trying situations:

1. Determine the type of emergency you're dealing with so you know how to proceed. You'll handle a building fire much differently than you would a computer crash.

2. Stay calm. No matter what type of emergency you're dealing with, don't panic so you can handle the situation.

3. Deal with safety issues first. If there is some physical hazard, find out who to contact for emergency aid.

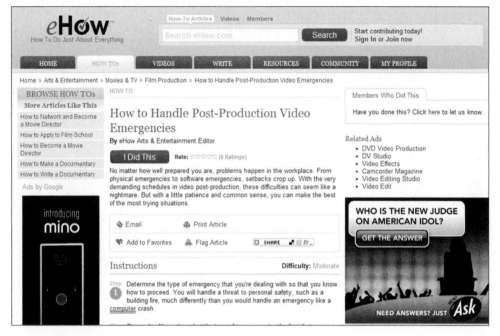

Figure 8.23 How to Handle Post-Production Video Emergencies

4. Figure out what you were doing when the problem occurred. What were you working on? Where you were in the video production process when the problem occurred? What equipment were you using when error messages appeared?

5. Check for simple, obvious problems like loose cables or unplugged equipment. If your video production equipment uses batteries, make sure they're working.

6. Decide if this is a problem you can fix yourself or if you need technical support. When you call tech support, get an estimate of how long it will take to fix. This will give you an idea of how the emergency will affect your video production deadline.

7. Talk to your clients and let them know what the problem is. Apologize for any delays. Offer solutions if you can, and if you can't, explain what happened. Most clients will understand as long as you're honest with them.

Also, the technical editor of this book says, "Make sure you have a backup of the original footage. And Google the problem to see if others have experienced it before with the software you're using. You'll often find forums or comment threads where people are helping one another figure it out."

Now that we've covered video production basics, tips, techniques, and frequently asked questions, let's tackle the next step in the process: how to become a YouTube partner and video advertiser.

Month 7: Become a YouTube Partner and Video Advertiser

YouTube partners are independent video creators and media companies who meet YouTube's qualifications. YouTube also offers video advertising opportunities that enable marketers to connect with their audience in a targeted way at a massive scale. In this chapter, you will learn how to become a YouTube partner, which gives you the ability to share in ad revenue from your YouTube videos. We will also take a look at some of the YouTube ad opportunities to discover how your brand can converse with this vibrant community. Finally, you will learn why this model is a natural fit for the YouTube community, which is why you will never hear a YouTube partner say, "Unfortunately, a few years back we had to start accepting advertising."

Chapter Contents:

Like Super Bowl Commercials?

Somehow, it seems only fitting that the first draft of this chapter was written on a Super Bowl Sunday. That's the one day a year I sit down in front of my television to watch TV commercials.

Now, I'm not an NFL football fan. I grew up watching the Detroit Lions, the worst regular-season team in NFL history, which killed my interest in the game. After moving to Boston, I admit I watched the New England Patriots from time to time, until Tom Brady (a University of Michigan alumnus) got injured.

And this year, I couldn't have cared less if the Pittsburgh Steelers were 7-point favorites over the Arizona Cardinals and ended up winning 27-23. Heck, I wasn't even a member of an office football pool.

So when I tuned into to NBC that afternoon to watch TV, it was to see the Super Bowl commercials. I've been a big fan since I first saw the Apple 1984 commercial that launched the Macintosh during Super Bowl XVIII.

My son Brendan and I couldn't wait to discover if Conan O'Brien shilling for Bud Light in Swedish, the homemade Doritos Crystal Ball ad, or the Budweiser Clydesdales Generations saga would be among the highlights of Super Bowl XLIII. And my wife couldn't wait to hear Bruce Springsteen during the Super Bowl half-time show.

Perhaps that's why 32 Super Bowl advertisers paid NBC a record $206 million for 69 advertising spots, even though marketers faced "the combination of a no-big-name matchup, the terrible economy, elevated expectations for marketing return on investment, and a growing sentiment against irresponsible spending," as Joe Grimaldi, the president and CEO of Mullen, told Brian Steinberg of the *Boston Globe* on the day before the 2009 game.

The 2009 Super Bowl commercials were purchased for between $2.4 million and $3 million per 30-second spot in the hopes of reaching an audience of 100 million viewers. That was a $24 to $30 CPM (or cost per thousand, because M is the Roman numeral for 1,000). When you add the cost of producing each spot, estimated to be $1 million to $2 million, this means marketers thought they'd get a decent bang for the buck by spending $34 to $50 for a thousand impressions.

-marketing for *PC Computing* from 1988 to 1991 and then worked for William Ziff, Jr. as the director of corporate communications for Ziff-Davis from 1991 until he retired in 1993.

He often said a special-interest magazine was a like a magnet and a screen: it attracted readers interested in a topic but also sifted out those who weren't as interested. This created an audience that endemic advertisers could reach cost-effectively, because a high percentage of readers were interested in their products.

John Battelle, who was a reporter at *MacWeek* when it was acquired by Ziff-Davis, wrote about this phenomenon in his Searchblog on May 25, 2004:

What's inherent in this interaction is the intention of all parties to be in relationship with each other. This creates and fosters a sense of community—the best publications always have what are called 'endemic' advertisers—those that 'belong' to the publication's community, that 'fit' with the publication's voice and point of view. I've found that in the magazines and sites I've helped create, my readers enjoyed the ads nearly as much as the editorial, because the ads served them, seemed to understand who they were in relation to the community the publication created.

So, what does this mean to veteran marketers and new YouTubers? We've already learned that social marketing is fundamentally different from mass marketing. Does online video advertising need to be fundamentally different from TV commercials?

These are the right questions to ask and, while it is still "early days" for online video advertising, this chapter will look for some tentative answers. The definition of "early days" is an early period of development. In Chapter 1, I used the term "early days" to describe video search in 2005, so I'm using it again to describe online video advertising, which has lagged in development by a few years.

Week 1: Become a YouTube Partner

YouTube's Partner Program is a revenue-sharing program that allows creators and producers of original content to earn money from their videos on YouTube. You can earn revenue from relevant advertisements that run against your videos using Google's proprietary technology. YouTube uses a variety of criteria to review applications, including the size of your audience, quality of content, and consistency with its Community Guidelines and Terms of Use.

On December 10, 2008, Brian Stelter of the *New York Times* wrote an article entitled "YouTube Videos Pull in Real Money." He wrote, "One year after YouTube, the online video powerhouse, invited members to become 'partners' and added advertising to their videos, the most successful users are earning six-figure incomes from the Web site." Stelter interviewed Michael Buckley, the host of "What the Buck?" who said he was earning over $100,000 from YouTube advertisements. We'll take a closer look at his success story in the 11th chapter of this book. (Ironically, the term *Chapter 11* means something very different.)

On December 18, 2008, Greg Sandoval of CNET News wrote an article entitled "Universal Music seeing 'tens of millions' from YouTube." He reported that Rio Caraeff, executive vice president of Universal Music Group's eLabs, had said in an interview that YouTube had generated "tens of millions" of dollars for the recording company that year, up 80 percent from the previous year. We'll also examine this case study in the 11th chapter of this book.

And on March 15, 2009, Mike Shields of *MediaWeek* wrote an article entitled "YouTube Plays Partner." He interviewed John Evershed, CEO of Mondo Media, which makes Happy Tree Friends. Evershed said that Mondo was pulling in monthly revenue in the five-figure range on YouTube, which he saw quickly growing. We'll check out this example later in this chapter.

As Figure 9.3 illustrates, a wide variety of original content creators are YouTube Partners. Universal Music Group had close to 4 billion views as of May 5, 2009, making it the partner with the most views.

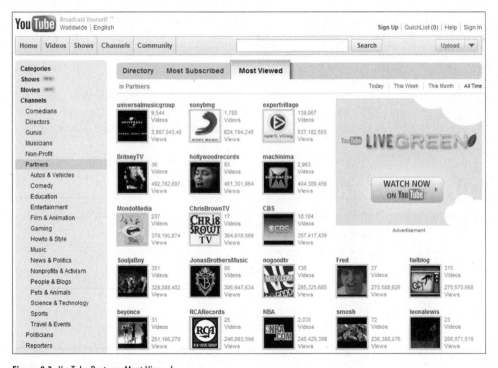

Figure 9.3 YouTube Partners Most Viewed

Monday: Sign up for YouTube Partner Program

Tuesday: Analyze cost-benefit of Partner Program

Wednesday: Create a destination

Thursday: Hold contests

Friday: Make money with Content ID

Monday: Sign Up for YouTube Partner Program

Today, we'll quickly cover the YouTube Partner Program basics. First, you need to meet the criteria for partnership:

- You create original videos suitable for online streaming.

- You own or have express permission to use and monetize all audio and video content that you upload. There are no exceptions to this criterion.

- You regularly upload videos that are viewed by thousands of YouTube users. This may be the toughest condition to meet.

- You live in the United States, Canada, or one of the other countries where the Partner Program is available.

In addition, YouTube uses AdSense to make revenue sharing payments to their partners, so you'll need to have an active AdSense account as well as a YouTube user account. Read the terms of use and other rules and regs to see if you are eligible. If so, then fill out an application at www.youtube.com/partners, but keep in mind that not everyone who applies for the program will qualify.

Your application will be reviewed to determine whether you fit YouTube's eligibility criteria. This may take some time, so you need to be patient. In the meantime, to help ensure that your application is approved, make sure that you have not violated YouTube's terms of use.

For example, do not use a photograph; any music; any movie or TV visuals; any artwork; or any play, theatrical work, or concert unless you have express permission of the person who created or produced it.

It's *not* okay to use someone else's material without permission, even if any of the following conditions apply:

- You edit together or "mash up" other works.

- You alter it by 10 percent, 20 percent, or 30 percent.

- You use only 30 seconds of a song or video clip.

- You found it on the Internet, because then it's in the public domain.

- You are performing a cover version of a song.

- Nobody sends you a copyright notice.

- You paid for it, so you can use it however you want.

- You give proper credits.

Are there exceptions to these rules? I'm not a lawyer, so you will want to go to http://www.youtube.com/t/content_management to read more about the YouTube Content ID system. It's a complex set of copyright policies and content management tools that attempts to balance the legal rights of copyright holders and the desire of people to express themselves online.

Lawrence Lessig, a professor of law at Stanford Law School, would describe the previous list as intellectual property (IP) "extremism." Professor Lessig says the content industry has convinced industry in general that extremism in copyright regulation is good for business and economic growth. He thinks that's false. In his book *Remix: Making Art and Commerce Thrive in the Hybrid Economy*, Professor Lessig describes the creative and profitable future that culture and industry could realize, if only we gave up IP extremism.

I emailed Professor Lessig some questions about his urgent, eloquent plea. And he emailed me his answers, which I posted to the Search Engine Watch Blog. Here is part of our Q&A:

Q: Who benefits and who is harmed by extremism in copyright regulation?

A: "Benefits: Lawyers (certainly). The record companies (maybe). Harmed: Artists, businesses, consumers—and a generation of (criminalized) kids."

Q: Why is IP extremism bad for business and economic growth?

A: "Practice moderation. When the lawyers in the room start insisting that the licenses you create must impose perfect control over everything you have, ask them to prove it. Ask them to demonstrate that the business return from that relationship of antagonism is higher than its cost. Don't give over your business' future to those who don't think like a business man or woman. Keep focused on the only undeniable truth: IP is an asset. Like any business asset, it should be deployed to maximize the value of the corporation."

Although I agree with Professor Lessig, you still can't violate YouTube's terms of use. To meet their criteria for partnership, you must own or have express permission to use and monetize all audio and video content that you upload.

However, on August 21, 2008, Bob Egelko of the *San Francisco Chronicle* wrote an article entitled "Woman can sue over YouTube clip de-posting." Here's what he said:

> *In a victory for small-time music copiers over the entertainment industry, a federal judge ruled Wednesday that copyright holders can't order one of their songs removed from the Web without first checking to see if the excerpt was so small and innocuous that it was legal. The ruling by U.S. District Judge Jeremy Fogel of San Jose was the first in the nation to require the owner of the rights to a creative work to consider whether an online copy was a "fair use" — a small or insignificant replication that couldn't have affected the market for the original — before ordering the Web host to take it down.*

Remember, I'm not an attorney, and the information I present here is not legal advice. I'm presenting it for informational purposes only.

Tuesday: Analyze Cost-Benefit of Partner Program

Today, let's analyze the benefits and costs of the Partner Program. According to YouTube, the benefits and costs include:

Effective monetization YouTube's automatically targeted, creative ad formats generate revenue while maintaining a positive user experience when your videos are viewed. The hidden cost is creating compelling video content.

Widest reach Your content can be discovered, watched and shared by the largest online video community in the world and via YouTube's syndication partners. The hidden cost is promoting videos to thousands of YouTube users.

Nonexclusive agreement YouTube doesn't restrict where you can upload and distribute your videos, so you can monetize it via YouTube and still use it elsewhere. The hidden cost is owning the copyrights and distribution rights to all the content that you upload.

Now, there are no guarantees under the YouTube Partner agreement about how much, or whether, you will be paid. Revenue is generated based on a share of advertising revenue generated when people view your videos. The more views you get, the more money you'll make. Nevertheless, there are some additional sources of revenue that you will want to know about.

When you enable revenue sharing on a video, YouTube may begin showing ads next to your videos on your YouTube video watch pages. By default, YouTube also enables three other sources of revenue, listed next, which I recommend leaving turned on to maximize your revenue potential.

Allow embedding Embedded videos also earn you money through ads. I recommend leaving this option turned on. Ads on embedded videos are similar in behavior to existing InVideo ads on YouTube. They can be composed of graphical overlays or they can be contextually targeted text ads. The overlays are contextually targeted to users based on various signals associated with the video, such as text, metadata, and other information that you provide directly through tagging. All earnings from embedded videos will be reported in your AdSense account on a daily basis under "AdSense for Content Host." Brad O'Farrell, the technical editor of this book, says, "After two years of YouTube, I've found that these kind of ads ultimately generate the most money, because you're always getting a slow trickle of views from embedded videos."

Allow InVideo advertising Allowing InVideo advertising means that YouTube may occasionally run transparent overlay ads on the lower portion of your video.

Allow AdSense overlay advertising AdSense overlay ads show both in your videos on your YouTube channel and on embedded videos on other websites. AdSense overlay ads are similar to InVideo ads and can be composed of graphical overlays or contextually targeted text. AdSense overlay ads can also be turned on or off in the same manner as InVideo ads.

Although YouTube Partners generally don't talk about how much ad revenue they get when people view their videos, it appears that revenue is being generated.

For example, MGM Worldwide Digital Media (MGM) and YouTube announced a multiple channel commitment on November 10, 2008. As Figure 9.4 illustrates, the Partner Program kicked off with Impact, a channel dedicated to promoting MGM's video on demand (VOD) high-octane action programming.

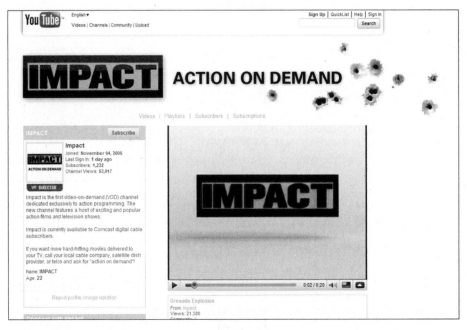

Figure 9.4 Impact: Action On Demand

MGM's Impact launched as a VOD offering in partnership with Comcast. It quickly became one of the cable operator's most popular on-demand offerings, amassing more than 12 million views since launching in August 2008.

The Impact channel on YouTube was an extension of the popular brand dedicated exclusively to action programming. The YouTube Impact channel features a host of exciting clips from classic MGM films such as *Rocky*, *Ronin*, *Legally Blonde*, and *The Magnificent Seven* as well as a sampling of exciting and popular action television show clips and full-length movies like *Lone Wolf McQuade* and *Bulletproof Monk*.

"We're looking to mine the breadth and depth of the MGM library to build out and promote branded, multiplatform opportunities on demand, online and wherever viewers consume their entertainment," Jim Packer, co-president, MGM Worldwide Television, said in a press release announcing the new partner. "Our agreement with YouTube opens the door to a number of themed broadband channels that will serve the consumers' growing appetite for entertainment media consumption in the digital space and 'on demand' space," he added.

Jordan Hoffner, director of content partnerships for YouTube, said in the press release announcing the new partner, "By partnering with MGM, YouTube is strengthening its position as an entertainment destination where Hollywood studios can reach a global audience and where our audience can watch their favorite full-length films, TV shows, and clips."

As Figure 9.5 illustrates, MGM also launched American Gladiators, a channel that showcases highlights and full episodes from the classic show that took America by storm during the 1980s and 1990s.

Figure 9.5 American Gladiators

Both the Impact and American Gladiator YouTube channels are ad supported. MGM has refreshed them with new videos every month and has plans to launch additional channels on YouTube in the near future. So I think it is safe to assume that "revenue is generated."

Wednesday: Create a Destination

Another option that you will want to consider is creating a Brand Channel. As this was written, a Brand Channel cost $200,000 or more in advertising commitments on YouTube for American advertisers targeting the United States market. Since all pricing minimums are subject to change, you should verify the current contract requirements with a YouTube ad sales representative.

If this cost commitment seems sort of steep, then consider that a 30-second ad on the Super Bowl cost $3 million in 2009. And YouTube gets a Super-Bowl sized audience month in and month out. So, a new YouTuber or small business might not pop for a Brand Channel, but then they might not pop for a Super Bowl commercial, either.

A variety of marketers have created brand channels. This includes:

- Disney Parks (http://www.youtube.com/disneyparks)

- Nike's LeBron James Channel (http://www.youtube.com/LeBron)

- Dunkin' Donuts (http://www.youtube.com/DunkinDonuts)

- United States Navy (http://www.youtube.com/UnitedStatesNavy)

- 100% Pure New Zealand (http://www.youtube.com/PureNewZealand)

Brand channels allow marketers to create a brandable and customized destination on YouTube. The basic brand channel functionality can also be integrated into a website by copying one line of HTML.

As Figure 9.6 illustrates, the design of Johnson's Baby Channel clearly communicates the brand's values. The channel info says, "Johnson's has been helping parents and doctors give babies a healthy, happy start in life for more than 100 years." And the invitation to submit videos lets them connect and create persistent relationships with their customers.

Figure 9.6 Johnson's Baby Channel is well customized to reinforce the brand.

Since it costs a ton of dough, a Brand Channel should provide you with a ton of features and benefits that you can't get on a regular channel. And it does, including:

- The featured video will play automatically when a user arrives at a Brand Channel, increasing views.

- When a user clicks on another video, that video will play within the Brand Channel, keeping the user within your branded space.

- Brand Channels can list up to 16 channel links, enabling you to cross-promote your other channels and websites.

- You can moderate all comments on a Brand Channel.

- You can limit the "related videos" on the Watch Page of each video on a Branded Channel to partner videos.

- To ensure brand safety, you can make a Brand Channel accessible only to users of a certain age or gender.

- As you learned in Chapter 6, you can customize Brand Channels with a channel banner at the top of the page, externally hosted background image, and branding box.

- A Brand Channel offers a 300×250 pixel side column image that can include a call to action like "Buy Now."

- The watch page for each video on a Brand Channel is branded with a 300×45 pixel banner, as well as a 55×55 pixel channel icon.

- Google Analytics is only available on Brand Channels to track and measure traffic.

In addition, YouTube has a selection of ready-made gadgets available for Brand Channels. These small web applications or rich media ads sit on a Brand Channel, offering deeper functionality for users. They include:

- Carousel: This encourages users to scroll through your videos. For an example, check out `http://www.youtube.com/live`.

- Video Wall: This displays up to 45 videos. To see a demonstration, go to `http://www.youtube.com/walldemo1`.

- Mosaic: This display hundreds of videos in a branded image. For a demo, look at `http://www.youtube.com/mosaicdemo2`.

- Mash-up: This allows users to make their own edits of your videos. Watch the W mashup contest at `http://www.youtube.com/wthefilm` to see what I mean.

- Gizmoz: This enables users to create, customize, animate and share 3D talking heads to express themselves in more imaginative ways. Go to `http://www.youtube.com/watch?v=ZwZZqWmwtyA` for a sample.

Although these features and benefits will help, the success of your Brand Channel is still highly dependent on the content you upload. So, you should:

- Have a dedicated person developing your YouTube channel.

- Emphasize the quality over the quantity of videos that you upload.

- Try to upload a couple of videos each week, keeping the content on your channel fresh and updated.

- Try to upload content on a regular schedule, helping users anticipate when they can come back to see the new content on your channel.

- Update your video library over time, encouraging repeat visits and additional views.

- Update the featured video on your channel as frequently as possible.

- Explain the types of content that are available on your channel.

To have a successful Brand Channel, you also need to be a fully vested member of the YouTube community. So, you should:

- Ask viewers to rate, share, and subscribe to each of your videos.

- Encourage viewers to post text comments and video responses to each of your videos.

- Rate videos by other YouTubers as your favorites if they have compelling content that is relevant to your brand channel.

- Interact with other members of the YouTube community who subscribe to your channel, post comments or video responses to your videos, or create relevant content on their channels.

- Tell other YouTubers when and why you might add their videos to your brand channel.

- Link to your website, blog, or profile from your brand channel and link from these online properties to your brand channel.

If creating a destination with a Brand Channel seems like it will take a lot of time and money, remember this: sometimes you gotta go big or go home.

Thursday: Hold Contests

YouTube contests are a core way of driving user interaction and deep engagement with your content. They can easily be integrated into your brand channel, creating one destination to reach your users with a unified message.

As Figure 9.7 illustrates, in the summer of 2008 Kmart encouraged "junior fashionistas" ages 13 and up to record and upload a 30- to 60-second commercial of themselves and up to four friends and enter it into the Show Your Back to School Style: Get in the Commercial contest on the official Kmart channel. The top vote-getting commercial was professionally produced and aired during *90210* on the CW network.

This is the type of active user interactions that brands and advertisers seek in order to reach new customers. As opposed to a more traditional advertising model, where advertisers actively search for their target audiences, YouTube contests actually bring interested users to advertisers.

As you learned in Chapter 7, there are a number of best practices to holding successful contests, including these guidelines for contest administration:

- Create compelling call-to-action videos for each contest phase.

- Assign resources to manage your contest and respond to customer inquiries. By clearly defining the contest rules, prizes, deadlines, and entry requirements, you will be able to reduce the need for resources.

- Review all contest entries to manage brand acceptability.

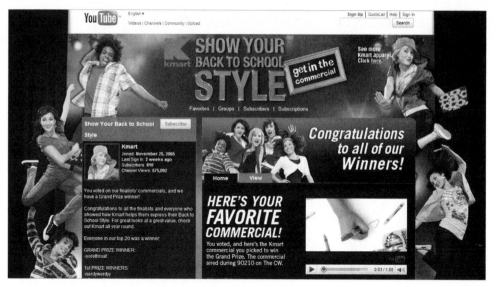

Figure 9.7 Kmart's channel, after the conclusion of its 2008 contest

As you learned in Chapter 7, there are a number of best practices to holding successful contests, including these guidelines for contest administration:

- Create compelling call-to-action videos for each contest phase.

- Assign resources to manage your contest and respond to customer inquiries. By clearly defining the contest rules, prizes, deadlines, and entry requirements, you will be able to reduce the need for resources.

- Review all contest entries to manage brand acceptability.

Frequently, publicity and recognition can be as valuable as financial prizes. The following list identifies several different types of prizes that have been awarded to previous YouTube contest winners:

- Winning videos have been broadcast on network television as ads for the brand running the contest.

- Contest winners receive experiences, such as the opportunity to meet or perform with a celebrity or band.

- Winners receive a prize package featuring the sponsor's products, such as a vacation package, musical equipment, or an automobile.

- Frequently, contest sponsors will combine a financial prize with another prize that provides some type of public recognition for the winners or winning videos.

As this was written, YouTube contests cost $500,000 or more. Again, all commitment minimums are subject to change, so verify current pricing directly with a YouTube ad sales representative.

My technical editor, Brad O'Farrell, adds, "A cash prize of at least a few thousand dollars is more likely to drive hundreds and hundreds of submissions than a feather-in-your-cap prize. As a member of the YouTube community, the only contests I ever hear about or am aware of are the ones with cash prizes."

A variety of other marketers have used contests to engage the community. This includes:

- HP's Project Direct, which got over 650 short films submitted and more than 3.8 million video views.

- Sierra Mist's Sketchies sketch comedy contest, which got over 5,000 submissions and more than 3.4 million views.

- Chrysler 300's Spin it Your Way, which got more than 70 video entries and 1.7 million video views.

Friday: Make Money with Content ID

You may need to use the Glossary in the back of this book for today's lesson because it contains terms only an experienced YouTuber would understand.

First, let's start with YouTube's "Content Identification and Management System," which is also called the YouTube "Content ID" system or "CID."

YouTube director: "Is this in the Glossary?"

Yes, it's in the Glossary.

Now, Content ID is a complex set of copyright policies and content management tools. It lets rights owners identify videos uploaded by users that are comprised *entirely* or *partially* of their content.

Search engine marketer: "How does it do that?"

I don't know. It's a mystery.

Content ID then lets rights owners select, in advance, what should happen when these user-uploaded videos are found: make money from them, get stats on them, or block them.

Entrepreneur: "How do you make money from them?"

I'll get to that.

One of Content ID's content management tools is called Video Identification, or Video ID. Rights holders give YouTube reference files of the video content they own, metadata describing that content, and what they want YouTube to do when a match is found. YouTube compares videos that have been uploaded against these reference files. Its technology mysteriously identifies their works and either monetizes, tracks, or blocks them.

Now, if copyright holders partner with YouTube, then Video ID can generate revenue for them. In fact, David King, YouTube product manager, said on the YouTube Blog on August 27, 2008, YouTube Partners were monetizing 90 percent of all claims created through Video ID. This led directly to a significant increase in monetizable part-ner inventory as more than 300 YouTube Video ID partners were seeing claimed content more than double their number of views, against which YouTube could run ads.

This meant that if a partner had, for example, 10,000 views of its content, leav-ing up videos claimed by the Video ID system will lead to an additional 10,000 views of that same content on average. YouTube calls this "partner uplift," and some part-ners have seen uplift as high as 9,000 percent.

This was confirmed by an article entitled "Some Media Companies Choose to Profit from Pirated YouTube Clips," by Brian Stelter (*New York Times*, August 15, 2008). Stelter wrote, "After years of regarding pirated video on YouTube as a threat, some major media companies are having a change of heart, treating it instead as an advertising opportunity."

Stelter reported that CBS, Universal Music, Lionsgate, Electronic Arts, and other companies had stopped prodding YouTube to remove unauthorized clips of their movies, music videos, and other content and had started selling advertising against them instead. He added, "CBS may be the most surprising new business partner in that its sister company, Viacom, is still pursuing its acrimonious billion-dollar copyright lawsuit against YouTube's owner, Google."

Here's how Video ID works: YouTube users who post content without permis-sion do not share in the advertising revenue generated by their posts. Instead, it is split between the media companies and YouTube.

The infringing user receives an email message saying, "A YouTube partner made a copyright claim on one of your videos." The email message explains that the media company has "authorized the use of this content" and that viewers may see advertising on the video.

Before Video ID, media companies would simply demand that their material be taken down. But the technology offers an alternative, allowing the companies to "claim" the videos and start showing ads alongside them, creating a new revenue stream for both YouTube and the content owners.

Stelter added, "Electronic Arts, the video game publisher, has taken Video ID a step further, using it to encourage user submissions. In a promotion for the coming video game Spore, E.A. encouraged gamers to upload original Spore creatures they cre-ated using a software program. There were more than 100,000 submissions, and some attracted hundreds of thousands of views. E.A. used Video ID to claim the most popu-lar user videos and share in the ad revenue on them."

As Figure 9.8 illustrates, the "Spore Space Video" featuring brand-new game-play footage as well as an in-depth interview with producer Kip Katsarelis had more than 460,000 views as of February 2009.

You can learn more about YouTube's Content Identification and Management System (CID) at http://youtube.com/t/contentid.

Figure 9.8 "Spore Space Video"

Week 2: Weigh YouTube Alternatives

As I've mentioned before, YouTube should be the center, but not the circumference, of your video marketing campaigns. So when you weigh the alternatives to YouTube, you have a range of strategic options:

- 40 percent YouTube, 60 percent alternatives
- 50 percent YouTube, 50 percent alternatives
- 60 percent YouTube, 40 percent alternatives
- 70 percent YouTube, 30 percent alternatives
- 80 percent YouTube, 20 percent alternatives

You'll notice that I didn't offer any alternatives above 60 percent or below 20 percent. That's because I think veteran marketers can't afford to ignore YouTube—and new YouTubers can't afford to ignore the alternatives. (Even Hulu.com, an online video service, has 170 videos on its huluDotCom's channel on YouTube.)

So this week, we'll look at case studies of organizations that are heading in different directions along this spectrum, which reflects YouTube's market share.

Monday: Examine PBS's website and channel

Tuesday: Visit Showtime's website and channel

Wednesday: Check out Mondo Media's websites and channel

Thursday: View Squeegees on YouTube and Hulu

Friday: Watch HBO...on YouTube and its website

Monday: Examine PBS's Website and Channel

For example, PBS features online videos of its programs and collections on its website at www.pbs.org/video and also uploads its best programs on PBS's channel on YouTube at www.youtube.com/pbs.

As Figure 9.9 illustrates, PBS Video includes featured videos of its award-winning national programming and locally produced shows. You can watch your favorite shows and catch the episodes you may have missed. You can also click Share to send your favorites to friends and post to social networks or purchase your own copy by clicking Own It.

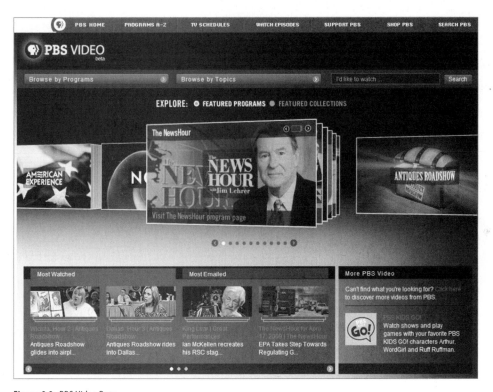

Figure 9.9 PBS Video Beta

Each week, PBS reaches more than 65 million Americans from every walk of life with a broad array of programs on its 356 member stations. In addition, www.pbs. org had close to 4.3 million unique visitors in March 2009 and almost 6 million visits, according to Compete.

Now, let's examine PBS's channel on YouTube. As Figure 9.10 illustrates, the broadcaster's channel was launched in March 2006. As of early May 2009, the more than 1,900 videos on PBS's channel had over 21.6 million views.

Figure 9.10 PBS

In January 2008, PBS announced it was adding more video content to its official YouTube channel, including selected online-only features, program excerpts, and extended previews from its award-winning series specials. PBS continued uploading longer segments of shows like *Tavis Smiley*, *NATURE*, and *Frontline/World* as well as documentaries from *Independent Lens* and *P.O.V.* With more than 18,000 subscribers as of early May 2009, PBS's decision to provide more video options followed greater demand for such content.

"Our channel on YouTube has enabled us to have a meaningful dialogue with viewers," John Boland, PBS's chief content officer, said in a press release. "It's critical that we engage as many people as possible with our programming. Posting PBS content on YouTube has helped us drive viewers back to watch the entire programs on our local stations' broadcast, and has helped increase usage of these programs' companion websites on pbs.org."

In October 2008, YouTube announced it had partnered with PBS to empower American voters to upload their Election Day voting experiences to YouTube. The initiative educated voters on the entire process and a wide array of issues associated with voting in America while enabling the world to watch pivotal moments in that historic election as they unfolded. In the first presidential election since YouTube's inception, this program gathered massive amounts of polling place video.

Some of the best videos were showcased on PBS television, as part of *The NewsHour with Jim Lehrer*'s Election Day broadcast. They were also used throughout PBS's election coverage, both on-air and online. YouTube users were asked to tag all events that hindered the voting process "pollproblem." These videos, as well as those documenting the spectrum of the entire voting process, were reviewed by analysts from PBS's political team, who then offered commentary on how the election played out.

In addition, YouTube and PBS distributed 1,000 Flip Video camcorders through Pure Digital Technologies, Inc.'s Flip Video Spotlight program so that participating nonpartisan nonprofit groups and local PBS stations across the country could also capture polling place activity.

Bringing enhanced PBS programming to a global YouTube audience furthers the broadcaster's mission of spreading awareness, unlocking mysteries, and exposing truths. Other broadcasters should take note.

Tuesday: Visit Showtime's Website and Channel

Today, we'll take a long look at Showtime's website and then pay a quick visit to Showtime's channel on YouTube.

For Showtime, online video serves not only to promote the network's cable channel programming, but also to create a new revenue stream of its own through advertising. As it establishes its website as a leading video content destination, Showtime's partnership with Brightcove helps to provide online audiences with the kind of premium experience its TV viewers have come to expect.

As I mentioned in Chapter 4, Brightcove provides video publishing tools to many big media companies. It has competitors, including PermissionTV and IVT, but Brightcove is used by more broadcast and cable networks, print and online media outlets, and music entertainment businesses and organizations worldwide to publish and distribute video on the Web.

In a case study on Brightcove's website, Chris Lucas, vice president and executive producer of digital media, says, "By working with Brightcove, we can create new experiences for the way people consume and interact with video."

Because Showtime is a premium network, its viewers expect an experience a cut above the norm. At the same time, building and maintaining its own state-of-the-art video player is beyond the company's core strength and an inefficient use of its resources.

"Showtime is a content company, not a technology company," says Lucas. "The Brightcove Platform allows us to focus on what we do best."

Showtime uses the Brightcove Platform to manage the large catalog of video content it delivers to viewers through the Showtime official site, which is www.sho.com. As Figure 9.11 illustrates, viewers enjoy near-HD quality through one of the largest players on the Web and can easily share their favorite content. Brightcove also makes it simple for Showtime to provide individual players to syndication partners such as cable affiliates and consumer portals without having to build custom applications for each partner.

Figure 9.11 The Showtime home page is managed using Brightcove software.

Brightcove has had a dramatic impact both internally, where it has helped Showtime free up three full-time positions, and among audiences, with page views for video content more than doubling in the first two months. The network can now more easily leverage and monetize the full depth of its archive while continuing to enhance its offerings.

Says Lucas, "Our relationship with Brightcove is very much a partnership, and we continue to work together on next-generation online video experiences."

Brightcove is used by hundreds of media companies, businesses, and organizations to power online video initiatives that reach over 100 million Internet users every month. The platform provides the following features:

Media management Built for producers, the Brightcove Media module provides content upload, video and playlist management, policy management, and image capture.

Publishing Built for designers, the Brightcove Publishing module allows users to create, manage, and customize video players without the need for development or IT resources.

Dynamic delivery To provide the best possible user experience, Brightcove detects end user connection speeds and optimizes video playback to deliver a high-quality experience.

Distribution You can reach a broad audience by syndicating content to Brightcove's network of distribution partners, enabling viral sharing, and letting major search engines index videos.

Advertising Built for ad ops professionals, the Brightcove Advertising module allows users to set and manage ad policies and integrate with leading ad servers and networks.

Analytics You can run reports to analyze performance and usage metrics across all videos or integrate with leading third-party analytics platforms.

APIs With Brightcove's suite of APIs and developer tools, users can create highly customized players and site navigation, boost SEO, and integrate with third-party systems.

Founded in 2004, Brightcove offers its online video platform in three editions:

Brightcove Basic This edition is for individuals and smaller organizations that are looking for a professional online video platform that is proven and affordable.

Brightcove Pro This edition extends the capabilities of Brightcove Basic and is designed for larger companies with a video or digital media team that operates a single web property.

Brightcove Enterprise This edition provides a set of capabilities designed for the publishers and conglomerates faced with complex requirements related to operating multiple web properties.

Meanwhile, the 202 videos on Showtime's channel on YouTube (Figure 9.12) had more than 110 million views as of May 2009, making it the #49 most viewed channel of all time. So, it appears that Showtime can have its popcorn and eat it too.

Figure 9.12 The Showtime channel on YouTube is similar in branding to its home page.

Wednesday: Check Out Mondo Media's Websites and Channel

Today, we'll spit our time checking out two of Mondo Media's websites and MondoMedia's channel on YouTube.

Cofounded by John Evershed and Deirdre O'Malley, Mondo Media is the Internet's leading multiplatform distributor of ad-supported animation for teens and young adults. The Mondo Mini Shows ad network comprises Mondo's own sites and a growing network of third-party sites, including these:

- mondominishows.com
- happytreefriends.com
- joecartoon.com
- spikeandmike.com
- newyorkercartoons.com

The Mondo Mini Shows channel is distributed across several major sites and platforms:

- YouTube.com
- MySpace.com
- Joost
- MondoToGo.com (mobile)
- iTunes podcasts

With over 30 million show views per month across all platforms, Mondo Media was the #6 most viewed and the #25 most subscribed YouTube channel of all time as of May 2009 as well as the #1 most downloaded video podcast on iTunes.

The official home of Happy Tree Friends and Mondo Mini Shows on YouTube is updated twice a week with new videos that are short, viral, and deadly funny. As Figure 9.13 illustrates, the 238 videos on MondoMedia's Channel on YouTube had 380 million views as of May 2009.

Figure 9.13 Mondo Mini Shows War Journal

Mondo Media has pulled over 500 million show views since launch with its flagship property Happy Tree Friends, which boasts 900,000+ online members, features global TV distribution in over 30 markets, and has sold over 1 million DVDs worldwide to date. Mondo Media's branded distribution partners include YouTube, Hulu, MySpace, Dailymotion, Metacafe, Bablegum, iTunes, iPhone, and Joost.

Mondo Media sells and manages advertising and sponsorships across its network of sites and syndication partners, procures licensing and merchandising deals, and sells and manages TV and DVD distribution rights.

Mondo Mini Shows (Figure 9.14) are distributed on an ad-supported, virtual animation channel via the Internet, podcasts, and mobile. Happy Tree Friends (Figure 9.15) is a TV series, home video line, mobile phenomenon, video game, and line of merchandise.

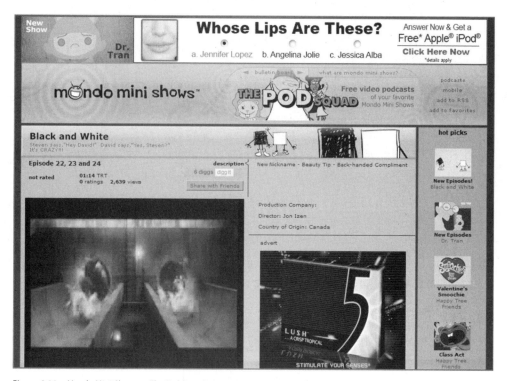

Figure 9.14: Mondo Mini Shows—The Pod Squad

As these two shows started gaining in popularity, Mondo Media looked to determine the best means to monetize their traffic and loyal audience. However, because the broadcaster was running campaigns from multiple video ad networks, it faced a few challenges:

- How could Mondo Media better monetize the number of video streams across both sites, improving its inventory fill rate?

- How could it maximize revenue from multiple sources (internal sales, ad networks, ad syndication feeds) and optimize by type of ad placement (pre-roll, mid-roll, interactive overlay)?

- How could it improve ad operations efficiency with respect to technical integration, campaign management, and reporting?

Figure 9.15 Happy Tree Friends

Mondo Media selected YuMe to address these challenges, and you can read the case study here:

www.yumenetworks.com/technology/mondo_media.php

Using YuMe's Adaptive Campaign Engine (ACE), Mondo Media is now able to maximize revenue from multiple ad sources: the broadcaster's own ad sales team, YuMe's ad sales team, third-party ad networks, and third-party syndication feeds.

ACE helped to solve Mondo Media's ad operations headache by providing a single integrated dashboard that reports on each feed's performance in real time, then automatically adjusts all feeds adapting to parameters set by the broadcaster to maximize each impression, increasing fill rate and effective CPMs. With ACE, Mondo Media is now able to achieve a 100 percent fill rate, and its overall effective CPM has increased by over 70 percent. ACE has also helped Mondo Media optimize ad performance and revenue in real time by matching video inventory with optimal ad placements.

Evershed says in the case study, "Our ability to fully monetize the popularity of content like 'Happy Tree Friends' depends on how well we can match each placement in our inventory to the best-performing available ad feed, no matter where it's coming from. With ACE, YuMe gives us both the real-time transparency and automation to make this possible, and the technology to make sure each ad ends up where it needs to be."

Thursday: View Squeegees on YouTube and Hulu

Today, we'll look at the Squeegees's channel on YouTube, and then we'll look at the Squeegees shows on Hulu.

In February 2008, the Disney-ABC Television Group announced the launch of Stage 9 Digital Media. Focused on creating original short-form programming, the studio's experimental new media content includes the comedy series *Squeegees*, which premiered the same day on ABC.com and YouTube. The series' initial coexclusive run was sponsored by Toyota.

Barry Jossen, an Academy Award–winning short-form producer and studio executive, was tapped as general manager of Stage 9. Jossen has produced both award-winning films and television series and received his Academy Award for the live action short film *Dear Diary*.

"While the new media space is loaded with UGC (user-generated content), we feel the audience is missing the quality experience found in other forms of exhibition, and we are answering their need," said Jossen in a press release announcing the launch of Stage 9.

"To have a storied company like Disney-ABC make new content for the YouTube community is quite groundbreaking and reflective of their unwavering imagination and YouTube's position as the home for quality professional video," added Jordan Hoffner, head of premium content partnerships for YouTube. Of course, he said this 14 months before Disney-ABC took a 27 percent stake in Hulu.

Squeegees comes from the brilliant minds of the comedy team Handsome Donkey, dubbed "Online Auteurs" by the *New York Times*. As Figure 9.16 illustrates, *Squeegees* is a character-driven ensemble comedy about entrepreneurial slackers and their fledgling window washing business.

Figure 9.16 *Squeegees*

The series premiered on February 28, 2008, and was the most subscribed new partner video on YouTube in its first week. New *Squeegees* episodes debuted every Monday and Friday on both sites.

After an exclusive nine-week first-run premiere on YouTube and ABC.com, Stage 9 Digital Media expanded exhibition of its debut series *Squeegees*, announcing web syndication partnerships with YouTube, Hulu, Zvue, eBaum's World, X-Box Live, and iTunes.

Squeegees's new expanded release significantly extended the comedy's reach. The new multiprogram deals also followed the studio's distribution strategy to partner with top broadband video sites and download services to maximize viewer accessibility and interaction.

"With the popularity of 'Squeegees,' Disney-ABC Television Group and Stage 9 proved that YouTube is a natural home for original, professional content," said Hoffner in a second press release issued that day.

"We're going after the digital generation whose quest for entertainment is extended across the Internet," said Jossen in this new press release. "This second, wider distribution takes 'Squeegees' to them wherever they are, on whatever device they're using. The strategy not only broadens the audience for the series, it builds interest in Stage 9's upcoming slate of programming."

As Figure 9.17 illustrates, the look and feel of *Squeegees* on Hulu is different than the Squeegees's channel on YouTube. In addition, 10 episodes have been uploaded to Hulu, while there are 15 videos on YouTube.

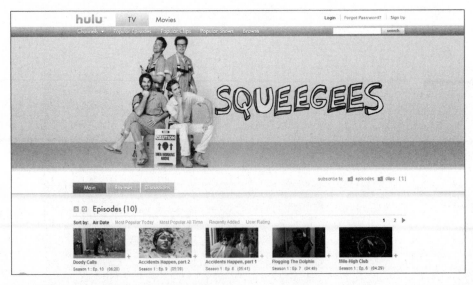

Figure 9.17 *Squeegees* on Hulu: a different approach

The studio's rollout of new short-form programming continued with *Voicemail 2*, the second season of ABC.com's first original series inspired by one man's decade-long collection of phone messages. The previously unpublished humorous snippets capture an uncanny insight into the life of a 20-something male slacker in pursuit of happiness...with no responsibility. *Voicemail 2* is executive produced by Angela Mancuso.

Also slated to debut in the spring of 2009 was the original science fiction action thriller *Trenches*, from Shane Felux, the critically acclaimed filmmaker and creator of "Pitching George Lucas" and "Star Wars Revelations," which became online sensations. Set in another time, on another planet, *Trenches* begins in the waning days of a grueling war. A botched rescue attempt forces a young soldier and his unit to team up with their enemy to survive a brutal threat and escape the planet.

The studio has an active slate of more than 20 programs in comedy, drama, animation, and reality ranging from traditional linear episodic storytelling to fully immersive interactive content geared toward the trend-setting 18 to 34 demographic.

Friday: Watch HBO...on YouTube and its Website

Today, we'll visit HBO's official YouTube channel, and then we'll visit HBO's official website.

On February 25, 2008, Home Box Office (HBO), Inc., and YouTube announced an agreement to offer select promotional content on HBO's new branded YouTube channel. This included videos from HBO shows, including *Flight of the Conchords*, *The Wire*, *Def Comedy Jam*, *Real Time with Bill Maher*, *Real Sports*, *Extras*, *Stand Up Comedy*, *Habla y Habla*, and *Entourage*.

Full-length episodes of HBO's original series *In Treatment* are also available on the channel, as well as promotional content from HBO Films and HBO Documentary Films. As Figure 9.18 illustrates, HBO's channel was used to promote a new comedy series, *Eastbound & Down*, which premiered on February 15, 2009.

Figure 9.18 HBO's channel

The HBO YouTube channel is populated with content from the company's most popular shows as well as special YouTube-only features.

Meanwhile, HBO's official website, which is powered by Brightcove, contains schedule information, original video content, episode guides, polls, contests, bulletin boards, celebrity chats, and more! As Figure 9.19 illustrates, HBO Online informs you that Danny McBride stars in *Eastbound & Down*.

Figure 9.19 HBO Online

"We are delighted to bring HBO content to the YouTube community and fans of our shows," Joseph Giraldi, HBO's director of digital distribution and partnerships, said in a February 2008 press release announcing the launch of the YouTube channel. "We invest significantly in developing HBO programs and are always searching for new promotional platforms."

This is worth remembering when trying to understand what happened a year later. Disney-ABC announced an agreement with YouTube in March 2009 and then announced in April 2009 that it had agreed to become a joint venture partner and equity owner of Hulu.

Although a multiplatform approach makes sense, there is still a lot of room between the strategic option of 40 percent YouTube / 60 percent alternatives and the strategic option of 80 percent YouTube / 20 percent alternatives.

"As the leader in online video, YouTube provides top media companies like HBO an opportunity to broadcast their content to an entirely new audience," Hoffner said in the February 2008 press release. "The YouTube community watches hundreds of millions of videos everyday and as that number increases, so does the demand for original, quality programming."

This is also worth remembering when trying to understand what happened 14 months later. YouTube announced a new destination for television shows in mid-April 2009 and then redesigned its home page later that same month.

Although YouTube needs to continue offering all the different kinds of video that users want to see, it is a delicate balance to reflect what is popular, from TV shows and music videos to bedroom vlogs and citizen journalism reports.

Week 3: Evaluate Advertising Opportunities

In addition to becoming a YouTube Partner and weighing the YouTube alternatives, you should evaluate all the YouTube video advertising opportunities.

Advertising on YouTube is about helping users, partners, and advertisers connect with each other through video. All advertisements must follow YouTube's Community Guidelines and advertising content policies.

For example, YouTube does not permit advertising for academic aids, adult or pornographic content, aids to pass a drug test, anabolic steroids, automated ad clicking, bulk marketing, counterfeit designer goods, data entry affiliate programs, dialers, drugs and drug paraphernalia, e-gold, escort services, fake documents, fireworks and pyrotechnic devices, gambling, hacking and cracking sites, inflating ad clicks or impressions, miracle cures, online video sites that compete with YouTube, prostitution, scams phishing for personal information, tobacco and cigarettes, traffic devices, or weapons.

In addition, ads may not have fake hyperlinks, resemble dialog boxes, simulate fake interactivity, contain content of a sexual nature, initiate downloads, be intrusive, advertise competitive content, or have misleading content.

YouTube has also tested lots of different kinds of advertising over the past few years, and it is constantly working to develop the right advertising format for the right content and environment on YouTube. But different experiences—like watching short videos or full-length videos, sharing videos and uploading videos, browsing related videos, and searching for videos—require YouTube to provide advertisers with lots of options. So, they've created many products that work in different ways:

Homepage Video Ads Reaches those coming to YouTube who just want to be entertained with anything engaging.

InVideo Ads Reaches those interested in content related to the short video they're watching.

Click-to buy Reaches those who want to find products and other information online related to the video they're watching.

Promoted Videos Reaches those who are searching for videos.

In-stream ads Reaches those who are willing to accept this kind of advertising experience when watching longer-form and premium content on YouTube, like TV shows and movies.

This week, we'll take a closer look at each of these options.

Monday: Welcome Homepage Video Ads

Tuesday: Investigate InVideo Ads

Wednesday: Check out click-to-buy

Thursday: Explore Promoted Videos

Friday: Inspect in-stream ads

Monday: Welcome Homepage Video Ads

Let's start by welcoming Homepage Video Ads, which are an up-front way to connect with users when they visit the site.

On August 22, 2006, YouTube unveiled brand channels and what was then called the Participatory Video Ad (PVA)—because it was designed to encourage dialogue between community and marketers.

YouTube's first brand channel partner was Warner Bros. Records, which created the Paris Hilton Channel for her debut album, *Paris*, which was released globally that day. The Paris Hilton Channel was sponsored by Fox Broadcasting Company's hit show *Prison Break*. (Hey, you can't make this stuff up.)

The pop singer created an original broadcast for the YouTube community taking advantage of the new PVA offering on the YouTube home page. Weinstein Company experienced great success with the first-ever PVA promotion on YouTube for the feature film *PULSE* with a campaign created by interactive agency Deep Focus. Fox Broadcasting, working with digital communications agency Organic, Inc., also utilized the new PVA in conjunction with the Paris Hilton sponsorship to promote the fall season launch of *Prison Break*.

"Our vision is to build a new advertising platform that both the community and advertisers will embrace. Our announcement today is just the beginning of the many new ad concepts we will be rolling out over the coming year," Chad Hurley, CEO and cofounder of YouTube, said in a press release. "This new medium requires finding a balance between traditional online advertising and new creative approaches that engage consumers in an active way. Advertisers now have a highly targeted opportunity for aligning their brands alongside the entertainment experience people are enjoying on YouTube."

The PVA was a user-initiated video advertisement with all of the YouTube community features enabled. Consumers could rate, share, comment, embed, and favorite advertising content that they found interesting, informative, and entertaining. Rather than interrupt a consumer's experience, YouTube created a model that encouraged engagement and participation.

The YouTube community was very receptive to this new advertising experience and propelled PVA videos to the top of the Most Viewed, Most Discussed, and Top Favorite video rankings. Advertisers had the opportunity to participate and moderate discussions around their creative.

The Warner Music Group and YouTube parted ways in December 2008 because they couldn't reach acceptable business terms. And the PVA is now called the Homepage Video Ad.

Although impressions are not guaranteed, the YouTube Homepage has been delivering around 30 million impressions and 11 million unique visitors a day in the U.S. The Homepage Video Ad is a great way to create awareness and reach a wide audience with your marketing message. And over time, some Video Ad best practices have emerged:

- **Keep it short:** Sixty seconds is a good yardstick. If the message is longer, the chances that users will tune out get higher.

- **Keep it engaging:** Users will watch most or all of a video if it interests and engages them. So, try to connect with your audience in a personal and targeted way.

- **Don't lecture, motivate:** A couple of minutes of talking heads isn't very effective. So, try to entertain, inform and inspire instead of just trying to educate.

- **Deliver your messages early:** Viewers are likely to tune-out near the end of a video, so deliver your key message early.

- **Include a call to action:** If your marketing objective is to increase visits to a destination, then give your audience a reason to go there. A call to action can be very effective, if it's appropriate.

Over time, ad specifications have emerged:

Video format	H.264, MPEG-2, or MPEG-4 preferred
Aspect ratio	Native aspect ratio without letterboxing (examples: 4:3, 16:9)
Resolution	640×360 (16:9) or 480×360 (4:3) recommended
Audio format	MP3 or AAC preferred
Maximum file size	1GB

And over time, advertisers have learned how a 300×360 YouTube Video Ad that runs in the top-right corner of the home page works:

- 300×35 companion ad that clicks through to an external URL.

- 300×225 video screen:

  - Advertiser can provide an optional 300×225 custom title card image (instead of showing a still from the video).

  - I highly recommend using the automatically generated mid-section thumbnail because this can improve your click-to-play rate.

- 300×100 info box under the video with the following elements:
  - The title of the video (60 characters, two lines max), which clicks through to the video's watch page.
  - A 50×50 profile channel icon, which clicks through to the advertiser's channel.
  - Rate the video option.
  - Full Screen option.
- If a user clicks the video for a second time, they can be directed to either the video's watch page or channel, depending on the advertiser's preference.

In addition, YouTube now offers a masthead ad. As a full-width unit in the most prominent space on YouTube, a masthead ad offers rich media interactivity and DoubleClick metrics. If you use a masthead ad, I recommend that it include a video and link to a watch page.

Tuesday: Investigate InVideo Ads

Today, let's investigate InVideo Ads, which are animated overlays that appear at the bottom 20 percent of a video shortly after launching. These ads are 80 percent transparent and appear 15 seconds into a video.

If users do not take action (the ad lasts approximately 10 to 15 seconds), the ad will disperse. If a user is interested, clicking on the overlay temporarily pauses the video and allows the user to launch a deeper interactive ad experience.

YouTube has found that less than 10 percent of users close the overlay, which has a click-through rate (CTR) 8 to 10 times the click-to-play rate of standard display ads. So, let's take a closer look at how YouTube InVideo Ads work.

YouTube InVideo Ads run on partner watch pages. The Flash overlay ad will appear 15 seconds into the video. The user can click to display a video ad or interactive Flash ad within the YouTube video player or go directly to a click-through URL. If the user doesn't click the overlay to play a video ad, the video will automatically play as post-roll.

Although a 300×250 companion display ad is optional, I highly recommend it. These elements are road-blocked for the same advertiser or campaign when presented together. As Figure 9.20 illustrates, Ford uses a InVideo Ad for the 2010 Fusion hybrid within "Beyonce - Single Ladies (Put A Ring On It)" and a companion display ad, ensuring that no other advertiser's creative will appear next to its overlay.

YouTube InVideo Ads provide marketers with the opportunity to reach users as they watch video content on the Web. Through an unobtrusive yet highly engaging ad unit, the YouTube InVideo Ad establishes an above-the-fold presence on partner watch pages and acts as an invitation for users to learn more.

Figure 9.20 An InVideo Ad with a companion display ad

There are some best practices on how to best use InVideo Ads:

Utilize a companion Click-through rates are very strong when a companion is used in tandem with an InVideo overlay. The 300×250 companion grabs the user's attention and invites them to learn more.

Use a strong call to action Use buttons or clearly marked sections in your ad to point users toward additional content. This works best when the Watch Video Now button is on for 10 seconds before the overlap minimizes.

Invite engagement Think of the overlay as an invitation to your content, not your entire message. Creativity and user engagement are critical.

Keep it fresh Rotate creative on a regular basis. The highest click-through and click-to-play rates are in the first five days of a campaign.

Wednesday: Check Out Click-to-Buy

Today, we'll check out click-to-buy, YouTube's first step in providing a viable e-commerce platform for users and partners. Adding click-to-buy links to the watch pages of thousands of YouTube partner videos gives users another way to discover new content on the site.

Introduced on October 7, 2008, in collaboration with iTunes and Amazon.com, click-to-buy also gives YouTube Partners new revenue opportunities related to their content on YouTube.

How does it work? When you view a YouTube video with a great sound track, you often see comments from YouTube users asking about the name of the song and where they can download it. Or, when users watch the trailer for an upcoming video game, they want to know when it will be released and where they can buy it.

Click-to-buy links just provide YouTube users with instant gratification. They are nonobtrusive retail links, placed on the watch page beneath the video with the other community features. Just as YouTube users can share, favorite, comment on, and respond to videos quickly and easily, now they can click to buy products—like songs and video games—related to the content they're watching.

YouTube got started by providing Amazon.com product links to the newly released video game Spore on videos from Electronic Arts. As Figure 9.21 illustrates, YouTube also got started by embedding iTunes and Amazon.com links on videos like "Katy Perry - I Kissed a Girl (Official Video)" from companies like EMI Music.

Figure 9.21 A click-to-buy link, offering the viewer the chance to buy the MP3 of the video they're watching

This was just the beginning of building a broad, viable e-commerce platform for users and partners on YouTube. The YouTube eCommerce Platform will be rolled out on a larger scale over the coming months to allow partners across all industries—including music, film, TV, and publishing—to generate additional revenue from their content beyond the advertising YouTube serves against their videos.

Thursday: Explore Promoted Videos

Today, let's explore YouTube Promoted Videos, an advertising program that enables all video creators—from the everyday user to a Fortune 500 advertiser—to reach people who are interested in their content, products, or services with relevant videos. You can use Promoted Videos to make sure your videos find a larger audience whether you're a startup band trying to break out with a new single, a film studio seeking to promote an exciting movie trailer, or even a first-time uploader trying to quickly build a following on the site.

With 15 hours of video uploaded to YouTube every minute and millions of viewers watching hundreds of millions of videos every day, the popularity of YouTube can be a mixed blessing for users. Although it's easier to get your 15 minutes of fame (or more, depending on who you are), it's also harder for people to find your video in the first place, even if it's exactly what they're looking for.

But what if you could promote your video on YouTube and make it easier for people to find it? YouTube announced a way to do just that in November 2008 when it introduced Promoted Videos.

So how do Promoted Videos work? Easy-to-use automated tools allow content owners to decide where they'd like their videos to appear, place bids in an automated online auction, and set daily spending budgets. Then, when people search for videos, YouTube displays relevant videos alongside the search results. These videos are clearly labeled as promoted videos and are priced on a cost-per-click basis.

Promoted Videos is a self-serve advertising platform that allows you to promote your video to the audience you are interested in reaching in an easy, effective, democratic, and affordable way. It takes just a few minutes to set up, and you can set your budget at any level you wish. Visit https://ads.youtube.com to start your own Promoted Videos campaign.

As Figure 9.22 illustrates, when people use YouTube to search for movie trailers, YouTube displays a Promoted Video for the "Angels & Demons" trailer at the top and four other Promoted Videos on the right of the results page.

> **Note:** You can learn more about these tools in the video entitled "YouTube Sponsored Videos Overview"— Promoted Videos used to be called Sponsored Videos—which features Matthew Liu, product manager of YouTube.

As I mentioned earlier, YouTube is constantly working to develop the right advertising format for the right content and experience on YouTube. That's why the primary focus with Promoted Videos is to build a platform consistent with the site's search and discovery experience. Just as AdWords provides people with relevant, nonobtrusive advertising, YouTube hopes that Promoted Videos will provide useful, engaging content, accessible to advertisers of all kinds.

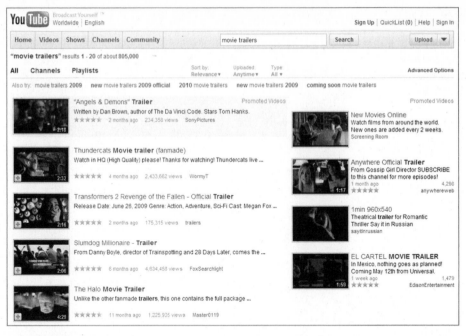

Figure 9.22 When people search for videos, YouTube displays the most relevant Promoted Videos alongside the results.

Friday: Inspect In-Stream Ads

Finally, let's inspect in-stream ads, advertising that runs within the video content, as a pre-roll, mid-roll, or post-roll.

In October 2008, the YouTube Blog announced that the video sharing site was starting to test full-length programming. Apparently, YouTubers have been asking "to be beamed up with Scotty, to devise a world-saving weapon using only gum and paperclips, and to get their grub on at 'The Peach Pit.'"

Note: Hey, I'm not making this up. Go to the YouTube Blog or read my post entitled "Beam me up, YouTube!" on the Search Marketing News Blog at Search Engine Watch (http://blog.searchenginewatch.com/081011-072603).

Through a deal with CBS, YouTube started offering *Star Trek: The Original Series*, *MacGyver*, and *Beverly Hills, 90210*. The YouTube Blog added, "These shows will be available in the new Theater View style we rolled out earlier this week, which provides optimal experience for watching full-length programming on your computer."

Now, these full-length CBS shows had been available elsewhere online for a long time via websites that are part of CBS's partner syndicate. So the big news wasn't the fact that I and other trekkies could now watch 70 full episodes and catch up with Kirk and Spock in the original *Star Trek* (Figure 9.23).

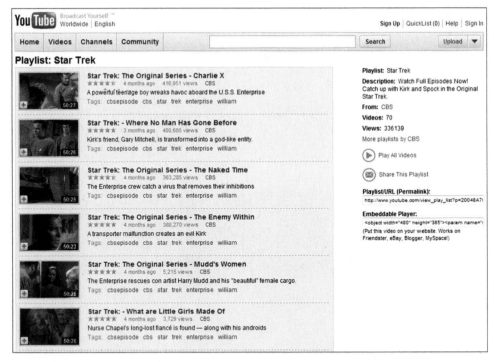

Figure 9.23 Playlist: Star Trek

No, the big news was the fact that they were being shown on YouTube, which generally limits the length of regular video uploads to 10 minutes.

And what does this means to veteran marketers and new YouTubers? The answer to this question was posted to the YouTube Blog, which said, "As we test this new format, we also want to ensure that our partners have more options when it comes to advertising on their full-length TV shows. You may see in-stream video ads (including pre-, mid- and post-rolls) embedded in some of these episodes; this advertising format will only appear on premium content where you are most comfortable seeing such ads."

Aha! You knew there was a catch!

Still, in order to make it clear to viewers, YouTube labeled all full-length videos with a Film Strip symbol so they would know what kind of content they're choosing to watch and what type of ads they might see.

Why all the caution? It's because most viewers see most pre-rolls, mid-rolls, and post-rolls as just new forms of nonendemic advertising. Or, to translate this from the language of marketing into the vernacular, most viewers see most in-stream video ads (most of the time) the same way that most people see most TV commercials (on most days)—as unrelated, untargeted, and unwanted as junk mail, telemarketers, and pop-up ads.

So, who would cross the Bridge of Death must answer me these questions three.

As Figure 9.24 illustrates, "Twins Brandon and Brenda Walsh experience a very special kind of culture shock when they move from Minnesota to Beverly Hills and begin their new lives at West Beverly High" in "Beverly Hills 90210 - Pilot Parts 1 and 2." Do viewers experience culture shock when they see a pre-roll for Nature Valley Chewy Trail Mix, made with pure and simple ingredients, before they watch the online video?

Figure 9.24 "Beverly Hills 90210 – Pilot Parts 1 and 2"

As Figure 9.25 illustrates, "A mysterious explosion demolishes an underground lab" in "MacGyver - Pilot." Will viewers be blown away when they see a mid-roll for the BlackBerry Bold, which embodies elegant design without sacrificing the features or functionality you expect from a premium smartphone, as they're watching the online video?

As Figure 9.26 illustrates, "Kirk's friend, Gary Mitchell, is transformed into a god-like entity" in "Star Trek - Where No Man Has Gone Before." Are viewers transformed when they see a post-roll for Fiber One, or does yogurt help you live long and prosper?

The answers to these questions depend on whether in-stream ads are the right advertising format for the right content and environment on YouTube. In other words, the answer depends on whether a specific pre-roll, mid-roll, or post-roll is endemic—or non-endemic—advertising.

When I watched the original *Star Trek* series from 1966 to 1969, all 80 episodes included TV commercials. But that was before TV remotes and TiVo helped eliminate "long, annoying commercials." Today, most viewers aren't willing to accept this kind of advertising experience when watching longer form content on YouTube like TV shows and movies—unless it is endemic.

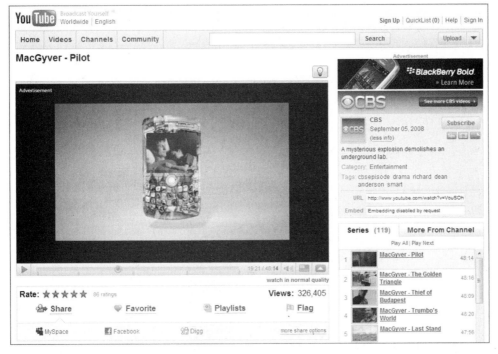

Figure 9.25 "MacGyver – Pilot"

Figure 9.26 "Star Trek – Where No Man Has Gone Before"

Week 4: Check Out Advertising Case Studies

This week, we'll check out some video advertising case studies.

Before we do that, let's take a look at some independent research conducted in December 2008 that measured the engagement power and positive brand benefits of advertising on YouTube.

Partnering with Motorola and its agency Mindshare and General Motors Europe, the Online Testing Exchange (OTX) conducted research that quantified user engagement on YouTube and TV and measured the combined impact of YouTube and TV advertising on brand perceptions and considerations. The four key findings were as follows:

YouTube is a "lean forward" platform. Using eye tracking technology and unique biometrics data, users were found to be 1.5 times more attentive on YouTube than TV and are more engaged (positively and negatively) with ads on YouTube than on TV, confirming the value of YouTube as a lean forward platform, where consumers actively choose the content they watch.

YouTube has a multiplier effect on and over TV advertising. For both GM Europe and Motorola, when viewers watched an ad on YouTube, ad recall and attribution was up to 14 percent higher than it was when they watched the same ad on TV. Additionally, ads on YouTube can shift perceptions of hard-to-reach audiences such as young men and infrequent TV viewers.

Advertising on YouTube has a 'halo' effect. It increased brand perceptions such as "innovative," "cool," "dynamic," and "unconventional." For Motorola, the addition of YouTube ad impressions drove brand metrics up to four times higher than TV alone. For GM Europe, Opel/Vauxhall Corsa, metrics were driven three times higher.

Ads on YouTube are well integrated into the site. They do not annoy consumers, yet they still manage to have strong cut-through, with high recall and attribution rates.

Benjamin Faes, head of YouTube and display for Google EMEA, said in a press release that "consumers are highly engaged with YouTube and its ads are having a multiplying effect on the brand impact of television advertising. I hope more marketers follow Motorola and GM's lead and grasp the exciting, innovative and brand enhancing advertising opportunities that YouTube has to offer."

Monday: Make a Splash with Homepage Video Ads

Tuesday: Enter Hyboria with InVideo Ads

Wednesday: Click to buy Monty Python's DVD

Thursday: Don't scratch Promoted Videos

Friday: Don't bet on the "pre-roll"

Monday: Make a Splash with Homepage Video Ads

YouTube offers an opportunity to connect with your audience in a personal and targeted way—and the ability to do so at massive scale. As I mentioned earlier, the YouTube Homepage has been getting around 30 million impressions and 11 million unique visitors a day in the United States. Although impressions aren't guaranteed, a variety of marketers are using YouTube Video Ads to deliver a big impact and drive attention to content, trailers, or advertising.

As Figure 9.27 illustrates, the Homepage Video Ad like the one for the Sony Pictures movie *Angels & Demons* is a great way to create awareness and reach a wide audience with your marketing message.

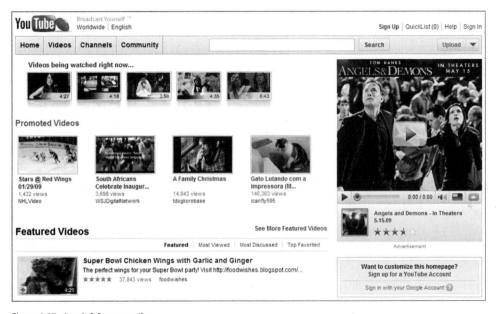

Figure 9.27 *Angels & Demons* trailer

Other advertisers are also making a splash with Homepage Video Ads. For example, Laurie Sullivan wrote an article for MediaPost's Online Media Daily on March 20, 2009, entitled, "YouTube's Home Page Masthead Ad a Hit with Studios, Networks."

She told the story of Lionsgate Pictures, which had used a Hompage Tandem Masthead Unit, or "Cross-Talk" unit, to promote "The Haunting in Connecticut" horror/thriller film, which opened in March 2009.

The "Cross-Talk" unit consists of a 960×250 pixel in-page ad unit that runs the full width of the YouTube homepage below the navigation bar along with a complementary 300×250 ad unit that sits below the masthead on the right and works in tandem with it. The two units can deliver a single message and are in sync with animation and a call-to-action.

According to Sullivan, "The placement is part of a growing trend by studios and networks to take advantage of the site's 30 million daily views of the home page." She added, "Many people come to YouTube without having a particular video in mind to view. They land on the home page to search through the site for videos that grab and pull them in."

So, yes, the YouTube homepage is a little like broadcast TV in this respect. But, a feature in the "Cross-Talk" ad for "The Haunting In Connecticut" let viewers type in their ZIP code to find the nearest haunted building in their area. Broadcast TV can't do that.

Although it's not clear if the "Cross-Talk" ad creates a higher click-through rate (CTR) for studios, it's worth noting that the movie opened ranked #2, with a gross of over $23 million, despite the review aggregator Rotten Tomatoes rating the film as "rotten," with a 19 percent positive rating based on 91 reviews.

YouTube has been experimenting with other ways to promote and advertise movies and television shows on its homepage. For example, Showtime used a standard 300×250 YouTube video ad unit on January 12, 2009, to premiere the show "United States of Tara," a comedy about a housewife with multiple personalities.

According to Sullivan, "The premiere received about 500,000 views on YouTube in one day in the United States and about 880,000 views on TV." But, YouTube Insight revealed that people were pausing in specific areas during the program, providing information that could let Showtime change its marketing efforts down the road. Broadcast TV can't do that.

On May 8, 2009, Sullivan wrote another article for Online Media Daily, this one entitled "Sprint Takes Over YouTube Home Page with UG Human Clock." So, the growing trend to take advantage of YouTube's 30 million daily views of its homepage now extends beyond just studios and networks.

Sprint's Homepage Masthead unit on YouTube, which was created by Goodby Silverstein & Partners, embedded user-generated content in a human clock to promote Sprint's "Now Network." Users who wanted to participate were assigned a number, and could then upload videos of themselves to the clock.

The numbers were strung together in a series of video vignettes placed in a digital clock to represent the time. Sullivan explained, "For example, at 12:09 the ad would display four people, each holding up one number to represent '1,' '2,' '0' and '9.' As seconds, minutes and hours click by, the user-generated videos change based on the time zone."

Videos were screened by Sprint as they were uploaded and could appear several times during the days that the ad ran. Sullivan added, "The ad will become a widget at sprint.com/nownetwork—which provides the local time in multiple ways—as well as facts and figures about hair growth, planes in the air, top searches on Google, tweets on Twitter, shopping days until Christmas, and a staggering amount of other minutiae." Broadcast TV can't do that.

Although YouTube's Homepage Masthead Unit was launched in January 2009 during the second-worst recession in the last half-century, it has already been used by 17 advertisers, including ABC, Apple, Electronic Arts, Fox, Honda, Las Vegas, Lionsgate, McDonald's, Nike, Sprint, Sony, Universal, Verizon, and Volvo. Several chose to buy the unit more than once.

Zal Bilimoria, YouTube's product manager for the home page, told Sullivan that these rich media masthead units had interaction rates of 14 percent on average, compared to an industry average for similar-size units of just under 5 percent, according to DoubleClick, which is also owned by Google.

How do you account for that? Well, Volvo ran a live Twitter feed in its Homepage Masthead ad. Broadcast TV, you've got some 'splainin' to do!

Tuesday: Enter Hyboria with InVideo Ads

Today, we'll look at how Age of Conan entered the era of InVideo Ads.

As Figure 9.28 illustrates, Age of Conan: Hyborian Adventures is a massively multiplayer online role-playing game (MMORPG) based on the world and works of acclaimed author Robert E. Howard. In Age of Conan, players enter Hyboria with thousands of their friends and enemies to live, fight, and explore the dark and brutal world of King Conan.

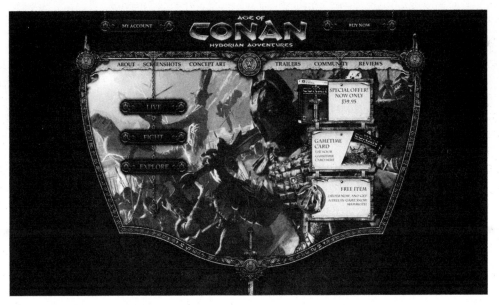

Figure 9.28 Age of Conan: Hyborian Adventures

Funcom, a leading independent developer and publisher of computer and console games, was looking to score big with the release of its latest online game, Age of Conan. It faced an eternal challenge encountered by marketers: how to reach the right audience with the right message at the right time to maximize its ROI.

It found a new age solution on YouTube. To reach the gamer community, Funcom opted to run an InVideo Ad campaign on niche gaming content from Machinima.com, a YouTube partner and the #6 most viewed Partner channel with more than 405 million views as of May 2009.

"It was important to us to target ads to a special demographic that would be most likely to respond by visiting Funcom's web site to learn more. We know that gamers love YouTube and Machinima.com, so this was a natural fit for our media plan," says Terri Perkins, director of marketing and advertising at Funcom.

As you saw earlier in this chapter, InVideo Ads are YouTube's solution for reaching the video-engaged community right where they are watching: within the video player. The InVideo Ad unit is a graphical overlay that occupies 20 percent of the video display area for 20 seconds. InVideo overlay ads have lower abandonment rates and up to 10 to 15 times greater click-through rates than standard display ads.

Click-through rates on the Age of Conan ads were impressive, exceeding 2.37 percent. InVideo Ads are well received by audiences on YouTube.

"We have never received a complaint from our users about ads we run with our videos. Moreover, the click-through rates we've recorded have proven that our audience is interested in interacting with high quality advertising units," said Philip DeBevoise, president of Machinima.com.

"The ads looked good, hit the right audience and drew our desired group to our web site. We will absolutely use InVideo ads on YouTube again," said Perkins. "The style draws our audience in without being annoying and captures their attention in a world dulled by traditional ads." More importantly, Funcom boosted sales of its latest online game.

Wednesday: Click to Buy Monty Python's DVD

"YouTube content partners now have the ability to promote and monetize their content in a new and exciting way and create a deeper distribution channel for their content online," Chad Hurley, cofounder and CEO of YouTube, said in a press release on October 7, 2008. "Our goal is to improve the overall YouTube experience by connecting consumers with relevant information and entertaining content. The addition of retail links will enhance the viewing experience and allow people to engage more deeply with the content they want to consume."

The same day, Glenn Brown, YouTube strategic partner development manager, and Thai Tran, YouTube product manager, said in a post to the Official Google Blog: "Our vision is to help partners across all industries—from music, to film, to print, to TV—offer useful and relevant products to a large, yet targeted audience, and generate additional revenue from their content on YouTube beyond the advertising we serve against their videos."

So, YouTube has a goal and a vision. But, does click-to-buy work?

On January 21, 2009, the YouTube Team posted this answer to the YouTube Blog: "Last year we launched our eCommerce platform for YouTube, which allows users to easily 'click-to-buy' products—like songs and movies—related to the content they're watching on the site. The past few months have demonstrated that great content on YouTube leads to increased sales. For example, when Monty Python launched their channel in November, not only did their YouTube videos shoot to the top of the most viewed lists, but their DVDs also quickly climbed to No. 2 on Amazon's Movies & TV bestsellers list, with increased sales of 23,000 percent," as Figure 9.29 illustrates.

Figure 9.29 The Monty Python channel

YouTube is also expanding and improving the ways in which these links are displayed. You may have started to see click-to-buy links appearing as semitransparent overlays that appear in the bottom of the video for a short period of time. This increased visibility should help even more people take advantage of this program.

YouTube has already experimented with links to purchase music, DVDs, and video games, and it intends to experiment with links to additional types of products soon. Those partners who use YouTube's Content Identification and Management System can also enable retail links on claimed videos that they choose to leave up on the site.

We examine the Monty Python success story in the 11th chapter. In the meantime, to apply for a grant to develop your own pay-per-click links, please visit "The Ministry of Silly Walks." Speak to the man in the bowler hat.

Thursday: Don't Scratch Promoted Videos

Today, let's review a case study from a company that is "zealous about great gadgets" and says, "When others zig, we ZAGG!"

Started in 2005, ZAGG Inc. has grown from a backyard workshop to a publicly traded trendsetter in developing creative solutions for people to enjoy their beloved gadgets. ZAGG Inc.'s flagship brand, the invisibleSHIELD, is a clear, protective film used to protect gadgets from nicks and scratches. With the release of new touch-screen smartphones such as Apple's iPhone and T-Mobile's G1, sales of the invisibleSHIELD have exploded online, and the company has quickly grown to over 200 employees.

Like many companies with a new and innovative product, ZAGG's main objective was to raise awareness and demonstrate the power of its offering. By leveraging the power of sight, sound, and motion, ZAGG hoped to illustrate the protective value of invisibleSHIELD in a series of scratch-test demo videos. The company looked to drive traffic to its commercial site and increase sales by illustrating the invisibleSHIELD scratch-resistant qualities.

As the 6th largest Internet destination in the United States, according to Nielsen/NetRatings data for December 2008, YouTube has the audience for virtually every product. Getting your videos seen by the right audience becomes the next challenge. To accomplish this, ZAGG looked to Promoted Videos.

Promoted Videos allowed ZAGG to bid on relevant keywords so that the product's video demo would be surfaced when users were searching for content relevant to the invisibleSHIELD offering. Rather than spending time, energy, and money on a complex ad unit, ZAGG recognized that the demo video itself worked as an ad. Based off the AdWords system, the creation of ZAGG's Promoted Videos program was not only seamless, but also cost-effective.

The Promoted Videos campaign "has been a great opportunity for us to rise above the thousands upon thousands of videos that are uploaded to YouTube daily," says Cameron Gibbs, director of online marketing at ZAGG Inc. "By targeting viewers searching for the content relevant to our product, we were able to drive quality traffic to our videos and ultimately to our site."

As a result of this program, ZAGG has not only witnessed higher view counts on its videos, but also increased traffic to the company site and more sales. It's easier to sell a product when customers can actually see how it works.

The targeted and intent-based nature of Promoted Videos provided ZAGG with an ad platform on YouTube that just made sense. ZAGG's Promoted Videos campaign was a huge success. "We were able to drive qualified leads and success was easy to measure. In fact, our campaign on YouTube performed better than many of our text ad programs on other search engines," Gibbs adds.

Friday: Don't Bet on the "Pre-Roll"

Finally, it's too soon to know if the majority of advertising embedded in full-length TV shows will be endemic or nonendemic in-stream video ads (including pre-, mid-, and post-rolls). So, don't bet too heavily on the "pre-roll," the 15- to 30-second ad viewers commonly sit through before watching a video.

Despite the rapid growth of digital video advertising, marketers are still learning how to use the medium most effectively. In December 2008, the Internet Advertising Bureau (IAB) Research Council undertook a study of a video advertising campaign for an unnamed major retail brand.

This research sought to provide insights into which combinations of lengths and placements of digital video advertising are most effective. The IAB commissioned Millward Brown and Dynamic Logic to undertake this research, which published the findings as a case study on digital video ad effectiveness.

The findings of the study include the following:

- Fifteen seconds seems to be an optimal length for digital video creative in the pre-roll position. Although 30-second spots risked turning off a viewer waiting to watch something else, 5-second spots had trouble conveying a message.

- Thirty-second spots do well at conveying a complex or emotionally resonant message, but they work best in user-initiated placements where viewers display more patience for long messages—in other words, when the user must take an action, like clicking on an ad or rolling over an in-text link, to begin playing the ad.

- Pre-roll, in-text, and in-banner video ad placements can all contribute to achieving the goals of a campaign. However, different placements may perform optimally with different creative lengths.

As a single campaign case study, the IAB says these findings do not represent definitive conclusions. However, they do offer useful guidance for the industry and point in productive directions for further research in the area of digital video creative length and placement.

So, "What Works in Online Video Advertising?" That was the headline of an article by Douglas MacMillan in *BusinessWeek* on January 27, 2009. MacMillan wrote:

> *When it comes to advertisements in online videos, Web surfers don't know what to expect. Watch an episode of* The Office *on Hulu, and you'll get a couple of 15-second ads from sponsors like Target. View a National Geographic Channel clip about emperor penguins on YouTube, and you might see clickable ads for an Arctic cruise company across the lower portion of the video. Other sites opt for a lowly display ad off to one side of the screen.*

With so many different formats for video online, some companies are avoiding online video advertising altogether.

In order to reduce the incremental production costs of developing the right advertising format for the right content and environment, a number of advertisers have joined the Pool, an effort among marketers and web publishers to agree on a standard format for online video ads. They hope that by working together, the group will more efficiently find out what kinds of ads work best, thereby giving marketers more reason to shift ad dollars toward the Web.

Proponents of a common standard liken their quest to the search 40 years ago to make the 30-second spot the gold standard for television advertising. The Pool, which includes Starcom MediaVest, Microsoft, Yahoo!, Hulu, CBS Interactive, Discovery Communications, AOL, and Broadband Enterprises, proposed a total of 30 different types of ads. The group then invited advertisers, including Allstate, Applebee's, and Capital One, to the table, and took a group vote on which ads they believed would be most effective.

On January 21, 2009, the Pool began testing the top five candidates with panels of viewers in various U.S. cities and plans to announce a winner in February 2010. Although the Pool has declined to name which formats are still in the running, it has said the competing formats are being tested against one of the most common kinds of online video ad, the pre-roll.

I wish them well, but trying to pick the "winning" video ad format smacks of one-size-fits-all thinking. It may have worked in the mass marketing era, but it is dysfunctional in the social marketing era.

As MacMillan observed in his article, "The similarity of pre-rolls to television commercials is part of the appeal to advertisers, some of whom are looking for the easiest way to shift ad spending from television to online. But some argue that pre-roll ads don't take advantage of the unique opportunities afforded by the Web, like interactivity and customization." I agree. And I would encourage you to continue testing lots of different kinds of video advertising and continue developing different advertising formats for different content and environments.

Different experiences—watching short videos or full-length videos, sharing videos, browsing related videos, and searching for videos—require different advertising products that work in different ways. As Figure 9.30 reminds us, 1984 was a long, long time ago.

Figure 9.30 "1984 Apple's Macintosh Commercial"

Month 8: Trust but Verify YouTube Insight

10

Galileo once wrote, "Count what is countable, measure what is measurable. What is not measurable, make measurable." This is still controversial advice 400 years later. In this chapter, we will look at what is countable by YouTube Insight and what is measurable by TubeMogul and Visible Measures. We'll also look at other tools that make measurable what is not measurable by these tools. But we will need to continue explaining, "The chart, of course, is nonrepresentational," until currently available metrics get more robust.

Chapter Contents:

The Map Room

Galileo once said, "Count what is countable, measure what is measurable. What is not measurable, make measurable." That was controversial advice 400 years ago, when the dominant view was geocentric (the Earth is the center of the universe), not heliocentric (the sun is the center of the solar system). In fact, Galileo's ability to make measurable Copernicus's heliocentric hypothesis, which was not measurable before telescopic observation, got Galileo in trouble with the Roman Inquisition.

Another historic figure who discovered how difficult it is to make measurable what is not measurable was Winston Churchill. At the beginning of World War II, Churchill inherited a navy that counted only capital ships and measured only victories over other fleets—pretty much the same as it had since the Battle of Trafalgar in 1805.

But Churchill understood that victory depended on getting a higher percentage of Allied convoys through German U-boats and surface raiders. So, in 1941, he coined the term *Battle of the Atlantic* to get the Admiralty to focus more attention on this strategic threat.

Churchill had a large map of the Atlantic Ocean hung on the southern wall in the Map Room down the hall from his War Cabinet Rooms. It was used to plot the position of convoys and the movements of individual warships—and the thousands of pinholes left by markers still mark the principal convoy routes, which could be seen from the other end of the room.

The Map Room remained open day and night, and the chief task of the officers manning this room was to collate and summarize all relevant information on the progress of the war and present it on maps, which would be constantly updated. In other words, Churchill required the map keepers to make as measurable as possible what was often not easily measurable.

This, in turn, kept the pressure on the chiefs of staff to develop new weapons, tactics, and countermeasures, which eventually drove the German surface raiders from the ocean by the middle of 1941 and decisively defeated the U-boats in a series of convoy battles between March and May 1943.

As Churchill wrote afterward, "The only thing that ever frightened me during the war was the U-boat peril.... It did not take the form of flaring battles and glittering achievements, it manifested itself through statistics, diagrams, and curves unknown to the nation, incomprehensible to the public."

Veteran marketers and new YouTubers are fighting similar battles today. Whether your YouTube video has 10 or 10 million views, you will want to know the answers to these questions: Who's watching this? Where do these viewers come from? How did they find my video?

The battles to answer these questions are part of a larger war to develop a successful web analytics strategy. If you want to learn web analytics the right way, I strongly recommend that you read *Web Analytics: An Hour a Day* by Avinash Kaushik (Sybex,

2007). His thought-provoking analysis of the challenges and opportunities facing today's web analytics challenges conventional wisdom and debunks popular myths.

If you like Kaushik's book, you'll love his blog, Occam's Razor. He also has a day job: Kaushik is the analytics evangelist for Google. And on the swing shift, he's the cofounder and chief education officer for Market Motive, where I'm also on the faculty. Like Galileo and Churchill, Kaushik is one of my heroes, and I try to apply his thought-provoking recommendations to video marketing.

So, in this chapter, we'll look at what is countable by YouTube Insight, what is measurable by TubeMogul and Visible Measures, and what is not measurable by these tools...yet. As Figure 10.1 illustrates, veteran marketers and new YouTubers need to explain to colleagues and clients, "The chart, of course, is nonrepresentational," until currently available metrics get more robust.

"The chart, of course, is nonrepresentational."

Figure 10.1 "The chart, of course, is nonrepresentational." (Cartoon by Leo Cullum in *The New Yorker*, September 20, 2004.)

Week 1: Trust YouTube Insight

On March 26, 2008, Tracy Chan, product manager at YouTube, posted this item to the Official Google Blog: "I remember the first time a video I posted to YouTube cracked 100 views. I wasn't so much surprised as curious: Who were these people? How did they find this video? Where did they come from?"

Chan then announced YouTube's first step toward answering these questions by introducing YouTube Insight, a free analytics and reporting tool that enables anyone with a YouTube account to view detailed statistics about the audience for the videos that they upload to the site.

For example, uploaders can see how often their videos are viewed in different geographic regions as well as how popular they are relative to all videos in that market over a given period of time. Users, partners, and advertisers can also delve deeper into the life cycle of their videos, like what pages viewers were on before they navigated to a video, how long it takes for a video to become popular, and what happens to video views as popularity peaks.

Insight also gives video creators an inside look into the viewing trends of their audience on YouTube. This information can help video creators increase views and get better ratings. Partners can evaluate metrics to understand and better serve their audiences as well as increase ad revenue. And advertisers can study their metrics and successes to tailor their marketing—both on and off the video sharing site—in order to reach the right viewers. As a result, Insight turns YouTube into one of the world's largest focus groups.

How can this help you? Well, let's say you learn that new videos that play off your previous content become popular more quickly, your videos are most popular on Wednesdays and Thursdays, and you have a huge following in Canada. Using these metrics, there are some things you can do to increase your videos' view counts and improve the popularity of your channel:

- Create compelling new content that appeals to your target audience.
- Post these videos on days these viewers are on the site.
- Post your next video in French as well as English.

Brad O'Farrell, the technical editor of this book, finds that Insight doesn't report much variation from video to video. He says, "Most of the time Insight just tells me that videos are extremely popular in areas that are more populated and that their views spiked up when they were featured. I'm hoping they'll eventually add a weighted Insight feature."

Brad notices that video views dip down near the end of the week, spike up on Sunday, then remain steady until about Thursday at MyDamnChannel's channel (www.youtube.com/MyDamnChannel), which features "original originality by comedians, filmmakers, musicians, and photoshoppers."

I notice that video views dip down near the weekend, spike up on Monday, then remain steady until about Thursday at SESConferenceExpo's channel (www.youtube.com/SESConferenceExpo), which is a global conference and training series focused on search engine optimization and search engine marketing.

So, your mileage may vary, but I agree with Brad that YouTube needs to continue adding features and functionality to Insight. In April 2009, YouTube added a link that allows you to export your Insight data into CSV files. CSV files are open-format files that organize data so it can be moved and analyzed using spreadsheet software such as Microsoft Excel and Google Docs.

As Figure 10.2 illustrates, Chan also uploaded a video that provides a basic understanding of the YouTube Insight tool.

Figure 10.2 "YouTube Insight Overview"

Some of the features were made available fairly quickly—like the specific breakdown of how viewers discovered the video. Other features were rolled out over the first year. Let's take a closer look at some of the more important ones.

Monday: Count your video views

Tuesday: Measure your relative popularity

Wednesday: Discover how people find a video

Thursday: Determine the demographics of your audience

Friday: Figure out a video's hot spots

Monday: Count Your Video Views

To see YouTube Insight for your own videos, simply sign into your YouTube account, then click on My Videos, and click the YouTube Insight link to check out this analytics and reporting tool.

As Figure 10.3 illustrates, the default is set to display a summary page that shows how many views your videos were getting in the past week, your top 10 videos for the week, the demographics of the people watching the videos in your channel, and how popular your videos are relative to those of other uploaders.

Figure 10.3 YouTube Insight, Summary tab, SESConferenceExpo

If you click the Views tab, you'll see video views charted on an interactive time-line and map, allowing you to drill down into different geographic regions and see the viewing activity in those regions over selected time periods.

The Views graph captures the viewing trend of all your videos or a particular video in a specific geographic market over a certain period of time. The aggregate data includes views from YouTube as well as from embedded videos, if you have embeds. You can see how views have trended over a period of time by clicking on and dragging various settings (1 day, 5 days, 1 month, 3 months, 6 months, or 1 year). You can also check the Show Unique Users box to see the number of unique viewers across all your videos or for a specific video.

It's worth noting that unique user metrics are displayed as aggregated data. As with all Insight statistics, no personally identifiable information is collected or shared.

The Views map captures the distribution of views in a geographic market over a certain period of time. The aggregate data includes views from YouTube as well as from embeds, if you've got them. You can click a particular country or select a specific map to see how viewing for a particular video has trended over a period of time for that country.

As Figure 10.4 illustrates, the graph shows data over time for the geographic region defined by the map and the map shows geographic data for the time period defined by the slider on the graph. You can change various settings on the graph by pulling the slider bar to a different time frame; the colors on the map will change to reflect the new time period selected on the graph. Conversely, if you select a country (e.g., Canada) or a new map (e.g., USA), the graph will update to reflect the viewing trends in that geographic market.

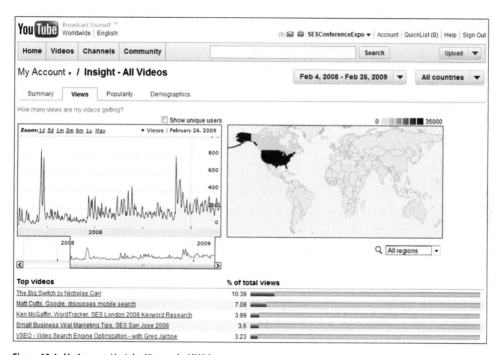

Figure 10.4 My Account / Insight, Views tab, All Videos

Tuesday: Measure Your Relative Popularity

If you click the Popularity tab above the graph display in YouTube Insight, you can compare the relative popularity of your videos in a given region to all other videos in that region.

As Figure 10.5 illustrates, Popularity is a relative measure between 0 and 100 of how the views for a particular video compare to all other videos or how the aggregated video views for your channel compare to all other channels.

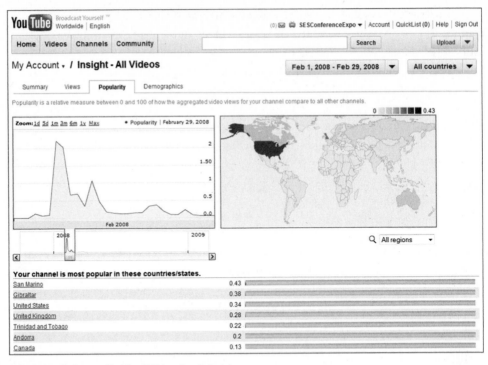

Figure 10.5 My Account / Insight, All Videos Popularity tab

The Popularity graph provides insight into how popular a particular video has been over time. This graph uses a popularity index, which measures how much more or less popular a particular video is compared to overall videos in that geographic market. For example, if my video is indexed at 96 on the graph, this means that only 4 percent of all videos in the selected region and timeframe have been viewed more than my video.

The Popularity map shows the relative popularity of a particular video within the different countries of a region. The scale is again relative, so the country within which the video is most popular will be dark green and the one in which it is least popular will be light green.

Before we go to the next tab in YouTube Insight, are there any questions?

Search Engine Marketer: "Can I find out how many video responses, text comments, and ratings all the videos on my channel have received?"

I'm glad you asked that question. In March 2009, YouTube Insight added a feature: a Community tab that allows you to see how YouTube users engage with your content over time. You can see total numbers related to ratings, comments, and favorites as well as the average number of actions the community takes per view of your video.

YouTube Director: "Can I compare popularity indexes for one group of videos with indexes for another group of videos?"

Currently, reporting is available for only one video at a time or all videos on a channel. But YouTube has said it will explore additional functionality and reporting options with future iterations of Insight.

Entrepreneur: "Can I get statistics for videos in other channels?"

Currently, reporting is available for only your own videos. But if YouTube explores additional functionality and reporting options, this feature could appear in future iterations of Insight.

Okay, now let's go to the next tab.

Wednesday: Discover How People Find a Video

Today, let's look at the Discovery tab in YouTube Insight.

The Discovery tab shows you how viewers "discovered" your video. They could have been searching on YouTube or Google, browsing under "Related Videos," watching it in an embedded player on a blog or website, or receiving a link to the video in an email from a friend or colleague.

As Figure 10.6 illustrates, the Discovery tab will give you insight into how people found your videos.

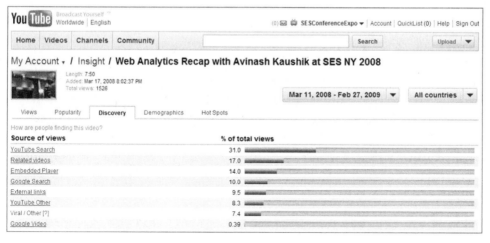

Figure 10.6 My Account / Insight, Discovery tab, "Web Analytics Recap with Avinash Kaushik at SES NY 2008"

If you click the links under Source of Views, you will see additional details about these aspects:

YouTube Search This section shows which terms viewers searched for on YouTube to find your video. For example, the top two search terms used to find the video in Figure 10.6 were *web analytics* and *avinash kaushik*.

Related Videos This section shows video content owners which related YouTube videos are driving views to your video. You can click through the Video ID to see these videos. The video in Figure 10.6 was found in Related Videos about SES NY 2008 and Avinash Kaushik.

Embedded Player This section shows what percentage of your views came from a YouTube player that is embedded on another site or blog. For example, the video in Figure 10.6 was embedded in the Search Engine Watch Blog.

Google Search This section shows which terms viewers searched for on Google to find your video. The top search term used to find the video in Figure 10.6 was *Avinash Kaushik.*

External Links This section shows which websites are driving views to your video. For the video in Figure 10.6, the top external link was www.kaushik.net.

YouTube Other This section represents different pages on YouTube.com that are driving views to your video.

Viral / Other This section represents direct links to your video, where there is no reference URL. These video views will come from users clicking links from emails or IMs.

Google Video This section shows which terms viewers searched for on Google Video to find your video.

Thursday: Determine the Demographics of Your Audience

On May 15, 2008, demographics became available in YouTube Insight.

In a post to the Official Google Blog, Nick Jakobi, product manager at YouTube, wrote, "When we first announced YouTube Insight, our free video analytics tool for YouTube, we were excited to see just how users, partners, and advertisers might creatively use information about the viewing trends of their videos. We've since learned that some users and partners are modifying their upload schedules based on when they know their audience is tuning in, and advertisers are studying geographic traffic patterns to assess the effectiveness of regional ad campaigns."

Jakobi backed this up by linking to two articles: one by Kim Hart in the *Washington Post* entitled "The Smart Money Watches You Watch Videos" and another by Zachary Rogers in ClickZ entitled "YouTube Analytics: Marketers Draw New Insights from Old Uploads."

Both articles told the story about how MSHC Partners had used YouTube Insight to discover that an old video clip promoting CleanMyRide.org, which featured comedian Sarah Silverman, had seen a sudden spike in views when she appeared on *Jimmy Kimmel Live* with a new video, dubbed "I'm F**king Matt Damon."

Jakobi then announced the addition of some new features to Insight. One was a new demographics tab that displays view count information broken down by age group (such as ages 18 to 24), gender, or a combination of the two to help you get a better understanding of the makeup of your YouTube audience. He added, "We show you general information about your viewers in anonymous and aggregate form, based on the birth date and gender information that users share with us when they create YouTube accounts. This means that individual users can't be personally identified."

In addition, some of the demographic data might represent the gender and age of the individual setting up a YouTube account for an organization instead of all the other people who might also be using it.

Plus, some people lie about their age. You need to be at least 13 years old to have an account; a younger kid might pretend to be older just to become a subscriber of Fred. I was born September 2, 1949, and have learned that it's not just the young who lie about their age; Jack Benny celebrated his 39th birthday 41 times. So, an older user might pretend to be Benny's age when signing up on YouTube.

Fortunately, Nielsen/NetRatings independently confirmed in December 2008 that YouTube's audience in the United States mirrors the demographics of the online population: 52 percent of YouTube visitors are male and 48 percent are female. And just as many are over the age of 55 as under 18:

- Eighteen percent are under the age of 18
- Twenty percent are 18–34
- Nineteen percent are 35–44
- Twenty-three percent are 45–54
- Twenty percent are over the age of 55

As Figure 10.7 illustrates, the default of the Demographics tab is to display age ranges for both genders and genders for all age groups. However, if you click male or female, you will see the age ranges of male or female visitors.

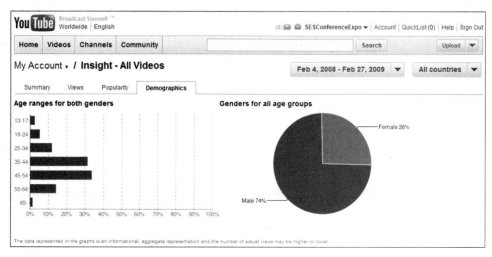

Figure 10.7 My Account / Insight, Demographics tab, All Videos

As with Insight's other features, this new information helps you learn how to create more compelling content that best engages the audiences you want to reach. Of course, it also helps to have been Kimmel's long-time girlfriend.

Friday: Figure Out a Video's Hot Spots

On September 30, 2008, YouTube added a new feature to Insight called Hot Spots. With Hot Spots, you can figure out which scenes in your videos are the "hottest," so you don't have to guess what viewers are watching. Insight also shows which parts of your videos are "coldest," so you can edit those videos to keep your audience engaged. You can find this new feature under the Hot Spots tab within the Insight dashboard.

What does *hot* mean? *Hot* shows that compared to other YouTube videos of similar length, fewer viewers are leaving your video at that point, and many viewers may even be rewinding on the control bar to see a particular sequence in your video again. *Cold* means that, compared to other YouTube videos of similar length, many viewers are moving to another part of your video or leaving the video entirely.

Figure 10.8 shows an example of Hot Spots in action. The Hot Spots tab in Insight plays your video alongside a graph that shows the ups and downs of viewership at different moments within the video. YouTube determines the "hot" and "cold" spots by comparing your video's abandonment rate at that moment to other videos on YouTube of the same length and incorporating data about rewinds and fast-forwards.

So what does that mean? Well, when the graph goes up, your video is hot: few viewers are leaving, and many are even rewinding on the control bar to see that sequence again. When the graph goes down, your content's gone cold: many viewers are moving to another part of the video or leaving the video entirely.

Figure 10.8 My Account / Insight, Hot Spots tab, "Web Analytics Recap with Avinash Kaushik at SES NY 2008"

You can see that viewers seemed to enjoy Kaushik's shout out to the Buckeyes; he got his MBA at The Ohio State University. But some started drifting off as he explains why it is getting harder to make a ton of money on the Web. The longer the video goes on, the more people tend to stay, generating a small hot spot as Kaushik predicts what's going to happen in the next 24 to 36 months and then a big hot spot as he talks about trying to measure "faith-based initiatives" like advertising in *Fortune* magazine. The final hot spot comes as he explains what he covers at his blog, Occam's Razor, and the dip at the end occurs as he talks about his book, *Web Analytics: An Hour a Day.*

Now, what can I do with this feedback? I could edit the video, keeping the "hottest" scenes. Or I could include a couple of well-timed annotations during the "coldest" scenes to let the audience know that Kaushik will be predicting what's going to happen in the next two to three years.

I could also leave this video alone but learn what parts of it viewers were watching and skipping so I can create better content in the future. YouTube is the world's largest focus group, so it makes sense to study the effectiveness of my interview.

Tracy Chan and Nick Jakobi are the YouTube product managers who cooked up Hot Spots. If either one of you read this, consider letting me compare my video to other videos of the same length *in the same category*. That way, I can use other 7-minute, 50-second videos from other reporters as my benchmark instead of videos of the same length in all categories.

Week 2: Verify with TubeMogul

YouTube Insight provides you with information that helps you better understand your audience: who they are, where they come from, what they watch, and when. However, if 20 to 60 percent of your video marketing campaigns are on other online video sites, then you will also want to analyze your overall marketing efforts—both on and off YouTube.

To do that, you can use TubeMogul, which not only distributes videos to more than 20 online video sites (including YouTube, Yahoo! Video, Veoh, Metacafe, MySpace, and Dailymotion), it also provides in-depth tracking and analytics for online video.

Although, if you upload an individual video without using TubeMogul, you can't retroactively add it to TubeMogul's Insight for your overall channel—"which is a pain," according to my technical editor.

As Figure 10.9 illustrates, this combination of syndication and analytics services enables TubeMogul to provide the SES Conference and Expo with independent information about online video performance on YouTube and other top video sharing sites.

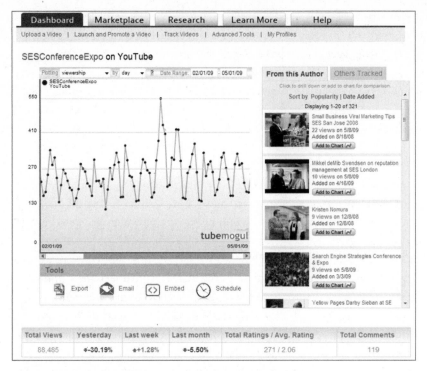

Figure 10.9 TubeMogul producer tracking of SESConferenceExpo on YouTube

Founded in 2006, TubeMogul aggregates video-viewing data from multiple sources, including YouTube, Yahoo! Video, Veoh, Metacafe, MySpace Video, Dailymotion, Revver, and Crackle. As TubeMogul's channel on YouTube says, this gives "publishers improved understanding of when, where and how often videos are watched," and they can "track and compare what's hot and what's not, measure the impact of marketing campaigns, gather competitive intelligence, and share the data with colleagues and friends."

Through its acquisition of Illumenix in October 2008, TubeMogul is also able to offer additional engagement and performance metrics. For sites that host their own video, TubeMogul InPlay can be set up in any Flash video player to track viewership metrics such as audience engagement, attention span, and site performance in real time.

In April 2009, TubeMogul landed $3 million in Series A funding from Trinity Ventures. This should enable the online video analytics and distribution company to address some of the growing pains created by over 75,000 users and tracking hundreds of millions of video streams.

Who uses TubeMogul? As I mentioned in the Introduction, 9 of the 100 most viewed channels on YouTube use TubeMogul: Machinima.com, Mondo Mini Shows, Fred's TubeMogul, HotForWords, Athene Wins, Barely Political, Philip DeFranco, Nuclear Blast USA, and Venetian Princess. TubeMogul's client list also includes CBS

Interactive, PBS, Ford Models, Universal McCann, AvenueA, Conde Nast, FreeMantle Media, Warner Bros., *The Onion*, Next New Networks, Revision3, Red Bull, Intel, Cisco, Home Depot, Green Peace, and the White House.

Although you can trust YouTube Insight, let's take a closer look at how you can use TubeMogul to verify the information and track far more than the traditional metric of video "views."

Monday: Understand your audience

Tuesday: Measure industry trends

Wednesday: Get rich metrics for your site's video player

Thursday: Use your audience metrics to drive innovation

Friday: Revise your ad revenues upward

Monday: Understand Your Audience

TubeMogul offers a number of features to help you understand your audience beyond the YouTube community:

Cross-Site Analytics TubeMogul provides you with a reporting dashboard to compare and contrast viewership information on your videos across multiple video sharing sites. Analytics include views, comments, and ratings trended over time. It also sends you daily emails that show changes in this data.

Data Export TubeMogul lets you export your analytics into Excel. YouTube didn't add this functionality until April 2009. You can also upgrade to one of TubeMogul's advanced product levels to export data that is more than 30 days old.

Data Feed TubeMogul lets you grab your raw data through a data feed set up to your specifications. If you want to merge your TubeMogul data with other data sets you're collecting, this is a pretty useful solution.

Link Intelligence TubeMogul also lets you see which blogs and websites are linking to your videos according to sites like Technorati, Google, and Digg. This can help you find out how link worthy your video content is, although I will show you another way to get this information in week 4.

Custom Video Groupings TubeMogul lets you group together any set of videos to aggregate viewership information for analysis. Common groupings are by episode, season, and sponsor. You can also upgrade to one of TubeMogul's advanced levels to create unlimited custom tracking units.

Event Reporting If you are wondering why your channel spiked with viewers, TubeMogul lets you see when your video was featured on more than 20 video sharing sites. You can also add your own markers to note events of significance to your video's success.

Audience Demographics TubeMogul enables you to learn your audience's gender, age, household income, ethnicity, education, and household size. This can help you get to know your viewers better and measure key segments.

Audience Geographics Finally, TubeMogul lets you see the geographic location of the viewers watching your videos on a world map. Who knows, you could be *big* in the United States but *huge* in Canada, eh?

As Figure 10.10 illustrates, Wallstrip, the popular online video show with a humorous and educational take on stocks and pop culture, uses TubeMogul data to help advertisers and investors understand the demographics of its audience, which is primarily male, 35 to 54 years old, and viewership trends across nine sites. Wallstrip also uses TubeMogul to benchmark its viewership against its competitors.

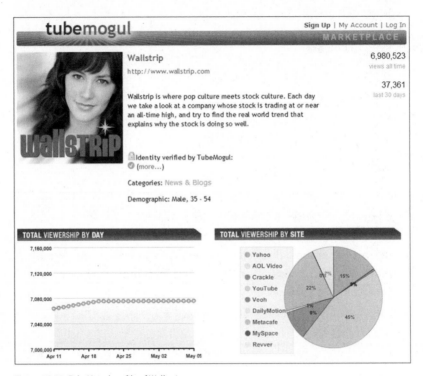

Figure 10.10 TubeMogul profile of Wallstrip

Tuesday: Measure Industry Trends

You can also track videos by producer on any site TubeMogul tracks, whether the video is yours or that of another producer. This might be your competitor's videos or any video that mentions a keyword. This feature allows you to track your own videos even if they weren't uploaded through TubeMogul.

For example, Home Depot uses TubeMogul to distribute videos to multiple sites rather than just uploading to YouTube alone, more than doubling their viewership.

Home Depot also utilizes TubeMogul's Keyword Intelligence to track all videos mentioning Home Depot.

As Figure 10.11 illustrates, over 7,000 videos with more than 28 million views had mentioned Home Depot as this was written.

Figure 10.11 Home Depot uses TubeMogul to track branded how-to videos

TubeMogul also enables you to track buzz in the world of user-generated content or compare your brand to your competitors' by tracking videos and viewership across the Internet based upon selected keywords. This is a significant timesaver for anyone manually collecting keyword statistics.

For example, Infuse Creative is one of the agencies that use TubeMogul. While working on a major theatrical release for a large Hollywood studio, Infuse Creative was asked to analyze the buzz created for keywords and tags on all videos across several video sharing sites.

Infuse Creative was already tracking the success of the studio's videos uploaded through TubeMogul to the studio's accounts at the video sites, but it also needed to track all the videos uploaded by fans and movie critics because the Hollywood studio wanted to get a picture of all views from all videos tagged with keywords pertaining to its new movie.

Infuse Creative used TubeMogul's Analytics by Keyword tool to gain competitive intelligence on all videos—regardless of video site or who uploaded them—tagged with specific words and phrases. The agency was able to share with its client data showing both the benefits of uploading theatrical trailers to the sharing sites and the subsequent buzz in the form of user-generated videos.

Although Infuse Creative couldn't share any of its client's charts, you can get an idea of the kind of competitive intelligence TubeMogul offers by looking at a chart that appeared in the TubeMogul Blog in March 2007.

The chart in Figure 10.12 illustrates what happened when the "Hillary 1984" attack video was posted on YouTube by an unknown party in March 2007. As you can see, the unanticipated consequence was a huge spike in daily views of the official videos by Democrats.

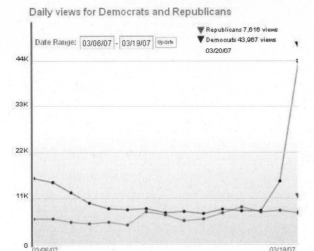

Figure 10.12 Daily views for Democrats and Republicans 03/19/07

The "Hillary 1984" attack video was widely distributed and had over 1.5 million views as of March 22, 2007. However, the buzz spilled over to the response videos officially put out by the Barack Obama and Hillary Clinton campaigns. The chart shows an aggregate of video views on YouTube of the top three Democrats (Obama, Clinton, and John Edwards) vs. that of the top three Republicans at the time (Rudy Giuliani, John McCain, and Mitt Romney).

Wednesday: Get Rich Metrics for Your Site's Video Player

Through its acquisition of Illumenix in October 2008, TubeMogul also offers InPlay to sites that host their own video. InPlay is a Flash-based analytics service that gives you an in-depth view into your site's video performance.

Able to be integrated with any Flash video player, InPlay tracks audience statistics and user interaction in real time. As Figure 10.13 illustrates, the metrics InPlay offers include viewed minutes, viewer attention, and per-stream quality.

One of the users of TubeMogul InPlay is eBaum's World, which was created by Eric Bauman and sold to ZVUE Corporation in August 2007 for $17.5 million. eBaum's World uses TubeMogul InPlay to track about 30 million streams per month on the online entertainment site.

At an individual video level, eBaum's World uses InPlay to track viewer engagement, including how much of a video is actually watched, what the most popular segments of a video are, when a viewer clicks away, and much more. Insights gleaned from these metrics allow eBaum editors to feature the most engaging videos as well as share rich viewership data with their video producers and sponsors.

At a sitewide level, eBaum's World also utilizes InPlay to track minutes viewed by category and viewer behavior around the content as a whole, leading to insights in everything from bandwidth delivery to optimal site structure.

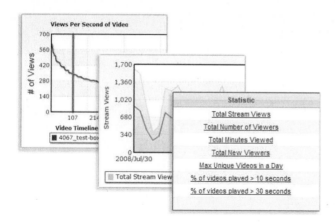

Figure 10.13 Illumenix became TubeMogul InPlay.

In January 2009, Bauman reported on his blog that ZVUE had decided to let him and the rest of this team go. He said, "We have been running eBaum's World for 10+ years so this is a very sad time for all of us. Without us, I am sure the site will not run nearly as smoothly anymore since there is a brand new team running it and they have no idea what they are doing."

According to Compete, unique visitors to ebaumsworld.com peaked at over 1.4 million in November 2008 and dropped to under 1.2 million in February 2009. So, getting rich metrics for your site's video player can help you handle some, but not all, of the things that go bump in the night.

Thursday: Use Your Audience Metrics to Drive Innovation

There are other benefits of using TubeMogul. As Figure 10.14 illustrates, *TV Week* is using TubeMogul's audience metrics to track within Brightcove's player.

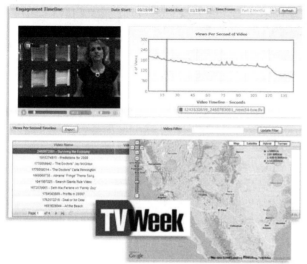

Figure 10.14 TubeMogul's audience metrics drive innovation at *TVWeek*

In December 2008, TubeMogul announced an integration and partnership relationship with Brightcove. When *TVWeek* heard the announcement, it jumped at the chance to start collecting in-depth viewership metrics of the video content it produces, including Daisy Whitney's show "New Media Minute." Like many sites, the company hosts the videos on its site using Brightcove's platform player.

In a press release, Greg Baumann, editor of *TVWeek* and the Brightcove plug-in's first user, said, "TubeMogul InPlay statistics are infinitely useful. In an instant, I know how many new viewers we have, our salespeople know by geographic region where our most engaged viewers are and our technical team knows who is experiencing errors."

A case study on TubeMogul's site provides some additional details about the benefits that *TVWeek* has seen:

Editorial *TVWeek*'s editors now measure audience engagement. By examining each video's audience retention at a per-second level, editors can figure out what makes the most popular videos successful. At a macro level, editors are able to establish benchmarks like overall minutes viewed, peak times of day, unique and repeat viewers, and referral sites/keywords.

Sales *TVWeek*'s ad sales team now provides objective reporting to advertisers. *TVWeek* is able to offer third-party metrics like "viewed seconds," which is a statistic that measures audience engagement at every moment and is unlike commonly cited data points like "impressions" or "views," which don't necessarily guarantee that anyone ever actually saw an ad.

Video delivery *TVWeek*'s engineers now know where in the world viewers are having slow load times. The engineers have access to video delivery metrics, such as download speeds, the number of users that experienced "rebuffers," and the peak times of day to avoid shuffling in new content.

Friday: Revise Your Ad Revenues Upward

Finally, the video-player metrics of TubeMogul InPlay have enabled Revision3 to make data-driven production decisions. This in turn has enabled Revision3 to revise its ad revenues...upward.

Effective measurement of video performance became much more important as the economy contracted and ad spending worsened. Few companies know this better than Revision3, the TV network for the Internet generation, which is posting record revenues amid industry projections of declining ad spending.

Revision3 uses TubeMogul to syndicate many of its shows to YouTube, MySpace, Yahoo!, Metacafe, and other sites as well as track the results (Figure 10.15).

According to a case study on TubeMogul's site, Revision3 utilizes TubeMogul InPlay for its own video player, tracking rich data on viewer behavior that occurs on its site. Using InPlay, Revision3 is able to track typical viewers' experiences, including per-stream data for how much of a video is actually watched, where in the world people are watching, and average download speeds.

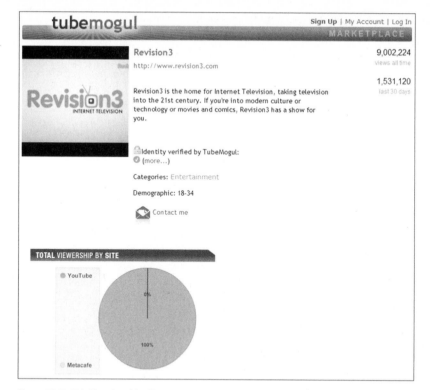

Figure 10.15 TubeMogul profile of Revision3

This enabled Revision3 shows to garner a record number of views for 2008 and helped launch its hit programs—including *Diggnation*, *The Totally Rad Show*, and *Tekzilla*. Views of Revision3's programs increased more than 140 percent year over year to over 46 million views in 2008 from 19 million views in 2007. In addition, the network reported a whopping 129 million segments viewed and nearly 1 billion minutes of engagement in 2008.

This, in turn, powered Revision3's impressive growth for 2008. With revenue tripling in the past year, viewership growing to 140 million minutes of engagement monthly, and more than 60 advertising partners, Revision3 enjoyed strong momentum and increased market penetration as the company moved into 2009.

With reach doubling in 2008, Revision3 continued to maintain a strong connection with the male, age 18 to 34 audience. Revision3 also delivered the most effective advertising products in the industry, with 99.9 percent audience sponsor recall. In addition, 48 percent of Revision3's audience has purchased a product or service from one of the company's sponsors.

All this has helped to fuel Revision3's strategic partnerships with Adobe, the Air Force, Anheuser-Busch, Axe, Carmex, Dolby, Dr. Pepper, EA, Go Daddy, Microsoft, Sony, Virgin America, and Zune.

Week 3: Verify with Visible Measures

Another tool that can help you analyze your overall marketing efforts—both on and off YouTube—is Visible Measures.

Coincidentally, TubeMogul and Visible Measures were both launched at Demo 08 on the same day: January 30, 2008. In a column entitled "Visible Measures and Tube-Mogul measure video usage," on the Between the Lines Blog on ZDNet.com, Dan Farber, said, "TubeMogul doesn't get inside the videos like Visible Measures."

The weekly *Ad Age* Viral Video Chart (Figure 10.1) uses data from Visible Measures about brand-driven viral video ads that appear on online video sharing destinations. Each campaign is measured on viewership of both brand-syndicated video clips and viewer-driven social video placements. The data is compiled using the Visible Measures Viral Reach Database of analytic data on more than 100 million Internet videos across more than 150 video sharing destinations.

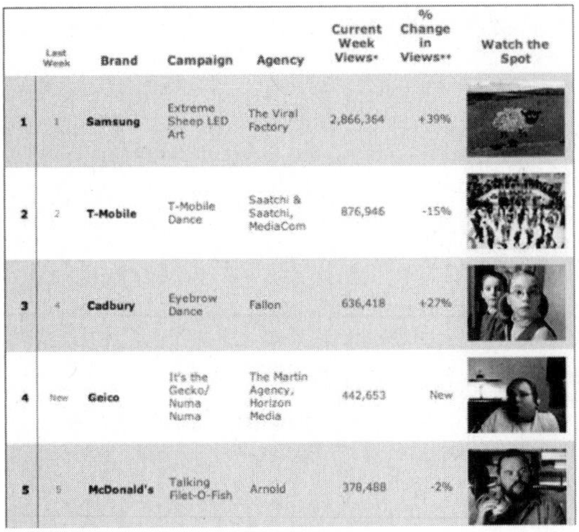

Last Week	Brand	Campaign	Agency	Current Week Views*	% Change in Views**	Watch the Spot
1 1	Samsung	Extreme Sheep LED Art	The Viral Factory	2,866,364	+39%	
2 2	T-Mobile	T-Mobile Dance	Saatchi & Saatchi, MediaCom	876,946	-15%	
3 4	Cadbury	Eyebrow Dance	Fallon	636,418	+27%	
4 New	Geico	It's the Gecko/ Numa Numa	The Martin Agency, Horizon Media	442,653	New	
5 5	McDonald's	Talking Filet-O-Fish	Arnold	378,488	-2%	

Figure 10.16 The *Ad Age* Viral Video Chart for April 2, 2009

Founded in 2005, Visible Measures is an independent third-party measurement firm that specializes in measuring the consumption and distribution of Internet video. In March 2009, Visible Measures raised $10 million in Series C financing. In April 2009, the company announced that it had become the online video measurement platform of record for MySpace.

The company's Internet video measurement solutions are powered by three core technologies: its Video Placement Multiplier, Viral Reach Database, and Video Metrics Engine. Let's take a closer look.

Monday: Distribute your video content

Tuesday: Count your true reach

Wednesday: Measure your video engagement

Thursday: Measure brand exposure

Friday: Measure audience behavior

Monday: Distribute Your Video Content

According to Visible Measures, Video Placement Multiplier distributes your video content to "over 40 of the top video sharing sites in a single step." Although the company doesn't list those sites by name, it says they range "from the hottest video sharing sites to tightly targeted niche destinations."

The first step in the company's automated video placement process involves providing Visible Measures with your video assets and metadata by filling out a form about the meta tags, titles, descriptions, and categories you want to use for your videos. This allows Visible Measures to prepare your videos for distribution and gives you control over brand placement.

Video Placement Multiplier classifies and categorizes every video sharing site supported by Visible Measures. This gives you control over where and how your brand is seen, helping you reach your target audience while staying clear of undesirable content.

To distribute your video content, Video Placement Multiplier uses an automated viral seeding technique that targets 40 of the top video sharing sites. These video destination sites are continuously monitored to ensure functionality and compatibility with your video content.

Video Placement Multiplier is integrated with the Visible Measures Viral Reach Database. As Figure 10.17 illustrates, this means that after your video content is seeded, you can immediately begin tracking how the community responds, no matter where it goes or how it changes.

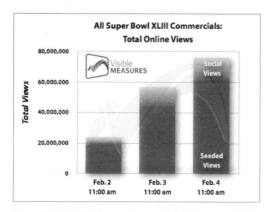

Figure 10.17 Visible Measures's analysis of All Super Bowl XLIII Commercials

As you can see from the figure, the Super Bowl XLIII commercials got about 60 million seeded views on the top 40 video sharing sites and another 15 million social views on blogs and social networking sites.

Tuesday: Count Your True Reach

According to Visible Measures, "Viral Reach Database gives you the ability to track your viral video campaign wherever it goes online and however it looks."

The Viral Reach Database collects data from over 150 video sharing destinations. This process finds tens of thousands of new video clips every day, constantly growing its video repository. This allows Visible Measures to detect and monitor responses, remixes, spoofs, parodies, mashups, and other derivative videos created by the community that are related to your campaign.

When this discovery process finds new videos, Visible Measures collects the publicly available analytic data and adds it to its video data storage center. Each clip produces more than a dozen data points, including title, comments, view count, rating count, and duration.

The company's constantly growing Viral Reach Database currently houses information for more than 100 million unique videos. The database stores all the data for every video Visible Measures discovers, ranging from daily stats to metadata. These statistics allow you to benchmark your campaign.

The Viral Reach Database also enables Visible Measures to provide detailed reports on viral video distribution, community participation, and audience growth. The ability to see the "True Reach" of a campaign enabled the company to create the Visible Measures 100 Million Views Club (Figure 10.18), which lists the online video campaigns that have accumulated a nine-figure total viewership.

It's worth noting that "Susan Boyle (Britain's Got Talent)" became a member of the 100 Million Views Club in less than a month. By comparison, the four videos ranked ahead of her took 14 to 21 months to earn their top positions.

Rank	Title	Type	Label / Studio	True Reach	Months Available	Watch
1	Soulja Boy: Crank That	Music Video	Universal	356,300,000	21	
2	Twilight	Movie Trailer	Summit	266,500,000	14	
3	Mariah Carey: Touch My Body	Music Video	Universal	230,200,000	14	
4	Jeff Dunham: Achmed the Dead Terrorist	User Generated	-	196,500,000	19	
5	Susan Boyle (Britain's Got Talent)	TV Show	Freemantle/iTV	186,000,000	0.7	

The Visible Measures 100 Million Views Club: May 1, 2009

Figure 10.18 The Visible Measures 100 Million Views Club: May 1, 2009

Wednesday: Measure Your Video Engagement

According to Visible Measures, its Video Metrics Engine captures "every interaction with every video everywhere in your online video network." As my technical editor points out, it's impossible to track when someone emails or IMs a video URL to a friend unless they use a built-in "share" tool. So, let's just say that the company's Video Metrics Engine is able to provide "best-in-class" Internet video metrics through a straightforward instrumentation process with your video player.

This process, led by a team of integration experts from Visible Measures, involves inserting Video Metrics Engine code into your video player. Once the code is inserted, virtually every interaction by every viewer with all of your videos is collected by the Video Metrics Engine. In addition, the code works with your player wherever it goes online—from blogs and embeds to social networking sites.

As soon as your player is instrumented, the Video Metrics Engine begins collecting data. Every time a viewer interacts with your video, the player sends information to the data collection system. This means that every pause, play, rewind, fast-forward, replay, copy, embed, repost, forward, share, and comment is collected by the Video Metrics Engine from every video, user, and site and stored for processing in the Visible Measures computational grid.

Information collected by the data collection system is stored on a distributed file system within the computation grid. This grid receives, processes, and stores information on millions of video streams every day. This means that regardless of the size of your content catalog or audience, the Video Metrics Engine is able to produce your video metrics data immediately.

Data that has been aggregated and processed by the computational grid is then loaded into the data warehouse. Once the data has been loaded, it can be viewed by a Web-based dashboard for analysis as users interact with your video content in real time.

The dashboard is the face of the Video Metrics Engine. As Figure 10.19 illustrates, it shows you visualizations of key metrics like engagement, captive viewing time, day parting, initial attention, play-through rate, title reach, stickiness, and many more.

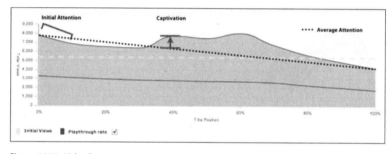

Figure 10.19 Video Engagement

These metrics can help you make better decisions regarding future Internet video investments and drive increases in audience growth, content consumption, viewing time, and the discovery of new revenue opportunities.

Thursday: Measure Brand Exposure

By combining what Visible Measures calls "True Reach" analysis with the audience interaction data, the company can estimate a campaign's aggregate viewing time, which represents total brand exposure.

For example, Nike recently launched a viral video in support of its Hyperdunk basketball shoe. As Figure 10.20 illustrates, the video featured basketball superstar Kobe Bryant recklessly leaping over a speeding Aston Martin.

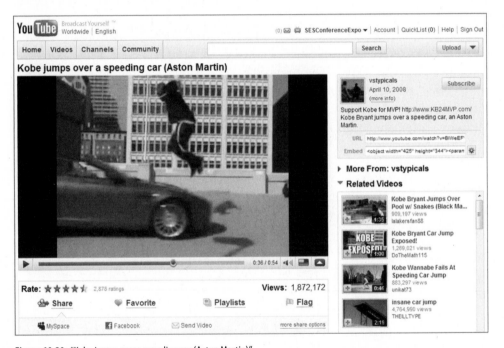

Figure 10.20 "Kobe jumps over a speeding car (Aston Martin)"

The company's Viral Reach Database captured well over 250 unique placements for the Kobe video. The brand appeared to be responsible for posting just over a dozen of these placements, so the remaining 240 placements were community driven.

Of these, 60 percent were copies of the original video and 40 percent were derivative videos, ranging from reenactments of the stunt and parodies of the clip to a truth squad of viewers determined to reveal the video as a fake. The large number of viral placements reflects the clip's overall audience appeal.

The original and viral placements of the Hyperdunk campaign accumulated more than 16 million views in aggregate. The original Kobe clips posted by Nike generated less than 40 percent of the overall reach. The viral placements increased the campaign reach by over 200 percent.

All told, the Nike Hyperdunk viral video campaign attracted over 35,000 comments. Based on a term frequency analysis, the audience reacted strongly to the campaign. Many of the comments collected reflect admiration ("best," "must-see"), skepticism ("fake," "real," "stunt"), and note the product placement of both the Aston and the Hyperdunk shoes ("Aston," "car," "Nike," "shoes").

The so-called "engagement curve" for the Hyperdunk video also illustrates a number of viral phenomena. First, the clip's initial attention score indicates significant audience abandonment during the clip's opening. However, as Kobe takes flight, the engagement curve spikes significantly, indicating substantial rewind behavior as viewers rewatch the stunt—most likely to try to see if it was real or not. Finally, the downward slope at the end of the clip indicates moderate concluding abandonment as users realize the fun is over and click away from the video.

As a result, the estimated engaged reach of this campaign was a whopping 375,000 hours of total viewing time. For perspective, the original 54-second clip drove well over 40 viewing years in aggregate!

Friday: Measure Audience Behavior

Here is another example. Boston.com, one of the most visited regional portals in the United States, uses Visible Measures to capture new data about its audience's interaction with viral videos. Boston.com is part of the business unit that also publishes the *Boston Globe*, which is owned by the New York Times Company.

In April 2009, the New York Times Company threatened to stop the presses of the *Globe* for good unless union workers agreed to $20 million in cuts. The newspaper, which has been printed for 137 years, had been saddled with reader flight and a drop in advertising—problems echoed in newsrooms across the country.

As Figure 10.21 illustrates, Boston.com's mission is to provide audiences with trusted editorial content from the *Globe* and other sources. Increasingly, video has become an important component of the editorial mix for Boston.com.

For several years video content has been delivered through strategic relationships with local broadcasters New England Cable News and New England Sports Network. More recently, as the appetite for video content increased, Boston.com has been expanding the use of video that it produces itself as well as video content that is user generated. Video is becoming a more important component in such areas as entertainment, special news reports, sports, and even breaking news.

Over the years, Boston.com has adopted a stable of measurement best practices and technologies to capture data on web page viewers. However, page view metrics alone do not tell a complete story for Internet video. An early adopter in an emerging market, Boston.com is working to develop a fuller assessment of its Internet video audience's in-stream behavior by partnering with Visible Measures.

Figure 10.21 Boston.com

Using VisibleSuite, Boston.com is capturing new data about its audience's access to, consumption of, and engagement with individual videos. For instance, early results show that Internet video audience engagement is not necessarily tied to video length. In the world of online news, fresh new content is more critical.

With VisibleSuite, Boston.com has identified viewing patterns associated with demographics, editorial design, and day-of-the week and time-of-day viewing that will have a profound effect on marketing and promotion of Internet video content. This audience behavior measurement data will allow Boston.com to continually refine its Internet video content, create more compelling packages for advertisers, and promote video content through its distribution partners more effectively.

Unfortunately, it may not prevent the *Globe* from following the *Rocky Mountain News*, which has shut down completely, the *Christian Science Monitor*, which is no longer printed on a daily basis, or the *Seattle Post-Intelligencer*, which has gone to a web-only version. Nevertheless, refining the Internet video content may be the last best hope of saving Boston.com no matter what happens to the *Globe*. And it may be the last best hope in other cities too.

In February 2009, ReelSEO released an in-depth report sponsored by EveryZing on how online video can help newspaper companies to grow their Internet audience and advertising base. Written by Senior Analyst Grant Crowell, "Business Models for

New Realities: The Newspapers Industry's Video SEO Opportunity" is the culmination of more than two years of industry research along with interviews with editors and publishers of newspaper companies nationwide.

I was one of the analysts who was interviewed for the report and was quoted in a press release when it was announced. I said, "If you do a SWOT analysis of newspapers, their strengths are in print, their weaknesses are online, but their opportunities are in online video, and their threats are legion. That's why newspaper executives should read this report today, not tomorrow."

I wrote that two months before The New York Times Company threatened to shutter the *Globe*. Today let me repeat my urgent request.

Week 4: Build an Integrated Trinity Platform

You should use YouTube Insight to count what is countable. And you should use TubeMogul or Visible Measures to measure what is measurable. But what can you do to make measurable what is not measurable by these tools?

The answer is to start building an integrated Trinity platform. What's that? In *Web Analytics: An Hour a Day,* Kaushik calls Trinity a mindset and a strategic approach. He says, "The central raison d'être of the Trinity strategy is something radical: actionable insights and metrics."

He adds, "Actionable insights and metrics are the über-goal simply because they drive strategic differentiation and a sustainable competitive advantage."

- The first component of this strategic approach is *behavior analysis*. The goal of behavior analysis is to infer the intent of video viewers or website visitors based on the data we have about them.

- The second component of the Trinity mindset is *outcome analysis*. You want to know the outcomes for your target audience and your company. We look at some dramatic outcomes in Chapter 11.

- The third component of this strategic approach is *experience analysis*. You need to get into the heads of your viewers, visitors, and customers to gain insights about why they do the things they do.

As Kaushik says and Figure 10.22 illustrates, "In the end, the Trinity mindset drives the fundamental *understanding of the customer experience* so that you can *influence the optimal customer behavior* that will lead to *win-win outcomes* for your company and your customers."

So, how do we start building an integrated Trinity platform? Kaushik says, "The entire framework will not come into existence overnight. Typically, you'll diagnose what you currently have and will work toward putting the missing pieces of the puzzle together."

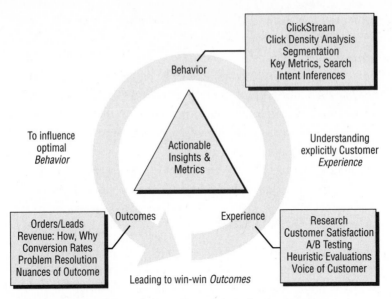

Figure 10.22 Understanding experience to influence behavior for win-win outcomes.

This week, we'll look at other tools that make measurable what is not measurable by YouTube Insight, TubeMogul, or Visible Measures. These tools can help you put the missing pieces of the puzzle together.

Monday: Monitor social media with Radian6

Tuesday: Track inlinks with Yahoo! Site Explorer

Tuesday: Get competitive intelligence from Hitwise

Thursday: Install Google Analytics

Friday: Get a DIY dashboard from KDPaine & Partners

Monday: Monitor Social Media with Radian6

One of the missing pieces of the puzzle is finding out who's talking about your brand in the online communities that surround the YouTube community. There are a number of solutions, including BuzzLogic and Trackur. But I'm currently using Radian6, an automated solution that monitors and analyzes a variety of social media.

Founded in 2006, Radian6 provides a social media monitoring platform, flexible dashboard, and as-it-happens alerts. Various analysis widgets give users the ability to uncover the top influencers as well as measure which conversations are having an impact online.

Radian6 has the ability to analyze buzz about your company, products, issues, and competitors and the outcomes of specific marketing campaigns and social media investments. You can know immediately which content is making an impact and what needs to be managed. You can uncover the opinion leaders online by topic, based on user-determined formula weightings. You can listen and learn more about these opinion leaders and decide on a path of engagement tracking the steps along the way.

Radian6 enables you to monitor all forms of social media, from video sharing sites like YouTube to blogs, discussion forums, opinion sites, social networking sites such as MySpace and Facebook, microblogging sites like Twitter, and photo sharing sites like Flickr. This gives you the ability to listen, measure, and decide which customers to engage across the entire social web.

In April 2009, Radian6 announced a partnership with Webtrends Open Exchange to offer Webtrends Social Measurement, powered by Radian6. This offers businesses a more complete view of customer engagement, in terms of both what's happening within their own website and what's happening outside their domain across the social web.

As Figure 10.23 illustrates, I interviewed Amber Naslund, director of community of Radian6, at SES New York 2009. I asked her why it is important for small businesses to use social media monitoring tools. She said the cost of these tools is relatively low and using social media is a great way to connect with smaller communities.

Figure 10.23 "Amber Naslund, Radian6, on the importance of social media for small businesses at SES New York"

Tuesday: Track Inlinks with Yahoo! Site Explorer

Another one of the missing pieces of the puzzle is finding a better way to track the comments and inlinks to your videos and channel.

On any video's watch page, you can find out what the top five sites linking to a video are under Statistics & Data. Also, with YouTube Insight, you can see what the top sites embedding one of your videos are. You can contact these sites and establish a relationship, and they may continue to post your future videos.

Also, you can check the comments on your videos. You can skim the comments to pick up on helpful information. If a popular user in the YouTube community comments on one of your videos, you can contact them and see if they would be interested in future collaboration or cross promotion. This requires you to be an avid community member, of course.

You can also check the content of the comments for memes—cultural references to specific communities—to figure out what kind of audience you're getting. For example, check out "Play him off, keyboard cat" on Brad OFarrell's channel at www.youtube.com/watch?v=2ndx_Id1UQU. Even though none of the Insight or reference data mentions 4chan.org, a lot of the comments contained references to 4chan memes, which you can find at http://en.wikipedia.org/wiki/4chan#Memes.

O'Farrell says, "So I knew the audience were '4chan people' and as such I modified my video's metadata to react to that. I changed the title to name the cat 'keyboard cat' since that's the naming convention 4chan memes often have (e.g., "long cat" or "speedy cat") so that it would be more consumable to the 4chan audience. I also put in the extra effort to get it monetized (I had to obtain the rights) and featured, and enabled video responses without my approval."

As Figure 10.24 illustrates, "Play him off, keyboard cat" had over 670,000 views as of May 2009 and it became a meme: over 790 parodies of the video have been made as of that date.

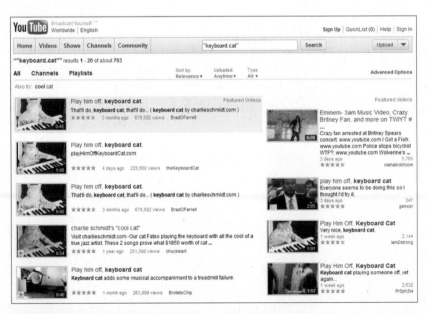

Figure 10.24 YouTube Search results for *keyboard cat*

Now that YouTube allows you to export your Insight data into CSV files, it's easier to move and analyze it using spreadsheet software. But Insight doesn't provide data for the sites linking to your channel. And YouTube doesn't report what sites are linking to other channels or more than the top five sites linking to a popular video.

So use Yahoo! Site Explorer (`https://siteexplorer.search.yahoo.com`) to track sites that link to a channel or watch page. Exploring a channel or watch page is as easy as doing a web search, but instead of entering a query term, you enter the URL into the Explore URL Search box and click Explore.

What's different about Site Explorer is that it does not return the same kind of results as a web search. Instead, the Site Explorer results page shows all the indexed inlinks to the URL.

By default Site Explorer provides 50 results per page. You can view the live or cached version of any result. You can also export the data to a tab-separated value (TSV) file for further analysis. And you have the option to download up to 1,000 results into a TSV file at once—and avoid having to page through the results.

How you format or specify the URL that you submit to Site Explorer influences what kind of results you get. So you should specify URLs in different forms to display different results in Site Explorer.

For example, when I pasted `http://www.youtube.com/user/huluDotCom` into Site Explorer, it found close to 57,000 inlinks to HuluDotCom's channel on YouTube in May 2009, but when I pasted `http://www.youtube.com/huluDotCom` into Site Explorer, it found only 138 inlinks.

When I pasted `http://www.youtube.com/watch?v=lich59xsjik` into Site Explorer, it found 2,188 inlinks to "Family Guy - Cool Whip," and I could export the inlinks to a TSV file for further analysis.

Wednesday: Get Competitive Intelligence from Hitwise

Another one of the missing pieces of the puzzle is finding out what your key competitor is doing online. There are several good services that provide this information, including comScore and Nielsen Online. But the one that I keep going back to for more competitive insights is Hitwise.

As Figure 10.25 illustrates, Hitwise provides its 1,500 clients with daily insights on how 10 million Internet users in the United States interact with more than 1 million websites, across more than 165 industries as well as how 100,000 Internet users in Canada interact with 85,000 websites in 160 industry categories. And Hitwise clickstream data provides extensive reports on the upstream traffic to and downstream traffic from a specific website, industry, or custom category.

Founded in 1997, Hitwise is now an Experian company. Instead of monitoring a sample of 10,000 to 50,000 Internet users, Hitwise works with ISP networks to monitor millions of Internet users. As a result, while many other measurement companies have data on the top 1,000 websites, Hitwise has data on over 1 million online businesses.

Figure 10.25 What you don't know *can* hurt you.

Hitwise offers a range of products and services that help marketers improve their online performance. The Hitwise flagship product is its online Competitive Intelligence Service.

Although Hitwise doesn't publish the cost of its service on its website, a typical subscription costs from $20,000 to $50,000 a year, depending on the features purchased. Veteran marketers will want to evaluate the benefits as well as the cost of Hitwise. However, new YouTubers might agree with Rebecca Kelley, who posted a review to the SEOmoz Blog on March 2, 2007, entitled, "Hitwise: Damn Expensive, but Damn Cool."

There are a couple of less-expensive alternatives. First, you can go to the Hitwise Research Store (http://researchstore.hitwise.com) and purchase a report on your competitor starting at $695 per report. Second, you can subscribe to the free monthly Hitwise newsletter to receive industry statistics, market trends, and other competitive intelligence data.

In addition, I strongly recommend reading the Hitwise Intelligence Analyst Weblogs. I do. You'll find posts entitled "Hulu and the Older Early Adopter" by Bill Tancer and "YouTube Site Search - Lil Wayne Tops" by Heather Hopkins.

Or, go to the Hitwise Press Center. Yes, there's plenty of good data there too, including the press releases "Google Closing in on 73 Percent of U.S. Searches in April 2009" and "Hitwise Launches Internet Measurement Service for Canada."

Thursday: Install Google Analytics

If one of the missing pieces of the Trinity mindset is "outcome analysis," then one of the tools you need is web analytics. As Figure 10.26 illustrates, Google Analytics can help you find out what happens after they click.

Figure 10.26 What happens after they click?

Google Analytics offers a number of features and benefits:

Advanced segmentation You can isolate and analyze subsets of your traffic. For example, you can select from predefined custom segments such as "Visits with Conversions" or create new custom segments with a flexible, easy-to-use segment builder. You can apply segments to current or historical data and compare segment performance side by side in reports.

Motion charts You can select metrics for the x-axis, y-axis, bubble size, and bubble color and view how these metrics interact over time.

Custom reports You can create, save, and edit custom reports that present the information you want to see organized in the way you want to see it. A drag-and-drop interface lets you select the metrics you want and define multiple levels of subreports.

Keyword and campaign comparison You can track and compare all your ads, email newsletters, affiliate campaigns, referrals, paid links, and keywords on Google and other search engines.

Internal site search You can find out how your visitors search your site, what they look for, and where they end up.

Benchmarking You can find out whether your site usage metrics underperform or out-perform those of your industry vertical. Opt-in benchmarking compares your key metrics against aggregate performance metrics while preserving the confidentiality of your data.

Trend and date slider You can compare time periods and select date ranges without losing sight of long-term trends.

E-commerce tracking You can trace transactions to campaigns and keywords, get loyalty and latency metrics, and identify your revenue sources.

Funnel visualization You can find out which pages result in lost conversions and where your would-be customers go.

Site overlay You can see traffic and conversion information for every link as you browse your site.

GeoTargeting You can find out where your visitors come from and identify your most lucrative geographic markets.

Getting started is relatively straightforward—if you know how to add tracking code to your website. If you don't, ask your webmaster to do it or find someone who has passed the Google Analytics Individual Qualification (IQ) test.

Go to www.google.com/analytics if you know how to add tracking code and sign up to access Analytics. Remember, even if it isn't as easy as Google says, it is free.

Installing the tracking code is a 10-step process:

1. Create a Google Analytics account.
2. Configure your profile.
3. Edit the tracking code for custom website setups.
4. Add the tracking code to your pages.
5. Link with your AdWords account.
6. Create goals and funnels.
7. Tag your advertising campaigns.
8. Create filters.
9. Grant access to other users.
10. Enable e-commerce transaction tracking.

If you look at the preceding list and think, "I can do that," then go right ahead. If not, don't be too proud to ask for help. Remember, just because you didn't pass the Google Analytics IQ test doesn't mean you aren't "wicked smart" when it comes to YouTube and video marketing.

Friday: Get a DIY Dashboard from KDPaine & Partners

The final missing piece of the puzzle is a dashboard that helps you measure your success across an integrated Trinity platform. And to get one, you will want to beat a path to the door of Katie Delahaye Paine.

Paine is the founder and CEO of KDPaine & Partners, a New Hampshire–based communications measurement company. She is the publisher of KDPaine's Measurement Blog and The Measurement Standard. And back in 1986, she was the director of corporate communications for Lotus Development Corporation. Yep, she was my immediate predecessor at Lotus, which may explain why we both got interested in measuring the effectiveness of marketing.

One of the products and services that KDPaine & Partners offers is DIY Dashboard software. Version 3.0 has a couple of features that you will want to check out. One is the ability to track content from YouTube as part of social media reports. Another is an automated metrics tool, dubbed KdPI, which translates thousands of data points into a simple table, which can be customized around your specific Key Performance Indicators (KPIs).

Advanced versions of DIY Dashboard 3.0 offer the ability to integrate data from web server statistics, sales lead programs, and survey research. Additionally, if a client outgrows the Do-It-Yourself version, KDPaine & Partners also offers custom coding and analysis to relieve the burden of data entry. Pricing for the DIY Dashboard starts at $300 per month.

The Measurement Standard used DIY Dashboard 3.0 to cover the YouTube video presidential primary race in New Hampshire. As Figure 10.27 illustrates, Republican hopeful Ron Paul was ahead in YouTube videos that mentioned New Hampshire, with more than 3 million views as of December 2007. But John McCain's reply, "Thanks, you little jerk," to a question about his age at a stump speech in New Hampshire was the most-viewed of any video. It was watched more than 300,000 times.

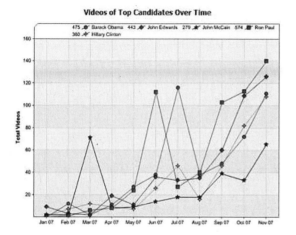

Figure 10.27 Videos of top candidates over time

Making measurable what is not measurable won't be easy. But it can yield some "insights" that you might miss if you use only YouTube Insight.

For example, The Measurement Standard reported in December 2007, "Videos posted by the campaign of front-runner Hillary Clinton were among the least favorably rated among the democratic candidates by YouTube users, who score each video on a one to five scale. Clinton's videos received an average rating of 3.47, compared to 4.80 for videos posted by Paul's campaign."

It also reported, "Although viewers have access to as many as 400 videos in a month, less than 10 percent of videos account for 80 percent of views, a trend that is also true among the other YouTube channels."

Measure Outcomes vs. Outputs

11

Although it is useful to measure views and ratings, how many of these "outputs" do you need to make the cash register ring? In this chapter, we'll look at some individuals and organizations that have used YouTube and video marketing to generate measurable "outcomes." But before we do that, we'll question the Dude at the watercooler with sunglasses, no pants, a cigarette, and a martini, who says, "When you're nailing the numbers, they don't ask questions."

Chapter Contents:

Nailing the Numbers

I learned the difference between measuring outputs and outcomes over 20 years ago. Back in 1986, I became the director of corporate communications at Lotus Development Corp. Actually, I became the company's 13th director of corporate communications, and that was when Lotus was only four and a half years old.

After my first month on the job, I took a very thick report on about 700 magazine and newspaper clippings that we'd generated, walked down the short hall to the chairman, president and CEO's office, and casually dropped it on Jim Manzi's desk.

My clipping report measured PR success in advertising value equivalency (AVE), which is calculated by measuring the column inches (in the case of print), or seconds (in the case of broadcast media) and multiplying these figures by the respective medium's advertising rates (per inch or per second). The resulting number was what it would have cost Lotus to place advertisements of that size or duration in those media. In short, I was nailing the numbers.

As Figure 11.1 illustrates, measuring outputs made me feel like the dude at the water-cooler with sunglasses, no pants, a cigarette, and a martini, who says, "When you're nailing the numbers, they don't ask questions."

"When you're nailing the numbers, they don't ask questions."

Figure 11.1 "When you're nailing the numbers, they don't ask questions." (Cartoon by C. Covert Darbyshire in *The New Yorker*, October 2, 2006.)

Manzi took a quick look and said, "Jarboe, these are just little pieces of paper. If I could deposit them in a bank, they'd be worth something. But, until you can measure the value of PR in cold, hard cash, don't waste my time with these so-called reports."

Although I'd worked in high-tech public relations at Wang Laboratories, Stratus Computer, and Data General for five years before joining Lotus, I'd never encountered this lack of faith in PR before. But then I'd never worked for a CEO who was a former journalist as well as a former McKinsey consultant before.

And I had to admit, Manzi was right. He was focused on outcomes.

Around that time, my father was the director of marketing at Oldsmobile. His ad agency, Leo Burnett, had created the memorable TV commercial, "It's not your father's Oldsmobile."

The folks at Leo Burnett were measuring the success of their ad campaign in gross rating points (GRPs), which represents the percentage of the target audience reached by an advertisement. If the advertisement appears more than once, the GRP figure represents the sum of each individual GRP. In the case of a TV commercial that is aired five times reaching 80 percent of the target audience, it would have 400 GRPs = $5 \times 80\%$.

But sales of Oldsmobiles were falling from 1.2 million in 1986 to 800,000 in 1988 and then to under 600,000 in 1990. At one point, my dad asked his ad agency, "How many GRPs do we need to sell a car?"

My dad was asking the right question. He was focused on outcomes.

But the folks at Leo Burnett were focused on outputs. Like the dude at the watercooler, they thought they were nailing the numbers back then. But, with 20/20 hindsight, it's now clear the ad campaign was "unselling" Oldsmobiles every year it ran by informing older customers the brand wasn't targeted at them anymore and reminding younger prospects the brand had been driven by old fogies for a generation. This had a negative impact on the brand preference of Olds.

So, as I started writing this book, I also started looking for case studies of YouTube channels and video advertising that did more than nail the numbers and generate measurable outputs. I looked for success stories about creating a positive impact on brand preference and generating measurable outcomes.

Win the Presidency of the United States: Barack Obama

On November 4, 2008, at 9:27 p.m., Barack Obama won the state of Ohio and the outcome of the presidential election became crystal clear. Sean Quinn of FiveThirtyEight. com observed, "That's the ballgame folks. He will be the next president of the United States. Barack Obama will be the next president of the United States."

Today, the whole world knows that Obama won the Democratic Party's nomination after a close campaign against Hillary Rodham Clinton in the 2008 presidential primaries and caucuses. Obama then defeated Republican candidate John McCain in the 2008 general election to become the first African-American elected president. And we also know that the 1,800 videos on BarackObamadotcom's channel on YouTube had been viewed over 110 million times as of November 4, 2008. But did the videos impact what happened next: Obama won 69.5 million popular votes and 365 electoral votes?

To understand the impact of YouTube and video marketing on candidate preference and election outcomes, the person I wanted to interview for this book was Arun Chaudhary. He's been called "Obama's auteur" by Aswini Anburajan of *National Journal Magazine* (April 19, 2008) and "Obama's video guru" by Michael Learmonth of *Silicon Alley Insider* (July 17, 2008).

As Figure 11.2 illustrates, Chaudhary's official title on the campaign was New Media Road Director of Obama for America (OFA). Today, he is the White House videographer.

Figure 11.2 "Online Video Production Best Practices - A Discussion with Arun Chaudhary From Obama for America"

Barack Obama started using YouTube and video marketing even before officially announcing his candidacy for the presidency of the United States on February 10, 2007.

On January 16, 2007, Obama announced via video on YouTube and his website that he had formed a presidential exploratory committee. As Figure 11.3 illustrates, the 3-minute, 7-second video has more than 1.8 million views and over 11,000 ratings.

With 4,500 text comments, "Barack Obama: My Plans for 2008" was the #3 most discussed video out of the more than 1,800 videos on BarackObamadotcom's Channel as of April 18, 2009. It had also been favorited more than 1,400 times.

Figure 11.3 "Barack Obama: My Plans for 2008"

The fact that a preannouncement video could create such an impact indicates that the "invisible caucus" that I described in Chapter 2 may have been held a month before the "invisible primary" that Linda Feldmann described in the *Christian Science Monitor* on February 26, 2007.

But, is there any hard evidence that the results of early jockeying for opinion leaders in YouTube's News & Politics category influenced the outcome of the early jockeying for money, top campaign staff, and high-profile endorsements? There could be, but it's buried in the list of close to 25,000 friends and 170,000 subscribers to BarackObamadotcom's channel.

Although you can find out when someone made a campaign donation or public endorsement, YouTube doesn't give you the ability to see the exact date when they became a friend or subscriber to a YouTube Channel. Yes, the earliest friends and subscribers are on the last page, but no, I don't have the time to go through 25,000 friends and 170,000 subscribers. So as with the chicken and the egg, let's just say we don't know which came first.

We do know that Chaudhary, a 32-year-old New York University film-school professor, took a leave of absence in the summer of 2007 to work for OFA.

In his April 19, 2008, cover story, "Obama's Auteur," Anburajan wrote, "Before Obama, Chaudhary—the son of an immigrant Indian father and a Jewish mother, both scientists—had tried to interest New York-area politicians in his scripts for political ads and Internet videos but to no avail. Then came the senator from Illinois."

Chaudhary lobbied hard for a position in the Obama campaign. He even interrupted both his wedding rehearsal dinner and his wedding day in May 2007 to sell himself to Joe Rospars, OFA's director of new media.

Rospars decided to hire a pro with real film experience to add something fresh to Obama's YouTube and video marketing campaign. "There's a lot of open space to be creative in a campaign and people don't take advantage of it," Rospars told Anburajan.

So Chaudhary became the full-time $40,000-a-year director of field production for the campaign, crisscrossing the country alongside the candidate with two other videographers, making videos that sought to pull supporters into the campaign by letting them peer through his lens.

"Why do you need to see someone with a mike in their hand telling you what Barack Obama said today, when you can see for yourself what Barack Obama said today?" Chaudhary told Anburajan.

Chaudhary also told Anburajan about a Chinese-American rapper named Jin the Emcee, who decided to join the Obama campaign after spending a night viewing all of the candidate's campaign videos on his computer.

This provides at least anecdotal evidence for my "invisible caucus" theory.

Of course, the campaign was also being waged offline as well as online. On November 21, 2007, Obama announced that Oprah Winfrey would be campaigning for him. As word spread that Oprah's first appearance would be in Iowa, polls released in early December revealed Obama taking the lead in that critical state. Although celebrity endorsements typically have little effect on voter opinions, the Oprah-Obama tour drew record-setting crowds in Iowa and dominated political news headlines.

On January 3, 2008, Obama won the Iowa Democratic caucus, the first contest in the Democratic nomination season. Obama had the support of 37.6 percent of Iowa's delegates, compared to 29.7 percent for John Edwards and 29.5 percent for Hillary Clinton.

In his remarks to his followers that evening, he said, "On this January night, at this defining moment in history, you have done what the cynics said we couldn't do." He added that in the future Americans will look back on the 2008 Iowa caucuses and say, "This is the moment when it all began."

This brings us to Obama's "Iowa Caucus Victory Speech" on January 3, 2008. As Figure 11.4 illustrates, the 14-minute, 7-second video has close to 2.4 million views and over 9,400 ratings.

This was the #2 most discussed video on BarackObamadotcom's channel, with more than 5,300 text comments as of April 2009. It had also been favorited more than 1,600 times.

Although news and political junkies could watch the entire speech live at 11:04 p.m. EST, opinion leaders could also share the entire speech with their followers the following day. This means the medium enabled the YouTube community to get a more complete message than you could get from the typical "sound bite," which had dominated political discourse for more than 40 years.

Figure 11.4 "Iowa Caucus Victory Speech"

Now, this didn't shorten the Democratic nomination process, which continued until June 7, 2008. But it did change it.

On July 16, 2008, frog design, *Fast Company*, and NYU's Tisch Interactive Telecommunications Program hosted an event at NYU entitled "Obama and Politics 2.0: Documenting History in Real-Time." It featured a conversation with Chaudhary and Ellen McGirt, a senior writer for *Fast Company*.

The following day, Learmonth posted a story about the event entitled "Obama's Video Guru Speaks: How We Owned the YouTube Primary." According to Chaudhary, Obama's organization took online video seriously from the outset, which put them ahead of previous efforts. The Clinton campaign would have had just one staffer videotaping an event; Obama's had between two and four people shooting, editing, and posting video in order to get multiple camera angles. They were fast in getting video posted (as fast as 19 minutes from shoot to post) and fast in alerting voters when new video was up. Wrote Learmonth:

> *Obama's YouTube and web site metrics show that his online viewers aren't pups. The average viewer is 45 to 55 years old, Chaudhary said, a fact he found "shocking." And while Chaudhary made plenty of humorous clips, they weren't the most popular. Invariably the videos that got the most views were long clips of speeches, unscripted moments, or, say, an appearance on "Ellen" or "Oprah." The viewing reflects a hunger not to be entertained, but to know something about the candidate.*

This brings us to the "Obama Speech: 'A More Perfect Union.'" As Figure 11.5 illustrates, the 37-minute, 39-second video has more than 6 million views and 28,500 ratings.

Figure 11.5 *"Obama Speech: 'A More Perfect Union'"*

Obama spoke in Philadelphia at the National Constitution Center on matters not just of race and recent remarks but of the fundamental path by which America can work together to pursue a better future.

His speech was given on March 18, 2008, and was the #1 most discussed video on BarackObamadotcom's channel with more than 10,000 text comments as of April 18, 2009. It has also been favorited more than 3,250 times and ranks #35 Most Viewed (All Time) in the News & Politics category.

Just nine days later, the Pew Research Center called the speech "arguably the biggest political event of the campaign so far," noting that 85 percent of Americans said they had heard at least a little about the speech and that 54 percent said they heard a lot about it.

On June 15, 2008, a report by the Pew Internet & American Life Project found 35 percent of Americans said they had watched online political videos—a figure that nearly tripled the reading the Pew Internet Project got in the 2004 race.

The report also found that 39 percent of online Americans had used the Internet to access "unfiltered" campaign materials, which included video of candidate debates, speeches, and announcements as well as position papers and speech transcripts.

In Chapter 3, you saw that BarackObamadotcom's channel had more than a five-to-one lead over JohnMcCaindotcom's channel in videos and close to a four-to-one lead in views. So what impact did YouTube and video marketing have on candidate preference and election outcomes?

Just after the election, Jose Antonio Vargas wrote an online column for the *Washington Post* (November 14, 2008) entitled "The YouTube Presidency." In it, he quoted Steve Grove, head of news and politics at YouTube, who said, "The Obama team has written the playbook on how to use YouTube for political campaigns. Not only have they achieved impressive mass—uploading over 1,800 videos that have been viewed over 110 million times total—but they've also used video to cultivate a sense of community amongst supporters."

On April 15, 2009, the Pew Internet & American Life Project reported on the Internet's role in campaign 2008. Here are the findings of its postelection survey of 2,254 adults conducted by Princeton Survey Research Associates International from November 20 to December 4, 2008:

- Forty-four percent of online Obama voters had watched video online from a campaign or news organization, compared to 39 percent of online McCain voters.

- Thirty-nine percent of online Obama voters had watched video online that did not come from a campaign or news organization, compared to 35 percent of online McCain voters.

- Twenty-one percent of online Obama voters shared photos, video, or audio files online related to the campaign or election, compared to 16 percent of McCain voters.

Aaron Smith, a research analyst with the Pew Internet Project, said, "Due to demographic differences between the two parties, McCain voters were actually more likely than Obama voters to go online in the first place. However, online Obama supporters were generally more engaged in the online political process than online McCain supporters."

He added, "Among internet users, Obama voters were more likely to share online political content with others, sign up for updates about the election, donate money to a candidate online, set up political news alerts and sign up online for volunteer activities related to the campaign. Online Obama voters were also out in front when it came to posting their own original political content online—26% of wired Obama voters did this, compared with 15% of online McCain supporters."

Smith also observed, "In 2008, nearly one in five internet users posted their thoughts, comments or questions about the campaign on a website, blog, social networking site or other online forum." He called this group "the online political participatory class." I'd call them "opinion leaders." They helped Obama win the presidency of the United States.

Q&A with Arun Chaudhary, New Media Road Director of Obama for America (OFA)

In spring 2009, I got my opportunity to ask Chaudhary questions about OFA's YouTube and video marketing campaign. We conducted the interview via email.

Jarboe: You took leave from NYU to become Barack Obama's director of video field production. How did you first get involved in the campaign?

Chaudhary: An old friend of mine, Kate Albright-Hanna, had taken the position of Director of Video for the OFA New Media Department. She thought that I might be a good fit to join the team, which was lucky for me because as a film academic and primarily a maker of fiction, I may not have looked like an obvious choice on paper. Video production on the campaign developed very organically as according to need more than by grand design, so the separation of the "Road Team" which I led as the New Media Road Director, wasn't something that was anticipated when I joined the campaign. I was more of the short, funny, creative things guy.

Jarboe: After two years on the campaign trail, you've posted more than 1,000 videos on the BarackObama.com website and on YouTube. What are your most memorable ones?

Chaudhary: There are two videos that always stand out to me.

One I shot on the eve of the Iowa Caucuses (Figure 11.6). President (then Senator) Obama wanted to visit a caucus location so we went about 45 minutes north of Des Moines to Ankeny, Iowa, not taking any press with us. It was a magic moment, not a single vote of any kind had been cast in the election and we had been campaigning for almost a year, hoping and trusting the American people were hearing the campaign's message. The air was full of anticipation, and when Barack walked in and everyone flocked to him and said they were caucusing for him, we knew that something serious had begun. The little video we made of this visit was posted to YouTube within minutes of it happening but was drowned out in all the attention of the Iowa Victory Speech that was posted almost immediately afterward. There is a lesson in there somewhere.

The second video would be our online response to the Clinton campaign's "3 a.m. Girl" ad (Figure 11.7). Senator Clinton had made a political ad about a 3 a.m. phone call that occurred "while your children are asleep." In a strange turn of events, the child in the stock footage the ad used had grown up to be an Obama supporter. The young woman was actually an Obama precinct captain in Washington State. I went to Tacoma to see her, and within 20 hours, travel included, we had a response piece up in YouTube. It was really fun and interesting to do it as a web piece because we had screen time enough to really play around with the material. The final product was as much of a deconstructing of the typical negative ad, as much as it was the young girl's story.

Figure 11.6 "Caucus Night: Barack in Ankeny"

Figure 11.7 "Hillary's '3 A.M. ad' Girl Doesn't Approve of that Message"

Jarboe: Who was your target audience? Was it opinion leaders in the YouTube community or political activists who also watched online video? Did your target audience change from 2007 to 2008 or from the primaries/caucuses to the general election?

Chaudhary: Our target audience was voters, all kinds of voters. While YouTube community folks and political activists were probably vocal commenters on our work, I don't think it would make sense to think of them as a target audience. We wanted to appeal to a wide variety of folks. When you have a candidate as exciting and dynamic as Barack Obama was, the most important thing you can do is get him in front of as many people as possible. We used to say the YouTube or live stream hits of his speeches were like adding thousands of extra seats in the room. Especially in the early states, the sort of people you want to watch an event are folks who couldn't physically make it for some reason. Rather than fishing for viral success you'd rather have real prospective voters see your candidate make his or her case.

Jarboe: Did you optimize your videos for YouTube? Were there search terms that you put in your title, description and tags of your videos on YouTube? Were there search terms that were used to optimize videos for Google?

Chaudhary: We tried to be very specific. Location and date of the speech was very important because you really hope that folks who weren't physically able to make the rally are able to find the footage. Topic is very important as well, because a lot of folks looking for political content online are hoping to find answers to their specific questions (what is the candidate's position on health care?) in that way; the candidate's websites are very much a modern update of campaign literature, or maybe even a bit like the voting guides various groups used to publish close to election times (Figure 11.8). You really can't be too specific with your titling, though of course there are only so many words you can actually have in the title itself. I also think it's important to include information in the peice itself. With emerging technologies and when posting videos on many different platforms, you never quite know what will happen. One of the format rules for BarackObama.com that was designed and enforced by Kate Albright-Hanna was that the opening card for every video would be the date and location. I remember thinking that it was maybe a little too austere, but she was absolutely right. If you lived in Keokuk, Iowa, and a friend forwarded you a video link, the first thing you would see when you clicked on it would be November 20th, 2007 Keokuk Iowa, and immediately know why it was relevant to you.

Jarboe: What was the most compelling video content of the campaign? Was it "Yes We Can - Barack Obama Music Video" or "Obama Speech: 'A More Perfect Union'"?

Figure 11.8 "Barack Obama on Health Care"

Chaudhary: I think I better leave the awarding of superlatives to folks who were the audiences of these movies, but between the two you mentioned I would have to go with "A More Perfect Union." The Will.i.am piece (which was not produced by the campaign; it was made by the artists themselves) was really great and I think a lot of people found it very inspiring and accessible, but we had consistent calls from the public to put up speeches in their entirety. As time went on we found that some of the effort of finding specific clips and producing them with cut shots was better spent trying to get entire speeches and town halls online. Folks really seemed to respond to being allowed to see the candidate unedited. In a sense they wanted to see the candidates in the raw and make their own decision, not to feel like they were being fed media. With a candidate as compelling as Barack Obama was, it made a lot of sense to let them see him in this manner. The more people actually saw him speak and hear his views, the more likely they were to vote for him. With a different candidate one might need to take a different strategy, but for us Barack Obama was always the star; we were just the backup singers.

Jarboe: What was your channel strategy? How much effort was focused on BarackObamadotcom's channel on YouTube versus BarackObama.com/tv/? Did this change from 2007 to 2008 or from the primaries/caucuses to the general election?

Chaudhary: There was a change. As we began seeing that the strongest case we could make for Barack Obama was being made by Barack Obama himself, we spent more time and video resources on the road with the candidate. The team that I led, the Road Team, consisted of 6 folks who did all the videotaping, still photography, and blogging from the trail itself, putting up YouTube clips from every event, whether it be a speech, a town hall, or even a visit to a local diner.

There was another video team (the one led by Kate Albright-Hanna) who made video content from headquarters, often the more produced pieces. The YouTube channel ended up being dominated by material from the Road Team simply because of the huge volume of video's we produced, although everything was on it. BarackTV was curated by Kate Albright-Hanna (using a higher quality player than YouTube) with an eye towards the more produced content (Figure 11.09). It was meant to be a complete viewing experience rather than campaign literature.

Figure 11.9 Organizing for America

Jarboe: In addition to creating compelling video content, did you engage in any outreach effort with the YouTube community or bloggers? Was there any effort to give opinion leaders a "heads up" when a new video was uploaded?

Chaudhary: There was some effort put into blog outreach, mostly from the HQ side; I can't really speak to it, because I wasn't involved with it, nor was it something we thought about much on the road.

Jarboe: What production challenges did you face and overcome? Was video produced in the field but uploaded from headquarters? Are there any tips or tools that you used to get videos uploaded on a daily basis?

Chaudhary: The production challenges were immense. We would often arrive at events with about 10 minutes to go before a speech would start and need to set up our cameras and live-streaming computer as fast as we could. If everything went right it was just about possible. Editing was just as challenging. The Road Team edited in the field on laptops and uploaded with aircards. On an airplane you can only upload to about 30,000 feet before losing all signal, so time was always of the essence. The watchword on our team was "workflow." Because we were doing so many events and traveling so constantly, we had a lot of opportunity to improve the workflow; see what order things should be done in, what tasks the computer could handle doing at the same time, figure out how to fill what little time we had to its fullest. Redundancy also helped. Every Road Team member had a camera, a laptop, and an aircard. That way we weren't reliant on any one person to get the job done; we were all able to do what we needed to do. It was definitely a process. By the end of the campaign, it was taking us minutes to upload what was taking hours at the beginning. There was no magic formula, it was just experience. The thing about doing a process over and over and over is that eventually you get better. A tip I would definitely offer others is to always worry about the audio first; once you have that everything else is fixable. Bad video can seem like a choice while bad audio is always a mistake.

Jarboe: Did you take advantage of any video advertising opportunities?

Chaudhary: This isn't really anything I can speak to directly; Joe Rospars and our on-line ad guys Michael Organ and Andrew Bleeker did a lot of amazing things, even putting up Obama posters in video games, but it wasn't something the Road Team got involved with other than providing footage—something we did for the television folks as well.

Jarboe: How did you measure your video campaign? Did you use YouTube Insight, TubeMogul, or other analytics for online video? Did you use web analytics on BarackObama.com? What feedback did these tools give you that led you to change what you were doing?

Chaudhary: We did pay attention to the analytics. In fact, there was an entire section of the New Media department devoted to analyzing all the data.

On a personal level, I was never quite sure how accurate the metrics of YouTube Insight or TubeMogul were, but I think it can show you some general trends and that can be quite useful. Seeing that folks would actually watch entire speeches and not just clips was very useful, especially as it is slightly counterintuitive. Also finding out that our core audience was much older than the 18–25 demographic was very interesting. According to the YouTube Insight tool, our main audience was 40 to 50, which is what you would expect from normal political media but not necessarily online. It has certainly reinforced my notion that online political video was essentially the modern replacement for the printed campaign guides of the past. I think a lot of folks went to all the websites to compare and contrast the candidates' views and make an informed decision.

Jarboe: I see President Obama using YouTube (Figure 11.10) as effectively as President Roosevelt used radio when it was still a new medium. How do you see President Obama's use of online video?

Chaudhary: Without getting into specifics I will say that President Obama has said that he is committed to the idea of a more open, more transparent administration and that online video can certainly be an effective means to achieve that end.

Figure 11.10 Whitehouse's channel

As Figure 11.11 illustrates, *Fast Company* named Obama's presidential campaign team #1 in The Fast 50 for 2009. The magazine said, "This year's most successful startup took a skinny kid with a funny name and turned him into the most powerful new national brand in a generation."

Fast Company said, "The team has become the envy of marketers both in and out of politics for proving, among other things, just how effective digital initiatives can be." It added, "The community that elected Obama raised more money, held more events, made more phone calls, shared more videos, and offered more policy suggestions than any in history. It also delivered more votes."

Figure 11.11 The Fast 50 2009: #1 Team Obama

Although YouTube and video marketing was just part of a much larger political process, it was a significant new part. At an early stage, it helped a former community organizer's presidential campaign take off when a critical mass of opinion leaders started sharing his videos with others.

Increase Sales of DVDs 23,000 Percent: Monty Python

"And now for something completely different."

It's Monty Python, another group that has used YouTube and video marketing to generate measurable outcomes. Yes, yes, the six comedians: Graham Chapman, John Cleese, Terry Gilliam, Eric Idle, Terry Jones, and Michael Palin.

The group created *Monty Python's Flying Circus*. I saw their first show on the BBC when it aired on October 5, 1969. I was a student at the University of Edinburgh back then. Some of my favorite sketches are "Dead Parrot," "The Spanish Inquisition," and "The Ministry of Silly Walks."

The Pythons went on to make such movies as *Monty Python and the Holy Grail* (1975), *Monty Python's Life of Brian* (1979), and *Monty Python's The Meaning of Life* (1983). And Idle wrote *Monty Python's Spamalot*. I bought a T-shirt at the musical that says, "I'm not dead yet."

But I never expected to see the Pythons in this book until January 21, 2009. That was the fateful day the YouTube Blog mentioned, "When Monty Python launched their channel in November, not only did their YouTube videos shoot to the top of the most viewed lists, but their DVDs also quickly climbed to No. 2 on Amazon's Movies & TV bestsellers list, with increased sales of 23,000 percent."

That was exactly the kind of success story that I knew you, the reader, would want to read. But, I didn't know how to contact Cleese, Gilliam, Idle, Jones, or Palin. (Chapman is deceased.)

So, I poked aimlessly about MontyPython's channel (shown in Figure 11.12) on YouTube hoping to find a way to connect with one of the comedians.

Figure 11.12 The Monty Python Channel

I have a YouTube account, so I could have sent them a message. But I thought that would make me look like just another fan of their sketch comedy.

Then, I discovered that, as Figure 11.13 illustrates, the most viewed and most discussed video on their channel was entitled "The Monty Python Channel on YouTube." That didn't seem right. It should have been "Always Look On The Bright Side of Life" or "He's Not The Messiah."

I watched the 2-minute and 29-second video and then read the channel information box. One was a close imitation of the language and thoughts of the other. Based on my extensive research, I concluded that the Pythons had created the YouTube channel in November 2008 to stop YouTubers from ripping them off. Here's an edited transcript "lovingly ripped off" from their remarks:

For three years, you YouTubers have been ripping us off, taking tens of thousands of our videos and putting them on YouTube....

We know who you are....

Figure 11.13 "The Monty Python Channel on YouTube"

We know where you live....

We could come after you in ways too horrible to mention....

But being the extraordinarily nice chaps we are, we've figured a better way to get our own back....

It's time for us to take matters into our own hands....

By launching our very own Monty Python channel on YouTube....

No more of those crap quality videos you've been posting. We're giving you the real thing - high quality videos delivered straight from our Monty Python vault....

What's more, we're taking your most viewed clips and uploading brand new high quality versions....

And what's even more, we're letting you see absolutely everything for free....

But we want something in return....

We want you to click on the links and buy our movies and TV shows....

Only this will soften our pain and disgust at being ripped off all these years.

As of April 18, 2009, "The Monty Python Channel on YouTube" had more than 2.2 million views, had over 4,000 ratings, and had been favorited almost 3,000 times. There were also 49 video responses and almost 2,000 text comments.

Meanwhile, Aaron Zamost in Google Corporate Communications put me in touch with John Goldstone, who I initially thought was Monty Python's PR person but who turned out to be their producer. In fact, Goldstone has been collaborating with the Monty Python team since 1974.

I emailed Goldstone some questions and he promptly emailed me back some answers. His email included a Pythonesque image of Mr. Gumby (Figure 11.14), so I know it was authentic.

Figure 11.14 Monty Python's Mr. Gumby

Q&A with John Goldstone, Producer of *Monty Python and the Holy Grail*

Jarboe: What's your background? How did you first get involved in Monty Python's channel on YouTube?

Goldstone: I have been working with Monty Python over the last 35 years. I produced the three movies—*Monty Python & the Holy Grail, Life of Brian*, and *The Meaning of Life*—and because we were able to keep the copyright in the movies and the 45 episodes of *Monty Python's Flying Circus*, I was able, when DVD became the primary format for home entertainment, to revisit the movies and TV shows and give them a whole new life both technically and with a considerable amount of new content. As the power of DVD started to recede last year, it was time to review our digital strategy, and apart from initiating a program of making the titles available for digital download, we felt the time had come to deal with the "YouTube problem." On the one hand, we were surprised at the number of clips that had been uploaded to YouTube in clear infringement of our copyright, and while we didn't want to be spoilsports, it was getting pretty much out of control and we could see no real benefit. So I arranged a trip to meet the YouTube guys on the Google campus in San Jose and discovered that they had a program that would enable us to have our own Monty Python channel on YouTube where we could put up clips from the movies and TV shows of far greater quality and order that might also encourage viewers to want to see whole movies or TV episodes via links to Amazon and iTunes and expand our Monty Python fan base.

Jarboe: Who was your target audience? Was it opinion leaders in the YouTube community or Monty Python fans who also watched online video? Did your target audience change from when the channel was launched to now?

Goldstone: Because Monty Python has been around for almost 40 years (October 2009 is the 40th anniversary of the first broadcast on BBCTV of *Monty Python's Flying Circus*), there are possibly now six generations of Monty Python fans around the world, so it wasn't a question of targeting but more about letting YouTube do its miraculous thing and bring its very wide audience into our net.

Jarboe: Did you optimize your videos for YouTube? Are there search terms that you put in the title, description, and tags of your videos?

Goldstone: We gave each clip as much cross reference as possible to make the search that much easier.

Jarboe: What is the most compelling video content on MontyPython's channel? Is it one of the most viewed or most discussed videos? Is it one of your playlists?

Goldstone: Certainly the most compelling, viewed, and discussed is the new introduction video we created for the launch of the channel. I had written the mission statement for the channel, which became the commentary for the introduction video, and we drew on interviews with the Pythons to tell the story. We used the playlist option as a way to create themes, which we continue to populate with new videos.

Jarboe: What is your channel strategy? How much effort was focused on Monty Python's channel on YouTube versus http://pythonline.com/ Figure 11.15? Has this changed since the channel was launched? Will it change going forward?

Goldstone: We have been developing PythOnline, which Eric Idle started in 1996, from its original form into a more interactive, user-generating platform and are about to go for a full launch of the MashCaster, which the folks at New Media Broadcasting Company who manage PythOnline for us have developed as a downloadable software program that enables Terry Gilliam–type animation to be created, shared, broadcast, and uploaded on PythOnline and of course YouTube. User-generated content is therefore a big part of our future direction.

Jarboe: In addition to creating compelling video content, have you engaged in any outreach effort with the YouTube community or bloggers? Do you give opinion leaders a "heads up" when a new video is uploaded?

Goldstone: So far we have preferred to provide new content on a regular basis to which YouTube subscribers to the Monty Python Channel are automatically alerted.

Figure 11.15 Pythonline

Jarboe: What production challenges have you faced and overcome? Are there any tips or tools that you used to get videos uploaded?

Goldstone: Maintaining high-definition quality has been the biggest challenge. Our mission statement criticized the inferior quality of so many of the clips that had been uploaded before the launch of the Monty Python Channel and we wanted to show how good they could and should be.

Jarboe: The YouTube Blog says your "DVDs quickly climbed to No. 2 on Amazon's Movies & TV bestsellers list" when you launched your channel, "with increased sales of 23,000 percent." Why did you take advantage of YouTube's click-to-buy platform? Did you also use Yahoo! Video ads, InVideo Ads, contests, or other high-profile placements?

Goldstone: The click-to-buy ability was exactly what we were looking for to make the link from video to the right Amazon page much more effective than the URL by the side of the video description. We are only now beginning to address premium advertising, which is only possible when you can show the size, composition, and consistency of your viewers.

Jarboe: How did you measure your video campaign? Did you use YouTube Insight, TubeMogul, or other analytics for online video? Did you use web analytics on http://pythonline.com/? What feedback did these tools give you that may have led you to change anything you were doing?

Goldstone: The analysis tools have been very useful for identifying where in the world our viewers are, although, because our DVDs have been available in many countries of the world, we have known for some time where our major audience bases are.

Jarboe: I've been a fan of the Pythons since Monty Python's Flying Circus *first aired on the BBC. Did the Pythons create a YouTube channel just to stop their content from being released illegally on the Internet, or is this the beginning of a new chapter in the quest for Global PythoNation?*

Goldstone: It certainly started as a way to control what was going on, but the extraordinary response we got to launching our own channel has opened up broader ideas to reach and expand our audience.

That is serious advice from a man who has been producing comedy films in England since the mid-1970s. But, perhaps I should make an appointment with the Argument Clinic (Figure 11.16), because I'd like to have a 5-minute argument with Goldstone about one of his statements.

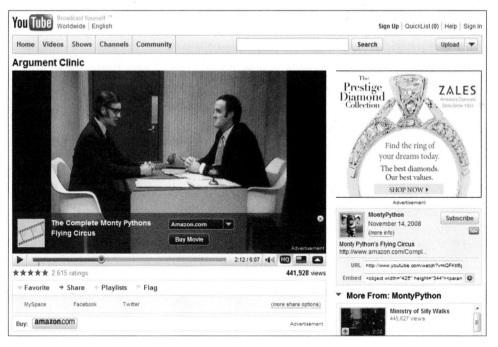

Figure 11.16 "Argument Clinic"

He said, "There are possibly now six generations of Monty Python fans around the world." But that's highly unlikely for a group that's been around for only 40 years, unless those fans are baboons. According to Wikipedia, a new generation of baboons comes along every five to eight years. So, it's possible that six generations of baboons have been born since 1969.

Deliver 700 Percent Increase in Sales: Will It Blend?

Before I proceed, are there any questions?

> **YouTube Director:** "What if the star of my video isn't as exciting and dynamic as Barack Obama?"

> **Search Engine Marketer:** "What if the content my video isn't as compelling as the Monty Python Channel on YouTube?"

> **Entrepreneur:** "And what if I have to launch my YouTube and video marketing campaign on a bare-bones budget?"

Would you want to hear a single success story that answers each and every one of your questions?

> **All:** "Yes!"

Well, let me tell you the story of Blendtec, a division of K-TEC that makes high-performing, durable blenders for commercial use and a newer line of home appliances. Although you may not have heard of this small, Utah-based manufacturer, there's a good chance you've had a smoothie, cappuccino, milkshake, or other frozen drink made with a Blendtec blender.

Tom Dickson, the company founder, describes himself as a "geek." And Kate Klonick of *Esquire* described him as "an otherwise bland grandfatherly-type from Utah" in an article on May 3, 2007. In other words, the star of Blendtec's videos isn't as exciting and dynamic as Barack Obama.

 Note: Brad O'Farrell, the technical editor of this book, thinks the star of the videos isn't Dickson, it's the Total Blender. So, maybe Blendtec's videos are as exciting and dynamic as no-drama Obama.

George Wright, Blendtec's first director of sales and marketing, created a YouTube and video marketing campaign called "Will It Blend?" Wearing the white lab coat and safety glasses, Dickson takes everything but the kitchen sink, sticks it in a blender, and says, "Will it blend? That is the question." While the item is blended, he smiles and waits for the process to end. When it does, he empties out the contents, and the subtitle "Yes, it blends!" appears. In other words, Blendtec's video content isn't as compelling as the Monty Python Channel on YouTube–.

When Blendtec hired Wright in January 2006, the company relied on demonstrations at trade shows and word-of-mouth referrals. On October 30, 2006, Wright created Blendtec's YouTube channel and spent $50 creating the first five "Will It Blend?" videos. He bought a white lab coat, the URL, and a selection of items to be blended, including marbles, a rake, a Big Mac Extra Value Meal, a "cochicken" (12 oz. can of Coke and half a rotisserie chicken), and some ice. In other words, Wright had a bare-bones budget.

"Will It Blend?" has since been called "the best viral marketing campaign ever." It's been featured on the *Today* show, *The Tonight Show*, and The History Channel.

As Figure 11.17 illustrates, the 84 videos on Blendtec's channel on YouTube had more than 73.5 million views in April 2009, making it the #90 most viewed of all time. The channel also had over 182,000 subscribers, making it the #38 most subscribed of all time.

As Figure 11.18 illustrates, the most viewed and most discussed video in the series, "Will it Blend? - iPhone," had more than 6.7 million views and almost 17,000 ratings as of April 2009. It also had also been favorited over 17,600 times, had two video responses, and more than 12,200 text comments.

Figure 11.17 "Will It Blend?"

Figure 11.18 "Will It Blend - iPhone"

And as Figure 11.19 illustrates, this doesn't count views on or subscribers to the official Will It Blend? site (www.willitblend.com).

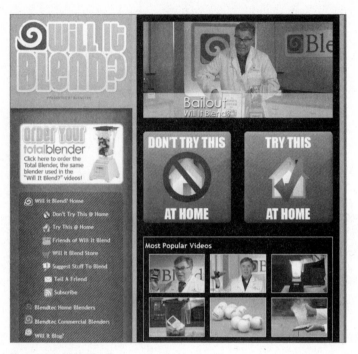

Figure 11.19 Will It Blend?

I first met Wright on October 3, 2008, at the Digital PR Next Practices Summit in New York City. At the *PR News* conference, he talked about building community and reputation online with social media tools and I discussed improving your search engine marketing and PR.

I'd already seen "Will it Blend? - iPhone." And I'd already written: "Unless you are one of the Blendtec guys, don't try using their humorous viral marketing techniques at home."

But, before Wright spoke, I still wasn't sure if he had been lucky or good. Slide 3 of his presentation outlined the critical components of his "Will it Blend?" viral marketing campaign. It clearly showed me that Wright was good. Here's a quick idea of what he said about each critical component:

Entertaining "A viral video doesn't have to be funny, but it has to be worth watching! You gotta check this out! That's the test."

Business objective "'Will it Blend?' generates revenue. Nike has offered to pay us money to blend one of their new shoes."

Honesty in claims "When we said we'd blended neodymium magnets, we got email telling us they were ceramic magnets."

Keep it real "We try to be ourselves and our videos are not overproduced. We try to be a little bit edgy, but not too slick."

Interactivity "People suggest things to blend, like the new iPhone. They aren't just viewers; they're engaged."

Simple user subscription "We have more than 200,000 subscriptions to our YouTube channel and our own 'Will it Blend?' website."

Then Wright said, "This new form of marketing has delivered a 700 percent increase in sales for Blendtec." During the network break between our presentations, I asked Wright if he would be interested in providing one of the case studies for this book. And he asked me, "Have you read the profile on Blendtec in Michael Miller's new book, *YouTube for Business* (Que, August 2008)?"

As a matter of fact, I had read the book. And Miller had also profiled me in another one of his books, "Online Marketing Heroes" (Wiley, March 2008). But I wanted to interview Wright a year after Miller had, hoping that there would be new developments or more details to share with my readers. Wright agreed to be interviewed in the spring of 2009 and then headed out to the lobby to blend a wooden rake handle for all the other conference attendees.

Six months later, I called Wright at his office in West Orem, Utah. As I had hoped, there were new developments and more details for us to talk about. For starters, Wright is now the company's vice president of marketing and sales. And as Figure 11.20 illustrates, Blendtec has used YouTube and video marketing in the past year to transform itself from being focused on business-to-business (B2B) to being focused business-to-consumer (B2C) sales.

Figure 11.20 Blendtec

Q&A with George Wright, Vice President of Marketing and Sales, Blendtec

Here are my questions and his answers:

> *Jarboe: What's your background? What did you do before joining Blendtec? How did you first get the idea for "Will It Blend?"*

Wright: My background is in heavy industry. Before joining Blendtec, I handled PR at a steel mill and marcom for a major pump and valve manufacturer. My budget was huge at these other companies. But that was different at Blendtec, which had a wonder product but no marketing. However, we did have a video producer and equipment already to create instructional videos for our commercial customers. Then I happened upon owner Tom Dickson feeding a 2×2-inch wooden board into a commercial blender as part of a destructive test and found it fascinating. I thought that others might get a kick out of watching the process, and the idea for creating a video was born. I wrote a marketing strategy entitled "Blending Marbles." Then, as I said last October, I spent $50. The most expensive things I bought were half a rotisserie chicken and 12 ounces of Coke. At the time, I said, "Dang, this is good cochicken. This is the best I ever tasted." But then a month later, we transmogrified half a dozen oysters in the whole shell. It was better than anything else (Figure 11.21).

Figure 11.21 "Will It Blend? - Oysters"

Jarboe: Who is your target audience? Is it opinion leaders in the YouTube community or customers who also watch online video? Has your target audience changed from when the channel was launched to now?

Wright: Our target audiences were existing customers, potential customers, and employees. We needed to explain complicated pieces of equipment to both B2B and B2C market segments. Although our target audience now includes homemakers as well as our wholesale dealer network and key accounts, all these people are already interested in our product.

Jarboe: Do you optimize your videos for YouTube? Are there search terms that you put in the title, description, and tags of your videos on YouTube? Are there search terms that you use to optimize videos for Google?

Wright: We have optimized around our product. We created the "Will It Blend?" brand name. But blending an iPod was also part of our search engine optimization strategy (Figure 11.22).

Figure 11.22 "Will It Blend? - iPod"

Jarboe: What is the most compelling video content on Blendtec's channel? Is it one of the most viewed or most discussed videos? Is it your playlist?

Wright: I'm always blown away by "Will It Blend? - Marbles." That was the question I asked in my original marketing strategy. We put a bag of 50 marbles into a Blendtec blender. And yes, it blends! Blending a dozen glow sticks was also fun. When we turned the lights off for effect, our 12-hour lantern was engaging. For live blends, we always blend a rake with a wooden handle because it is visual from a distance. Blending a baseball was funny. But some of the best videos we have done to date are in our playlist (Figure 11.23).

Figure 11.23 Cream of the Crop

Jarboe: What is your channel strategy? How much effort is focused on Blendtec's channel on YouTube versus www.willitblend.com? *Has this changed since the channel was launched? Will it change going forward?*

Wright: We are focused on our own Will It Blend? website, which we control. The analytics are better. And our website gets more views than our YouTube channel. Now, YouTube is a great place to reach new people. But, the website has links to our e-commerce website, so they can buy our product.

Jarboe: In addition to creating compelling video content, have you engaged in any outreach effort with the YouTube community or bloggers? Do you give opinion leaders a "heads up" when a new video is uploaded?

Wright: We have more than 200,000 subscribers. They automatically get a "heads up" whenever we upload a new video. Although we did let the folks at Nike know when we decided to remix their Air Max 90 Current (Figure 11.24). But they'd asked us to do that.

Jarboe: What production challenges have you faced and overcome? Are there any tips or tools that you used to get videos uploaded?

Figure 11.24 "Will It Blend? - Nike"

Wright: Keep it real, keep it short, and get to the point. "Will It Blend?" That's as complicated as it gets. On blending day, we won't let Tom know what we're blending. That keeps it real.

Jarboe: Have you taken advantage of any video advertising opportunities? Have you used Yahoo! Video ads, InVideo Ads, contests, or other high-profile placements?

Wright: We haven't taken out any ads. We did put up a billboard on the side of our factory, but YouTube is a social channel. So, we let it work its magic.

Jarboe: How do you measure your video campaign? Do you use YouTube Insight, TubeMogul, or other analytics for online video? Do you use web analytics on www.willitblend.com? *What feedback have these tools given you that may have led you to change anything you were doing?*

Wright: It's hard to pay for fancy analytics when you only spending $50 to start with. So, on our Will It Blend? website, we use Google Analytics because it's free.

Jarboe: I've already got the "Will It Blend - "The First 50 Videos" DVD. What else should I get?

Wright: You could get a "Will It Blend?" T-shirt, which you can wear while pondering life's important questions. What is the purpose of life? What is the airspeed velocity of an unladen swallow? And, of course, Will It Blend?

As you learned in Chapter 2, it's important to ask the right questions.

Book $100 Million in Revenue: Universal Music Group

Another organization that has used YouTube and video marketing to make the cash register ring is Universal Music Group (UMG). UMG (a unit of Vivendi) is the world's leading music company.

UMG owns the most extensive catalog of music in the industry, with recordings going back 100 years. Its record labels include Decca, Interscope Geffen A&M Records, Island Def Jam Music Group, MCA Nashville, Universal Motown Republic Group, Universal Music Latino, Universal Records South, and Verve Music Group.

As Figure 11.25 illustrates, the 9,500 videos on universalmusicgroup's channel on YouTube had 3.9 billion views as of April 2009, making it the #1 most viewed channel of all time.

Figure 11.25 Universal Music Group

UMG's music video channel also had more than 671,000 subscribers, making it the #4 most subscribed of all time.

As Figure 11.26 illustrates, UMG's most viewed video is "Rihanna - Don't Stop The Music," which had more than 175,000 ratings and close to 87 million views as of April 2009, making it the #7 most viewed video of all time.

The music video had been favorited over 285,000 times, making it #13 top favorited of all time. It also had over 101,000 text comments, making it the #45 most discussed video of all time.

These are impressive outputs. But what is even more impressive is the amount of advertising revenue that YouTube is sharing with UMG. On December 18, 2008, Greg Sandoval wrote an article for CNET News entitled, "Universal Music seeing 'tens of millions' from YouTube." He said, "For the first time, there are signs that YouTube is driving significant revenue for itself and some of the video site's partners."

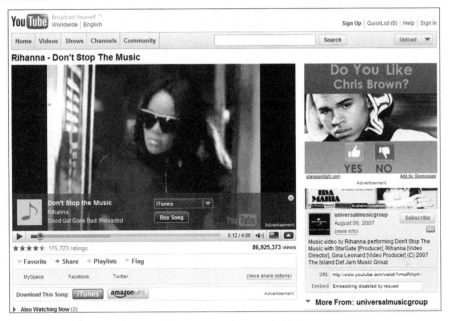

Figure 11.26 "Rihanna - Don't Stop The Music"

Sandoval added that Rio Caraeff, executive vice president of Universal Music Group's eLabs, had said UMG was bringing in "tens of millions of dollars" from YouTube. Caraeff added, "Since 2005, Universal has gone from making zero dollars on music videos to nearly $100 million."

"But the big question is whether the growth in music-video revenue says more about the music industry than it does about YouTube," Sandoval observed.

This big question is likely to be answered in the coming months. On April 9, 2009, UMG and YouTube announced that they are working together to launch VEVO, a music and video entertainment service that will feature UMG's premium video content.

VEVO (Figure 11.27) will be a premium online music video hub when it is launched later this year. It will blend UMG's broad catalog of top artists and content with YouTube's video technology and user community. How? This content will be available through a special VEVO branded embedded player.

Figure 11.27 VEVO

YouTube also renewed and extended its successful partnership with UMG and the two companies will share advertising revenue on VEVO as well as YouTube.

What does all this mean? According to Sandoval, "YouTube's traffic machine may finally be turning into a cash machine."

Earn $100,000: What the Buck?!

Individuals are using YouTube and video marketing to make the cash register ring too. One of them is Michael Buckley, the host/writer/producer of What the Buck?!

As Figure 11.28 illustrates, WhatTheBuckShow's channel is one of the most popular entertainment channels on YouTube with more than 102 million views and over 411,000 subscribers as of April 2009.

Figure 11.28 What The Buck?!

There are close to 300 videos on the channel. As you can see in Figure 11.29, the most viewed video is "Hanna Montana Naughty Tape? Kim Kardashian Burping PSA!" It had more than 6.5 million views as of April 2009.

Buckley creates the show in the second bedroom of his home in Connecticut. As his channel info says, "Whether accusing Demi and Selena of hacking Miley's Iphone or telling Madonna to pluck her daughter's eyebrow, he is not afraid to tell stars to go Buck themselves. He also does a great Terri Seymour impression, knows how to fix American Idol and likes to show his naked knees!"

In October 2007, Buckley "broke all records" of YouTube ratings when four of his shows ended up on the week's 10 top-rated videos. In March 2008, he won a 2007 YouTube Award for best commentary with the video "LonelyGirl15 is Dead!"

Figure 11.29 "Hanna Montana Naughty Tape? Kim Kardashian Burping PSA!"

In September 2008, Buckley quit his low-paying day job as an administrative assistant for Live Nation, a music promotion company, and is now earning more money as an online entertainer.

In a *New York Times* article of December 10, 2008, Buckley said he was earning over $100,000 from YouTube advertisements. This prompted CNN to feature Buckley on December 16. As Figure 11.30 illustrates, the interview was entitled, "YouTube Pays."

Figure 11.30 YouTube Pays

Finish #1 at the Box Office: Rob Zombie's *Halloween*

Last but not least, advertisers are using YouTube to generate measurable outcomes. One of the classic examples is Palisades Interactive Media's ad campaign for Rob Zombie's *Halloween*, which was released by Dimension Films in August 2007.

To put butts in seats, Palisades needed to establish online awareness and build up the prerelease excitement for the film for the opening weekend. The agency also needed to engage with the YouTube community to create strong buzz around the film and create an "afterlife" for the trailer that would extend beyond the marketing campaign.

So, Palisades uploaded the trailer to YouTube and then used YouTube InVideo Ads to drive traffic to the trailer, where the YouTube community could comment, rate, and share the video.

The agency also targeted YouTube users watching rock and heavy metal music. The graphical overlay ran within a Linkin Park music video, accompanied by a 300 250 display banner. The YouTube InVideo Ads achieved a 50 percent share of voice on rock/heavy metal music videos.

The ads also struck a chord with the rock and heavy metal audience. The click-to-play (CTP) rates to watch the trailer were very strong, achieving 1.1 percent CTP rate within the first five days and 0.9 percent CTP rate over the entire campaign. In addition, with the support of the graphical overlay, the companion ad also saw strong click-through rates (CTRs), achieving a 0.76 percent CTR.

By increasing awareness of the film and the trailer through a targeted InVideo Ads campaign, Palisades Interactive Media was able to drive the video into YouTube's most viewed page, bringing even greater exposure to the film's trailer and allowing the video to sustain its popularity.

The advocacy of opinion leaders in the YouTube community ensured continual awareness and engagement of the trailer after the marketing campaign. For example, Zombiedeadman75 commented, "This movie is going to be the best movie of the year. Can't wait to see it."

With just under 2,000 ratings, 3,000 comments, and over 1 million total views, the InVideo Ads' support of the trailer had the impact Palisades Media sought to achieve.

Most importantly, Rob Zombie's *Halloween* finished in the #1 spot at the box office, bringing in $31 million for Dimension Films in the opening weekend.

Two years later, you can still hear the cash register ring.

Mysteries of Online Video Revealed

It took me eight months to write this book, and it's supposed to take you an hour a day for eight months to read. So I'm not surprised if you are saying, "Enough storyboarding. Let's shoot something." But, whether you learn by reading or learn by doing, you will quickly discover there's always more to learn. New developments at YouTube and continual changes in video marketing mean the mysteries of online video can never be revealed once and for all. In this final chapter, we will look at the right questions you need to continue asking in the days, weeks, and months ahead.

Chapter Contents:
Who Discovers, Watches, and Shares New Videos?
What Categories or Types of Video Do They Watch?
When Do They Discover New Videos?
Where Do They Share New Videos?
Why Don't More New Videos Go Viral?
How Does Marketing with Video Work?

Who Discovers, Watches, and Shares New Videos?

This is the last chapter, and I know you are eager to get started. You have already spent an hour a day over eight months learning what I can currently teach you about YouTube and video marketing. Like the fellows in Figure 12.1, you are ready to say, "Enough storyboarding. Let's shoot something."

"Enough storyboarding. Let's shoot something."

Figure 12.1 "Enough storyboarding. Let's shoot something." (Cartoon by Leo Cullum in *The New Yorker*, June 4, 2001.)

I hear you. But there is one more important lesson you need to learn: There is always more to learn.

New developments at YouTube and continual changes in video marketing mean the mysteries of online video can never be revealed once and for all. So you need to continue asking questions in the days, weeks, and months ahead.

Shortly after I started writing this book, my firm started promoting a search engine strategies (SES) webcast with Bill Tancer, the general manager of global research at Hitwise and one of the keynote speakers at Search Engine Strategies Chicago 2008. In order to encourage Q&A, we offered to give away 10 copies of Tancer's new book, *Click: What Millions of People Are Doing Online and Why It Matters* (Hyperion, September 2008) to participants who asked the best questions.

To prepare for the event, I read *Click* and felt an overwhelming level of shock and awe as I read Chapter 10, which is entitled "Finding the Early Adopters." Tancer had also read *Diffusion of Innovations* by Everett Rogers.

Click even included an expanded version of the chart I used in Chapter 1 (Figure 12.2) showing the market share of visits to YouTube, Yahoo! Video, and Google Video from July 23, 2005 to December 15, 2007.

The only thing missing from the chart was the brief threat from MySpace Video. But that data, which I presented in Chapter 2, had also come from Hitwise.

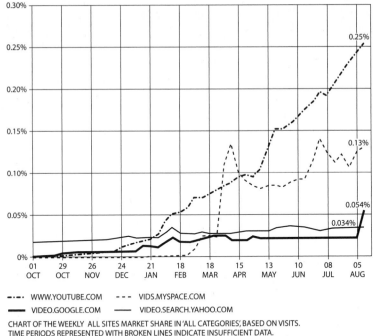

0.30%
0.25% — 0.25%
0.20%
0.15%
0.13%
0.10%
0.054%
0.05% — 0.034%
0%

01 OCT — 29 OCT — 26 NOV — 24 DEC — 21 JAN — 18 FEB — 18 MAR — 15 APR — 13 MAY — 10 JUN — 08 JUL — 05 AUG

-·-· WWW.YOUTUBE.COM — - - - VIDS.MYSPACE.COM
——— VIDEO.GOOGLE.COM — ——— VIDEO.SEARCH.YAHOO.COM

CHART OF THE WEEKLY ALL SITES MARKET SHARE IN 'ALL CATEGORIES', BASED ON VISITS.
TIME PERIODS REPRESENTED WITH BROKEN LINES INDICATE INSUFFICIENT DATA.
GENERATED ON: 08/16/2006. COPYRIGHT 2006 (C) 'HITWISE PTY LTD'.

Figure 12.2 Market Share of Visits to youtube.com, videosearch.yahoo.com, and video.google.com

Tancer also observed, "Sometime between November 2005 and January 2006, the diffusion of YouTube use moved from Innovator to Early Adopter, and then crossed over to the Early Majority."

The difference between Tancer's analysis and mine is that he uses terms and concepts like *early adopter* that Rogers explains in Chapter 7 of *Diffusion of Innovations* while I use terms and concepts like *opinion leaders* that Rogers explains in Chapter 8. This may seem like a distinction without a difference, but they are as unlike each other as the *individual* adoption of a new *video search engine* versus the *social* adoption of a new *video sharing site*. This difference also enables me to add some incremental value in my book, although Tancer and I are just standing on different shoulders of the same giant.

Using another Hitwise tool, clickstream analysis, Tancer was also able to examine what sites Internet users were on just prior to visiting YouTube and where they went immediately afterwards. This enabled him to understand how word of this new site spread and describe the mechanism in *Click*.

In October 2005, 52 percent of the traffic to YouTube came from social networking sites like MySpace and Facebook. "Within just one month, the method by which users arrived at the YouTube site began to shift dramatically," wrote Tancer. Traffic from email services like Hotmail and Yahoo! Mail started contributing 17 percent of the traffic to YouTube, while traffic from social networking sites declined to just 30 percent. "On the YouTube site, once users viewed a video, they had the ability to send an email to friends that included a link back to the video that they had just viewed," Tancer observed.

I attribute this to opinion leaders sharing links to videos with their followers. I outlined the characteristics of opinion leaders in Chapter 2, showed you how to identify them in Chapter 3, and illustrated the role they play in Chapter 7. The influence of these opinion leaders also explains why video sharing sites were eating the lunch of video search engines in this critical period.

Tancer found more clues about YouTube's meteoric rise hidden in the data. "Along with social networking and email traffic, visits from Google were showing up in YouTube's clickstream in January 2006."

For the four weeks ending January 28, 2006, 5 of the top 10 search terms that sent traffic to YouTube were *Lazy Sunday* (#4), *Narnia Rap* (#7), *SNL Lazy Sunday* (#8), *Chronicles of Narnia SNL* (#9), and *SNL Lazy Sunday* (#10). The other five search terms were navigational—variations of *YouTube* or *YouTube.com.*

In other words, opinion leaders were still buzzing about the skit by Chris Parnell and Andy Samberg on NBC's *Saturday Night Live,* which had aired the same week that YouTube debuted, and their followers were searching to find it.

As I pointed out in Chapter 1, LeeAnn Prescott of Hitwise had reached the same conclusion and posted similar data in her analysis weblog back in December 2005 and January 2006. And with 20/20 hindsight, you use Google Insights for Search (http://www.google.com/insights/search/#) to see this for yourself by typing *Lazy Sunday* or *Narnia Rap* into the search box.

You can see a similar pattern in more recent searches for *Susan Boyle*, which wasn't a search term on April 8, 2009, spiked on April 15, continued at a high level through April 22, declined on April 29, and declined again on May 6. And as we saw in Chapter 7, tweets on Twitter spiked on April 15, and posts to blogs spiked on April 16.

Veteran marketers can use Hitwise data to identify opinion leaders and see what this segment is doing today. However, new YouTubers and aspiring entrepreneurs shouldn't be surprised that it costs about $20,000 a year to get access to Hitwise insights on how 10 million U.S. Internet users interact with more than 1 million websites, across 165+ industries.

For less than $30, you can buy *Click* and find out that 39 percent of the early adopters of online video sharing in late 2005 and early 2006 were 18 to 24 years old, 57 percent earned less than $60,000 a year, and 25 percent lived in California. There were also significant percentages of segments that Claritas PRIZM calls the "Bohemian Mix," "Money and Brains," and "Young Digerati."

In *Click*, Tancer looked at what these segments were doing in early 2008. He found they were willing to test other online video sites beyond YouTube, including Veoh, Wikimedia Commons, Stickam, WebcamNow, and Bix.

I interviewed Tancer in December following his keynote at SES Chicago 2008 (Figure 12.3) about his latest findings. He said that the pattern had shifted again to sites that provided an editorial layer to surface video content that is specific to a particular viewpoint or interest.

Figure 12.3 "Bill Tancer on Search Patterns at SES Chicago 2008"

"It's as if these early adopters are telling us there's too much information out there and just relying on what's most popular on YouTube or just relying on search as a method to find what you are looking for may not work," Tancer said.

In his book, Tancer added, "This willingness to try new services demonstrates that this particular group of Internet users, while continuing to use mainstream services online, is always on the lookout for something better."

It's worth noting that many of the young and the restless aren't opinion leaders and many opinion leaders aren't young or restless. For example, even as far back as December 2005, comScore Networks announced that consumers between the ages of 35 and 54 years old accounted for more than 45 percent of all online video watched in August 2005. Their research also found that 35 to 54-year-olds were 20 percent more likely to watch online video than the average Internet user.

Recently, Tancer started writing a weekly column for the *Wall Street Journal* entitled *Click*. In his first piece, "Hulu and the Older Early Adopter," he addressed this phenomenon. When Hulu launched its public site in March 2008, the largest age group visiting the site was made up of Internet visitors over 55 years old, who accounted for 47 percent of all site visits, while traditionally younger early adopters accounted for only 17 percent of traffic.

"The content on Hulu—primarily network television shows from NBC and Fox— was already in the sweet spot of the so-called Greatest Generation," wrote Tancer.

On March 26, 2009, YouTube added a Share To Twitter button under the Share options so users can easily send a video into the Twittersphere.

The following month, comScore released some interesting data about Twitter. What came as no surprise was that Twitter traffic was rising. What was surprising was the top demographic driving adoption of Twitter was persons 45 to 54 years old, with 25 to 34-year-olds in second place, 35 to 44-year-olds in third, 55 to 64-year-olds in fourth, and the 18 to 24 demographic in fifth.

It's also worth noting that there are probably six times more YouTube opinion leaders today than there were three years ago. Where did I get this estimate?

According to comScore, 16 million Americans visited YouTube in July 2006. That figure grew to 107.1 million Americans in April 2009. If the total audience is now more than six times larger, then it is fair to assume that the number of opinion leaders has increased by at least a factor of six too. Unless, of course, the Pareto principle I mentioned in Chapter 2 has been repealed.

This means there are about 10 to 20 million YouTube opinion leaders today. The hub is made up of fully vested members of the YouTube community. The spokes include the online communities around YouTube: bloggers, journalists, and Wikipedians as well as the MySpace, Facebook, Twitter, Digg, and other communities.

As you saw in Chapter 7, the key to analyzing the nature of communication flows through this network of networks is seeing "who relays messages to whom." Or, Paul Revere to Dr. Samuel Prescott to Captain Isaac Davis. But we've also seen modern examples of this process throughout this book.

The key is identifying the people who bring new ideas from outside their social group to its members. As Professor Ronald S. Burt wrote in "The Social Capital of Opinion Leaders" (*The Annals of the American Academy of Political Sciences*, 1999), these people "carry information across the boundaries between groups. They are not people at the top of things so much as people at the edge of things, not leaders within groups so much as brokers between groups."

And according to a YouTube user profile study by Advertiser Perceptions, Inc., users are now evenly distributed East, South, Midwest, and West; 55 percent are suburban, 26 percent urban, and 19 percent rural; 71 percent are employed, 15 percent are students; 69 percent are college educated; and 47 percent are married. And as YouTube's audience has gone mainstream, it is logical to assume that the demographics of its opinion leaders probably mirror the demographics of the U.S. online population more closely too.

This doesn't mean that 18- to 24-year-old Californians have stopped using YouTube to discover the quirky and unusual. It means they have been joined by opinion leaders from other regions with different demographics, who are finding a wider spectrum of video content to share with 5 to 10 other people.

Here's what to look for if you want the names of some of these opinion leaders:

- Members of the YouTube community who posted video responses to Judson Laipply's "Evolution of Dance," which reclaimed its old #1 spot as the most viewed video on YouTube on April 30, 2009.

- YouTubers who left "driveling, mindless comments" on "The Monty Python Channel on YouTube."

- 4chanPeople, who made parodies of "Play him off, keyboard cat."

- Fans of Ryan Higa, who subscribed to nigahiga's channel, which reached 1 million subscribers on May 10, 2009.

- Supporters of Barack Obama's presidential campaign, who became Friends of BarackObamadotcom's channel.

- Online journalists who linked to HuluDotCom's channel on YouTube.

Nevertheless, it's worth paying attention to another observation by Tancer in Chapter 10 of his book: "YouTube's rise from the vast collection of unknown video sites didn't take years, or even months for that matter. The move from obscurity to ubiquity occurred in the span of just thirty-five days."

I agree and can only add this: once you identify the opinion leaders in your segment of the online video market, you need to continue watching them like a hawk. In a world where market leadership can be upended in a matter of days, you can't afford to be the last one to learn that Elvis has left the building.

What Categories or Types of Video Do They Watch?

It's also important to continue tracking what categories or types of video opinion leaders are watching these days, even if they continue going to YouTube.

Although YouTube started with a video entitled "Me at the zoo," which was uploaded by Jawed Karim on April 23, 2005, the video sharing site has since evolved into the world's most popular online video community.

On January 30, 2009, YouTube CEO Chad Hurley told Erick Schonfeld of TechCrunch that more than 15 hours of video content was being uploaded to YouTube every minute. If it was a television network, YouTube could broadcast more than 40,000 new half-hour-long TV programs a day. If it was Hollywood, YouTube could release over 75,000 new two-hour-long movies a week.

As the amount of video content has increased, so has the diversity. As Figure 12.4 illustrates, there are over 20,000 videos from over 100 of our leading university and college partners on YouTube EDU (www.youtube.com/edu).

In his interview with Schonfeld, Hurley also said, "Even on YouTube, you have a small percentage of the community uploading videos, and the majority consumes. It is in the range of 2 to 3 percent. But the audience is so large even that is a big number."

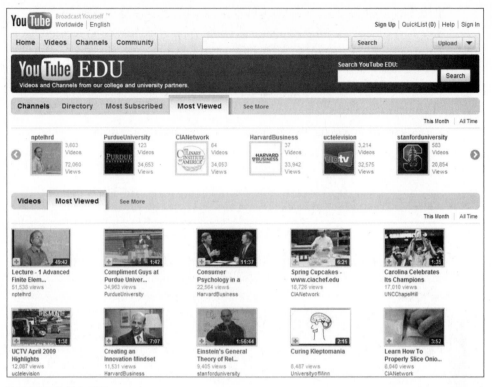

Figure 12.4 YouTube EDU

Yes, it is. With about 100 million U.S. Internet users watching videos on YouTube each month, this means about 2 to 3 million Americans are uploading videos to their YouTube channels. And since there are more than 300 million YouTube visitors worldwide, this means there could be an additional 4 to 6 million YouTube channels in other countries, or a total of about 6 to 9 million channels worldwide.

YouTube also has over 3,000 content partnerships. This includes older deals with content providers such as the BBC, CBS, NBA, Sony Music Group, Sundance Channel, and Universal Music Group. It also includes newer ones, including the ones announced in March 2009 with partners like these:

- Disney/ABC Television Group (www.youtube.com/ABC), including ABC Entertainment, ABC News, ABC Family and SOAPnet, and ESPN

- South by Southwest (www.youtube.com/sxsw), one of the premier music and film festivals in the country

- The Backstreet Boys (www.youtube.com/user/bsbofficial), who uploaded over 20 videos in their first month alone, including plenty of behind-the-scenes tour footage

- Hollywood.com (www.youtube.com/hollywoodstreams), which offers up-to-the-minute celebrity and entertainment news

- EPIC FU (www.youtube.com/epicfu), CHIC.TV (www.youtube.com/chictv), and TREND HUNTER TV (www.youtube.com/TrendhunterTV), which all report on the latest trends in pop culture
- Geek Entertainment TV (www.youtube.com/geekentertainmenttv), iTouchiPodz (www.youtube.com/iTouchiPodz), and TylersComputerShow (www.youtube.com/TylersComputerShow) for tech news
- Australian comedienne Miss Cupcake (www.youtube.com/misscupcake1) and her fiveandahalfgirls (www.youtube.com/fiveandahalfgirls) channel, a faux vlog in which she plays, well, five and a half different personalities
- Total-German-Shepherd.com (www.youtube.com/TotalGermanShepherd), 100+ videos of German shepherds playing in the great outdoors

During the same month, YouTube brought back Best in Jest. As Figure 12.5 illustrates, it's a destination for videos from some of YouTube's favorite comedy partners, presented by the movie *Observe and Report*.

Figure 12.5 Best in Jest

Best in Jest contains top-shelf comedic content like Obama Girl and Chad Vader from channels like The Onion (www.youtube.com/TheOnion), Barely Political (www.youtube.com/barelypolitical), Blame Society Films (www.youtube.com/blamesocietyfilms), and Waverly Films (www.youtube.com/waverlyflams) in a special player.

There were already a lot of ways to discover comedy content on YouTube: browsing the Comedy category, subscribing to comedy channels, exploring the related video suggestions when watching comedy videos, and tracking friend activity. But with Best in Jest, YouTubers have a new option: find a collection of guaranteed funny stuff all in one place, as Tancer has recommended.

YouTube is introducing a wider variety of styles in response to competition from Hulu (www.hulu.com), which is co-owned by NBC Universal, News Corp., and Providence Equity Partners. Hulu offers hit TV shows including *Saturday Night Live* (Figure 12.6).

Figure 12.6 Hulu

According to comScore Video Metrix, the number of unique video viewers to Hulu surged 42 percent in February 2009 to 34.7 million, driven in large part by its Super Bowl TV ad starring Alec Baldwin. This vaulted Hulu into fourth place, behind Google Sites (99 percent YouTube), Fox Interactive Media (77 percent MySpace) and Yahoo! sites but ahead of Microsoft sites.

YouTube started responding to this competitive threat in October 2008 when it announced a deal with CBS to test full-length programming, including *Star Trek*, *MacGyver*, and *Beverly Hills, 90210*. Or, as the YouTube Blog said, "You asked to be beamed up with Scotty, to devise a world-saving weapon using only gum and paper-clips, and to get your grub on at 'The Peach Pit.' So we're giving you full-length episodes of these shows and many others."

The test of this new format also gave YouTube's partners like CBS more options when it came to selling advertising in these full-length TV shows. YouTubers started seeing in-stream video ads (including pre-, mid-, and post-rolls) embedded in some of these episodes.

This was followed in November 2008 by a multiple-channel commitment by MGM Worldwide Digital Media (MGM) that kicked off with American Gladiators (www.youtube.com/americangladiators), a channel that showcases highlights and full episodes from the classic show, and Impact, a channel dedicated to promoting MGM's video-on-demand (VOD) action programming (www.youtube.com/impact).

The Impact channel on YouTube (Figure 12.7) features a host of video clips from classic MGM films such as *Rocky*, *Ronin*, *Legally Blonde*, and *The Magnificent Seven* in addition to a sampling of popular action television show clips and full-length movies like *Lone Wolf McQuade* and *Bulletproof Monk*. Impact is currently available to Comcast digital cable subscribers.

Figure 12.7 Impact Action on Demand

YouTube has come a long way, baby. The video sharing site that featured "lonelygirl15" from June 2006 to August 2008 has evolved into a platform fit for the Queen of England. So keep tracking the categories or types of video that opinion leaders are watching. They will continue to change too.

When Do They Discover New Videos?

Another one of the right questions that you need to continue asking is, When do opinion leaders discover new videos?

The average online video viewer watched 356 minutes of video in January 2009 according to comScore Video Metrix. In other words, the typical online video viewer watched 101 videos that month for an average of 3.5 minutes each.

And that's the average online video viewer. Opinion leaders need to watch even more new videos than their followers. Why? As Rogers observed, "Opinion leaders gain their perceived competency by serving as an avenue for the entrance of new ideas into their system." You won't maintain your opinion leadership very long if everyone else at work, at home, or at school has already seen the new video that you've just discovered.

Now, 356 minutes is almost 6 hours. So opinion leaders need to find significantly more than 6 hours each month to watch significantly more than 101 new videos. When do they find that kind of time?

Well, you've just spent a valuable amount of time reading this book. Could you afford to continue spending an hour a day watching new videos?

You could if the new videos were more entertaining, informative, and empowering than anything you could watch on television, read in newspapers, or hear on the radio. In other words, opinion leaders can afford to spend an hour a day watching new videos if this experience is or becomes a normal way for them to communicate and exchange ideas.

I believe this evolution is behind two recent YouTube initiatives, which appear aimed at strengthening its relationship with opinion leaders.

The first is YouTube Live (www.youtube.com/live), a celebration of the vibrant communities that exist on the site. As Figure 12.8 illustrates, the first YouTube Live was held on November 22, 2008, in San Francisco and streamed for a worldwide audience of millions.

Figure 12.8 YouTube Live

YouTube users have been gathering informally for years, but this was the first time that YouTube officially leaped off screens for an event unlike any other. With live performances, celebrity guests, original videos, surprise collaborations, and much more, the event mixed elements of a concert, variety show, and party, with YouTube phenomena always at the core.

So when do opinion leaders discover new videos? As you saw in Chapter 7, it can be when YouTube stages special events.

Held at the Herbst Pavilion in Fort Mason, YouTube Live featured Will.i.am, Esmee Denters, Fred, Soulja Boy Tell 'Em, and Tay Zonday, who were profiled in Chapter 5, as well as Katy Perry, Bo Burnham, Joe Satriani, MythBusters, and Akon, who were profiled in Chapter 7.

Other acts also joined this lineup:

Katers 17 Among the most popular U.K. YouTube personalities, who recently signed a contract for Starburst, Katers 17 represents the truly global nature of YouTube, bringing her Anglo style and unique Britishisms to her homespun videos.

The Spinto Band Independent music is alive and well on YouTube, as evidenced by the ongoing success of this Wilmington, Delaware, rock act. Their wistful harmonies and creative videos have generated some great response, with fans uploading their own versions alongside the band's official entries.

Jon M. Chu and The League of Extraordinary Dancers Step Up 2 The Streets director Jon M. Chu has been front and center for some of YouTube's most celebrated dance videos, including the biggest online dance battle in YouTube history between the Miley Cyrus / Mandy Jiroux Cru and his ACDC. He brought his unique choreographic style to the event by introducing his most ambitious project yet: The League of Extraordinary Dancers.

MC Hammer A pioneer in combining dance and hip-hop, three-time Grammy Award winner MC Hammer remains a powerful influence in music, as evidenced by the hundreds of YouTube videos in which users attempt to emulate his unique dance skills.

Brandon Hardesty Best known for his spot-on reenactments of scenes from Hollywood's most beloved films, Hardesty has quickly become a favorite not only of the YouTube community, but also of Jimmy Kimmel, for whom he did a series of re-creations leading up to last year's Academy Awards.

A global b-boy showcase featuring dancers from the movie *Planet B-Boy* dazzled the crowd, along with "Canon Rock" virtuoso Funtwo. In addition, the Vlog Squad offered exclusive, behind-the-scenes access from different areas of the venue. William Sledd, Michael Buckley, and Lisa Nova were part of this ace reporting team. Chad Vader, Juan Mann, Julia Nunes, Sick Puppies, Lisa Lavie, Beardyman, and Jason Latimer also made guest appearances. And Mike Relm served as house video jockey.

YouTube Live honored the most groundbreaking, creative, and buzzworthy videos and individuals from the site's early days through today. This is a smart way to keep YouTube's opinion leaders fully engaged while also creating new videos they can share with their followers.

What does this mean to the new YouTuber who isn't a YouTube star...yet? It means that there is an additional offline opportunity to get involved with the YouTube community just as you would with any other community. You could become one of the featured dancers or a member of the Vlog Squad. You could become one of the new acts invited to future YouTube Live events.

The second YouTube initiative may be less entertaining, but it may be more empowering. It is also strengthening the site's relationship with opinion leaders.

On January 12, 2009, the 111th United States Congress and YouTube announced the launch of official Congressional YouTube channels. Each member of the House and Senate will have the opportunity to create and control their own YouTube channel that citizens can locate on a Google Map interface on two new platforms: the House Hub (http://youtube.com/househub) and the Senate Hub (http://youtube.com/senatehub).

Recently, both houses of Congress adjusted rules regarding posting content to third-party websites, permitting the same access pioneered during the election season to carry over to government. As a result, all members of Congress can create, manage, and control their own individual YouTube channels. Several representatives and senators, who can be found at the House and Senate Hubs on YouTube, have already created YouTube channels, where they post videos of floor speeches, committee hearings, behind-the-scenes footage, and more.

The Democratic and Republican leadership of both the House and Senate announced the initiative in a YouTube video (Figure 12.9) that can be found at www.youtube.com/watch?v=avch-fRFmbw.

Figure 12.9 "Welcome to Congress, YouTube"

Steve Grove, YouTube's head of news and politics, posted this to the YouTube Blog: "So, why are your elected leaders coming to YouTube? The short answer is: you. Your use of YouTube and other online platforms to speak up on political issues and hold your leaders accountable has shown just how powerful this medium can be. You've shown your elected officials that in order to be in contact with you, they need to come to the platforms you use most, and engage with you directly." He added, "The House Hub and Senate Hub are the digital equivalents of a backstage pass to your government."

When should you take advantage of this new opportunity? When your senator asks you to make suggestions or your congressman solicits feedback, that's when. This is another new opportunity to become a fully vested member of the YouTube community.

Where Do They Share New Videos?

In Chapter 2, you learned that opinion leaders discover, watch, and share new videos at home, at work, and from a third place, such as a mobile phone.

According to the Multiplatform Video Report, which was released in June 2008 by Solutions Research Group, Americans are consuming more and more video content than ever and this growth will continue across various platforms and devices. The report showed that viewers tend to consume video content across various platforms, during very specific times of day and on specific days of the week. For example, viewers watch the most online video during weekdays and during the daylight hours. Users also utilize mobile devices for video during specific times—typically weekday mornings.

In addition, the report predicts that the total time spent consuming video via various interactive platforms, including mobile, desktop, and Internet video, will triple to a total of 2.9 hours a day by early 2013. This is based on such factors as greater access to and use of online video, significantly increased penetration for laptops, and proliferation of mobile video devices and Internet-enabled devices such as the iPhone.

This could dramatically shift where opinion leaders discover, watch, or share new videos—particularly in the news and sports categories.

Currently, the nuances of a mobile experience are drastically different than watching videos on a PC. Not only do users want quick access to content in the fewest number of clicks, they also want relevant content that is optimized for their phone's screen. For example, users might want a quick clip of the latest scores, injuries, news, and gossip about their favorite sports team—but it had better be sharp because their cell phone's screen is small, and it had better be short because their service provider is charging them an arm and leg for the data.

As Figure 12.10 illustrates, you can go to www.youtube.com/mobile to learn how to play YouTube videos on your phone as well as how to create YouTube videos from your phone.

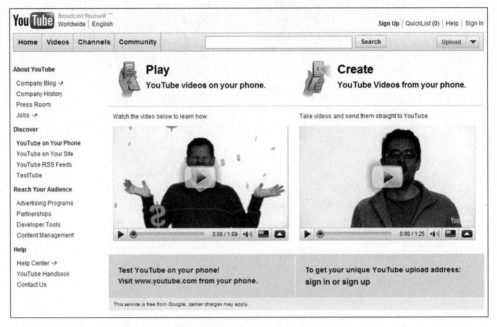

Figure 12.10 Play YouTube videos on your phone. Create YouTube videos from your phone.

If you're unable to find a video on the iPhone that you know is live on YouTube, it's possible the video hasn't been converted yet to the H.264 codec. As this was being written, YouTube was in the process of encoding videos on the site to the H.264 format so they'd be viewable on the iPhone in higher video quality.

YouTube is adding more of these encoded videos each week until its full library will be available in the H.264 format because the iPhone is transforming the mobile video landscape.

Six months after the iPhone was launched on June 29, 2007, it had already become the most popular device for accessing news and information by mobile phone users: 85 percent of iPhone users accessed news and information in the month of January 2008, according to M:Metrics.

M:Metrics also found that a staggering 30.9 percent of iPhone owners watched mobile TV or video that month versus a 4.6 percent market average and more than double the rate for all smartphone users. Usage of social networking was also popular among iPhone users: 49.7 percent accessed a social networking site in January 2008, nearly 12 times the market average. Twenty percent of iPhone owners accessed Facebook, one of the first Web properties to customize its content for the iPhone, versus 1.5 percent of the total mobile market.

Two of iPhone's featured apps, one for Google Maps and the other for YouTube, were extremely popular among iPhone users: 36 percent used Google Maps and 30.4 percent accessed YouTube. In comparison, only 2.6 percent of all mobile subscribers accessed Google Maps and 1.0 percent checked out YouTube.

M:Metrics also revealed the demographic composition of iPhone users. They are more likely to be male, be 25 to 34, earn more that $100,000, and have a college degree than the average mobile subscriber. In other words, a different demographic group of opinion leaders was driving iPhone adoption.

This group includes some of my friends and colleagues, who love discovering new iPhone apps and sharing this information with others. They remind me of the Apple Macintosh evangelists of the second half of the 1980s.

Mark Donovan, a senior analyst at M:Metrics, said in a press release announcing these findings, "In addition to the attributes of the device itself, another important factor to consider is the fact that all iPhones on AT&T are attached to an unlimited data plan. Our data shows that once the fear of surprise data charges is eliminated, mobile content consumption increases dramatically, regardless of device."

According to comScore, only 6.5 million Americans tuned into mobile video in August 2008. In a press release announcing these findings, Mark Donovan, a senior analyst at comScore, said, "While the most popular forms of mobile TV and video are genres such as music videos and movie trailers which offer short video snacks, the data also show a nascent audience for long-form mobile content such as TV shows." He added, "At under three percent penetration, the mobile video audience in the United States remains small, but it is composed largely of males between 18 and 34 years old, which could make it attractive to advertisers seeking to reach multi-tasking early-adopters who don't have time for appointment television."

The mobile video audience is growing rapidly, so you'll want to monitor it closely. This target audience may discover, watch, and share different categories or types of video at different times. You don't want to be the last to learn that Elvis has entered the building.

Why Don't More New Videos Go Viral?

Yet another right question you need to continue asking on the road from here is, Why don't more new videos go viral? Although the elements in Figure 12.11 appear to be train stations along a track, a more apt metaphor would be riverboat landings along the Mississippi. As Mark Twain observed in his book, *Life on the Mississippi* (1883):

> *The Mississippi is remarkable in…its disposition to make prodigious jumps by cutting through narrow necks of land, and thus straightening and shortening itself. More than once it has shortened itself 30 miles at a single jump! These cut-offs have…thrown several river towns out into the rural districts, and built up sand bars and forests in front of them. The town of Delta used to be three miles below Vicksburg: a recent cut-off has radically changed the position, and Delta is now two miles above Vicksburg.*

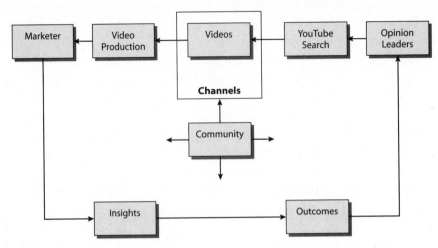

Elements in the communication process in the video sharing era

Figure 12.11 Elements in the communication process in the video sharing era

And YouTube, like the Mississippi, is also moving bodily sideways:

- The number of YouTube opinion leaders is growing and their demographics are shifting.
- YouTube is continually working to improve its algorithms to provide the most relevant results for user queries.
- More than 15 hours of video content is being uploaded every minute to YouTube in a wider variety of categories and types.
- The number of YouTube channels is growing, including one added in January 2009 for the pope (www.youtube.com/vatican).
- The YouTube community has held two YouTube Live events, but I've been told that they've stopped holding the annual YouTube Awards.
- YouTube has added HD/HQ and widescreen options, changing the formats you need to use for the best results.
- YouTube has added new advertising options, including click-to-buy links and sponsored videos.
- YouTube Insight has continued to add new features, including Hot Spots and Community tabs.
- More YouTube Partners and Sponsors are starting to share case studies and success stories that measure outcomes.

This means too many elements in the communication process are still changing too rapidly for veteran marketers and new YouTubers to successfully navigate their way from start to finish with any degree of predictability.

But wait, there's more! I reversed the old map of mass media to focus your attention on the behavior of opinion leaders, which is radically different from couch potatoes.

According to Wikipedia, Jack Mingo, coauthor of *The Official Couch Potato Handbook* and the minister of Information and Propaganda for Couch Potatoes, a California-based organization dedicated to television watching, says the spud was selected as his quasi-official organization's role model because "we're an underground movement, we're all eyes when planted in front of the TV, vegetation is an important part of our existence, and we're Tubers. Get it?"

But, you can't count on couch potatoes to lean forward and help new videos go viral. At least you couldn't until recently.

As Figure 12.12 illustrates, YouTube's most hyperactive star, the helium-voiced Fred Figglehorn, recorded its millionth subscriber on April 7, 2009, becoming the first YouTube channel to do so. What's even more amazing is that Fred's channel accomplished this in under a year.

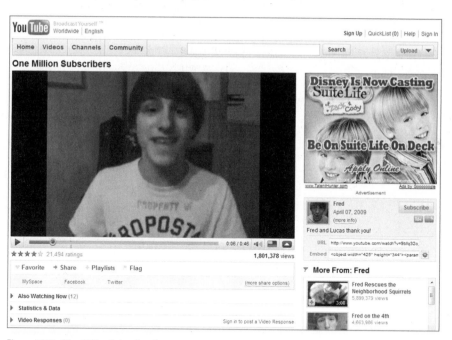

Figure 12.12 "One Million Subscribers"

Although Fred was profiled in Chapter 5, let's review a few facts: Fred is the creation of Lucas Cruikshank, a 15-year-old Nebraskan who was first spotted making videos with his cousins on JKLproduction's channel on YouTube (www.youtube.com/jklproduction). Featuring such smash-hit episodes as "Fred Goes Swimming" (over 23 million views as of April 9, 2009), "Fred Loses His Meds" (over 18 million views), and "Fred Goes to the Dentist" (over 13 million views), Fred's channel (www.youtube.com/Fred) is the fastest growing in YouTube history.

Fred's high-pitched episodes chronicle the misadventures of a pseudo six-year-old as he overreacts to friends, family, and schoolmates; events in his life; and the object of his nonreciprocated affection, Judy. Cruikshank releases his videos in traditional TV style, in 10-episode seasons that have become the schoolyard equivalent of must-see TV. His millionth subscriber joined the cult of Fred early in season three.

With more than a million subscribers, all Cruickshank needs to do is produce more of his new Fred videos for them to go viral. So, congratulations Lucas/Fred on achieving this notable milestone in the history of online video. As Figure 12.13 illustrates, you single-handedly forced me to revise my map to show that communication in the video sharing era is becoming a two-way street—or a push and pull process.

Nine steps to getting better results a higher percentage of the time

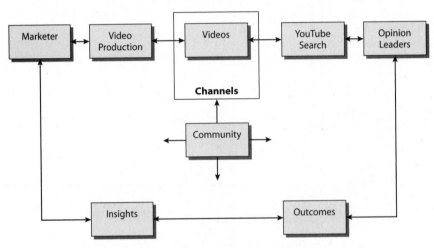

Figure 12.13 Nine steps to getting better results a higher percentage of the time

What does this mean to veteran marketers and new YouTubers? It means you can use a push-pull strategy now. You can push new videos to existing subscribers while optimizing them to pull in new viewers.

You should still start by identifying your target audience before choosing a message, but now you can broadcast an ad campaign on YouTube as well as create viral video content. You can combine blog outreach with video optimization.

In other words, you don't need to follow the nine steps in the map in Figure 12.13 in a linear, step-by-step fashion. Or, as one of the memorable quotes from *Ghostbusters* (1984) states:

Dr. Egon Spengler: "I have a radical idea. The door swings both ways, we could reverse the particle flow through the gate."

Dr. Peter Venkman: "How?"

Dr. Egon Spengler: "We'll cross the streams."

How Does Marketing with Video Work?

There's one last question that you need to continue asking on the road from here: How does marketing with video work?

I've been asking this question since December 2005, when I sat in the audience at a "Video Search" session at Search Engine Strategies Chicago (SES) and wrote about this upcoming online marketing tactic for Search Engine Watch. My article, which appeared in January 2006, was entitled "Video Search: Still Early Days." With 20/20 hindsight, I'm pretty happy that I wrote three-and-a-half years ago, "While it is still 'early days' for video search, this is the perfect time to start creating and optimizing content for this emerging category." This insight led me from writing about that SES session to three things:

- Uploading the *Christian Science Monitor*'s video "Hostage: The Jill Carroll Story" to YouTube in August 2006

- Teaching training workshops about Optimizing for Universal Search with Amanda Watlington of Searching for Profit in 2007 and 2008

- Speaking on panels about online video at SES San Jose 2008, SES Chicago 2008, SES London 2009, and SES New York 2009

Things are now starting to come full circle. As Figure 12.14 illustrates, Virginia Nussey, associate writer for the SEO Blog on Bruceclay.com conducted a Q&A with me on January 26, 2009, about my upcoming presentation at SES London 2009.

Figure 12.14 Six Questions with Greg Jarboe

Nussey asked, "You'll be speaking at the panel Online Video Update - The Next Wave. Do you think there will ever be industry standards on how to tag, organize, and find videos?"

I answered, "Yes, there are already de facto industry standards. They are YouTube's. According to comScore Video Metrix, YouTube has over 40% market share of the online video market and MySpace, which ranks #2, has less than 3%. So, whatever YouTube says about how to title, describe, tag, and otherwise optimize videos is the de facto industry standard. And YouTube says quite a bit, although it's often in Googlespeak, so you need a secret decoding ring to translate it."

Nussey: "What are the benefits of such standards?"

Jarboe: "You have a better shot at getting found in the roughly 2.9 billion search queries a month that are conducted on YouTube, according to comScore Media Metrix. By the way, that means there are more search queries conducted on YouTube than there are on Yahoo!—although Google itself is still king of the hill."

Nussey: "What are the drawbacks?"

Jarboe: "Once the de facto industry standards get out and everyone starts using them, then YouTube will change them. Hey, that's been the SEO's lot in life since Google was called BackRub."

Nussey: "Along with search engine optimization and public relations services, your company also does video production. What are some of the key tactics for video search optimization?"

Jarboe: "Encourage online publishers and bloggers to embed your videos in their websites and blogs. This may come as a surprise to some, but the number of hits a video gets is one of dozens of aspects that impacts its search result rankings in YouTube. So, the views an embedded YouTube video gets are added to its overall total."

So coming full circle again, let me put my journalist hat back on and provide a short report about the session entitled, "Video Search Engine Optimization: 2009 and Beyond," which was held at SES New York on March 24, 2009.

Greg Jarboe of SEO-PR

As Figure 12.15 illustrates, I said the latest comScore data showed 100 million Americans watched 6.3 billion videos on YouTube in January 2009.

Entrepreneur: "Which we learned in Chapter 2."

Correct. As Figure 12.16 illustrates, I shared a few tips to help your videos be discovered in search results and related videos.

Search Engine Marketer: "Which we learned in Chapter 4."

100 million U.S. viewers watch 6.3 billion videos a month on YouTube

"God, this is going to be all over YouTube."

- In January 2009, 100.9 million viewers watched an average of 62.6 videos per viewer on YouTube
- YouTube accounted for more than 99% of all videos viewed at Google Sites

Source: comScore, March 4, 2009

Figure 12.15 100 million U.S. viewers watch 6.3 billion videos a month on YouTube

---

Help your videos be discovered in search results and related videos

- Titles
  - Think of your title as a headline
  - If you want to include your brand name in the title, it should go last
- Tags
  - Be as detailed as possible
  - Include: Brand, City, topics
- Descriptions
  - Be as detailed as possible (short of offering the entire transcript)
  - Include URLs (with http://) to the Channel, Playlist, or another site
- Character Limits
  - Title: 120 characters
  - Tags/Keywords: 120 characters
  - Description: 1,000 characters

Source: YouTube Partner Help Center

Figure 12.16 Help your videos be discovered in search results and related videos

Correct again. And as Figure 12.17 illustrates, I used YouTube Insight to show YouTube Search was the source of 31 percent of views and Related Videos was the source of 17 percent for my video interview with Avanish Kaushik.

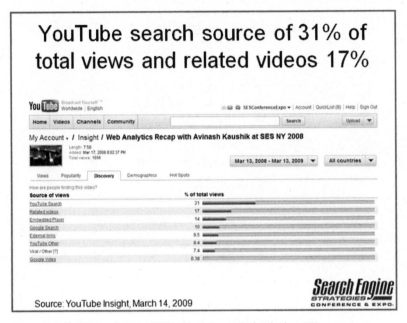

Figure 12.17 YouTube search source of 31% of total views and related videos 17%

YouTube Director: "Which we learned in Chapter 10."

All right, you caught me. But, you've spent eight months learning more about YouTube and video marketing than I could teach in just the eight minutes I had on that panel discussion. So you can also skip Mike McDonald's interview with me on the WebProNews Video Blog:

    http://videos.webpronews.com/2009/03/24/ses-ny-mysteries-of-online-video-
    revealed

Although Figure 12.18 says I revealed the mysteries of online video, you have already learned what I could reveal back then.

I'll need to come up with some new mysteries before I speak at the next SES event because, as Sheriff Bart said in *Blazing Saddles,* I "always like to keep my audience riveted."

Liana Evans of Serengeti Communications

The next speaker was Liana "Li" Evans, who was the director of Internet marketing for KeyRelevance back then and is now director of social media at Serengeti Communications. She is also the creator and main contributor to Search Marketing Gurus (www.searchmarketinggurus.com). I've interviewed her several times for SESConference-Expo's channel, including at SES London (Figure 12.19) in February 2009 (www.youtube .com/watch?v=7MRJTjCxGtc_).

Figure 12.18 "SES NY: Mysteries of Online Video Revealed"

Figure 12.19 "Liana Evans, KeyRelevance, on video branding strategy at SES London"

At SES New York 2009, Evans said optimizing titles, descriptions, and tags are fundamentals, so you need to go beyond. She said, "Being social is key."

Evans added, "Good videos are like wildfire," and shared one of a woman who freaked out when she missed her flight at Hong Kong International Airport (HKIA). As Figure 12.20 illustrates, it had over 5.4 million views back in March.

Figure 12.20 The Viral Aspect

Evans said, "Don't limit yourself to YouTube," and recommended distributing your videos using TubeMogul. She also told attendees to use niche video sites, including IMBroadcast (www.imbroadcast.com), which is dedicated to the Internet Marketing industry.

Evans also told attendees to check out Zoom and Go (www.zoomandgo.com), which is about inspiring travelers about where to go, what to see, what to do, and where to stay based on the experiences of other travelers or on the recommendations from locals around the world (Figure 12.21).

As Figure 12.22 illustrates, Evans concluded by saying, "No matter how small, branding matters!" And she showed The Swanky Bubbles restaurants and champagne bars in the Philadelphia area as an example of how even a small business could use video for branding in Google Maps.

Figure 12.21   Niche Video Shares

Figure 12.22   No Matter How Small — Branding Matters!

Gregory Markel of Infuse Creative

Gregory Markel, the founder and president of Infuse Creative, was the third speaker on the panel. My colleague Byron Gordon of SEO-PR interviewed Markel (www.youtube.com/watch?v=t8Vg1tLk1GQ) after the Video Search Engine Optimization (VSEO) panel at SES San Jose 2008 (Figure 12.23).

Figure 12.23 "Video Search Engine Optimization Panel Recap, Greg Markel"

At another conference, SES New York 2009, Markel discussed YouTube ranking factors. He said, "While keyword and tag optimization and view counts are still very important to ranking at YouTube, they are only two of the multiple ranking factors that influence ranking and popularity at YouTube as well as Google.com search results."

As Figure 12.24 shows, Markel listed 15 other YouTube ranking factors: rating, share, favorite, playlists, flagging, comments, age, honors, paid search, authority channel, links, embeds, responses, subscribers, and channel views.

Markel added, "Analyze the competition. Note their view numbers, ratings, playlists, comment numbers, response video numbers, favorited numbers, subscription numbers, honors/areas, and links. You will then need to meet or beat not only the numbers but quality where applicable." Markel then conducted an analysis of the video ranking #1 in a YouTube search for the term *race car* (Figure 12.25).

Figure 12.24 YouTube Ranking Factors

Figure 12.25 RANKING ANALYSIS: #1 for "Race Car"

And as Figure 12.26 illustrates, the video had 1.9 million views, over 3,000 ratings, and more than 3,500 comments. It had also been favorited almost 8,500 times and had 10 honors.

Figure 12.26 RANKING Analysis: #1 for "Race Car" results

Markel concluded, "We know why this video ranks the way it does. We can meet or beat this video's metrics." How? His recommendations:

- Use social media and websites within your control to "get the word out" about the video and build links (Facebook, MySpace, Twitter, article sites, PR sites, expert/profile sites).

- Post response videos to relevant video watch pages.

- Ask people to link, subscribe, rate, and favorite your video *within* your video.

Henry Hall of Microsoft

The fourth speaker was Henry Hall, the senior product manager of Microsoft Live Search (Figure 12.27). Hall said product videos, travel, sports, and full-length were joining user-generated content (UGC) as popular categories. And he cited eMarketer, which had reported that the top investment for online retailers in 2009 would be product-related videos.

Figure 12.27 Henry Hall of Microsoft (photo by Liana Evans, aka Storyspinn's photostream on Flickr)

He said Microsoft has conducted research on online video users to determine when, why, and where they seek and consume online video. Its Multimedia Modes Research found that there were basically 10 reasons. As Figure 12.28 illustrates, users seek online video for shopping, travel, recreation, tutorials and "how to," information and research, entertainment and leisure searching and browsing, research/comparison, and user-generated content viewing.

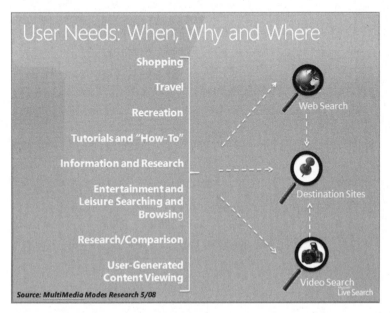

Figure 12.28 Users Needs: When, Why and Where

Hall added, "Going into this research, however, our assumption was that online video was primarily part of a leisure or entertainment scenario, such as catching up on missed TV shows, or watching viral videos. We found that these usage modes were in fact important, but the need for online video stretched far beyond entertainment, and often related to key tasks like shopping, travel, recreation, and productivity."

He then gave a demo of Live Video Search (http://search.live.com/video). As Figure 12.29 illustrates, it includes featured TV shows, music videos, most watched videos, recent news videos, and recent sports videos.

Hall also urged attendees of SES New York 2009 to visit the Live Search Webmaster Center (http://webmaster.live.com). As you can see in Figure 12.30, you can't upload your videos to Live Search Video, but you can "use the Webmaster Tools to troubleshoot the crawling and indexing of your site, submit sitemaps, and view statistics about your sites."

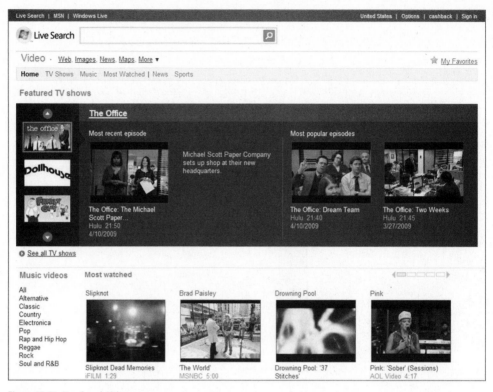

Figure 12.29 Live Search Video

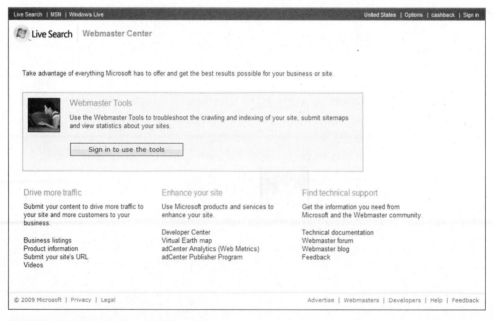

Figure 12.30 Webmaster Center—Live Search

Matthew Liu of YouTube

The fifth speaker was Matthew Liu, the lead product manager on YouTube Sponsored Videos. You may remember Liu from Chapter 9. As Figure 12.31 illustrates, I interviewed him (www.youtube.com/watch?v=CfP-PkstpP8) right after our panel at SES New York 2009.

Liu also covered the basics of improving video ranking on YouTube (Figure 12.32), but the basics had a lot more credibility coming from him.

Figure 12.31 "YouTube Product Manager, Matthew Liu, on YouTube's Insight and Sponsored videos"

Figure 12.32 The Basics to Improve Video Ranking on YouTube

As you can see, his recommendations are as follows:

Title

- Include an accurate and descriptive title.

Description

- Provide content that is descriptive, accurate, and unique.
- Use complete sentences.

Tags

- Include thorough descriptive keyword tags.
- Avoid keyword stuffing.

Community opinion

- Share videos with members of the community.
- Experiment with annotations, video responses, and thumbnails.
- Avoid spamming other video users, avoid rating your own videos.

Embeds

- Embed videos on websites to make your videos more discoverable and easier to find on the web.

Liu also talked about the Discovery tab in Insight. He said, "Understanding how people discovered your video is almost as valuable as getting your video viewed. You can see specifically which search terms on YouTube, Google or Google Video led the user to your video, which related videos led to your discovery, or which websites embed your videos!"

Liu touched on Insight's new Community tab. He said, "Understanding how users respond to your video enables you to refine and optimize your future videos."

Liu shared a case study, shown in Figure 12.33, of how Weezer had used Insight to get interesting insights into the discovery of "Pork and Beans."

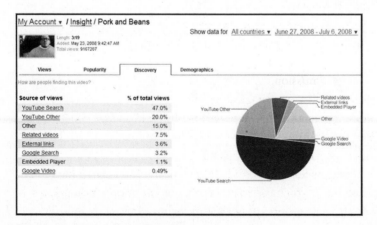

Figure 12.33 Insight—Weezer Case Study

Finally, Liu talked about Sponsored Videos, which he called "Paid search for YouTube" during the session and "AdWords for YouTube" during my interview with him afterwards. This *is* a distinction without a difference.

Liu discussed the Sponsored Videos self-service interface. He said, "After signing up for an account, select your video to promote, customize your descriptive text, and set your budget and CPC. Then see your promotion live in the search results."

Liu concluded by showing the ZAGG case study that we read in Chapter 9. As Figure 12.34 illustrates, it loses something when translated into PowerPoint.

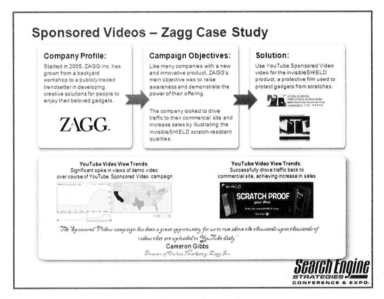

Figure 12.34 Sponsored Videos — ZAGG case study

What Should You Do Next?

So, what should you do next?

If you are interested in finding out how marketing with video works in an environment that is moving bodily sideways, then you should attend conferences like Search Engine Strategies. Even if the speakers merely confirm what you've already learned, it's worth the price of admission.

And don't be surprised to discover that even if the basics haven't changed, there will continue to be new developments at YouTube and other advances in video marketing that you will need to know about.

Now, there are other ways to keep up.

You will learn by doing. As Sophocles said, "One must learn by doing the thing; for though you think you know it, you have no certainty, until you try." Although his artistic career began in 468 BC, his observation still rings true today.

You can also continue to learn by reading. I recommend reading the YouTube Blog (www.youtube.com/blog) every business day. I also suggest reading Videomaker Enews (www.videomaker.com/news), a free e-newsletter. It will help inspire your video craft, keep you aware of what's happening in the video community, and provide all the tools and tips you'll need to create better video. Finally, I'd advise reading ReelSEO (www.reelseo.com), which is dedicated to video SEO and online video marketing.

Finally, I agree with Yogi Berra, who said, "You can observe a lot just by watching." So I've created a vlog on YouTube (www.youtube.com/seopr) and a video blog on my company's site (http://vlog.seo-pr.com) to share what I can observe by watching at lot of videos.

Although the new developments at YouTube or other advances in video marketing are unpredictable, they are not unexpected. The mysteries of online video can never be revealed once and for all.

Glossary

"Welcome to the YouTube Nation." As I mentioned in Chapter 1, not only does the YouTube community have its own language, YouTubers have their own culture and customs as well as their own folk heroes.

So, you need to learn how to "walk the walk" of video marketing as well as how to "talk the talk" of YouTube. That's why I've assembled this glossary of terms, tips, and Tubers instead of just appending a typical glossary.

Some of these come from YouTube itself, some from *Videomaker* magazine, and some from Wikipedia. And I've coined a few terms, created a couple of tips, and identified a handful of Tubers myself.

But let me warn you here and now that exploring YouTube and video marketing isn't like learning Latin and Roman history. Just when you think you've defined a term, described a tip, or depicted a Tuber, "shift happens."

This is the topic of a YouTube video created by Karl Fisch and modified by Scott McLeod entitled "Did You Know; Shift Happens - Globalization; Information Age" (Figure G.1).

Figure G.1 See how "shift happens."

The video shares the follow observations:

- According to the U.S. Department of Labor, one in four workers has been with their current employer for less than one year. One in two workers has been with their current employer for less than five years.

- According to former Secretary of Education Richard Riley, the top 10 jobs that will be in demand in 2010 didn't exist in 2004. We are currently preparing students for jobs that don't yet exist…using technologies that haven't yet been invented…to solve problems we don't even know are problems yet.

- The amount of technical information is doubling every two years. For students starting a four-year technical or college degree, this means that half of what they learn in their first year of study will be outdated by their third year of study.

"Did You Know; Shift Happens - Globalization; Information Age" had more than 4.7 million views as of June 2009.

So, here's a working glossary of terms, tips, and Tubers…for now:

account An account allows you to access special functions of YouTube. It contains all the information you provide, which is submitted upon signup. You can create a free YouTube account at `http://youtube.com/signup`.

account type There are several types of YouTube accounts, including Comedians, Directors, Gurus, Musicians, Non-Profits, Partners, Politicians, Reporters, and YouTubers.

action axis An imaginary line drawn between two subjects or along a line of motion to maintain continuity of screen direction. Crossing it from one shot to the next creates an error in continuity. It is also referred to as the "180-degree rule."

active sharing A YouTube feather that allows you to see who else is watching a video at the same time you are or explore users' recent histories.

annotations Plain-text notes added to videos after they've already been posted to YouTube as flash overlays. They come in various forms and have links and color variations. They are administrated by the video uploader but can potentially be added by anyone.

"Ask A Ninja Question 1 'Ninja Mart Store'" The first video in the *Ask a Ninja* series, it won a 2006 YouTube Award in the Series category.

AudioSwap You can use the AudioSwap tool to add music to your video from YouTube's library of licensed songs.

avatar, aka channel icon YouTube lets you use the thumbnail of any of your public videos as your avatar. You may also upload an avatar of your own choosing.

"Balloon Bowl" Video of person skateboarding in a skating pit filled with balloons. It was posted by davetheknave and won a 2007 YouTube Award in the Sports category.

"Battle at Kruger" Video of a pride of lions attacking a herd of buffalo, with an unexpected and dramatic twist near the end, posted by Jason275. It won a 2007 YouTube Award in the Eyewitness category.

"Blind Painter" Video of a local news piece on a blind University of North Texas student who is an excellent painter. It was posted by texascountryreporter and won a 2007 YouTube Award in the Inspirational category.

block This Content ID usage policy tells YouTube not to allow certain content.

Blocked Users page Displays all the users currently blocked from commenting on your videos and channel or sending you messages.

buffering The YouTube video player downloads a video as it plays. A buffer is a section of memory in your computer that allows for the simultaneous writing and reading of information—on YouTube the buffered section is represented by the red section of the video timeline. The YouTube video player reads video information from one section of the buffer while writing to another. This kind of multitasking allows for smoother playback of video during a continuous process of downloading and is especially helpful for slower connections.

bulletin A message posted on a user's channel that's also posted on their friends' channels.

camcorder Typically, a camcorder is the same thing as a video camera. When camcorders first came out, they consisted of a *cam*era and a cassette-re*corder*—hence the name, camcorder. These days, most video cameras record to some kind of digital format using an integrated recording medium such as a digital cassette or memory stick.

captions This feature allows you to give viewers a deeper understanding of your video. Adding captions and subtitles makes your videos more accessible to people who can't hear the audio or who speak another language.

categories A video can belong to one of several topic areas, called categories. This currently includes Autos & Vehicles, Comedy, Education, Entertainment, Film & Animation, Gaming, Howto & Style, Music, News & Politics, Nonprofits & Activism, People & Blogs, Pets & Animals, Science & Technology, Sports, and Travel & Events. YouTube added Movies to this list in October 2008 and Shows in April 2009, so this list is subject to change.

channel A YouTube channel is a user's page. It contains a user's profile information, videos, and favorites.

Channels tab This is at the top of most YouTube pages. It lists channels by account type.

"Chocolate Rain" This video of a baby-faced man singing an unusual song in an unexpectedly deep voice was posted by Tay Zonday. This video won a 2007 YouTube Award in the Music category.

close-up (CU) This is a tightly framed camera shot in which the principal subject is viewed at close range, appearing large and dominant onscreen. Pulled back slightly is a "medium close-up," while zoomed in very close is an "extreme close-up" (ECU or XCU).

Comedians (YouTube account type) In addition to performer information, Comedian accounts can publish a schedule of show dates.

comment This is a text response to a video (on a watch page) or a user (on a channel page).

Community Guidelines These describe what types of behavior are allowed or prohibited according to YouTube's terms of use.

Community tab Tab on YouTube where you can browse contests, groups, and community help forums.

composition Visual makeup of a video picture, including such variables as balance, framing, field of view, and texture, all aesthetic considerations. Combined qualities form an image that's pleasing to view.

compression This can be any form of compacting data. There are two main types of compression: The first is signal compression, which keeps a real-time signal such as audio within a designated amplitude range. The second is data compression, which is used to exclude redundant information, allowing for the efficient consolidation of data and a more effective format for transmission over communication networks. A good example of a data-compression format is MP3. Using MP3 compression, one can create files that contain audio data that can be downloaded over the Internet quickly and easily without much loss in clarity. You will want to compress your movie files before uploading them to YouTube in order to maximize your account's sharing capability. Most video editing software will allow you to apply some form of data compression over your video. You should take advantage of the full capabilities of your video editing software by reading the help documentation specific to the software. Doing so will allow for more ease in the uploading and sharing process involved in using YouTube.

contact list A list that includes other users on the site to whom you're linked through friend invitations as well as the email addresses of friends with whom you've shared videos.

Content ID YouTube's Content Identification and Management System.

Content Verification Program YouTube has created a Copyright Verification Tool that helps copyright owners to search for material that they believe has infringed their rights, and provids YouTube with reasonably sufficient information to permit the YouTube Teamto locate that material.

contests Users can submit videos to YouTube contests, and other users can vote on them.

cutaway This is a camera shot of something other than the central subject of a video. A cutaway can provide setup of the scenario in which the video takes place and helps to avoid monotony in lengthy scenes.

depth of field The range in front of a camera's lens in which objects appear in focus. Depth of field varies with subject-to-camera distance, focal length of a camera lens, and a camera's aperture setting.

description This is located to the right of the video, on its watch page. It is a field of text including information about the content of the video.

design (channel) You can customize the appearance of your YouTube channel.

developer APIs and RSS YouTube offers open access to key parts of the YouTube video repository and user community, via an open application programming interface (API) and RSS feeds. You can find this at http://youtube.com/dev.

Directors (YouTube account type) In addition to performer information, Director accounts have advanced options for branding videos and the user's YouTube channel with custom text and graphics. This is also an obsolete term for an old YouTube account with the ability to post videos that are over 10 minutes long; old Director accounts retained this ability even after the 10-minute limit was created.

Editors' Picks The YouTube Editors select featured videos on the home page. Users can apply to be guest editors and select the featured videos for a few days.

embedding You can have YouTube videos appear inside other web pages and blogs. The code for this is located on each watch page to the right of the video.

essential area This is an area defined by the boundaries within which contents of a video are sure to be seen regardless of masking differences in receiver displays. Also called the critical area or safe action area, it encompasses the inner 80 percent of the screen.

establishing shot This is the opening image of a program or scene. Usually, it's a wide and/or distant perspective that orients viewers to the overall setting and surroundings.

favorite From a YouTube watch page you can add a video you like to your list of favorites. Other users can browse your favorites on your YouTube channel page.

Featured Videos (home page) A section on the home page primarily populated with videos from YouTube's thousands of partners, although it can also include select user videos that are currently popular or that the YouTube Team has previously showcased in Spotlight Videos. YouTube automatically rotates these videos throughout the day to keep them fresh.

featured video (channel page) In your account settings, you can select a video to play at full size on your YouTube channel page.

flag as inappropriate If you believe a video violates YouTube's terms of use, you may flag it from the watch page. YouTube's administrators review all flagged videos. The same applies to groups and channel background images.

Flash The Flash player from Adobe Systems is a plug-in for your web browser. YouTube uses it to play videos.

follow focus Controlling lens focus so that an image maintains sharpness and clarity despite camcorder and/or subject movement.

framing Act of composing a shot in a camcorder's viewfinder for desired content, angle, and field of view.

free This term has two meanings. It can mean there is no cost, as in "Registering for YouTube is free." It can also mean not hampered, as in "YouTube encourages free speech." So be careful with how you use it.

"Free Hugs Campaign" Video of strangers hugging activist Juan Mann set to a song by the band Sick Puppies. It was posted by PeaceOnEarth123 and won a 2006 YouTube Award in the Inspirational category.

friends / friend invitations You can invite other users to be your friends. This allows you to share private videos with each other. You can send invitations from a user's YouTube channel page.

Google Video Originally, Google Video was a competitor to YouTube. Then, on January 14, 2009, Google announced that its video search engine would discontinue support for uploads. Google Video will continue to focus on search and search technology.

groups Groups allow users to share videos and have discussions on a common theme. They can be found under the YouTube Community tab.

"The Guild - Episode 1: Wake-Up Call" First video in *The Guild*, a web series about a group of friends who interact primarily through an online game. The series was created by Felicia Day and posted by watchtheguild. It won a 2007 YouTube Award in the Series category.

Gurus (YouTube account type) Like the other special account types, a Guru account has extended performer information and profiles.

headroom The space between the top of a subject's head and a monitor's upper screen edge. Too much headroom makes the subject appear to fall out of the frame.

Help The YouTube Help Center. If you can't find an answer to your question here, you can use YouTube's contact form to reach the support department.

"Here It Goes Again" This video of the band Ok Go dancing on treadmills won a 2006 YouTube Award in the Creative category.

history YouTube remembers the videos you have viewed recently. The link is at the very top of every page. You can clear your history by clicking the Clear Viewing History button on that page.

honors There are many different honors that are granted to the top videos and channels on YouTube. This includes video honors like most viewed, most discussed, most responded, top rated, and top favorited. It also includes channel honors like most viewed and most subscribed. When a video or a channel receives an honor, they appear on YouTube's browse pages.

"Hotness Prevails/Worst Video Ever" This video blog by thewinekone won a 2006 YouTube Award in the Commentary category.

"How to Solve a Rubik's Cube (Part One)" This video demonstrating an algorithmic solution to solving a Rubik's Cube, posted by pogobat, won a 2007 YouTube Award in the Instructional category.

Hulu Founded in March 2007, Hulu is a leading online aggregator of video content. In April 2009, Hulu and the Walt Disney Company announced that Disney, through its subsidiary ABC Enterprises Inc., had agreed to join NBC Universal, News Corporation, and Providence Equity Partners as a joint venture partner and equity owner of Hulu.

InVideo Ads YouTube InVideo Ads run on partner watch pages. If you allow InVideo advertising, YouTube may occasionally run transparent overlay ads on the lower portion of your video. These ads typically appear at the 15-second mark, they can be closed by the viewer if desired, and they will minimize automatically if the viewer does nothing.

JavaScript This is a scripting language used to create client-side web applications. To display videos, YouTube uses the Flash player, which relies on JavaScript. You will need to make sure the latest version of JavaScript is enabled in your browser in order to watch YouTube videos.

"Kiwi" This video of an animated Kiwi attempting to experience flight, posted by Madyeti47, won a 2006 YouTube Award in the Adorable category.

"Laughing Baby" This video of a laughing baby, posted by gsager1234, won a 2007 YouTube Award in the Adorable category.

Links (watch page) The Links section below your video displays the five websites within which your video has been embedded and is receiving the highest number of clicks.

"LonelyGirl15 is Dead!" This video of talking head Michael Buckley discussing the death of Lonelygirl15, one of the most watched fictional characters on YouTube in 2006, was posted by WhatTheBuckShow and won a 2007 YouTube Award in the Commentary category.

long shot (LS) This is a camera view of a subject or scene from a distance, showing a broad perspective.

medium shot (MS) This defines any camera perspective between long shot and close-up, viewing the subjects from a medium distance.

metadata This is data about your data. For videos on YouTube, this is the title, description, thumbnail, and tags. You can edit your videos' metadata even after posting them.

mobile (videos) These videos are available on Verizon Wireless.

Musicians (YouTube account type) In addition to performer information, a Musician account can publish a schedule of show dates.

"My Name is Lisa" Video about a young girl dealing with her mother's Alzheimer's disease. It was posted by sheltonfilms and won a 2007 YouTube Award in the Short Film category.

MySpace Video Introduced by MySpace in early 2007, MySpace Video is a video sharing site similar to YouTube. According to comScore Video Metrix, 47.4 million viewers watched 349 million videos on MySpace.com in March 2009.

Non-profits (YouTube Account Type) A status obtained by 501©3 nonprofit organization accepted into YouTube's nonprofit program.

nose room The distance between the subject and the edge of the frame in the direction the subject is looking. This is also called look room.

"The Original Human TETRIS Performance by Guillaume Reymond" This video of human beings imitating Tetris blocks with stop motion animation was posted by notsonoisy and won a 2007 YouTube Award in the Creative category.

over-the-shoulder shot View of the primary subject with the back of another person's shoulder and head in the foreground. Often used in interview situations.

pan Horizontal camera pivot, right to left or left to right, from a stationary position.

Partners (YouTube account type) There is a page under the Channels tab with videos from YouTube's major content partners. Partners can be large corporations or individuals. A partner can monetize videos but is held legally accountable for copyright infringements.

pedestal This camera move vertically lowers or raises the camcorder, approaching either the floor or the ceiling, while keeping the camera level.

performer information Several of the account types allow extended profiles so you can share more about you and your videos.

playlist You can add videos to playlists to play them in order or conveniently share the list of videos with your friends.

Playlists (watch page) Clicking this link will reveal a list of all user playlists that feature the video you are currently watching.

point-of-view shot (POV) Shot perspective whereby the video camera assumes a subject's view and thus viewers see what the subject sees.

Politicians (YouTube account type) The Politician account type was used by candidates for the 2008 United States presidential election. YouTube is exploring extending this to other election contests.

Post Video A button below each video on its watch page. You can use it to conveniently share the video on social bookmarking sites or your blog.

"Potter Puppet Pals in 'The Mysterious Ticking Noise'" This video of a Harry Potter–themed puppet show, posted by NeilCicierega, won a 2007 YouTube Award in the Comedy category.

private message YouTube has a system for messaging like email. You can read your messages from your account page. You send a message to a user from that user's channel page.

private video You can upload videos as private. These won't appear in search results and can be seen by only your friends.

processing time The time it takes a video, once uploaded to the site, to be fully entered into the YouTube system with all associated video information and representative thumbnails. Processing time varies greatly depending on the format of your original video, the file size, and upload traffic. It could take anywhere from a few minutes to several hours.

production This refers to the overall process of creating content. A producer is someone who oversees the entire process of creating content from start to finish. The

requirements of production can range from financial responsibilities to full implementation and execution of ideas and deadlines.

promoted videos This is what YouTube calls its self-service search advertising program. When people search on YouTube using one of your keywords, your promoted video may appear above or next to the search results. There's no minimum spending requirement and you're charged only if someone clicks your promoted videos promotion, not when the promotion is displayed.

QuickList QuickList is a playlist that can be easily added to and cleared so that you can save videos to watch later without having to navigate away from the page you were on. Whenever you see a + on a video's preview image, you can add the video to your QuickList by clicking the +.

rack focus Shifting focus between subjects in the background and foreground so a viewer's attention moves from subject to subject as the focus shifts.

rating You can rate YouTube videos by clicking the stars. More red stars mean better ratings. You can disable ratings for your videos, but this prevents you from getting Top Rated honors.

RealTime This setting allows you to share the video you are watching with your friends or other users who are also watching the same video.

related videos (watch page) Related videos are selected by a mysterious search algorithm. They might even be related to the video you're watching! Seriously, a new video's related videos will be decided by tags, but after it's been seen by multiple users, viewer histories will be used to decide what related videos appear.

remote Video shoot performed on location, outside a controlled studio environment.

Reporters (YouTube account type) This is for civilians or professionals who make videos about local or international news and current events.

rule of thirds This composition theory is based on dividing the screen into thirds vertically and horizontally and the placement of the main subject along those lines.

"Say It's Possible" Video of musician Terra Naomi singing a solo acoustic performance. It was posted by terranaomi and won a 2006 YouTube Award for Musician of the Year.

scene In the language of moving images, this is a sequence of related shots usually constituting action in one particular location. (See *shot*.)

search There is a search box at the top of every page. It accepts usernames, video titles, descriptions, and tags.

share video (watch page) You can have YouTube email a video link to a friend.

shot An intentional, isolated camera view. Collectively, shots make up a particular scene. (See *scene*.)

Shows tab YouTube created this new destination for television shows in April 2009. It allows you to browse shows by genre, network, title, and popularity.

"Smosh Short 2: Stranded" This video of a sketch comedy short by Smosh about a man stranded on a desert island was posted by Smosh and won a 2006 YouTube Award in the Comedy category.

spotlight videos The YouTube Team likes to highlight videos they think you'll want to watch—videos that hopefully inform, inspire, and entertain. Spotlight videos have top billing on category pages.

"Stop the Clash of Civilizations" Video promoting cultural tolerance between America and various Middle Eastern countries. It was posted by AvaazOrg and won a 2007 YouTube Award in the Politics category.

stream This term has two meanings. First, it refers to the stream of data which is transmitted over a network to allow play back in real time as it is transmitted. It can also refer to watching "streams" that other YouTube users are watching. This TestTube feature is essentially a chat room where videos can be posted for other users to check out and talk about. Get it? Got it? Good.

subscription You can subscribe to another user's channel or favorites or to a tag. You will see that user's videos/favorites, or videos with the tag, in your subscription center. The most recent will appear for you on the home page.

tag A tag is an associative heuristic. (A heuristic is just an informal method to help solve a problem.) You can subscribe to a tag to see new videos with that tag as they are added to a site. Tags also help decide if videos are related, and they facilitate search indexing.

TestTube This is where you can try out new YouTube features in development and let YouTube know what you think.

thumbnail This is a small picture that represents your video on YouTube. After your video has been uploaded, three video thumbnails will be generated automatically by the system. You can select one of them as your video thumbnail.

tilt This is vertical camcorder rotation (up and down) from a single axis, as on a tripod.

tracking Lateral camcorder movement that travels with a moving subject. The camcorder should maintain a regulated distance from the subject.

TubeMogul This service provides a single point for deploying uploads to the top video sharing sites and analytics on who, what, and how videos are being viewed.

two-shot This camera view includes two subjects. It's most generally applicable to interview situations.

upload This is content that is posted to a server. When you upload videos to YouTube, you are loading your video file onto its server, which will then host it for you to share with other users.

uploader The YouTube uploader is a tool you can use to upload multiple files at once. To use the uploader, you'll need to download YouTube's application to a Windows computer.

uploading time The time it takes for a video to upload from a user's computer to the YouTube servers.

VEVO In April 2009, YouTube and Universal Music Group (UMG) announced the launch of a music and video entertainment hub that will feature UMG's premium video content. This content will be exclusively available through VEVO.com and a new VEVO channel on YouTube, through a special VEVO branded embedded player.

video ads YouTube video ads, including standard autoplay, standard click-to-play, expandable autoplay, and expandable click-to-play, combine the benefits of a YouTube-hosted video (the cycle of virality and user engagement) with the benefits of a DART-hosted rich media ad (flighting, metrics, control).

Video Identification As a part of YouTube's initiative to protect copyright holders, this tool allows YouTube partners to identify and claim their copyrighted video content that was unofficially uploaded to the site. As proprietary videos are discovered and claimed, partners now have the option to place an ad on the video, offering a new revenue stream, or remove the video from the site. Video Identification also enables users to keep the uploaded video on their channel.

video response This is a video which is posted in response to another video, much like a text comment.

Videos tab This is at the top of most YouTube pages. It displays honored videos by category.

vignette A visual special effect whereby viewers see images through a perceived keyhole, heart shape, or diamond. In low-budget form, vignettes are achieved by aiming the camera through a cutout of a desired shape.

vlog (video blog) You can set a playlist as your vlog, and the videos on that playlist will appear on your YouTube channel along with optional descriptions you can add to them. The term *video blog* also refers to a variation of a web blog in which a person talks to a camera rather than writing their blog entry as text.

Visible Measures An independent third-party measurement firm that specializes in measuring the consumption and distribution of Internet video.

watch page The YouTube page with the full-sized video, all of the metadata, and comments.

web cam A video camera whose output may be viewed in real time over the World Wide Web.

whip pan (swish pan) Extremely rapid camera movement from left to right or right to left, appearing as an image blur. Two such pans in the same direction, edited together, one moving from and the other moving to a stationary shot, can effectively convey the passage of time or a change of location.

XML This stands for eXtensible Markup Language.Y

Yahoo! Video Although Yahoo! Video began as a video search engine, it is now a video sharing site similar to YouTube and MySpace Video. Yahoo! Video was redesigned and changed its focus to Yahoo!-hosted video only in February 2008.

Your Subscriptions (home page) When you subscribe to users' YouTube channels, the most recent videos those users have uploaded appear in this location.

YouTube This is the world's most popular online video community. According to comScore Video Metrix, 107.1 million viewers in the United States watched 6.8 billion videos on YouTube.com in April 2009. YouTube, LLC, is based in San Bruno, California, and is a subsidiary of Google Inc.

YouTube Blog The official YouTube blog is located at `http://youtube.com/blog`.

YouTubers (YouTube account type) The YouTuber account provides basic options. The term also means member of the YouTube community.

zoom This is the variance of focal length from wide-angle to telephoto, or vice versa, in one continuous move. *Zoom in* and *zoom out* are common terms.

Index

Note to the Reader: Throughout this index **boldfaced** page numbers indicate primary discussions of a topic. *Italicized* page numbers indicate illustrations.

INDEX